SLEEPY PRINCESS IN THE DEMON CASTLE

9

STORY & ART BY
KAGIJI KUMANOMATA

NIGHTS

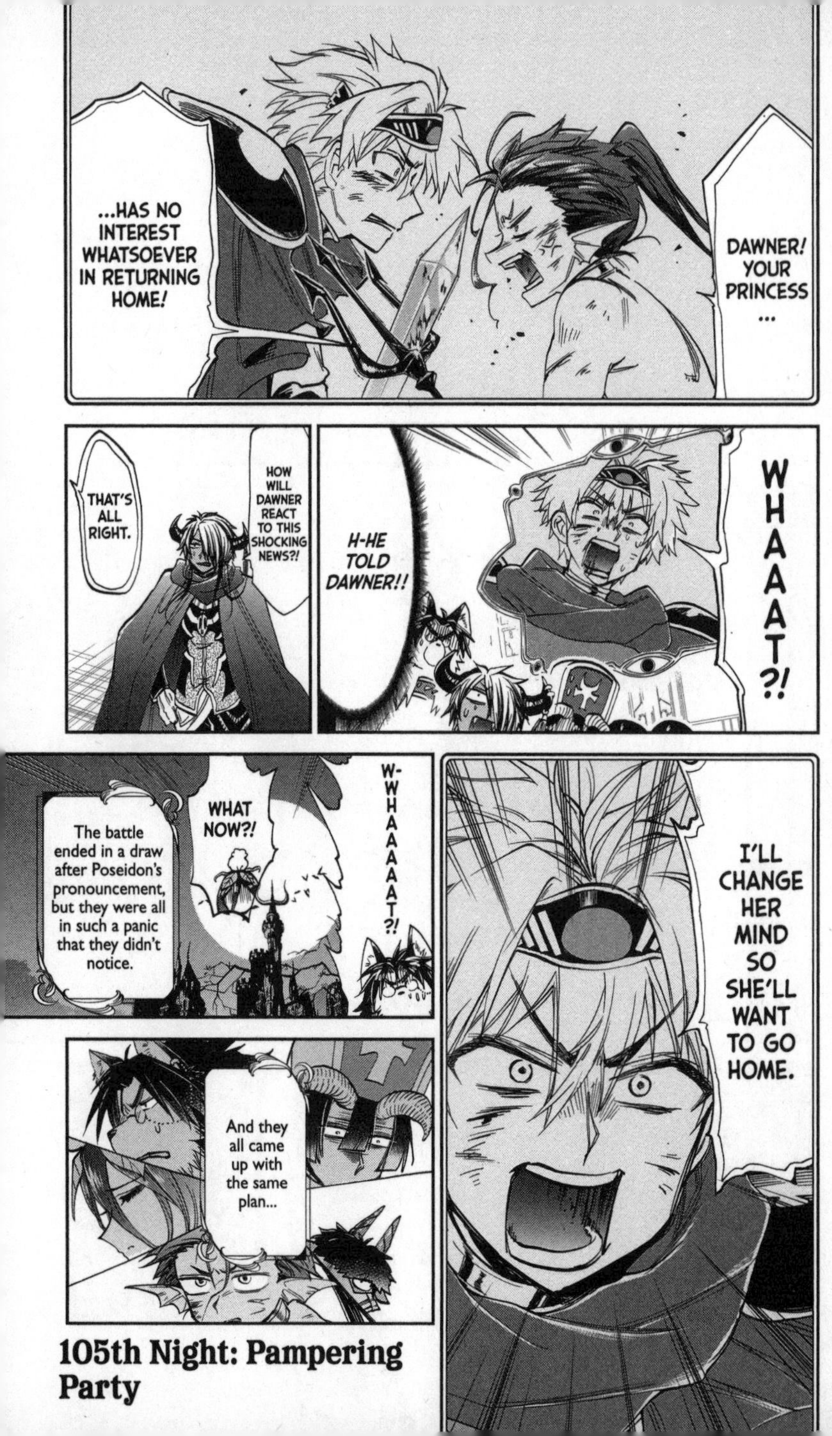
DAWNER! YOUR PRINCESS ...
...HAS NO INTEREST WHATSOEVER IN RETURNING HOME!
WHAAAAT?!
H-HE TOLD DAWNER!!
HOW WILL DAWNER REACT TO THIS SHOCKING NEWS?!
THAT'S ALL RIGHT.
I'LL CHANGE HER MIND SO SHE'LL WANT TO GO HOME.
W-WHAAAAAAAT?!
WHAT NOW?!
The battle ended in a draw after Poseidon's pronouncement, but they were all in such a panic that they didn't notice.
And they all came up with the same plan...

105th Night: Pampering Party

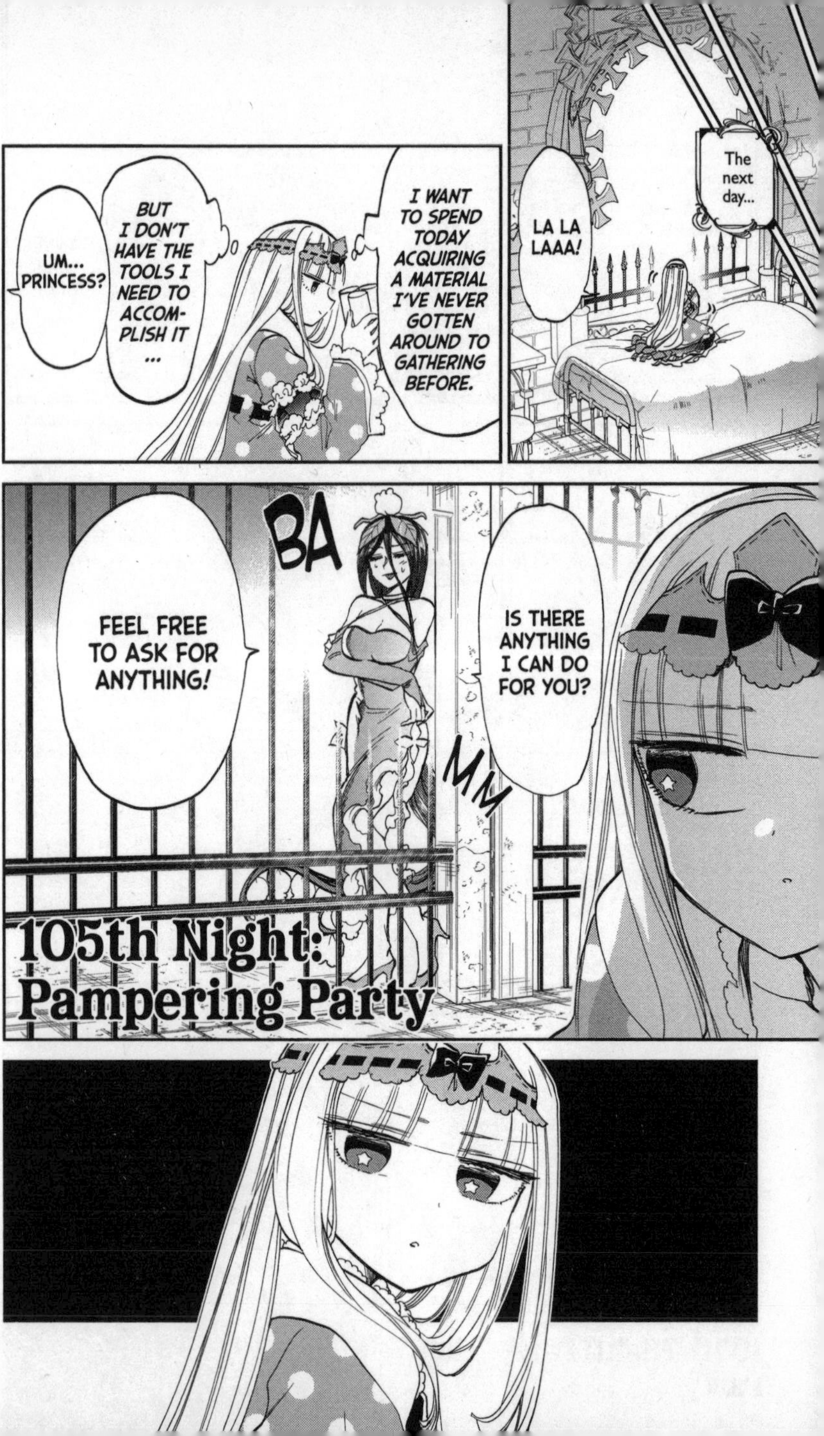
The next day...
LA LA LAAA!
I WANT TO SPEND TODAY ACQUIRING A MATERIAL I'VE NEVER GOTTEN AROUND TO GATHERING BEFORE.
BUT I DON'T HAVE THE TOOLS I NEED TO ACCOMPLISH IT ...
UM... PRINCESS?
IS THERE ANYTHING I CAN DO FOR YOU?
MM
BA
FEEL FREE TO ASK FOR ANYTHING!
105th Night: Pampering Party

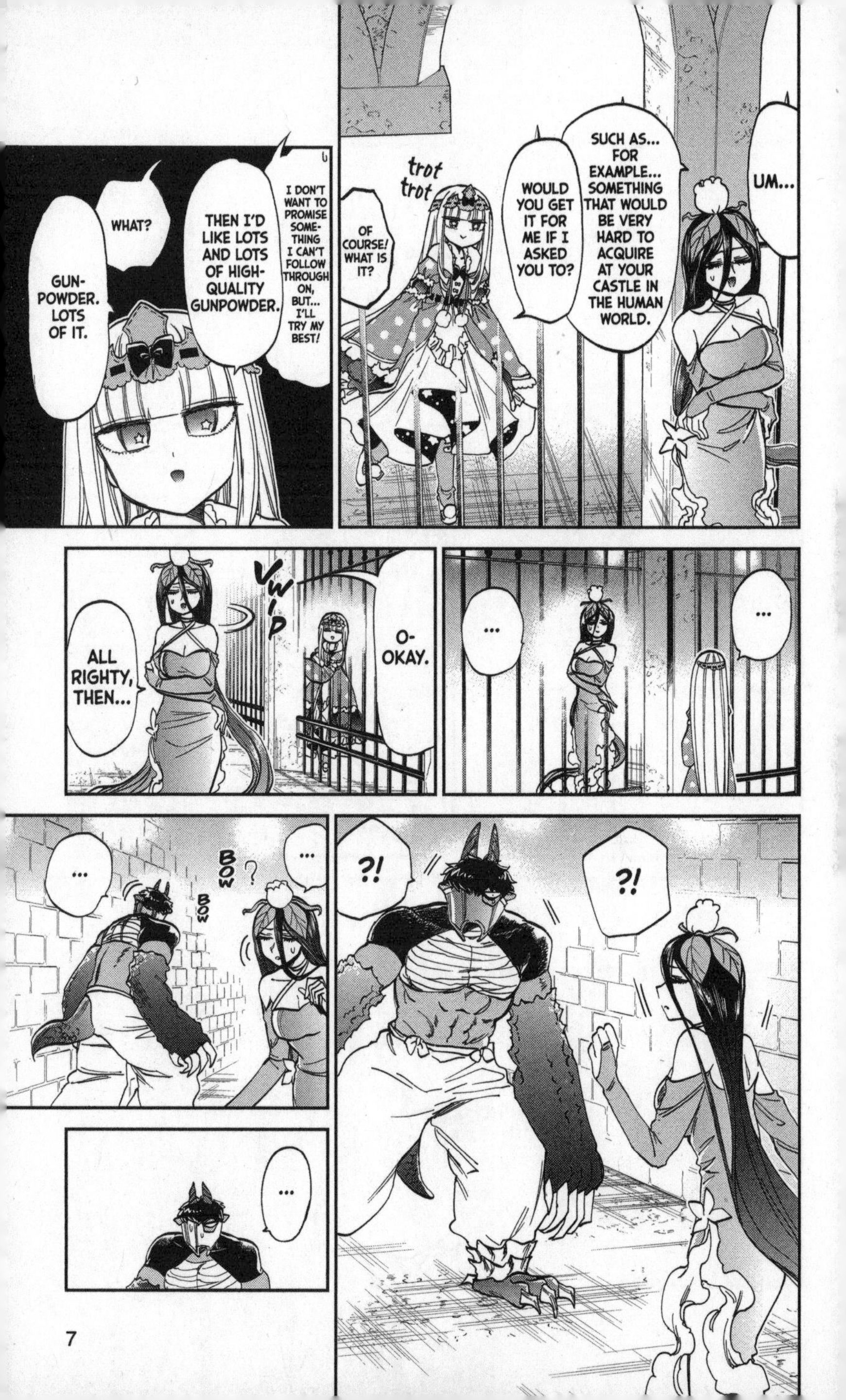
UM...
SUCH AS... FOR EXAMPLE... SOMETHING THAT WOULD BE VERY HARD TO ACQUIRE AT YOUR CASTLE IN THE HUMAN WORLD.
WOULD YOU GET IT FOR ME IF I ASKED YOU TO?
trot trot
OF COURSE! WHAT IS IT?
I DON'T WANT TO PROMISE SOMETHING I CAN'T FOLLOW THROUGH ON, BUT... I'LL TRY MY BEST!
THEN I'D LIKE LOTS AND LOTS OF HIGH-QUALITY GUNPOWDER.
WHAT?
GUN-POWDER. LOTS OF IT.
...
...
O-OKAY.
VWIP
ALL RIGHTY, THEN...
?!
?!
...
BOW BOW
?
...
...

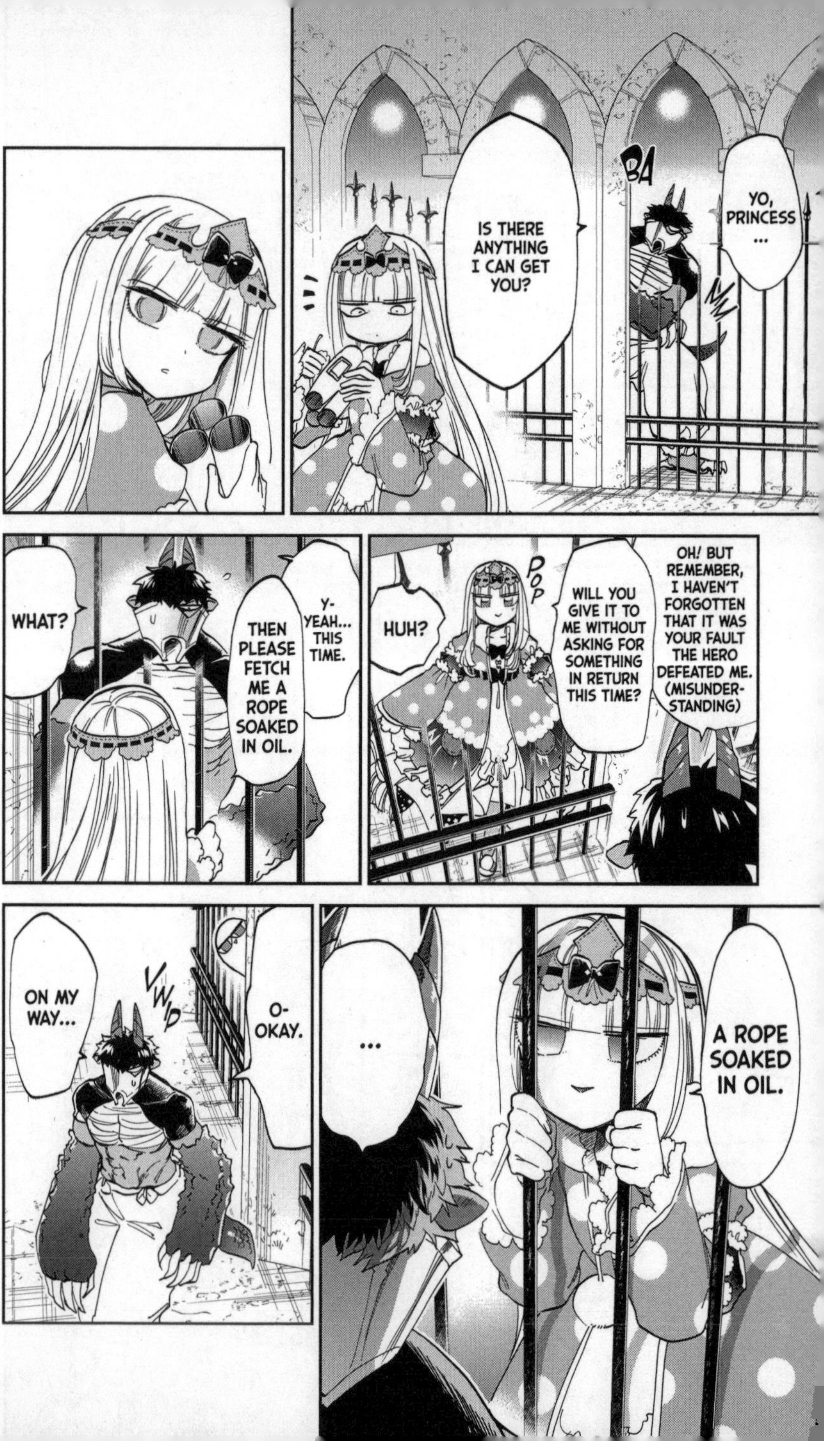
YO, PRINCESS ...
BA
IS THERE ANYTHING I CAN GET YOU?
OH! BUT REMEMBER, I HAVEN'T FORGOTTEN THAT IT WAS YOUR FAULT THE HERO DEFEATED ME. (MISUNDER-STANDING)
WILL YOU GIVE IT TO ME WITHOUT ASKING FOR SOMETHING IN RETURN THIS TIME?
POP
HUH?
Y-YEAH... THIS TIME.
THEN PLEASE FETCH ME A ROPE SOAKED IN OIL.
WHAT?
A ROPE SOAKED IN OIL.
...
O-OKAY.
VWIP
ON MY WAY...

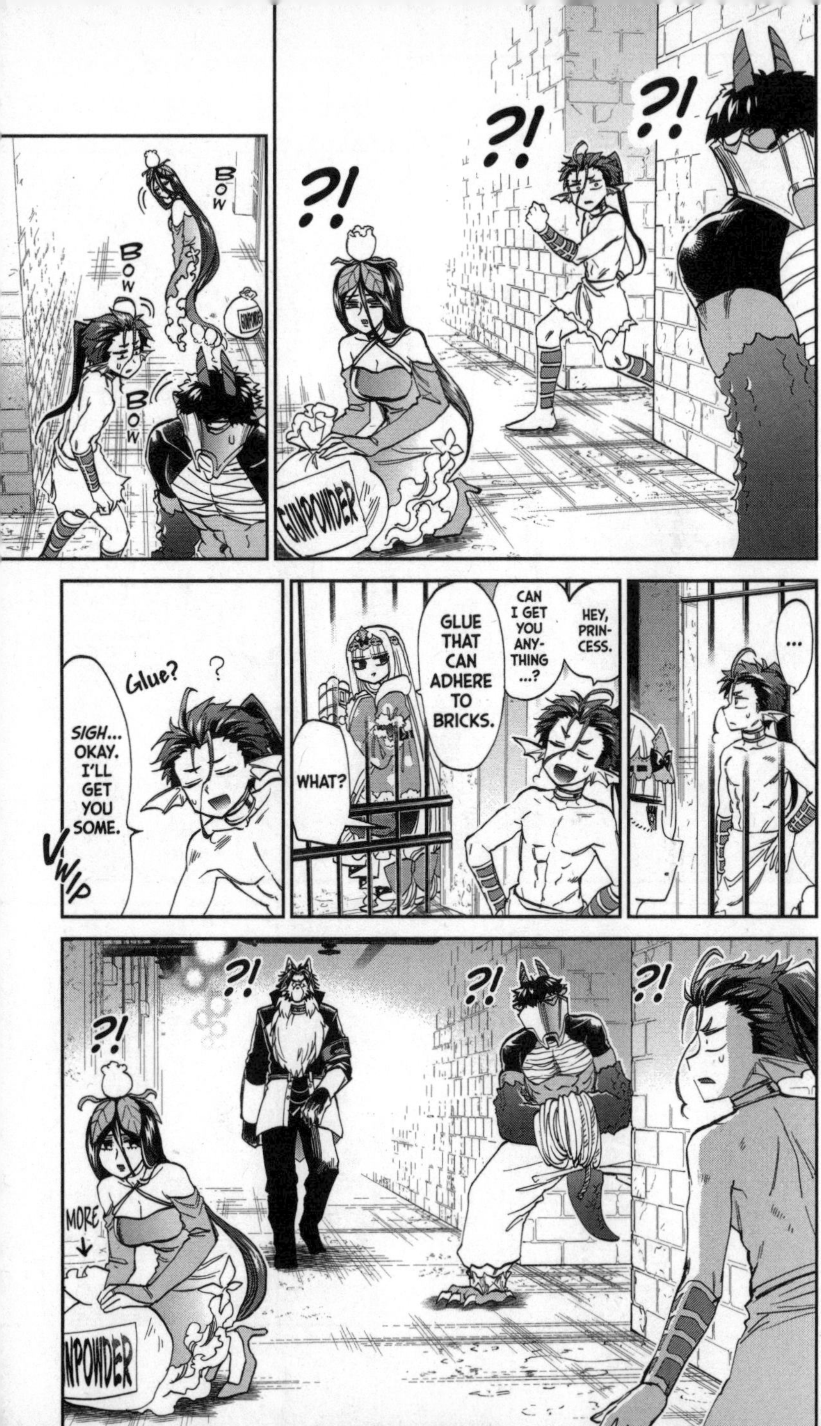
?!
?!
?!
GUNPOWDER
BOW
BOW
BOW
...
HEY, PRINCESS.
CAN I GET YOU ANYTHING ...?
GLUE THAT CAN ADHERE TO BRICKS.
WHAT?
Glue?
?
SIGH... OKAY. I'LL GET YOU SOME.
VWIP
?!
?!
?!
?!
MORE ↓
NPOWDER

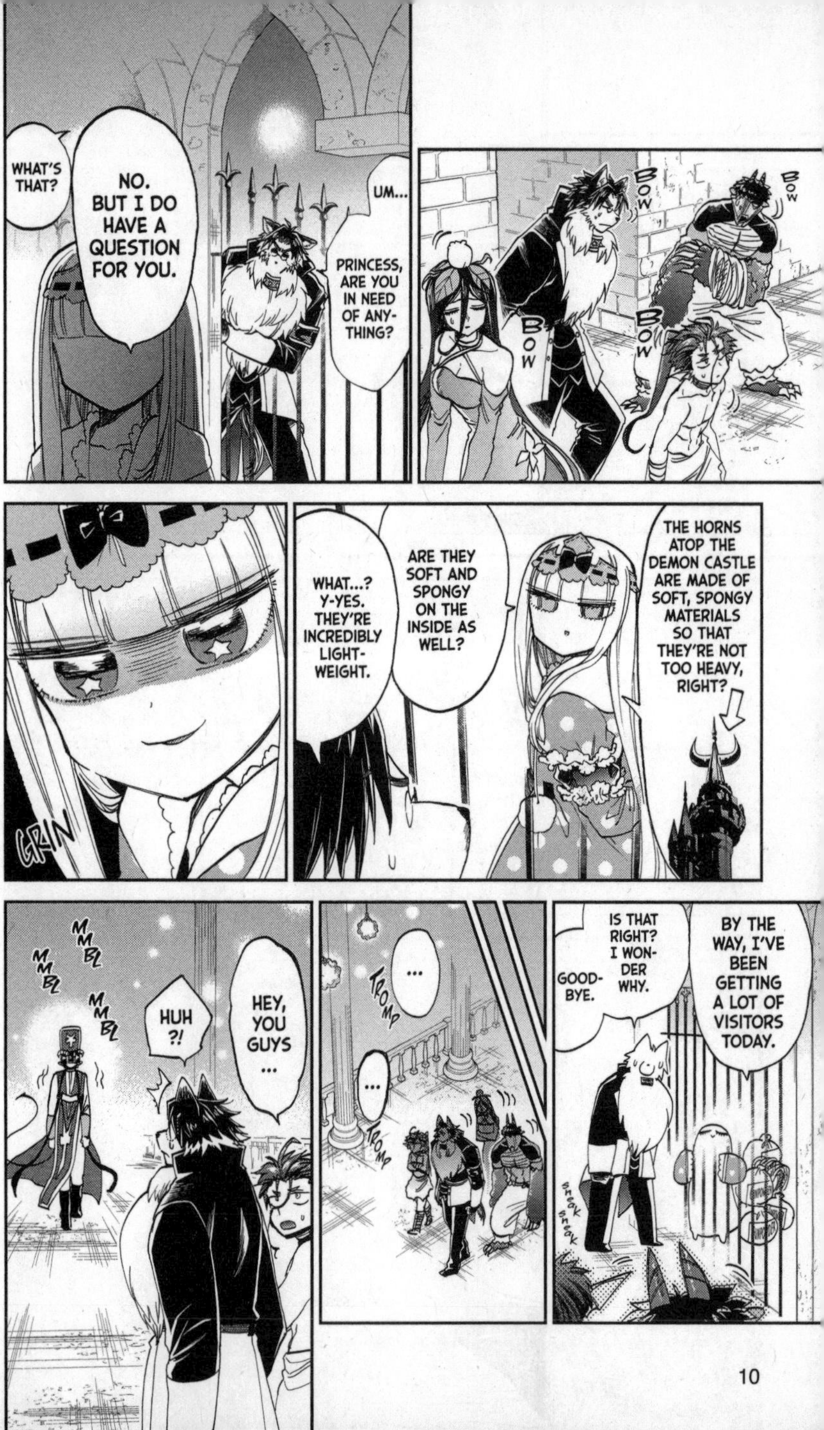
BOW
BOW
BOW
BOW
UM...
PRINCESS, ARE YOU IN NEED OF ANY-THING?
NO. BUT I DO HAVE A QUESTION FOR YOU.
WHAT'S THAT?
THE HORNS ATOP THE DEMON CASTLE ARE MADE OF SOFT, SPONGY MATERIALS SO THAT THEY'RE NOT TOO HEAVY, RIGHT?
ARE THEY SOFT AND SPONGY ON THE INSIDE AS WELL?
WHAT...? Y-YES. THEY'RE INCREDIBLY LIGHT-WEIGHT.
GRIN
BY THE WAY, I'VE BEEN GETTING A LOT OF VISITORS TODAY.
IS THAT RIGHT? I WON-DER WHY.
GOOD-BYE.
SHOK SHOK
...
TROMP
...
TROMP
HEY, YOU GUYS...
HUH?!
MMBL
MMBL
MMBL

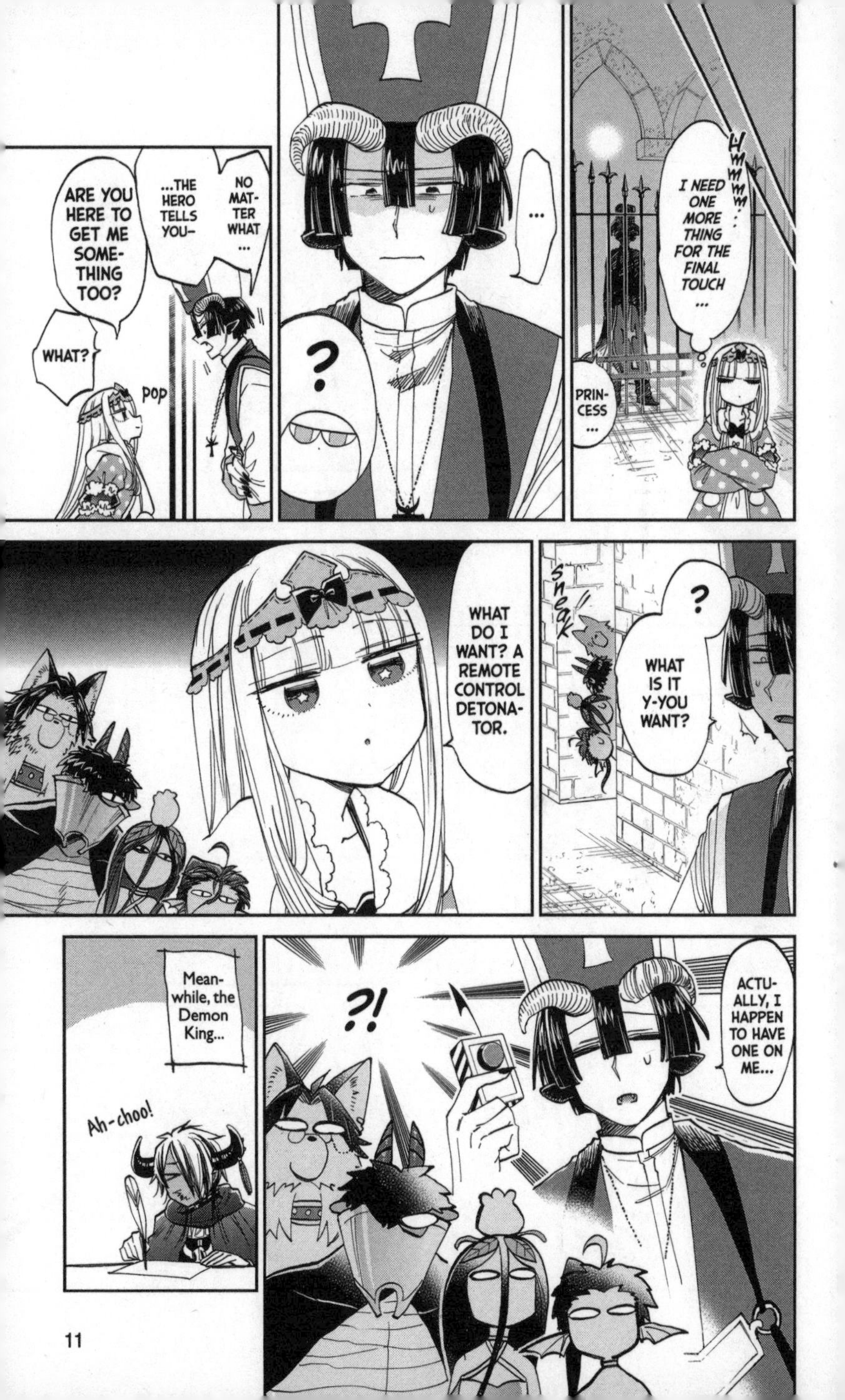
HMMMM...
I NEED ONE MORE THING FOR THE FINAL TOUCH...
PRINCESS...
...
?
NO MATTER WHAT...
...THE HERO TELLS YOU—
ARE YOU HERE TO GET ME SOMETHING TOO?
POP
WHAT?
?
WHAT IS IT Y-YOU WANT?
sneak
WHAT DO I WANT? A REMOTE CONTROL DETONATOR.
ACTUALLY, I HAPPEN TO HAVE ONE ON ME...
?!
Meanwhile, the Demon King...
Ah-choo!

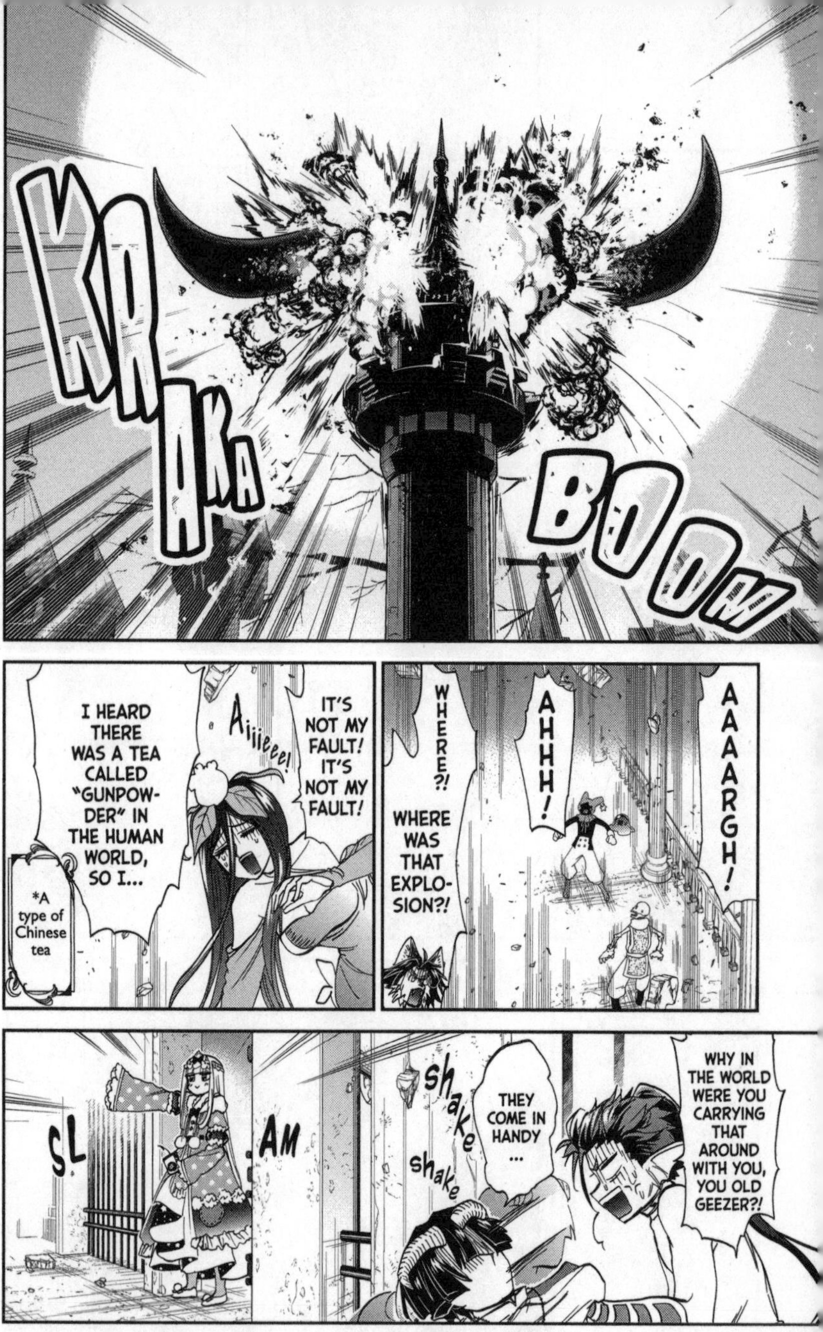
KRAKA
BOOM
AAAARGH!
AHHH!
WHERE?!
WHERE WAS THAT EXPLOSION?!
IT'S NOT MY FAULT! IT'S NOT MY FAULT!
Aiiieee!
I HEARD THERE WAS A TEA CALLED "GUNPOWDER" IN THE HUMAN WORLD, SO I...
*A type of Chinese tea
WHY IN THE WORLD WERE YOU CARRYING THAT AROUND WITH YOU, YOU OLD GEEZER?!
THEY COME IN HANDY ...
shake
shake
SLAM

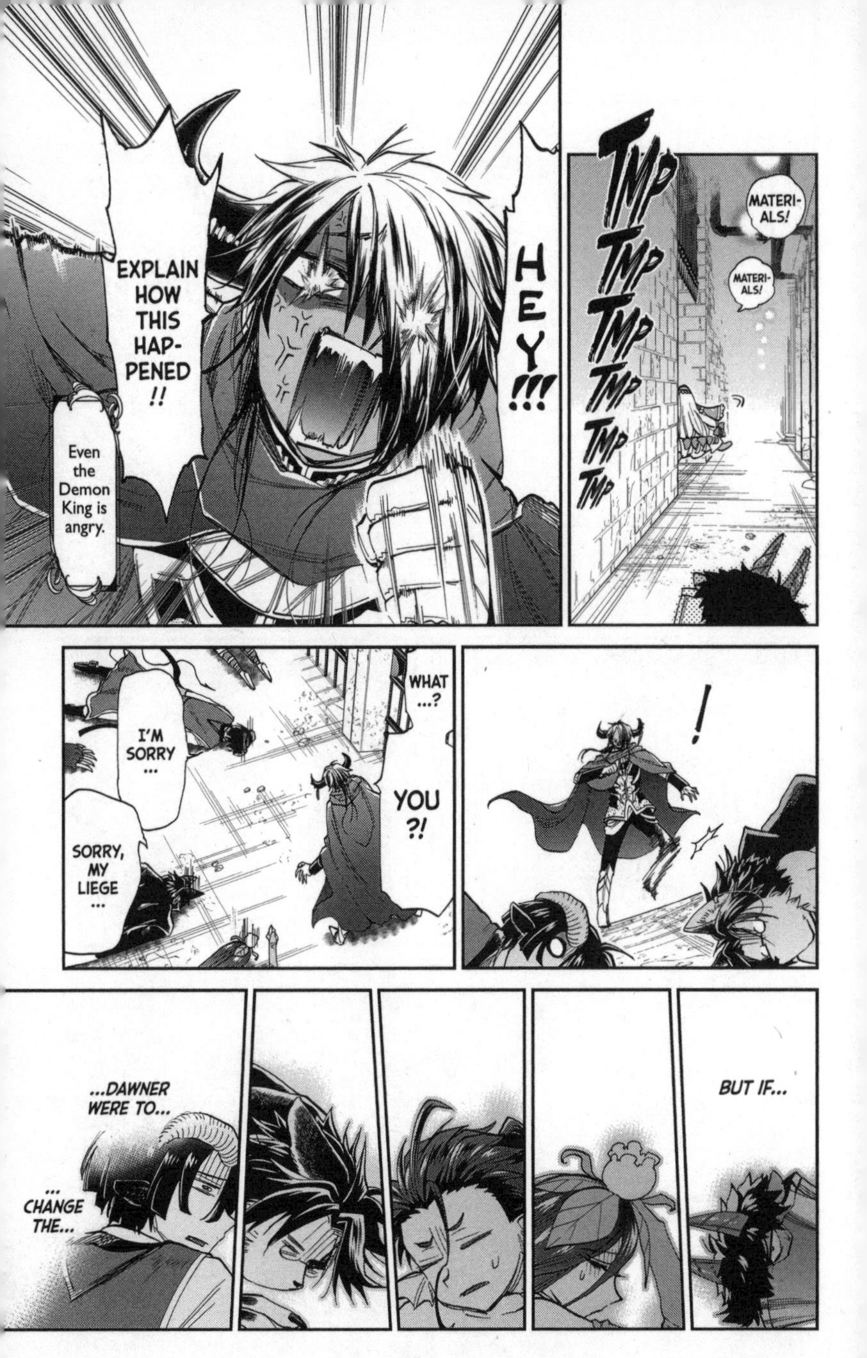
TMP TMP TMP TMP TMP TMP TMP
MATERI-ALS!
MATERI-ALS!
HEY!!!
EXPLAIN HOW THIS HAP-PENED!!
Even the Demon King is angry.
!
WHAT ...?
YOU?!
I'M SORRY ...
SORRY, MY LIEGE ...
BUT IF...
...DAWNER WERE TO...
...CHANGE THE...

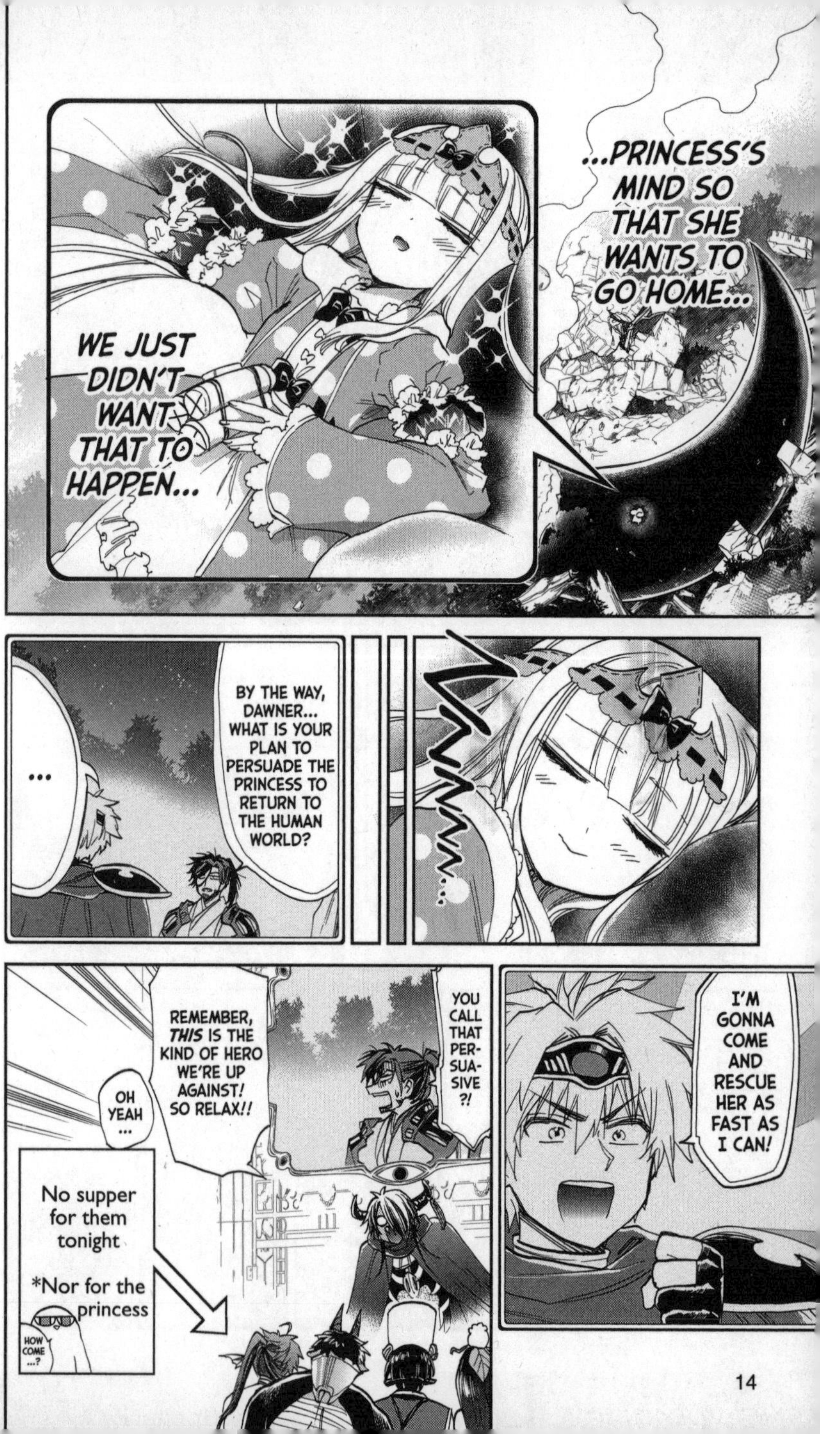

...PRINCESS'S MIND SO THAT SHE WANTS TO GO HOME...
WE JUST DIDN'T WANT THAT TO HAPPEN...
NNNNN...
BY THE WAY, DAWNER... WHAT IS YOUR PLAN TO PERSUADE THE PRINCESS TO RETURN TO THE HUMAN WORLD?
...
I'M GONNA COME AND RESCUE HER AS FAST AS I CAN!
YOU CALL THAT PERSUASIVE?!
REMEMBER, *THIS* IS THE KIND OF HERO WE'RE UP AGAINST! SO RELAX!!
OH YEAH ...
No supper for them tonight
*Nor for the princess
HOW COME ...?

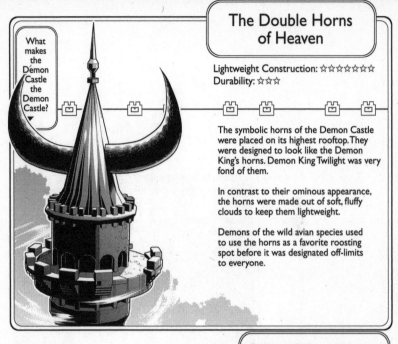

What makes the Demon Castle the Demon Castle?

The Double Horns of Heaven

Lightweight Construction: ☆☆☆☆☆☆☆☆
Durability: ☆☆☆

The symbolic horns of the Demon Castle were placed on its highest rooftop. They were designed to look like the Demon King's horns. Demon King Twilight was very fond of them.

In contrast to their ominous appearance, the horns were made out of soft, fluffy clouds to keep them lightweight.

Demons of the wild avian species used to use the horns as a favorite roosting spot before it was designated off-limits to everyone.

Problem until a few years ago:
"Demons of the wild avian species keep poking holes into the horns to store snacks."

Current problem:
"Maybe I should make them less springy so the princess doesn't..."

They decided to remove the broken horns...
...for renovation.
HEY! WHY DON'T WE TAKE THIS OPPORTUNITY TO REDESIGN THE HORNS?!
Yeah!
Fierce
SUDDENLY HE'S ALL ENTHUSIASTIC...
Weird style.

Would you like to change
your class?

11 changes
remaining

▶Yes

No ▼

Choir

"Sacred singing voice."

▼

106th Night: Deadlines Drive Everyone Crazy

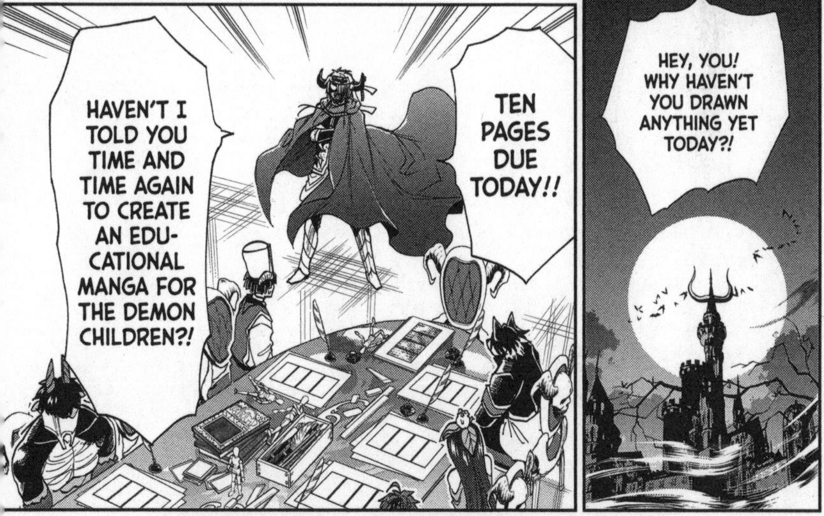

HEY, YOU! WHY HAVEN'T YOU DRAWN ANYTHING YET TODAY?!
TEN PAGES DUE TODAY!!
HAVEN'T I TOLD YOU TIME AND TIME AGAIN TO CREATE AN EDUCATIONAL MANGA FOR THE DEMON CHILDREN?!

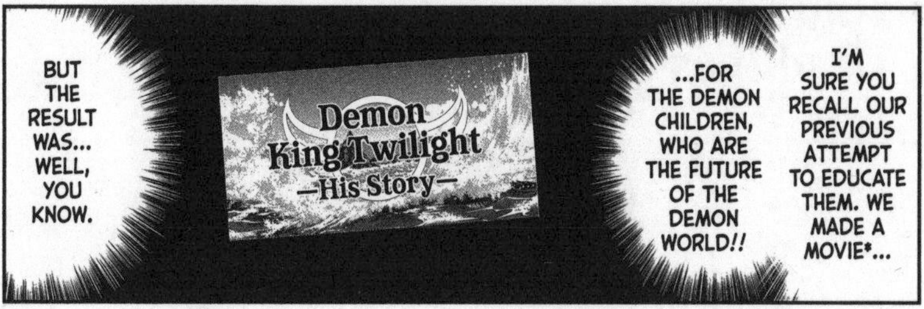

I'M SURE YOU RECALL OUR PREVIOUS ATTEMPT TO EDUCATE THEM. WE MADE A MOVIE*...
...FOR THE DEMON CHILDREN, WHO ARE THE FUTURE OF THE DEMON WORLD!!
Demon King Twilight
—His Story—
BUT THE RESULT WAS... WELL, YOU KNOW.

*See *Sleepy Princess in the Demon Castle* Vol. 7, 87th Night

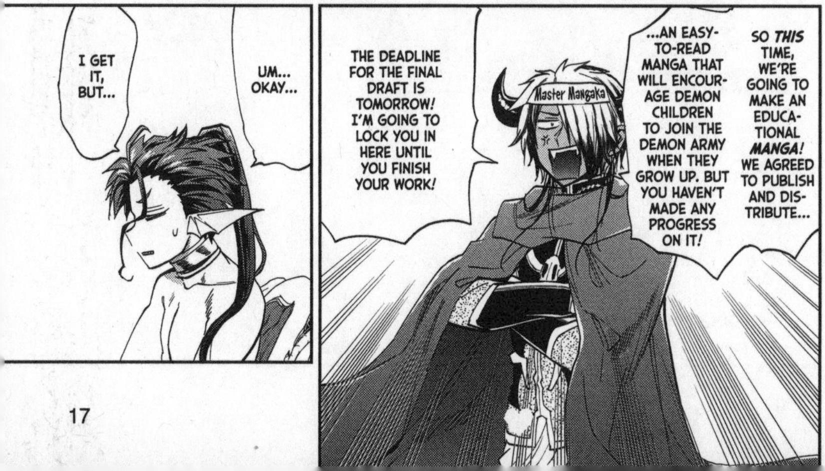

SO *THIS* TIME, WE'RE GOING TO MAKE AN EDUCATIONAL *MANGA*! WE AGREED TO PUBLISH AND DISTRIBUTE...
...AN EASY-TO-READ MANGA THAT WILL ENCOURAGE DEMON CHILDREN TO JOIN THE DEMON ARMY WHEN THEY GROW UP. BUT YOU HAVEN'T MADE ANY PROGRESS ON IT!
Master Mangaka
THE DEADLINE FOR THE FINAL DRAFT IS TOMORROW! I'M GOING TO LOCK YOU IN HERE UNTIL YOU FINISH YOUR WORK!
UM... OKAY...
I GET IT, BUT...

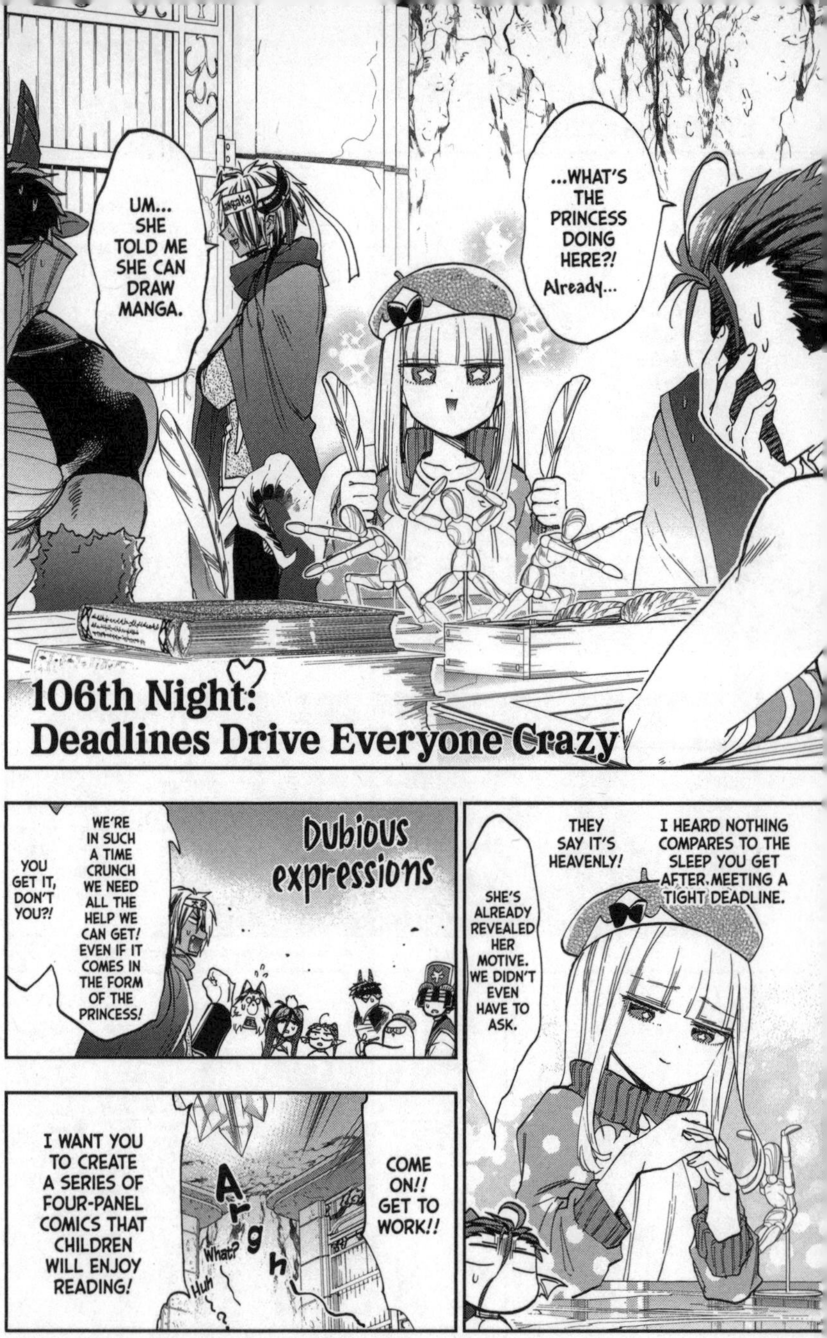
...WHAT'S THE PRINCESS DOING HERE?!
Already...
UM... SHE TOLD ME SHE CAN DRAW MANGA.
106th Night: Deadlines Drive Everyone Crazy
I HEARD NOTHING COMPARES TO THE SLEEP YOU GET AFTER MEETING A TIGHT DEADLINE.
THEY SAY IT'S HEAVENLY!
SHE'S ALREADY REVEALED HER MOTIVE. WE DIDN'T EVEN HAVE TO ASK.
Dubious expressions
WE'RE IN SUCH A TIME CRUNCH WE NEED ALL THE HELP WE CAN GET! EVEN IF IT COMES IN THE FORM OF THE PRINCESS!
YOU GET IT, DON'T YOU?!
COME ON!! GET TO WORK!!
Argh
What?
Huh
I WANT YOU TO CREATE A SERIES OF FOUR-PANEL COMICS THAT CHILDREN WILL ENJOY READING!

THEIR BEST ISN'T GOOD ENOUGH

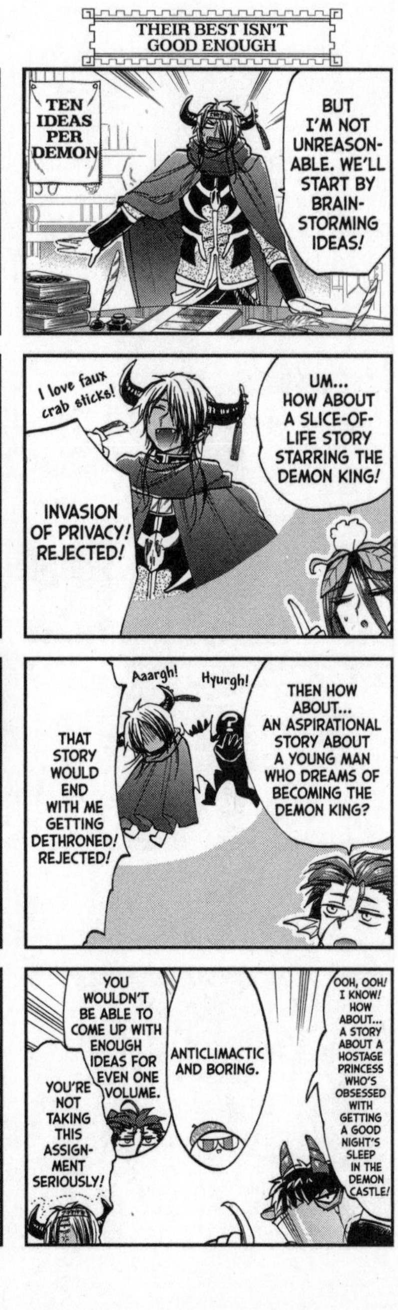
BUT I'M NOT UNREASONABLE. WE'LL START BY BRAINSTORMING IDEAS!
TEN IDEAS PER DEMON
UM... HOW ABOUT A SLICE-OF-LIFE STORY STARRING THE DEMON KING!
I love faux crab sticks!
INVASION OF PRIVACY! REJECTED!
THEN HOW ABOUT... AN ASPIRATIONAL STORY ABOUT A YOUNG MAN WHO DREAMS OF BECOMING THE DEMON KING?
Hyurgh!
Aaargh!
THAT STORY WOULD END WITH ME GETTING DETHRONED! REJECTED!
OOH, OOH! I KNOW! HOW ABOUT... A STORY ABOUT A HOSTAGE PRINCESS WHO'S OBSESSED WITH GETTING A GOOD NIGHT'S SLEEP IN THE DEMON CASTLE!
ANTICLIMACTIC AND BORING.
YOU WOULDN'T BE ABLE TO COME UP WITH ENOUGH IDEAS FOR EVEN ONE VOLUME.
YOU'RE NOT TAKING THIS ASSIGNMENT SERIOUSLY!

ALISALIS

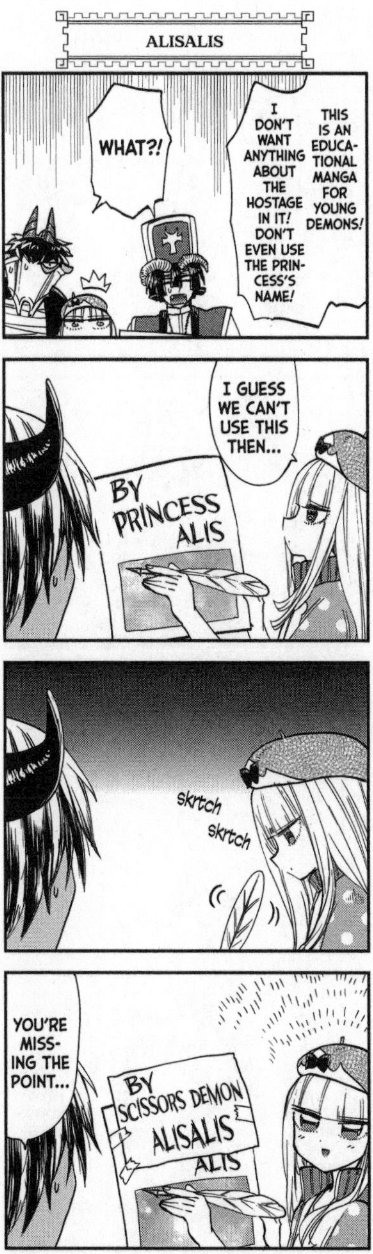
THIS IS AN EDUCATIONAL MANGA FOR YOUNG DEMONS!
I DON'T WANT ANYTHING ABOUT THE HOSTAGE IN IT! DON'T EVEN USE THE PRINCESS'S NAME!
WHAT?!
I GUESS WE CAN'T USE THIS THEN...
BY PRINCESS ALIS
skrtch
skrtch
BY SCISSORS DEMON ALISALIS
ALIS
YOU'RE MISSING THE POINT...

THE HEART OF A YOUTH

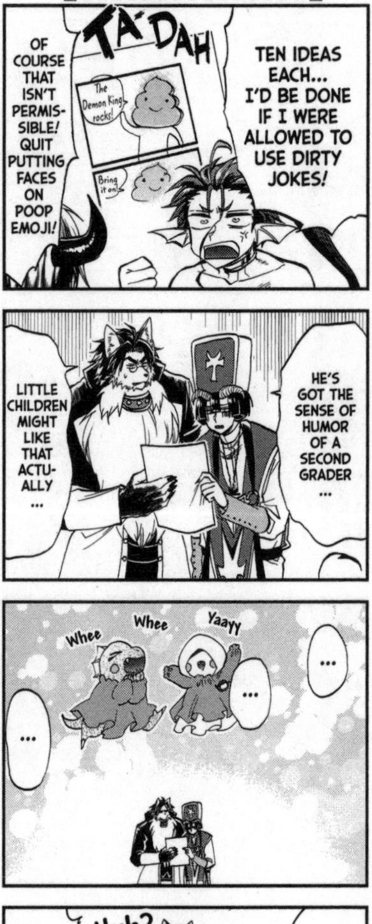
TEN IDEAS EACH... I'D BE DONE IF I WERE ALLOWED TO USE DIRTY JOKES!
TA-DAH
The Demon King rocks!
Bring it on!
OF COURSE THAT ISN'T PERMISSIBLE! QUIT PUTTING FACES ON POOP EMOJI!
HE'S GOT THE SENSE OF HUMOR OF A SECOND GRADER...
LITTLE CHILDREN MIGHT LIKE THAT ACTUALLY...
...
Yaayy
...
Whee
Whee
...
SO THIS IS NO GOOD THEN?
Huh?
I TOLD YOU THIS MANGA IS SUPPOSED TO BE EDUCATIONAL!!

OUT OF STYLE

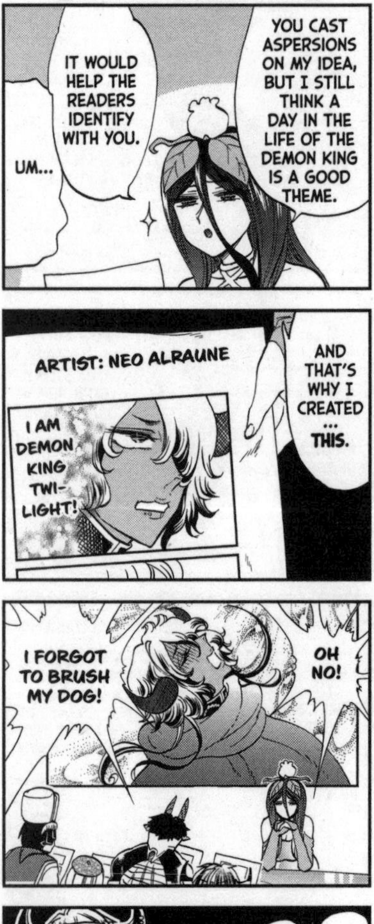
YOU CAST ASPERSIONS ON MY IDEA, BUT I STILL THINK A DAY IN THE LIFE OF THE DEMON KING IS A GOOD THEME.
IT WOULD HELP THE READERS IDENTIFY WITH YOU.
UM...
AND THAT'S WHY I CREATED ... THIS.
ARTIST: NEO ALRAUNE
I AM DEMON KING TWILIGHT!
OH NO!
I FORGOT TO BRUSH MY DOG!
...
UM... HOW OLD ARE YOU EXACTLY, SEXY GIRL?
Mmbl
Master Mangaka

THE DEMON KING'S SUNDAY ROUTINE

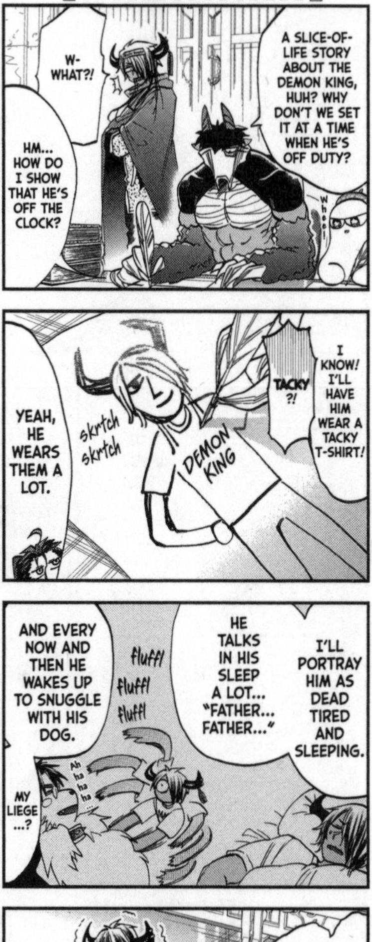
A SLICE-OF-LIFE STORY ABOUT THE DEMON KING, HUH? WHY DON'T WE SET IT AT A TIME WHEN HE'S OFF DUTY?
W-WHAT?!
HM... HOW DO I SHOW THAT HE'S OFF THE CLOCK?
I KNOW! I'LL HAVE HIM WEAR A TACKY T-SHIRT!
TACKY?!
DEMON KING
skrtch skrtch
YEAH, HE WEARS THEM A LOT.
I'LL PORTRAY HIM AS DEAD TIRED AND SLEEPING.
HE TALKS IN HIS SLEEP A LOT... "FATHER... FATHER..."
AND EVERY NOW AND THEN HE WAKES UP TO SNUGGLE WITH HIS DOG.
fluff! fluff! fluff!
Ah ha ha ha
MY LIEGE ...?
STOP ... IT ...
DON'T DRAW ME AS I TRULY AM...
The truth can hurt.

SECRET

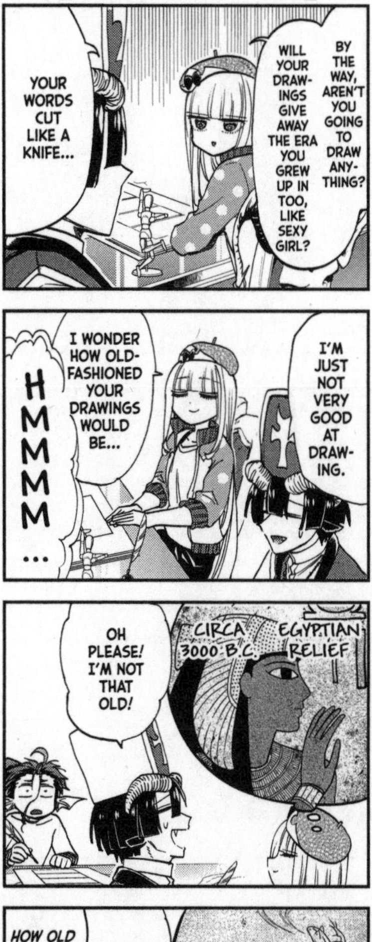
BY THE WAY, AREN'T YOU GOING TO DRAW ANYTHING?
WILL YOUR DRAWINGS GIVE AWAY THE ERA YOU GREW UP IN TOO, LIKE SEXY GIRL?
YOUR WORDS CUT LIKE A KNIFE...
I'M JUST NOT VERY GOOD AT DRAWING.
I WONDER HOW OLD-FASHIONED YOUR DRAWINGS WOULD BE...
HMMMM...
CIRCA 3000 B.C.
EGYPTIAN RELIEF
OH PLEASE! I'M NOT THAT OLD!
HEIAN ERA, KAMAKURA ERA
SCROLL OF FROLICKING ANIMALS
AND I'M NOT THAT GOOD!
HOW OLD ARE YOU THEN...?

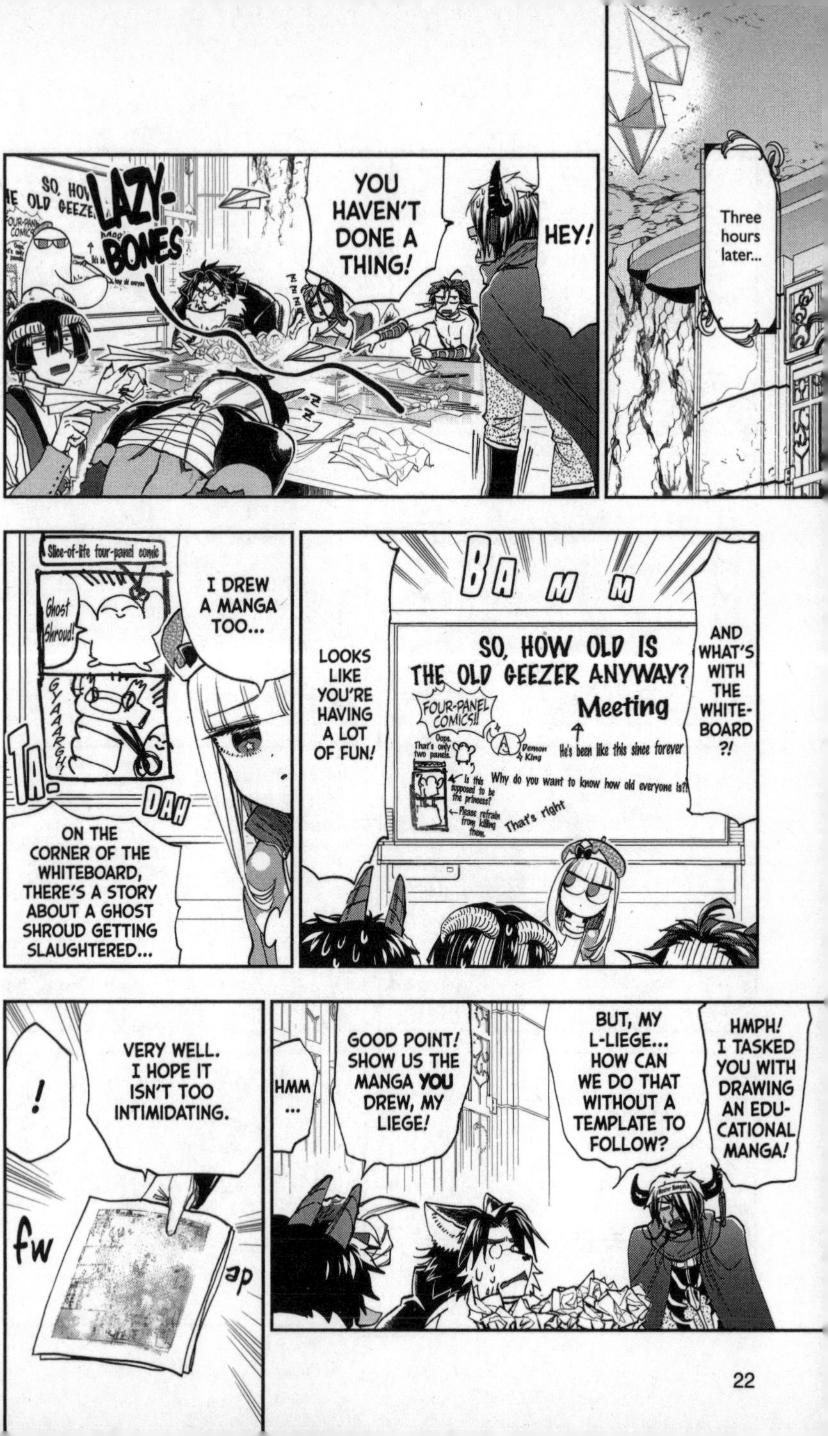
Three hours later...
HEY!
YOU HAVEN'T DONE A THING!
LAZY-BONES
SO, HOW OLD IS THE OLD GEEZER ANYWAY?
FOUR-PANEL COMICS
AND WHAT'S WITH THE WHITEBOARD?!
BAMM
SO, HOW OLD IS THE OLD GEEZER ANYWAY?
FOUR-PANEL COMICS!!
Meeting
Oops. That's only two panels.
Demon King
He's been like this since forever
Is this supposed to be the princess?
Why do you want to know how old everyone is?!
Please refrain from killing them.
That's right
LOOKS LIKE YOU'RE HAVING A LOT OF FUN!
I DREW A MANGA TOO...
Slice-of-life four-panel comic
Ghost Shroud!
GYAAARGH!
TA-DAH
ON THE CORNER OF THE WHITEBOARD, THERE'S A STORY ABOUT A GHOST SHROUD GETTING SLAUGHTERED...
HMPH! I TASKED YOU WITH DRAWING AN EDUCATIONAL MANGA!
BUT, MY L-LIEGE... HOW CAN WE DO THAT WITHOUT A TEMPLATE TO FOLLOW?
GOOD POINT! SHOW US THE MANGA **YOU** DREW, MY LIEGE!
HMM...
VERY WELL. I HOPE IT ISN'T TOO INTIMIDATING.
!
fwap

Ah, Demon Castle
Demon King Twilight
Hello, children!
I am Demon King Twilight.
The last time I drew a manga was way back when I was still but a child like you.
But today I would like to introduce myself to you with this manga.
I am Demon King Twilight.
Everyone calls me "my liege."
You are all much smaller than me.
I guess you're not this small (LOL).
Eat nutritious food, everyone!
The demon army is strong!
Demon King Twilight
I am Demon King Twilight.
The demon army is cool! Come join us!
We do battle with a human hero named Dawner.
I can't cover everything in this manga, but there's a movie version of this story too. Please watch it!
The demon army wants you!!
This message brought to you by Demon King Twilight

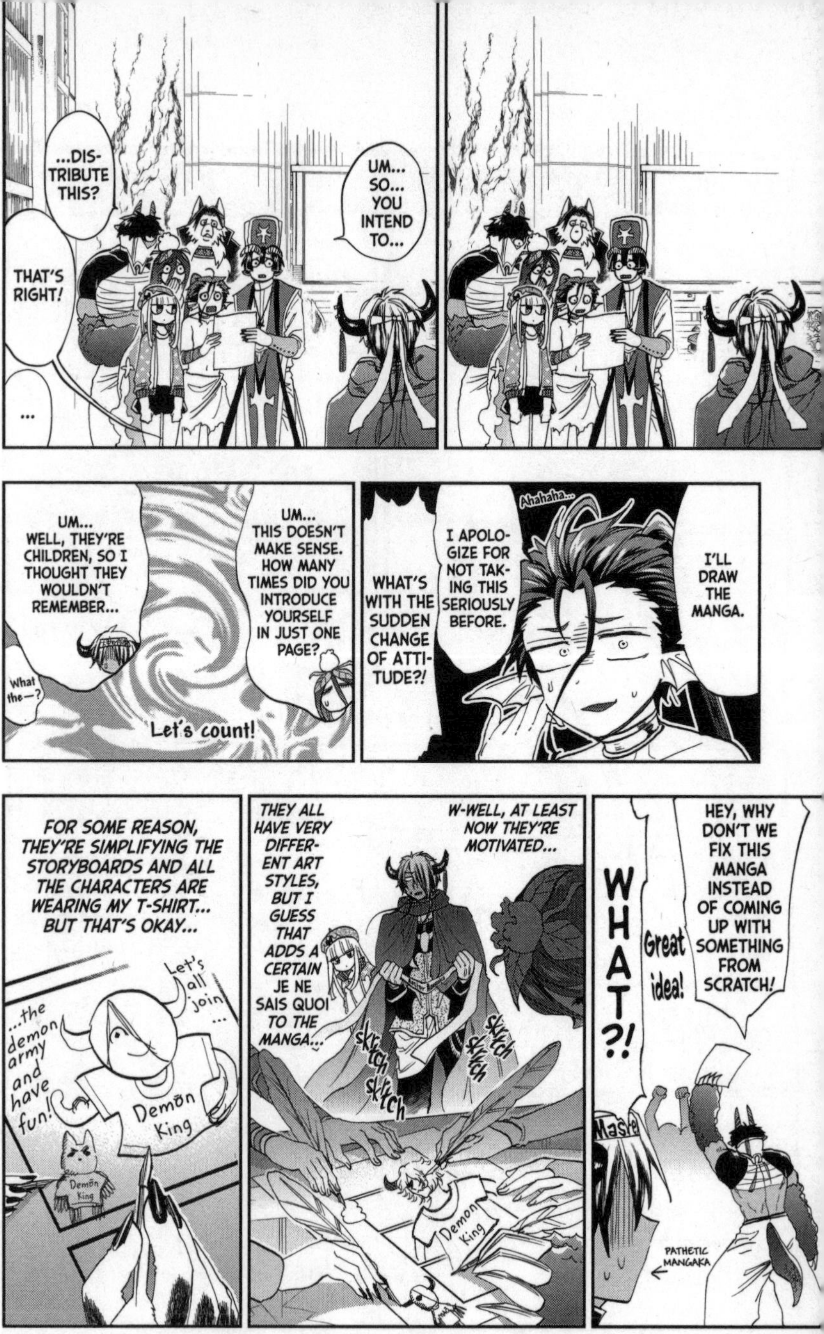
UM... SO... YOU INTEND TO...
...DIS-TRIBUTE THIS?
THAT'S RIGHT!
...
Ahahaha...
I'LL DRAW THE MANGA.
I APOLO-GIZE FOR NOT TAK-ING THIS SERIOUSLY BEFORE.
WHAT'S WITH THE SUDDEN CHANGE OF ATTI-TUDE?!
UM... THIS DOESN'T MAKE SENSE. HOW MANY TIMES DID YOU INTRODUCE YOURSELF IN JUST ONE PAGE?
UM... WELL, THEY'RE CHILDREN, SO I THOUGHT THEY WOULDN'T REMEMBER...
What the—?
Let's count!
HEY, WHY DON'T WE FIX THIS MANGA INSTEAD OF COMING UP WITH SOMETHING FROM SCRATCH!
Great idea!
WHAT?!
Master
PATHETIC MANGAKA
W-WELL, AT LEAST NOW THEY'RE MOTIVATED...
THEY ALL HAVE VERY DIFFER-ENT ART STYLES, BUT I GUESS THAT ADDS A CERTAIN JE NE SAIS QUOI TO THE MANGA...
skrtch skrtch skrtch skrtch skrtch
Demon King
FOR SOME REASON, THEY'RE SIMPLIFYING THE STORYBOARDS AND ALL THE CHARACTERS ARE WEARING MY T-SHIRT... BUT THAT'S OKAY...
Let's all join ...
...the demon army and have fun!
Demon King
Demon King

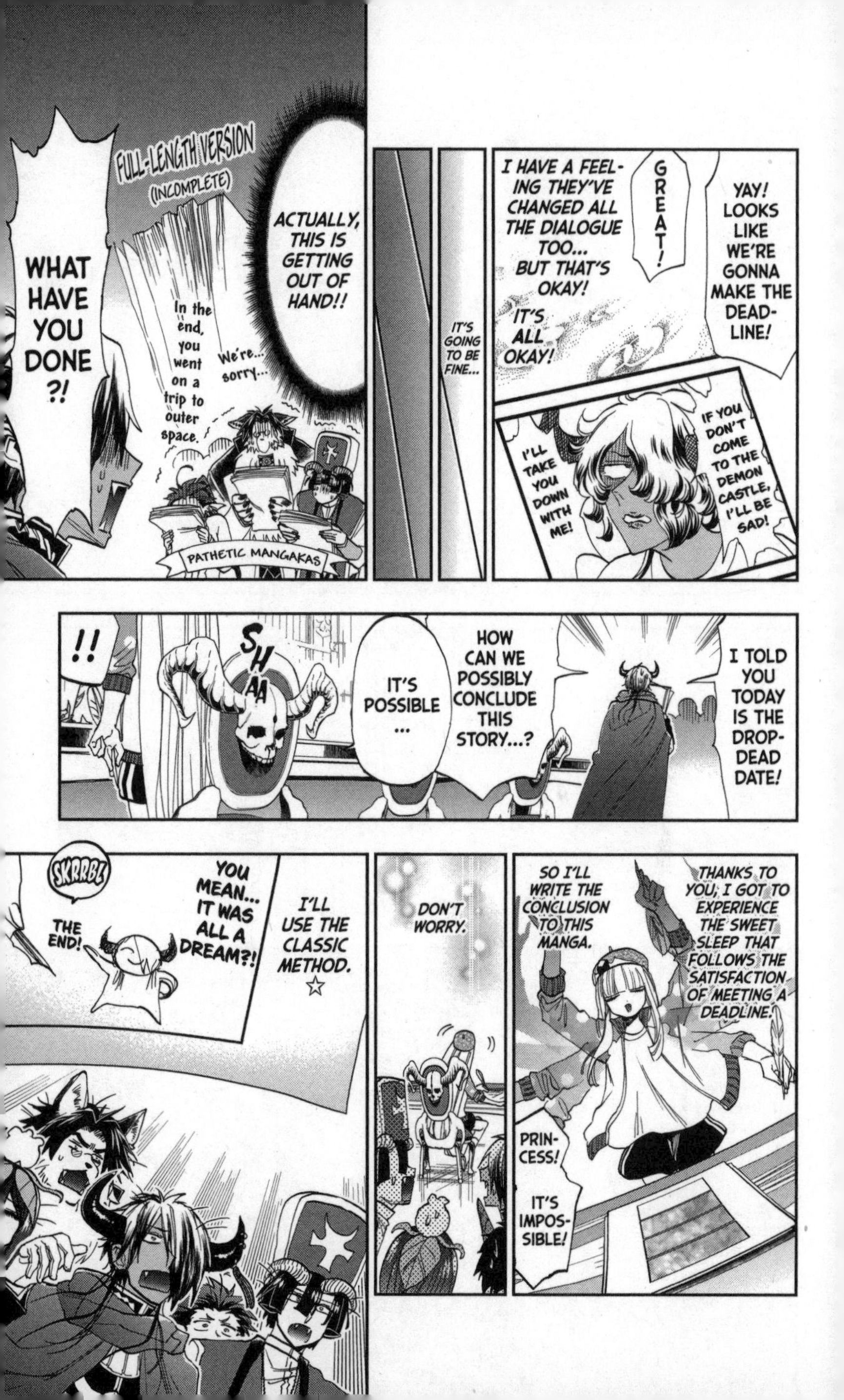
YAY! LOOKS LIKE WE'RE GONNA MAKE THE DEAD-LINE!
GREAT!
I HAVE A FEEL-ING THEY'VE CHANGED ALL THE DIALOGUE TOO... BUT THAT'S OKAY!
IT'S ALL OKAY!
IF YOU DON'T COME TO THE DEMON CASTLE, I'LL BE SAD!
I'LL TAKE YOU DOWN WITH ME!
IT'S GOING TO BE FINE...
FULL-LENGTH VERSION
(INCOMPLETE)
ACTUALLY, THIS IS GETTING OUT OF HAND!!
We're... sorry...
In the end, you went on a trip to outer space.
WHAT HAVE YOU DONE?!
PATHETIC MANGAKAS
I TOLD YOU TODAY IS THE DROP-DEAD DATE!
HOW CAN WE POSSIBLY CONCLUDE THIS STORY...?
IT'S POSSIBLE ...
SHAA
!!
THANKS TO YOU, I GOT TO EXPERIENCE THE SWEET SLEEP THAT FOLLOWS THE SATISFACTION OF MEETING A DEADLINE.
SO I'LL WRITE THE CONCLUSION TO THIS MANGA.
PRIN-CESS!
IT'S IMPOS-SIBLE!
DON'T WORRY.
I'LL USE THE CLASSIC METHOD. ☆
YOU MEAN... IT WAS ALL A DREAM?!
SKRRBL
THE END!

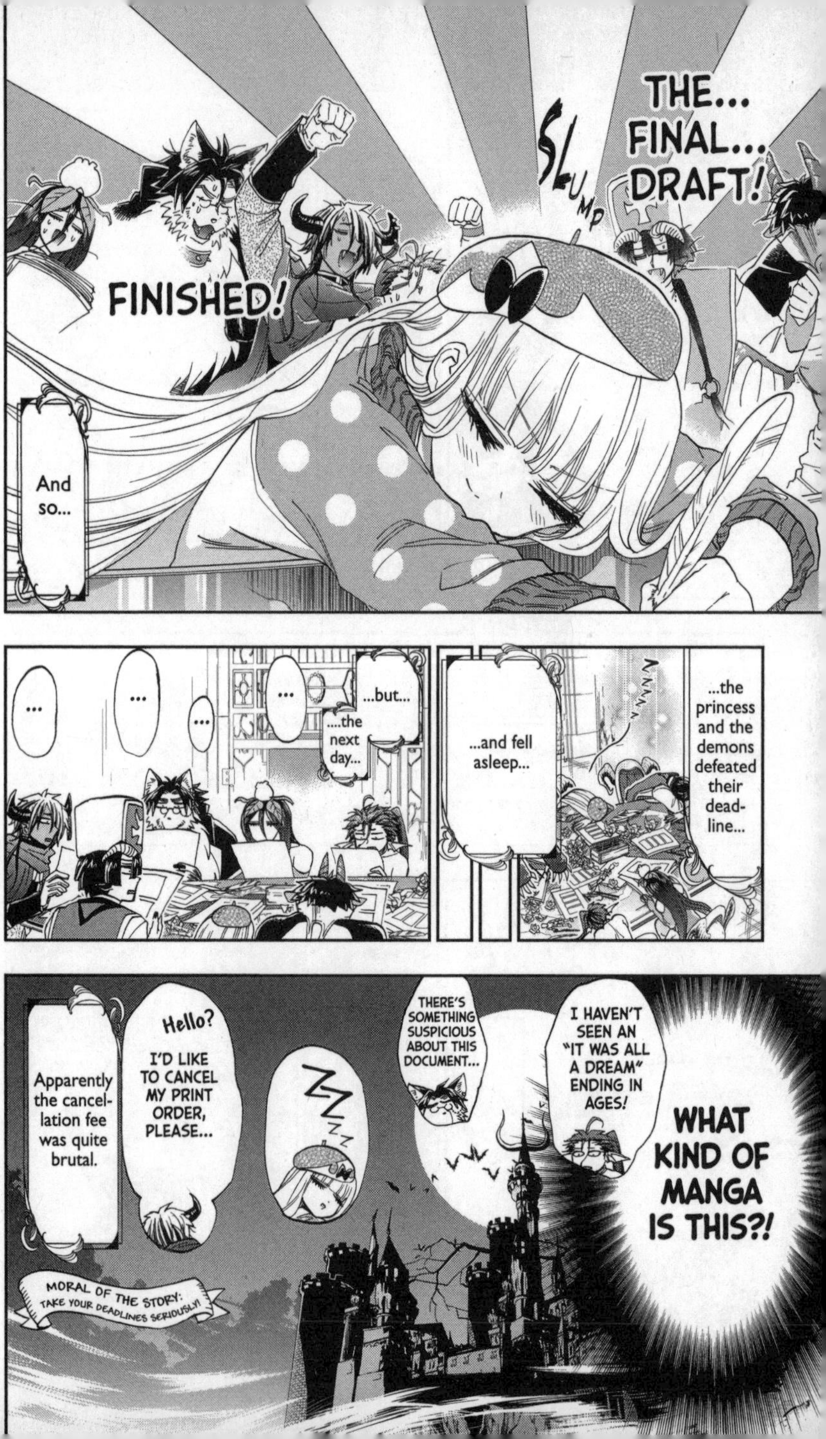
THE... FINAL... DRAFT!
SLUMP
FINISHED!
And so...
...the princess and the demons defeated their dead-line...
...and fell asleep...
...but...
....the next day...
...
...
...
...
WHAT KIND OF MANGA IS THIS?!
I HAVEN'T SEEN AN "IT WAS ALL A DREAM" ENDING IN AGES!
THERE'S SOMETHING SUSPICIOUS ABOUT THIS DOCUMENT...
ZZZ
Hello?
I'D LIKE TO CANCEL MY PRINT ORDER, PLEASE...
Apparently the cancel-lation fee was quite brutal.
MORAL OF THE STORY: TAKE YOUR DEADLINES SERIOUSLY!

The Demon King's Tacky Wardrobe

They're **all** his favorite.
D.K.
EVIL
It's Me

Comfort: ☆☆☆☆☆☆☆☆☆☆
Price: ☆☆

(1) The T-shirt I wear most often. Simple is best.

(2) Cute, isn't it? A yummy-looking, soothing T-shirt.

(3) I bought it because it looks a little like Great Red. Unfortunately, his fur stands up when I wear this while petting him.

(4) A souvenir from Hell Kusatsu. I thought it was cute.

(5) An alien with horns like me?! Cheerful and cute.

(6) I wear this during the cold season, but I bought it because I thought the summer motif was cute. Wearing it puts me in a summery mood.

(7) A shirt for someone who enjoys the great outdoors. The meat is kind of cute, isn't it?

PRINCESS
The princess is a little envious.
I wanna make one too!

I am Demon King Twilight. I have come to the conclusion that we are not suited to create manga.
It's important to know when to give up!

Anyway... the demon army needs you!
My room is somewhere around here.
Demon King Twilight

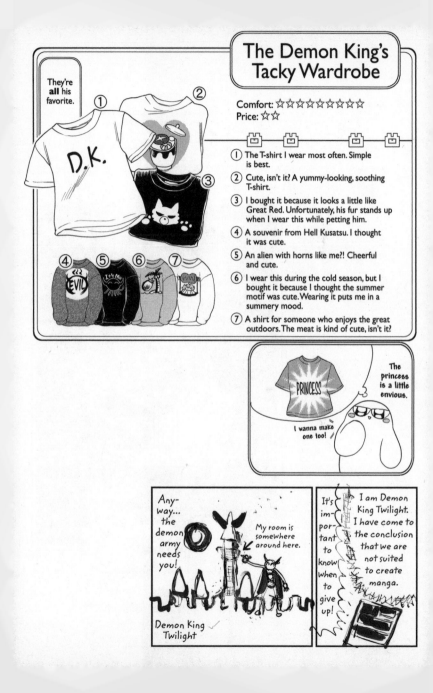

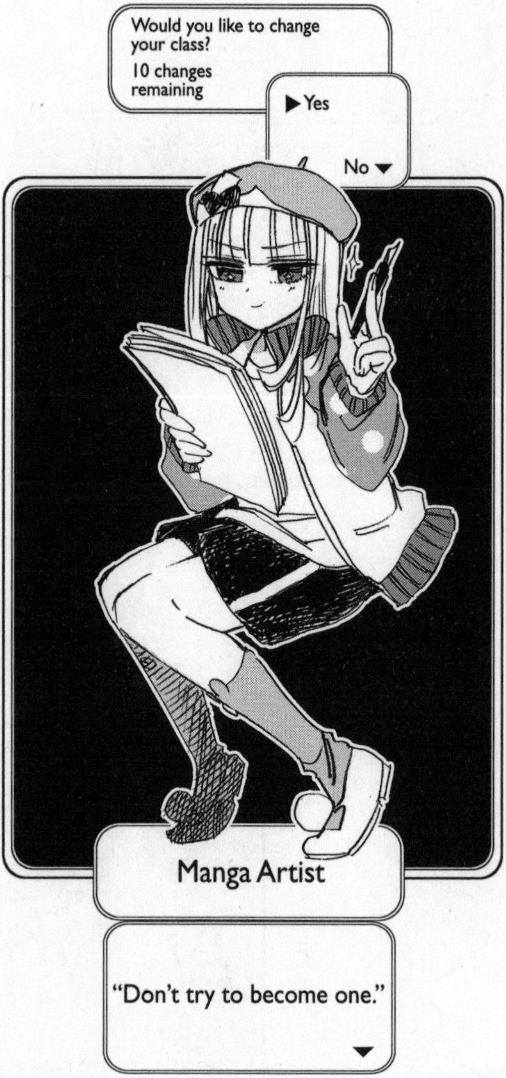
Would you like to change your class?
10 changes remaining
▶Yes
No ▼
Manga Artist
"Don't try to become one."

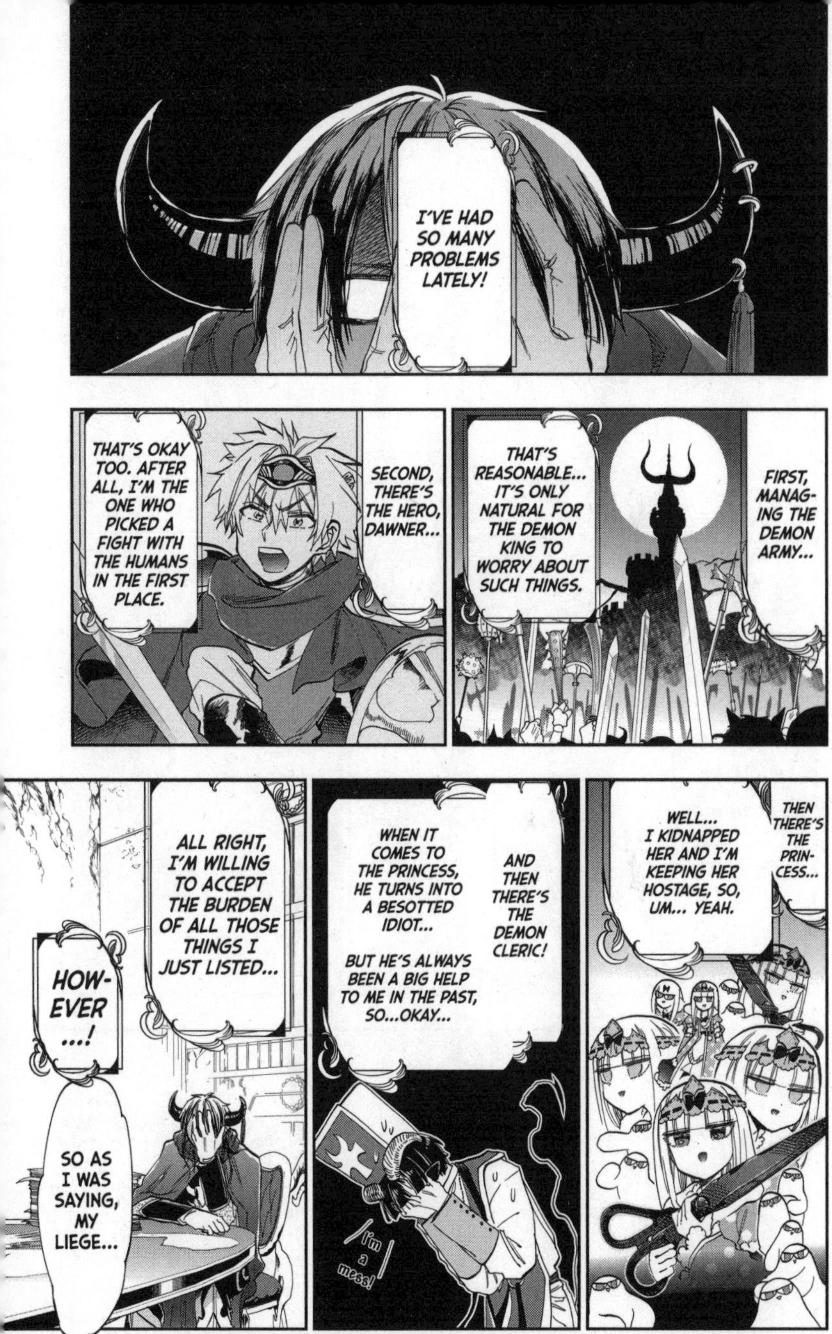
I'VE HAD SO MANY PROBLEMS LATELY!
FIRST, MANAGING THE DEMON ARMY...
THAT'S REASONABLE... IT'S ONLY NATURAL FOR THE DEMON KING TO WORRY ABOUT SUCH THINGS.
SECOND, THERE'S THE HERO, DAWNER...
THAT'S OKAY TOO. AFTER ALL, I'M THE ONE WHO PICKED A FIGHT WITH THE HUMANS IN THE FIRST PLACE.
THEN THERE'S THE PRINCESS...
WELL... I KIDNAPPED HER AND I'M KEEPING HER HOSTAGE, SO, UM... YEAH.
AND THEN THERE'S THE DEMON CLERIC!
WHEN IT COMES TO THE PRINCESS, HE TURNS INTO A BESOTTED IDIOT...
BUT HE'S ALWAYS BEEN A BIG HELP TO ME IN THE PAST, SO...OKAY...
I'm a mess!
ALL RIGHT, I'M WILLING TO ACCEPT THE BURDEN OF ALL THOSE THINGS I JUST LISTED...
HOW-EVER ...!
SO AS I WAS SAYING, MY LIEGE...

107th Night: V.I.D. (Very Important Demon)

107th Night: V.I.D. (Very Important Demon)

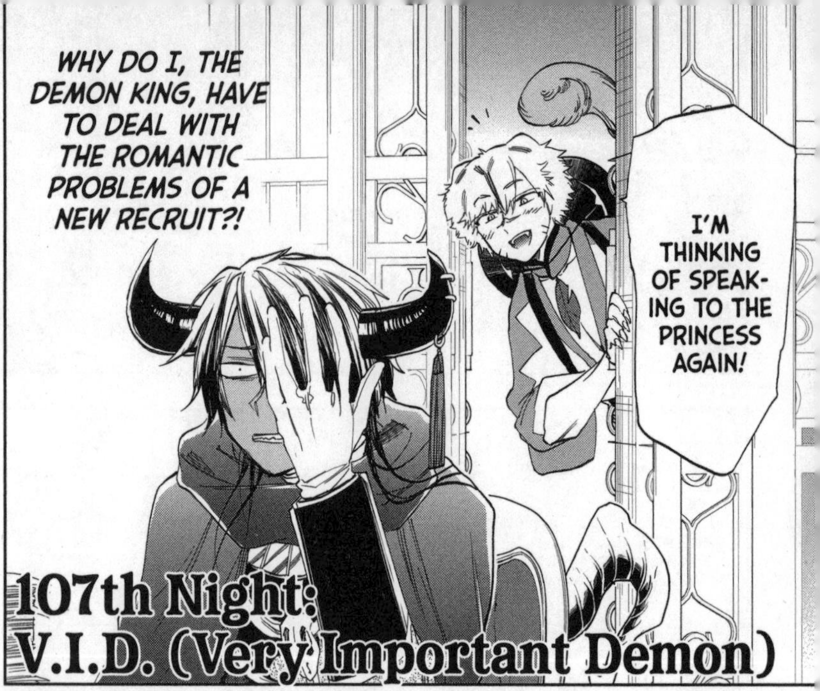
I'M THINKING OF SPEAK-ING TO THE PRINCESS AGAIN!
WHY DO I, THE DEMON KING, HAVE TO DEAL WITH THE ROMANTIC PROBLEMS OF A NEW RECRUIT?!
107th Night: V.I.D. (Very Important Demon)

*See *Sleepy Princess in the Demon Castle* Vol. 8, 101st Night

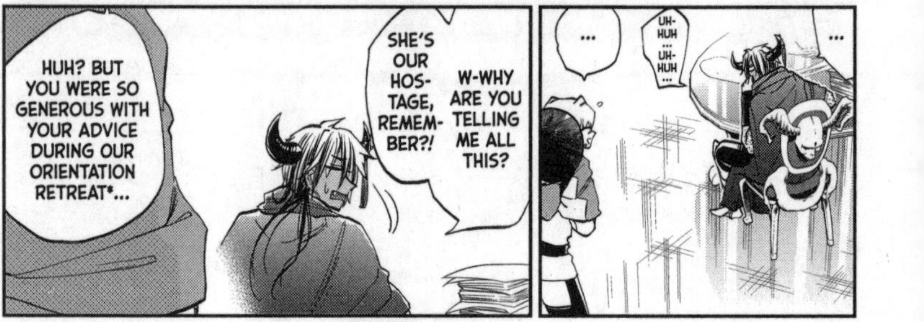
...
UH-HUH ... UH-HUH ...
...
W-WHY ARE YOU TELLING ME ALL THIS?
SHE'S OUR HOS-TAGE, REMEM-BER?!
HUH? BUT YOU WERE SO GENEROUS WITH YOUR ADVICE DURING OUR ORIENTATION RETREAT*...

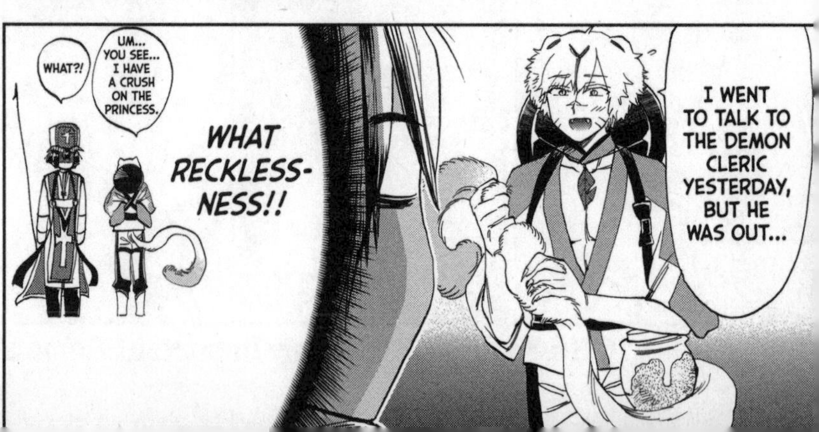
I WENT TO TALK TO THE DEMON CLERIC YESTERDAY, BUT HE WAS OUT...
WHAT RECKLESS-NESS!!
UM... YOU SEE... I HAVE A CRUSH ON THE PRINCESS.
WHAT?!

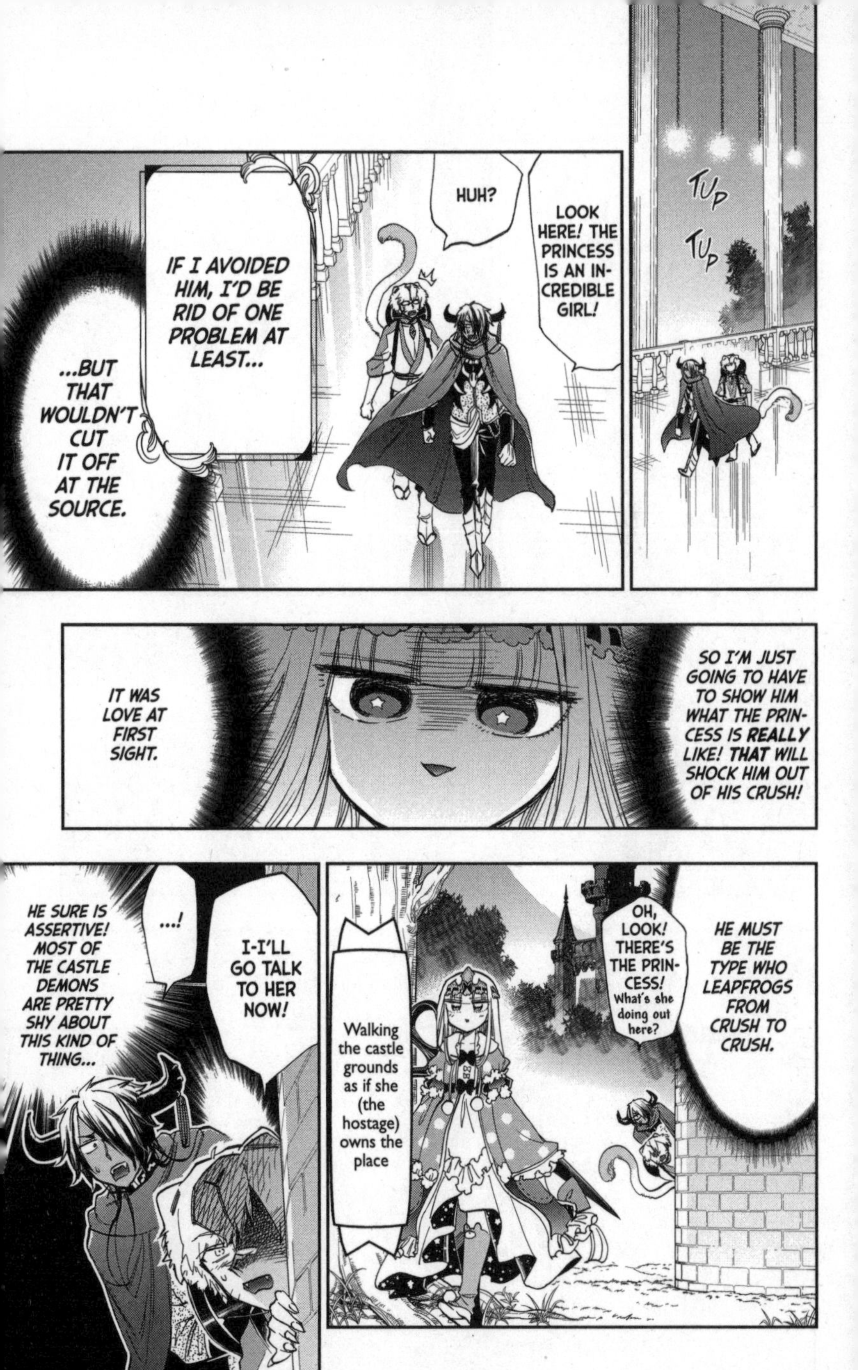
TUP
TUP
LOOK HERE! THE PRINCESS IS AN INCREDIBLE GIRL!
HUH?
IF I AVOIDED HIM, I'D BE RID OF ONE PROBLEM AT LEAST...
...BUT THAT WOULDN'T CUT IT OFF AT THE SOURCE.
SO I'M JUST GOING TO HAVE TO SHOW HIM WHAT THE PRINCESS IS REALLY LIKE! THAT WILL SHOCK HIM OUT OF HIS CRUSH!
IT WAS LOVE AT FIRST SIGHT.
HE MUST BE THE TYPE WHO LEAPFROGS FROM CRUSH TO CRUSH.
OH, LOOK! THERE'S THE PRINCESS!
What's she doing out here?
Walking the castle grounds as if she (the hostage) owns the place
I-I'LL GO TALK TO HER NOW!
...!
HE SURE IS ASSERTIVE! MOST OF THE CASTLE DEMONS ARE PRETTY SHY ABOUT THIS KIND OF THING...

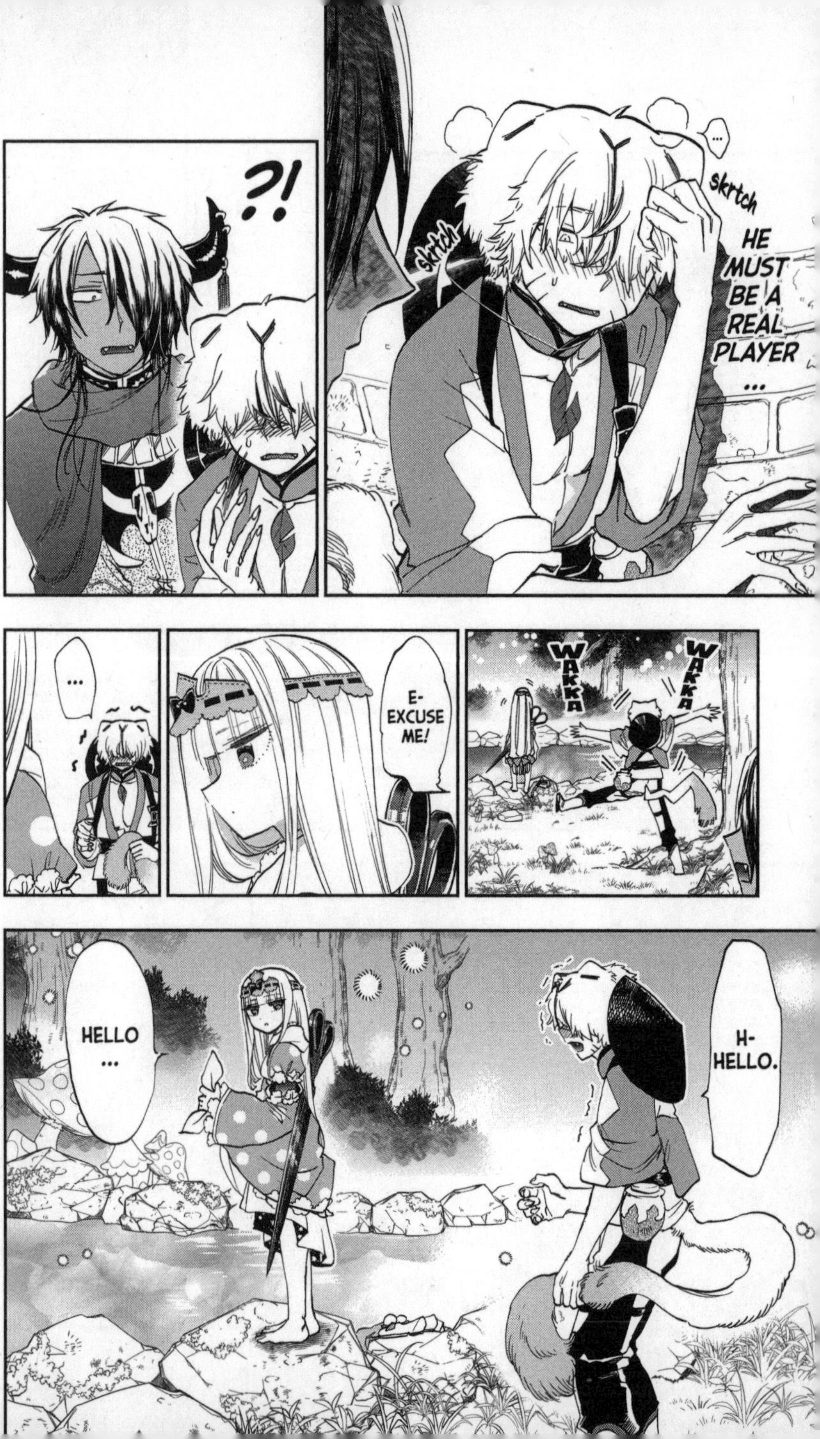
...
skrtch
HE MUST BE A REAL PLAYER ...
skrtch
?!
WAKKA
WAKKA
E-EXCUSE ME!
...
H-HELLO.
HELLO ...

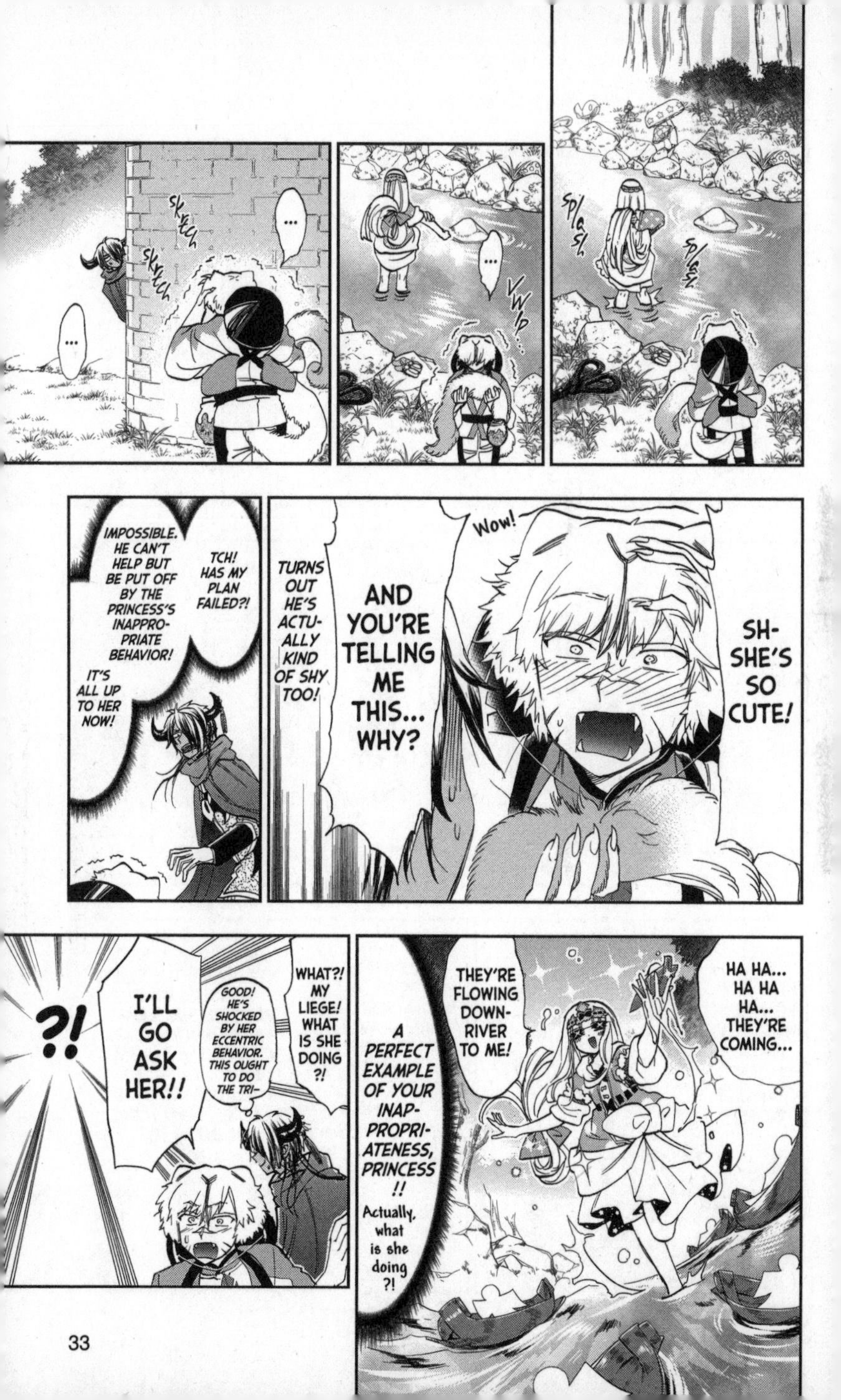
splash
splash
...
VWIP...
...
skrtch
skrtch
...
SH-SHE'S SO CUTE!
Wow!
AND YOU'RE TELLING ME THIS... WHY?
TURNS OUT HE'S ACTUALLY KIND OF SHY TOO!
TCH! HAS MY PLAN FAILED?!
IMPOSSIBLE. HE CAN'T HELP BUT BE PUT OFF BY THE PRINCESS'S INAPPROPRIATE BEHAVIOR!
IT'S ALL UP TO HER NOW!
HA HA... HA HA HA... THEY'RE COMING...
THEY'RE FLOWING DOWNRIVER TO ME!
A PERFECT EXAMPLE OF YOUR INAPPROPRIATENESS, PRINCESS!!
Actually, what is she doing?!
WHAT?! MY LIEGE! WHAT IS SHE DOING?!
GOOD! HE'S SHOCKED BY HER ECCENTRIC BEHAVIOR. THIS OUGHT TO DO THE TRI-
I'LL GO ASK HER!!
?!

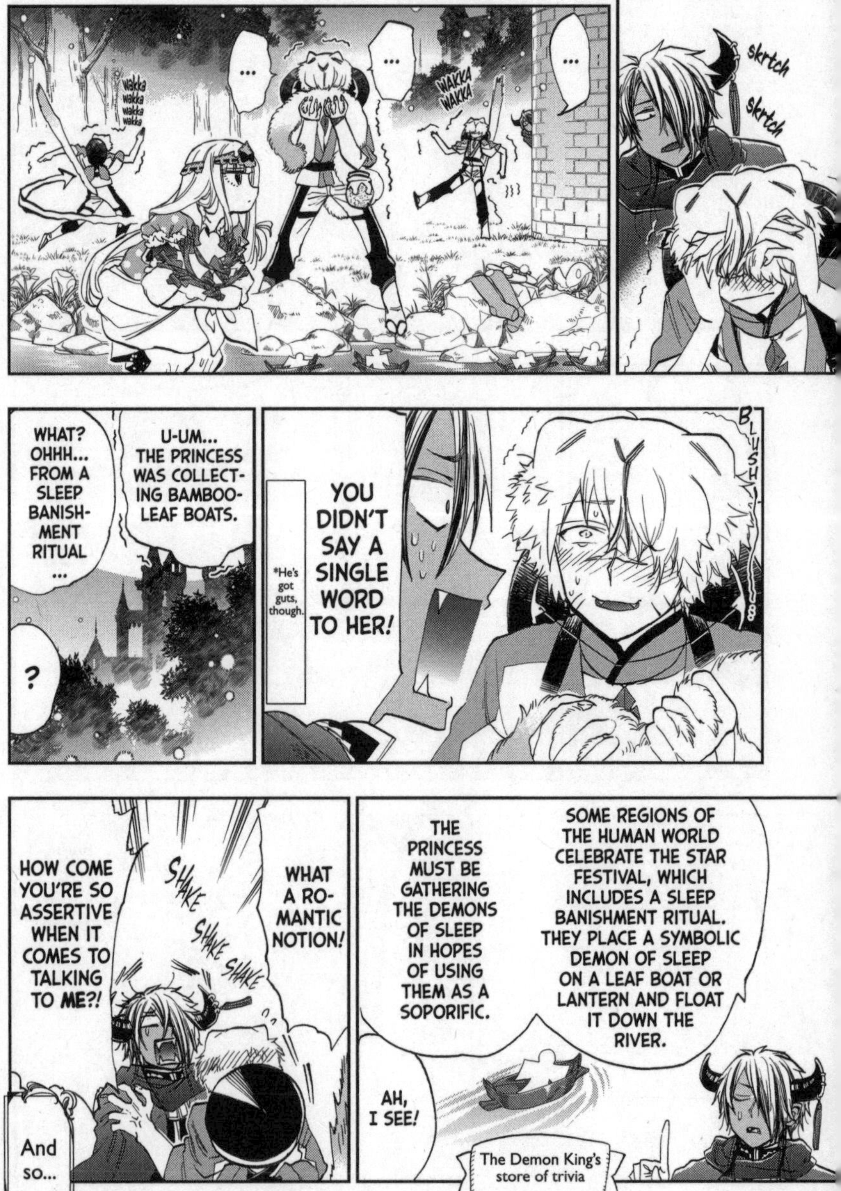

skrtch
skrtch
...
WAKKA WAKKA
...
...
wakka wakka wakka wakka
BLUSH
YOU DIDN'T SAY A SINGLE WORD TO HER!
*He's got guts, though.
U-UM... THE PRINCESS WAS COLLECT-ING BAMBOO-LEAF BOATS.
WHAT? OHHH... FROM A SLEEP BANISH-MENT RITUAL...
?
SOME REGIONS OF THE HUMAN WORLD CELEBRATE THE STAR FESTIVAL, WHICH INCLUDES A SLEEP BANISHMENT RITUAL. THEY PLACE A SYMBOLIC DEMON OF SLEEP ON A LEAF BOAT OR LANTERN AND FLOAT IT DOWN THE RIVER.
THE PRINCESS MUST BE GATHERING THE DEMONS OF SLEEP IN HOPES OF USING THEM AS A SOPORIFIC.
AH, I SEE!
The Demon King's store of trivia
WHAT A RO-MANTIC NOTION!
SHAKE
SHAKE
SHAKE
HOW COME YOU'RE SO ASSERTIVE WHEN IT COMES TO TALKING TO ME?!
And so...

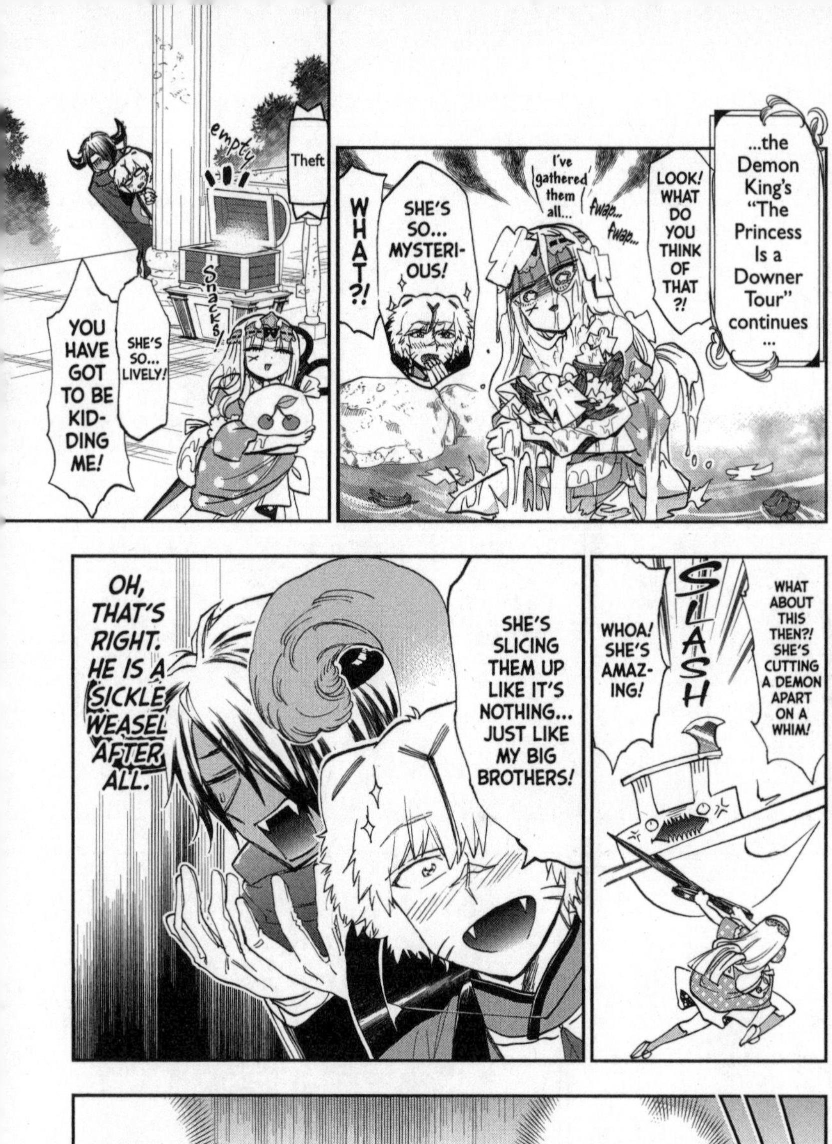
...the Demon King's "The Princess Is a Downer Tour" continues...
LOOK! WHAT DO YOU THINK OF THAT?!
I've gathered them all...
fwap... fwap...
SHE'S SO... MYSTERIOUS!
WHAT?!
Theft
empty
Snacks!
SHE'S SO... LIVELY!
YOU HAVE GOT TO BE KIDDING ME!
WHAT ABOUT THIS THEN?! SHE'S CUTTING A DEMON APART ON A WHIM!
SLASH
WHOA! SHE'S AMAZING!
SHE'S SLICING THEM UP LIKE IT'S NOTHING... JUST LIKE MY BIG BROTHERS!
OH, THAT'S RIGHT. HE IS A SICKLE WEASEL AFTER ALL.
NNGH...
IT'S NO USE. NOTHING SHOCKS HIM.
IN FACT, I THINK MY PLAN BACKFIRED.

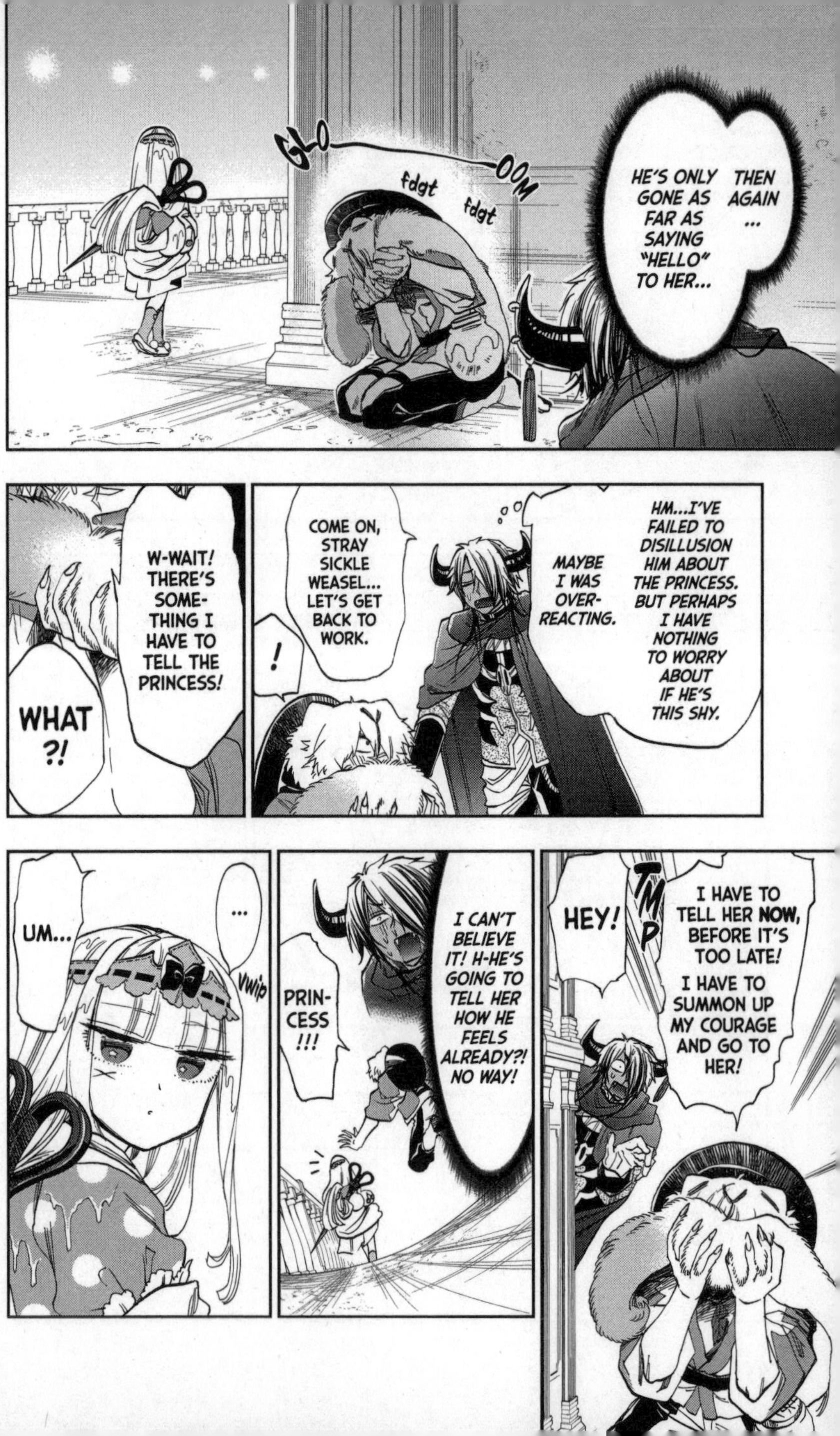
THEN AGAIN ...
HE'S ONLY GONE AS FAR AS SAYING "HELLO" TO HER...
GLO—OOM
fdgt fdgt
HM...I'VE FAILED TO DISILLUSION HIM ABOUT THE PRINCESS. BUT PERHAPS I HAVE NOTHING TO WORRY ABOUT IF HE'S THIS SHY.
MAYBE I WAS OVER-REACTING.
COME ON, STRAY SICKLE WEASEL... LET'S GET BACK TO WORK.
!
W-WAIT! THERE'S SOME-THING I HAVE TO TELL THE PRINCESS!
WHAT ?!
I HAVE TO TELL HER NOW, BEFORE IT'S TOO LATE!
I HAVE TO SUMMON UP MY COURAGE AND GO TO HER!
TMP
HEY!
I CAN'T BELIEVE IT! H-HE'S GOING TO TELL HER HOW HE FEELS ALREADY?! NO WAY!
PRIN-CESS !!!
Vwip
...
UM...

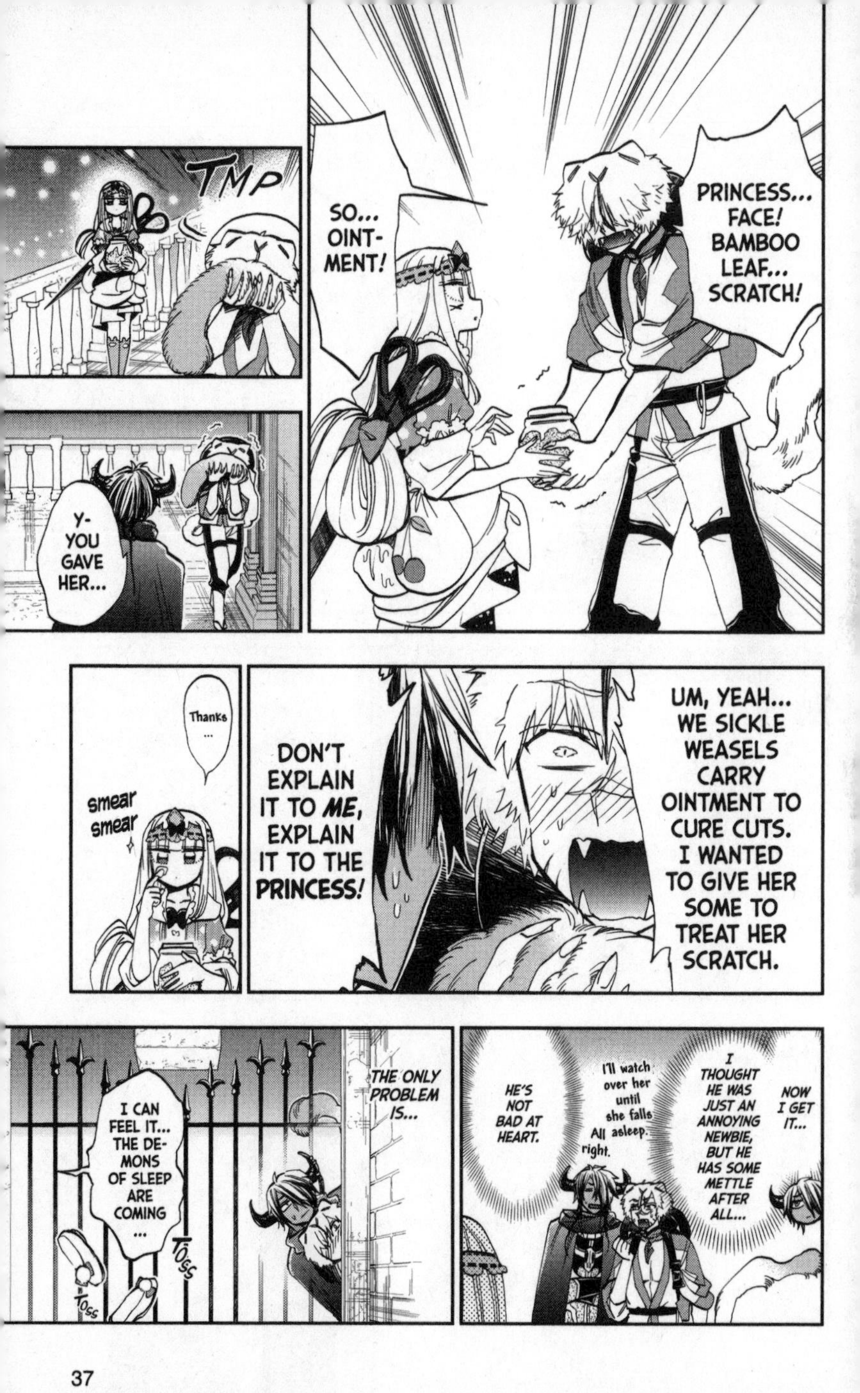
PRINCESS... FACE! BAMBOO LEAF... SCRATCH!
SO... OINT-MENT!
TMP
Y-YOU GAVE HER...
UM, YEAH... WE SICKLE WEASELS CARRY OINTMENT TO CURE CUTS. I WANTED TO GIVE HER SOME TO TREAT HER SCRATCH.
DON'T EXPLAIN IT TO *ME*, EXPLAIN IT TO THE PRINCESS!
Thanks ...
smear smear
NOW I GET IT...
I THOUGHT HE WAS JUST AN ANNOYING NEWBIE, BUT HE HAS SOME METTLE AFTER ALL...
I'll watch over her until she falls asleep.
All right.
HE'S NOT BAD AT HEART.
THE ONLY PROBLEM IS...
I CAN FEEL IT... THE DE-MONS OF SLEEP ARE COMING ...
TOSS
TOSS

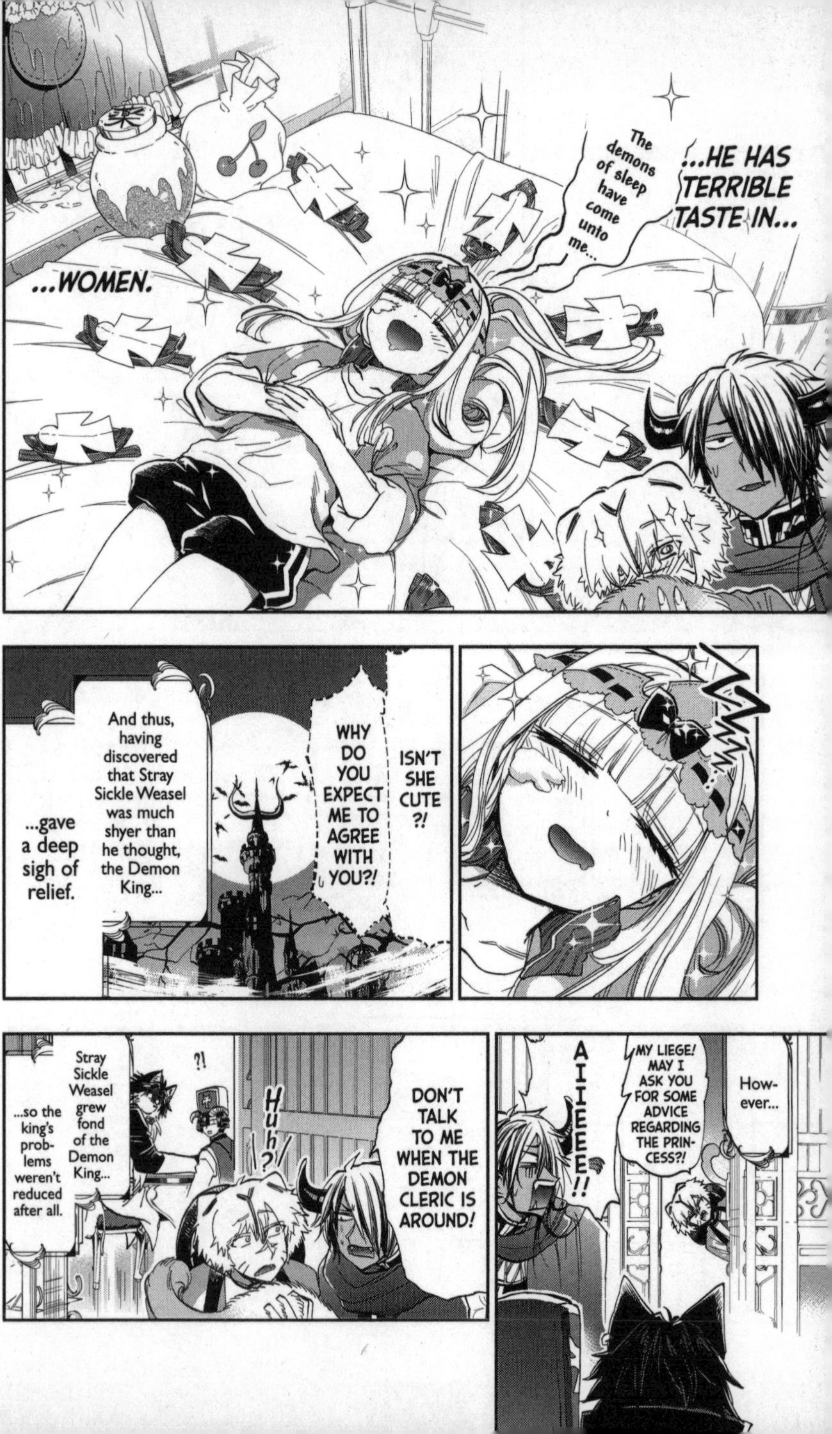
...HE HAS TERRIBLE TASTE IN...
The demons of sleep have come unto me...
...WOMEN.
ISN'T SHE CUTE?!
WHY DO YOU EXPECT ME TO AGREE WITH YOU?!
And thus, having discovered that Stray Sickle Weasel was much shyer than he thought, the Demon King...
...gave a deep sigh of relief.
However...
MY LIEGE! MAY I ASK YOU FOR SOME ADVICE REGARDING THE PRINCESS?!
AIIEEEE!!
DON'T TALK TO ME WHEN THE DEMON CLERIC IS AROUND!
Huh?!
?!
Stray Sickle Weasel grew fond of the Demon King...
...so the king's problems weren't reduced after all.

Sickle Weasel Ointment

Effectiveness: ☆☆☆☆☆☆☆☆☆☆
Kindness: ☆☆☆☆☆

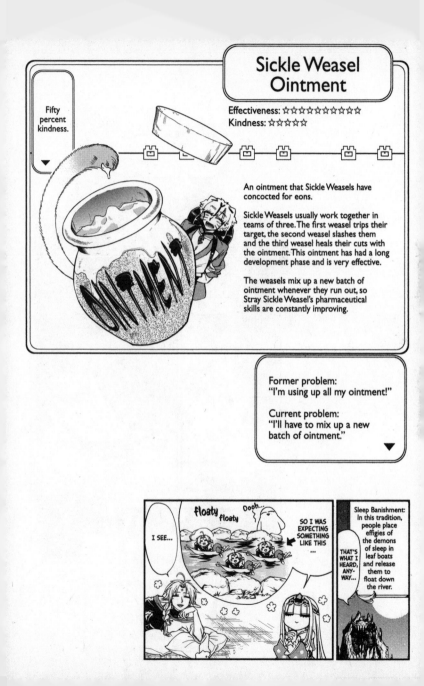

Fifty percent kindness.

OINTMENT

An ointment that Sickle Weasels have concocted for eons.

Sickle Weasels usually work together in teams of three. The first weasel trips their target, the second weasel slashes them and the third weasel heals their cuts with the ointment. This ointment has had a long development phase and is very effective.

The weasels mix up a new batch of ointment whenever they run out, so Stray Sickle Weasel's pharmaceutical skills are constantly improving.

Former problem:
"I'm using up all my ointment!"

Current problem:
"I'll have to mix up a new batch of ointment."

Sleep Banishment: In this tradition, people place effigies of the demons of sleep in leaf boats and release them to float down the river.
THAT'S WHAT I HEARD, ANYWAY...
SO I WAS EXPECTING SOMETHING LIKE THIS ...
Oooh...
floaty floaty
I SEE...

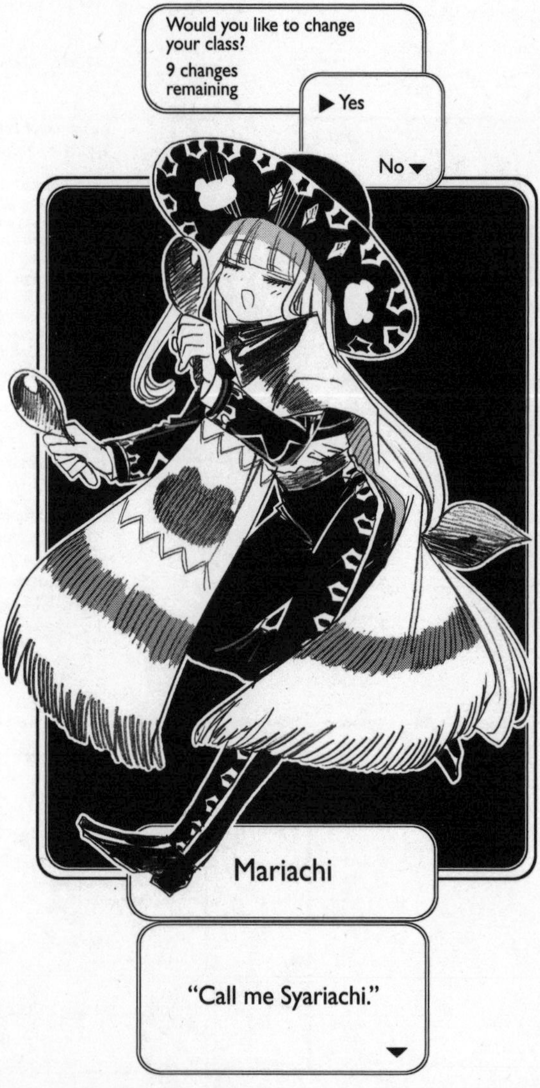
Would you like to change your class?
9 changes remaining
▶ Yes
No
Mariachi
"Call me Syariachi."

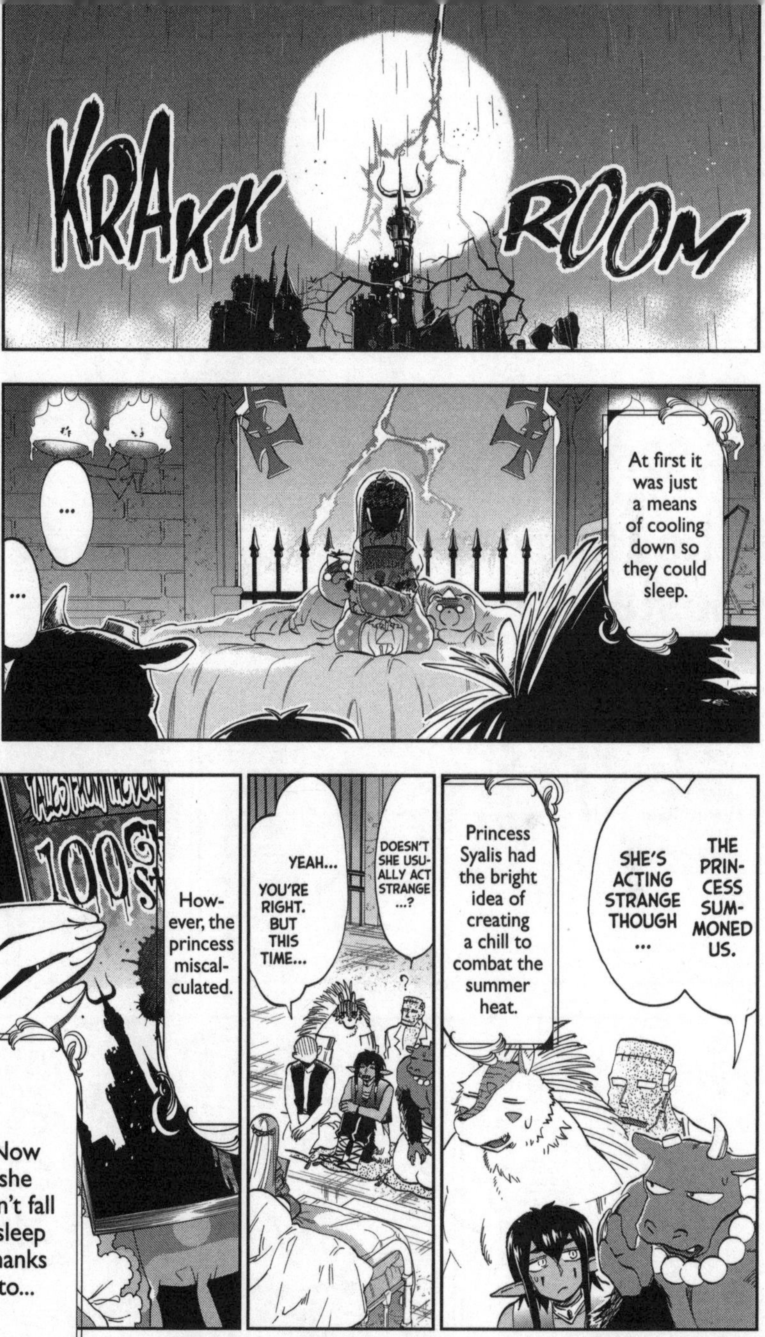
KRAKK
ROOM
At first it was just a means of cooling down so they could sleep.
...
...
THE PRINCESS SUMMONED US.
SHE'S ACTING STRANGE THOUGH...
Princess Syalis had the bright idea of creating a chill to combat the summer heat.
DOESN'T SHE USUALLY ACT STRANGE...?
YEAH... YOU'RE RIGHT. BUT THIS TIME...
?
However, the princess miscalculated.
Now she can't fall asleep thanks to...

108th Night:
The Horror of the Free-Range Hostage

108th Night: The Horror of the Free-Range Hostage

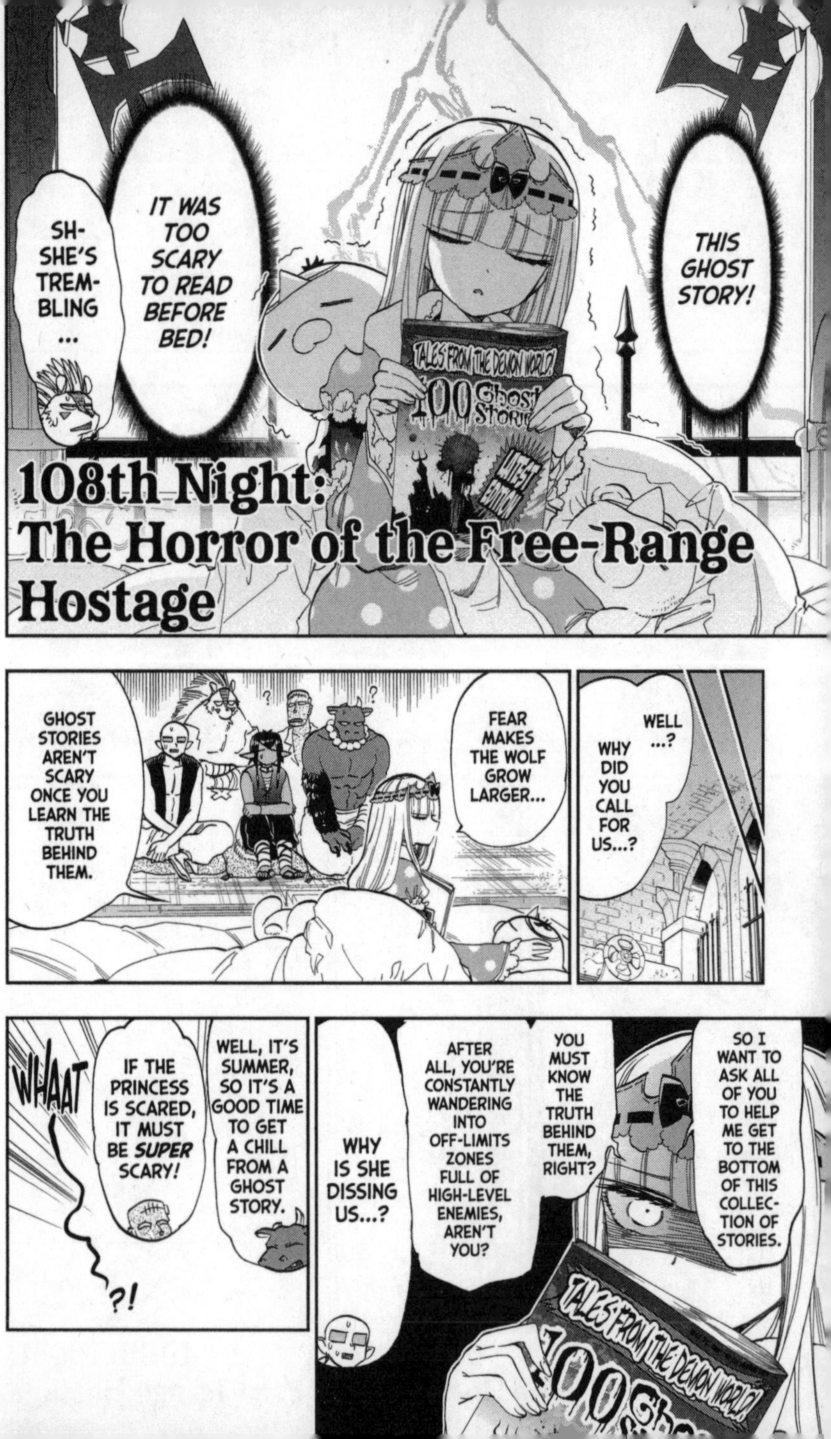
THIS GHOST STORY!
IT WAS TOO SCARY TO READ BEFORE BED!
TALES FROM THE DEMON WORLD!
SH-SHE'S TREM-BLING ...
WELL ...?
WHY DID YOU CALL FOR US...?
FEAR MAKES THE WOLF GROW LARGER...
GHOST STORIES AREN'T SCARY ONCE YOU LEARN THE TRUTH BEHIND THEM.
SO I WANT TO ASK ALL OF YOU TO HELP ME GET TO THE BOTTOM OF THIS COLLEC-TION OF STORIES.
YOU MUST KNOW THE TRUTH BEHIND THEM, RIGHT?
AFTER ALL, YOU'RE CONSTANTLY WANDERING INTO OFF-LIMITS ZONES FULL OF HIGH-LEVEL ENEMIES, AREN'T YOU?
WHY IS SHE DISSING US...?
TALES FROM THE DEMON WORLD!
WELL, IT'S SUMMER, SO IT'S A GOOD TIME TO GET A CHILL FROM A GHOST STORY.
IF THE PRINCESS IS SCARED, IT MUST BE *SUPER* SCARY!
WHAAT
?!

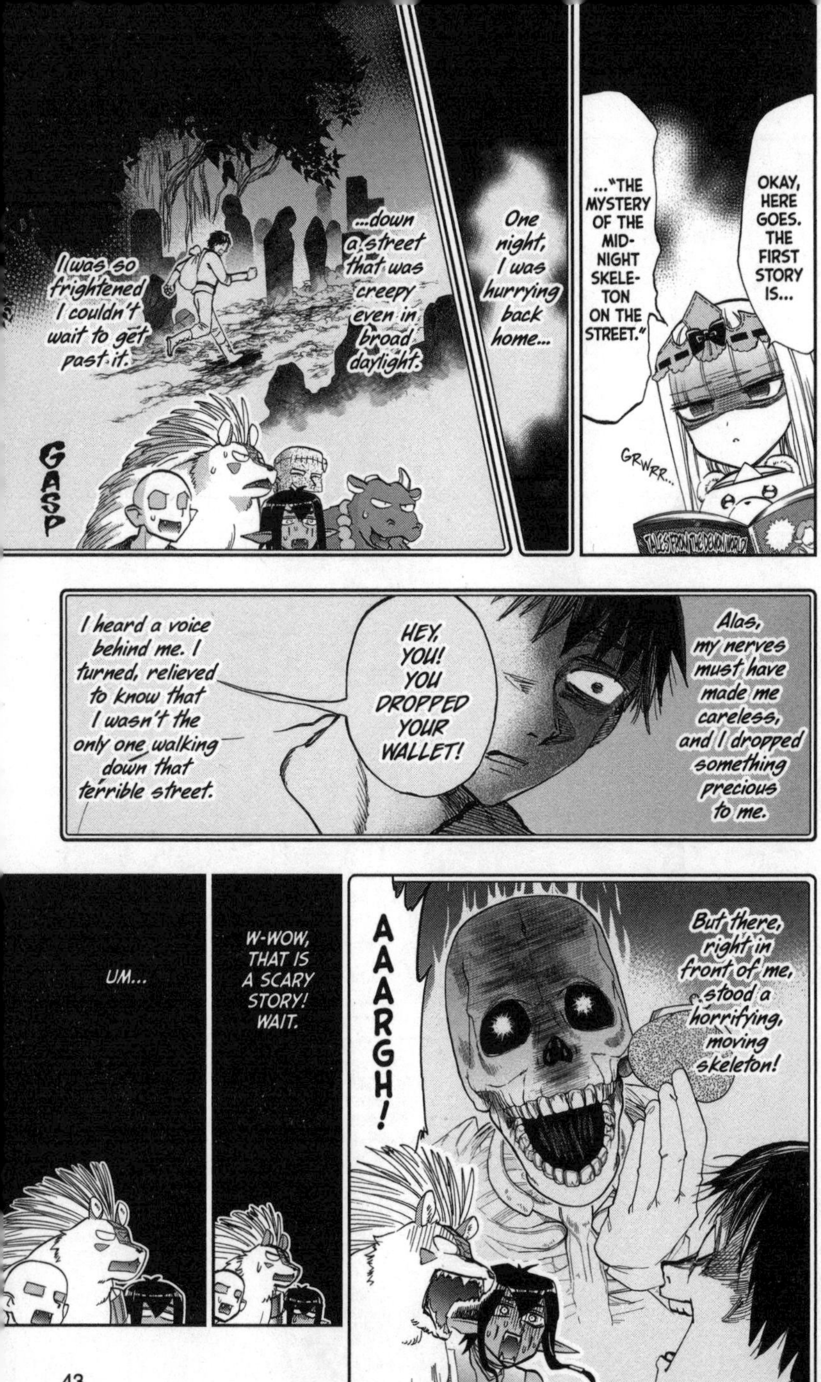
OKAY, HERE GOES. THE FIRST STORY IS...
..."THE MYSTERY OF THE MID-NIGHT SKELE-TON ON THE STREET."
GRWRR...
TALES FROM THE DEMON WORLD
One night, I was hurrying back home...
...down a street that was creepy even in broad daylight.
I was so frightened I couldn't wait to get past it.
GASP
Alas, my nerves must have made me careless, and I dropped something precious to me.
HEY, YOU! YOU DROPPED YOUR WALLET!
I heard a voice behind me. I turned, relieved to know that I wasn't the only one walking down that terrible street.
But there, right in front of me, stood a horrifying, moving skeleton!
AAAARGH!
W-WOW, THAT IS A SCARY STORY! WAIT.
UM...

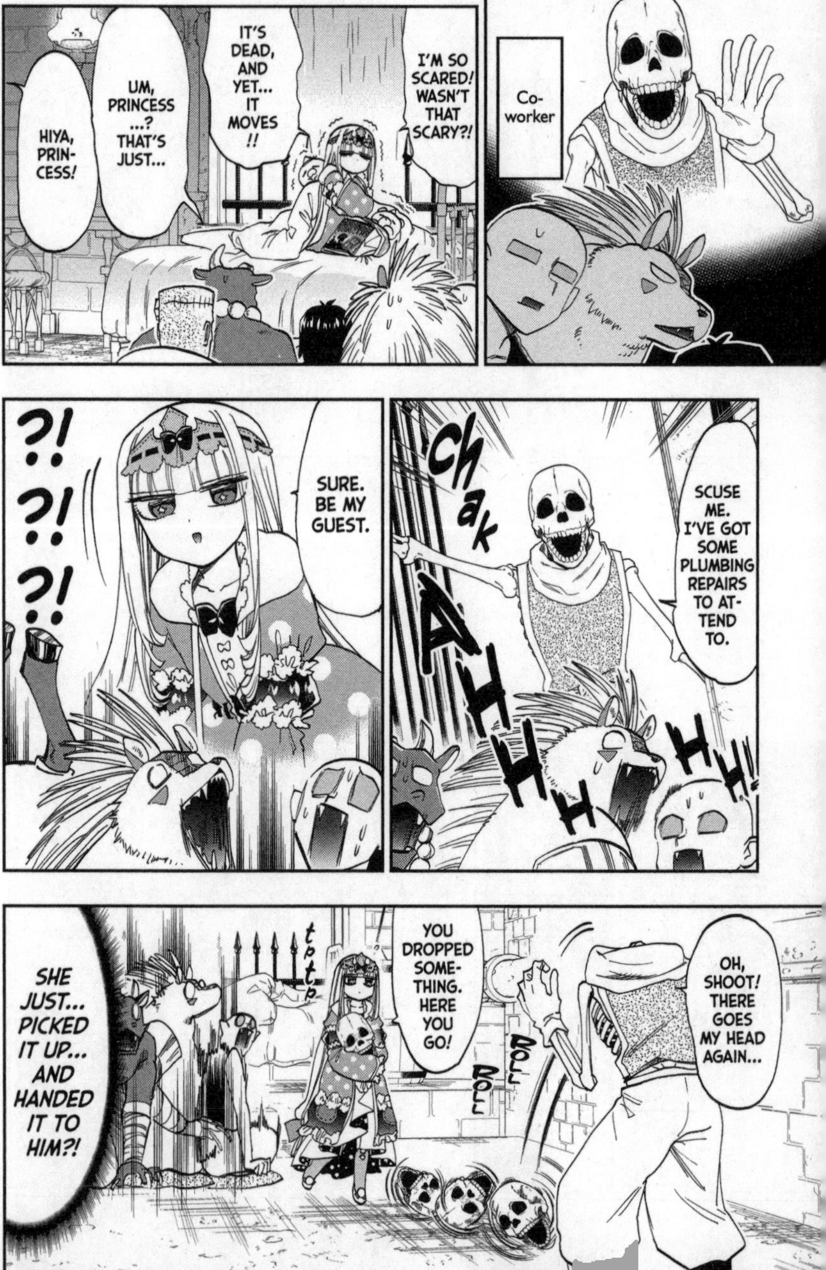
Co-worker
I'M SO SCARED! WASN'T THAT SCARY?!
IT'S DEAD, AND YET... IT MOVES !!
UM, PRINCESS ...? THAT'S JUST...
HIYA, PRINCESS!
Chak
SCUSE ME. I'VE GOT SOME PLUMBING REPAIRS TO ATTEND TO.
AHHHHHHHH!
SURE. BE MY GUEST.
?! ?! ?!
OH, SHOOT! THERE GOES MY HEAD AGAIN...
ROLL ROLL
YOU DROPPED SOMETHING. HERE YOU GO!
tptp
SHE JUST... PICKED IT UP... AND HANDED IT TO HIM?!

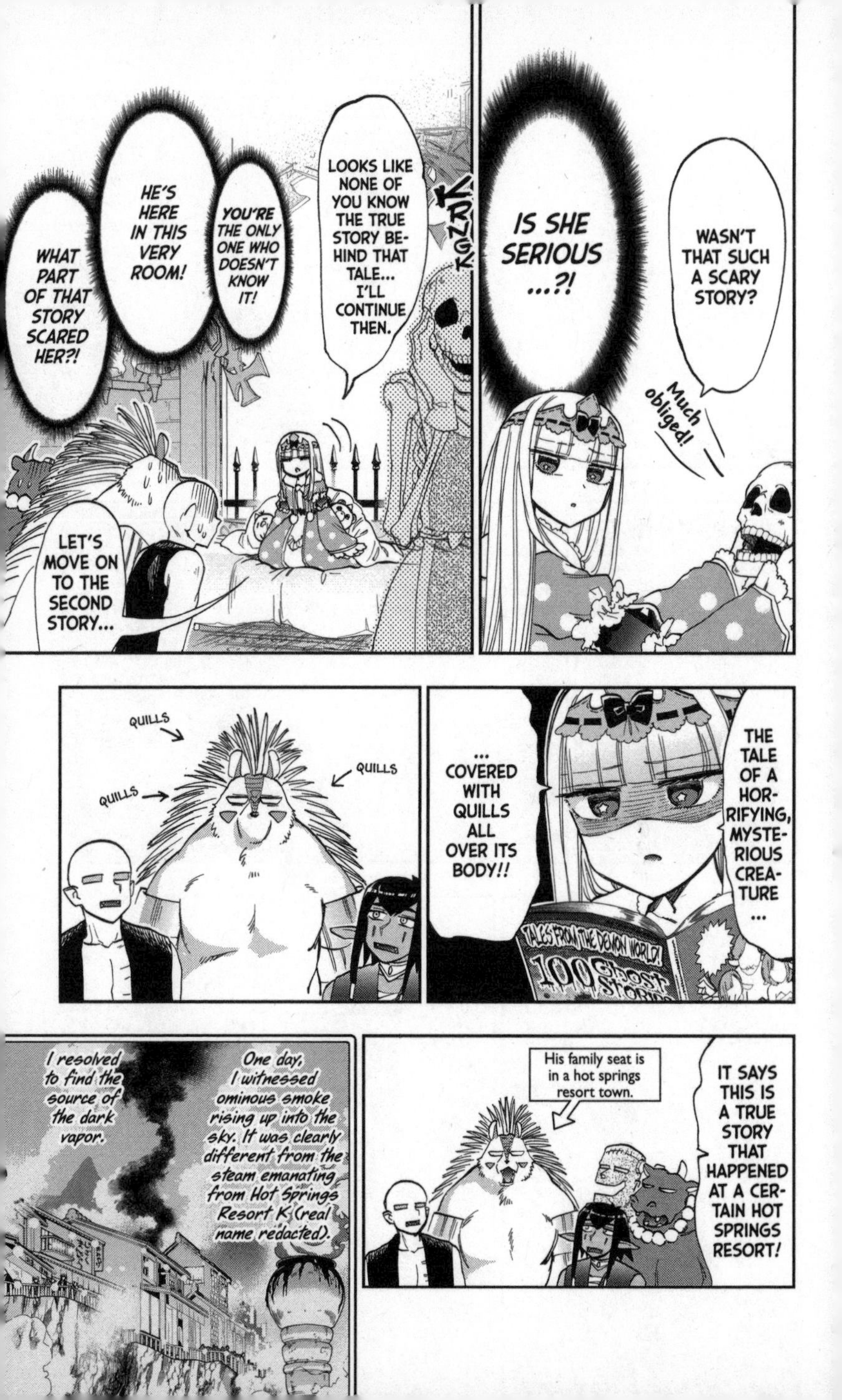
WASN'T THAT SUCH A SCARY STORY?
Much obliged!
IS SHE SERIOUS...?!
LOOKS LIKE NONE OF YOU KNOW THE TRUE STORY BEHIND THAT TALE... I'LL CONTINUE THEN.
KRNGK
YOU'RE THE ONLY ONE WHO DOESN'T KNOW IT!
HE'S HERE IN THIS VERY ROOM!
WHAT PART OF THAT STORY SCARED HER?!
LET'S MOVE ON TO THE SECOND STORY...
THE TALE OF A HORRIFYING, MYSTERIOUS CREATURE...
...COVERED WITH QUILLS ALL OVER ITS BODY!!
TALES FROM THE DEMON WORLD! 100 Ghost Stories
QUILLS
QUILLS
QUILLS
IT SAYS THIS IS A TRUE STORY THAT HAPPENED AT A CERTAIN HOT SPRINGS RESORT!
His family seat is in a hot springs resort town.
One day, I witnessed ominous smoke rising up into the sky. It was clearly different from the steam emanating from Hot Springs Resort K (real name redacted).
I resolved to find the source of the dark vapor.

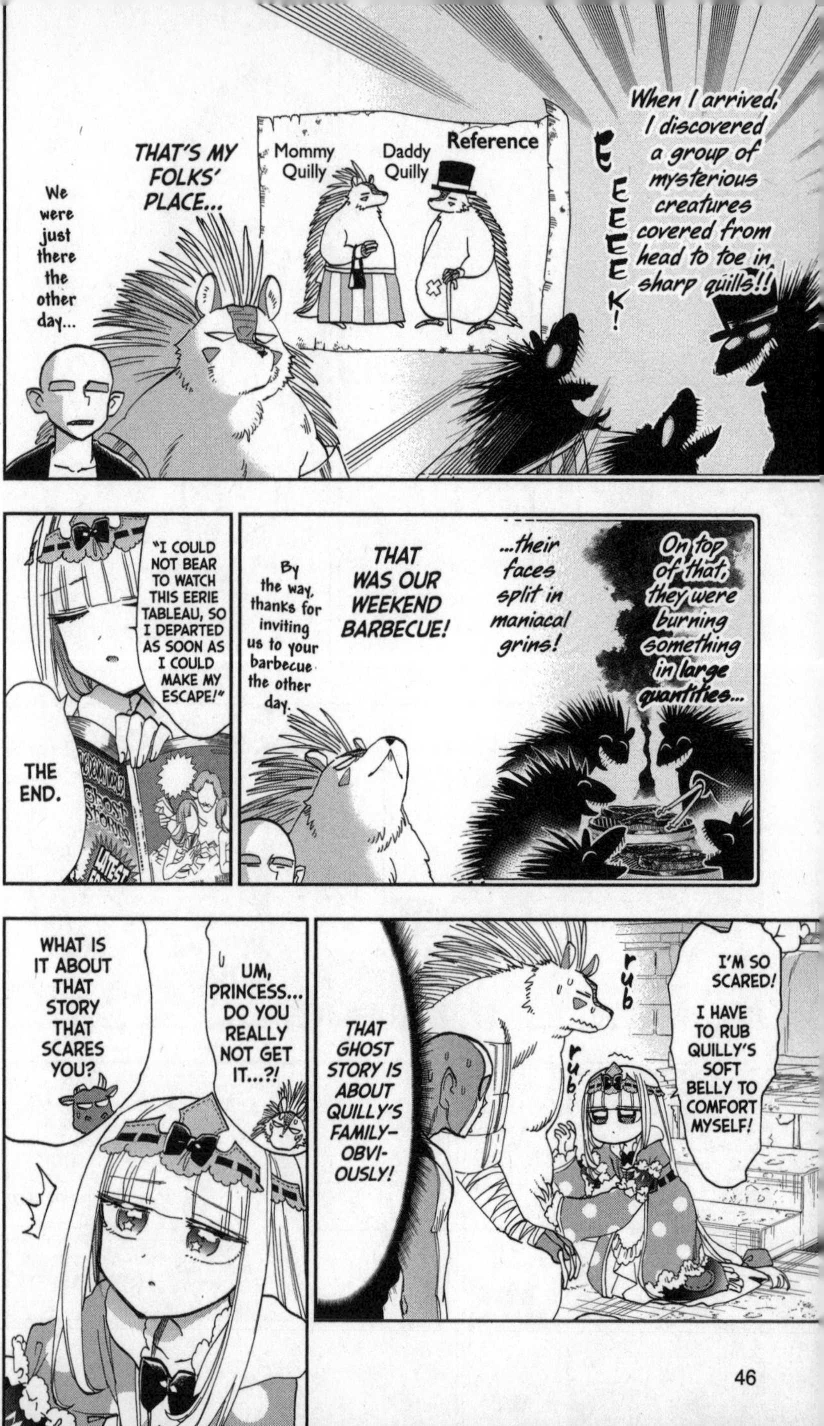
When I arrived, I discovered a group of mysterious creatures covered from head to toe in sharp quills!!
EEEEEK!
Reference
Daddy Quilly
Mommy Quilly
THAT'S MY FOLKS' PLACE...
We were just there the other day...
On top of that, they were burning something in large quantities...
...their faces split in maniacal grins!
THAT WAS OUR WEEKEND BARBECUE!
By the way, thanks for inviting us to your barbecue the other day.
"I COULD NOT BEAR TO WATCH THIS EERIE TABLEAU, SO I DEPARTED AS SOON AS I COULD MAKE MY ESCAPE!"
THE END.
I'M SO SCARED!
I HAVE TO RUB QUILLY'S SOFT BELLY TO COMFORT MYSELF!
rub
rub
THAT GHOST STORY IS ABOUT QUILLY'S FAMILY—OBVIOUSLY!
UM, PRINCESS... DO YOU REALLY NOT GET IT...?!
WHAT IS IT ABOUT THAT STORY THAT SCARES YOU?

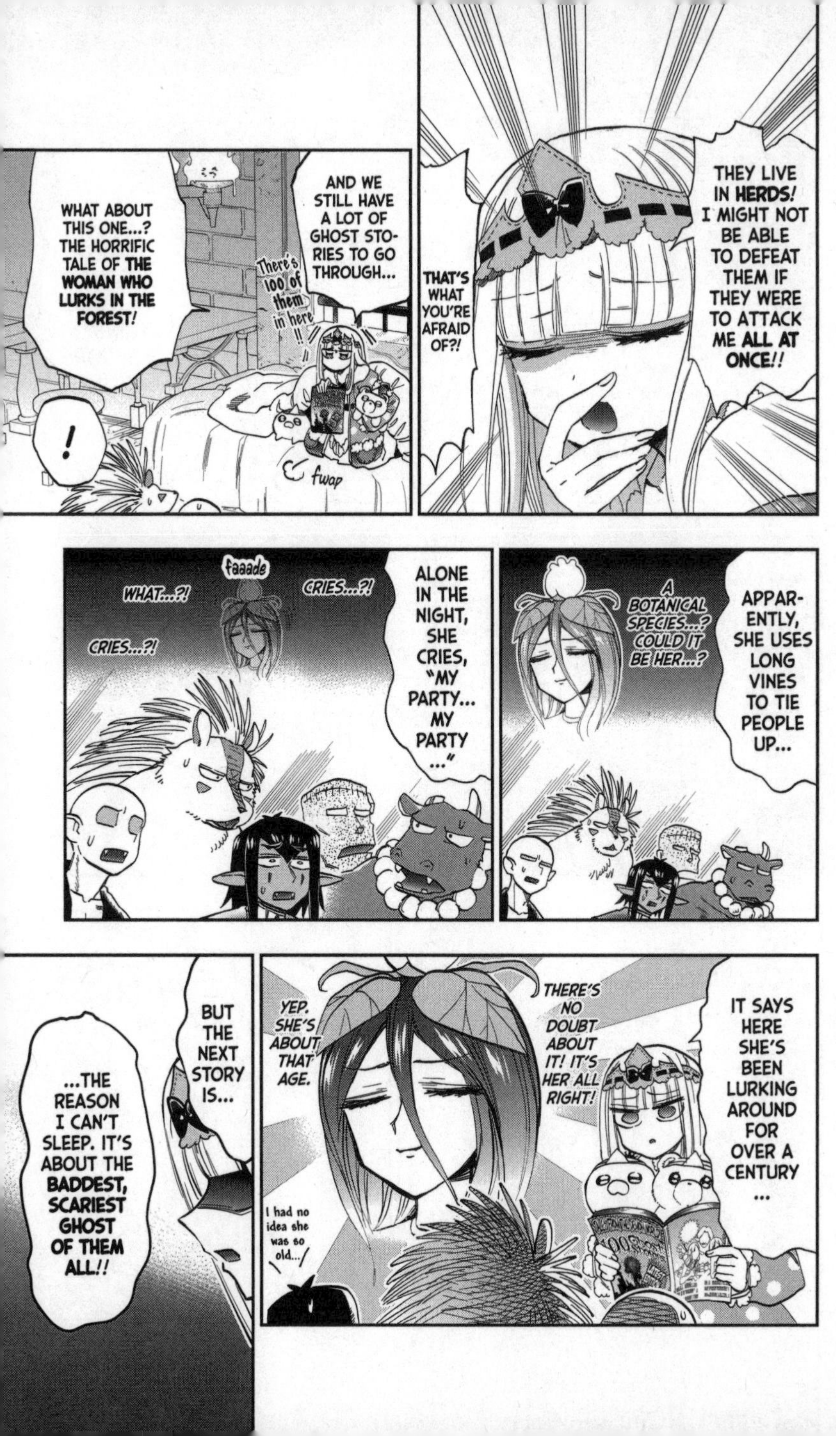
THEY LIVE IN HERDS! I MIGHT NOT BE ABLE TO DEFEAT THEM IF THEY WERE TO ATTACK ME ALL AT ONCE!!
THAT'S WHAT YOU'RE AFRAID OF?!
AND WE STILL HAVE A LOT OF GHOST STO-RIES TO GO THROUGH...
There's 100 of them in here!!
WHAT ABOUT THIS ONE...? THE HORRIFIC TALE OF THE WOMAN WHO LURKS IN THE FOREST!
!
fwap
APPAR-ENTLY, SHE USES LONG VINES TO TIE PEOPLE UP...
A BOTANICAL SPECIES...? COULD IT BE HER...?
ALONE IN THE NIGHT, SHE CRIES, "MY PARTY... MY PARTY..."
CRIES...?!
faaade
WHAT...?!
CRIES...?!
IT SAYS HERE SHE'S BEEN LURKING AROUND FOR OVER A CENTURY...
THERE'S NO DOUBT ABOUT IT! IT'S HER ALL RIGHT!
YEP. SHE'S ABOUT THAT AGE.
I had no idea she was so old...!
BUT THE NEXT STORY IS...
...THE REASON I CAN'T SLEEP. IT'S ABOUT THE BADDEST, SCARIEST GHOST OF THEM ALL!!

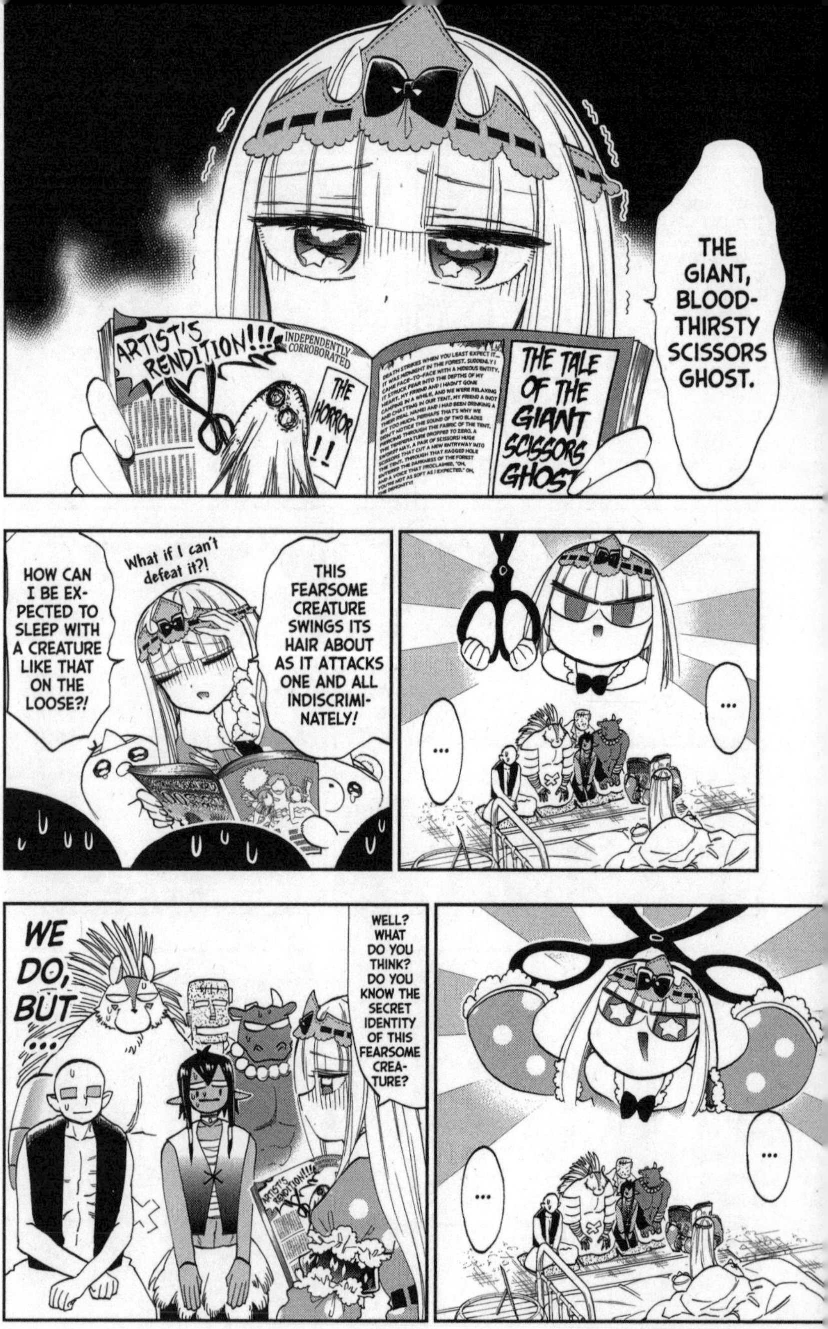
THE GIANT, BLOOD-THIRSTY SCISSORS GHOST.
ARTIST'S RENDITION!!!
INDEPENDENTLY CORROBORATED
THE HORROR!!
THE TALE OF THE GIANT SCISSORS GHOST
...
...
THIS FEARSOME CREATURE SWINGS ITS HAIR ABOUT AS IT ATTACKS ONE AND ALL INDISCRIMI-NATELY!
What if I can't defeat it?!
HOW CAN I BE EX-PECTED TO SLEEP WITH A CREATURE LIKE THAT ON THE LOOSE?!
...
...
WELL? WHAT DO YOU THINK? DO YOU KNOW THE SECRET IDENTITY OF THIS FEARSOME CREA-TURE?
WE DO, BUT...
ARTIST'S RENDITION!!!

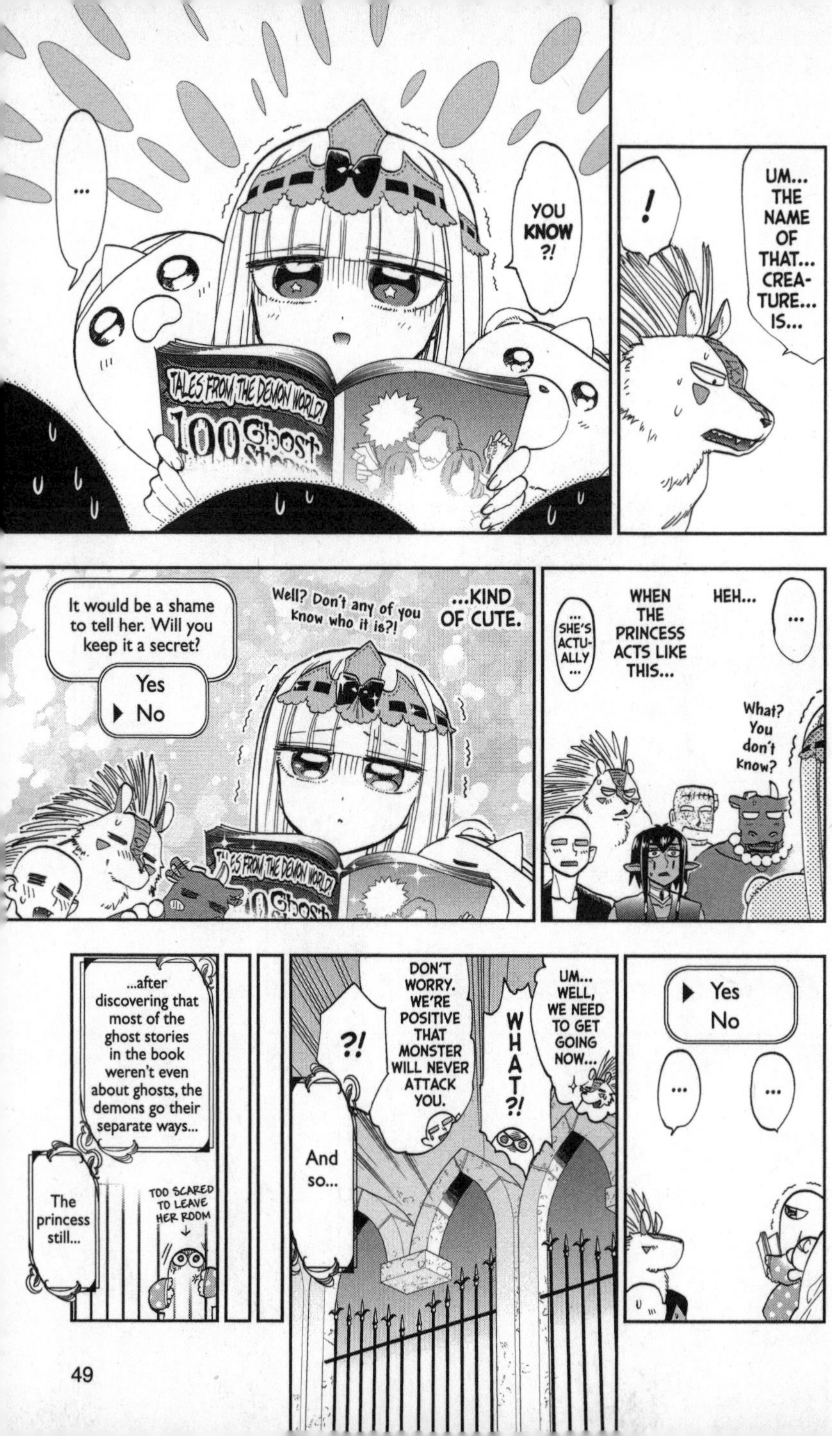

!
UM... THE NAME OF THAT... CREA-TURE... IS...
YOU KNOW?!
...
...
HEH...
WHEN THE PRINCESS ACTS LIKE THIS...
...SHE'S ACTU-ALLY...
What? You don't know?
...KIND OF CUTE.
Well? Don't any of you know who it is?!
TALES FROM THE DEMON WORLD! 100 Ghost Stories
It would be a shame to tell her. Will you keep it a secret?
Yes
▶ No
▶ Yes
No
...
...
UM... WELL, WE NEED TO GET GOING NOW...
WHAT?!
DON'T WORRY. WE'RE POSITIVE THAT MONSTER WILL NEVER ATTACK YOU.
?!
And so...
...after discovering that most of the ghost stories in the book weren't even about ghosts, the demons go their separate ways...
The princess still...
TOO SCARED TO LEAVE HER ROOM

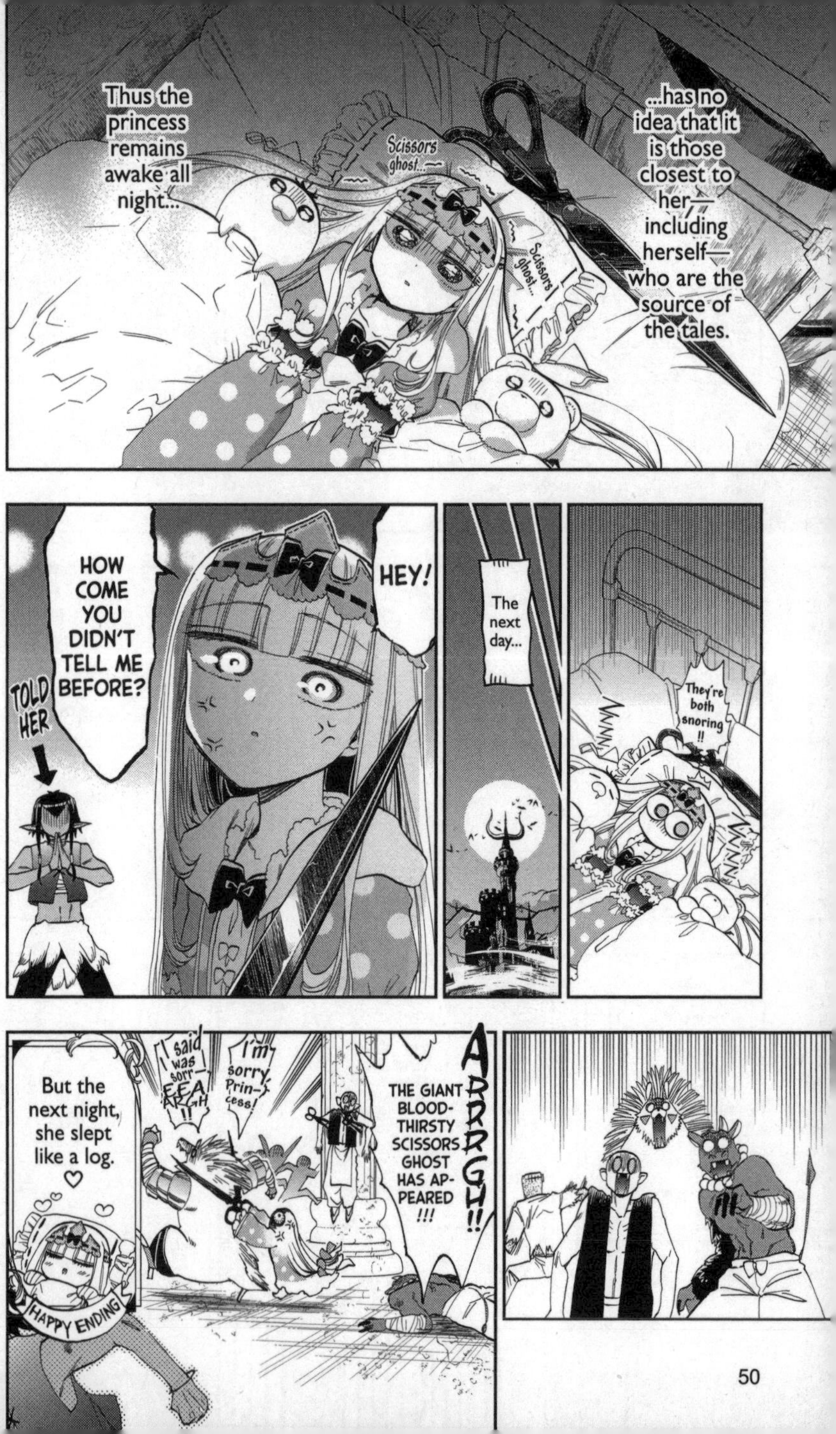
Thus the princess remains awake all night...
Scissors ghost...
Scissors ghost...
...has no idea that it is those closest to her—including herself—who are the source of the tales.
They're both snoring!!
NNNN
NNNN
The next day...
HEY!
HOW COME YOU DIDN'T TELL ME BEFORE?
TOLD HER
ARRRGH!!
THE GIANT BLOODTHIRSTY SCISSORS GHOST HAS APPEARED!!!
I'm sorry, Princess!
I said I was sorr— EEAARGH!!
But the next night, she slept like a log. ♡
HAPPY ENDING

Tales from the Demon World! 100 Ghost Stories

Truthfulness: ☆☆☆☆☆☆☆☆☆
Soothingness: ☆☆☆☆☆

A hundred stories in just one volume!

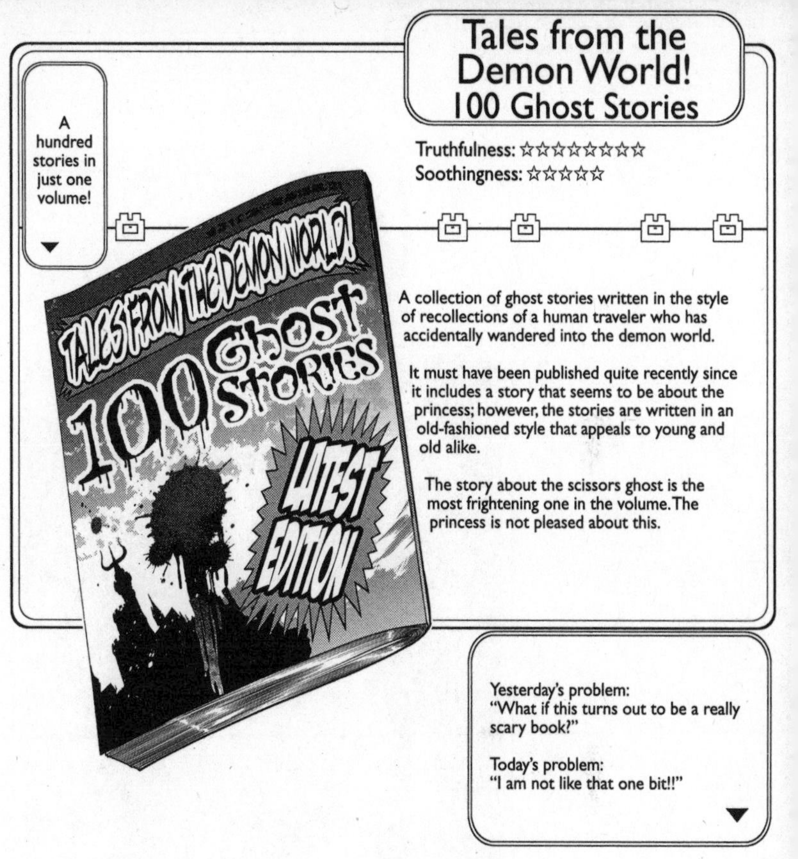
TALES FROM THE DEMON WORLD!
100 Ghost Stories
LATEST EDITION

A collection of ghost stories written in the style of recollections of a human traveler who has accidentally wandered into the demon world.

It must have been published quite recently since it includes a story that seems to be about the princess; however, the stories are written in an old-fashioned style that appeals to young and old alike.

The story about the scissors ghost is the most frightening one in the volume. The princess is not pleased about this.

Yesterday's problem:
"What if this turns out to be a really scary book?"

Today's problem:
"I am not like that one bit!!"

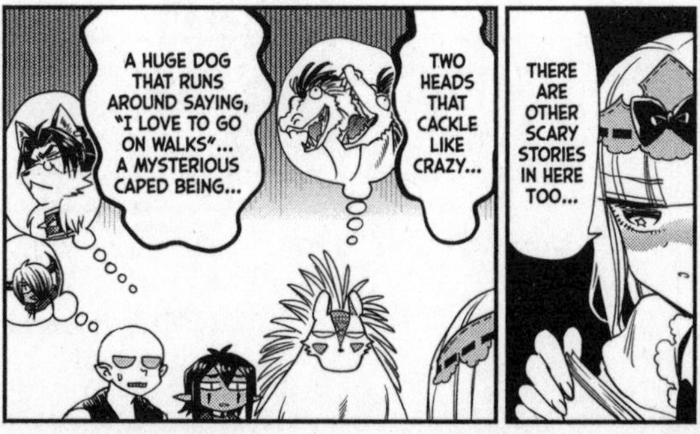
THERE ARE OTHER SCARY STORIES IN HERE TOO...
TWO HEADS THAT CACKLE LIKE CRAZY...
A HUGE DOG THAT RUNS AROUND SAYING, "I LOVE TO GO ON WALKS"... A MYSTERIOUS CAPED BEING...

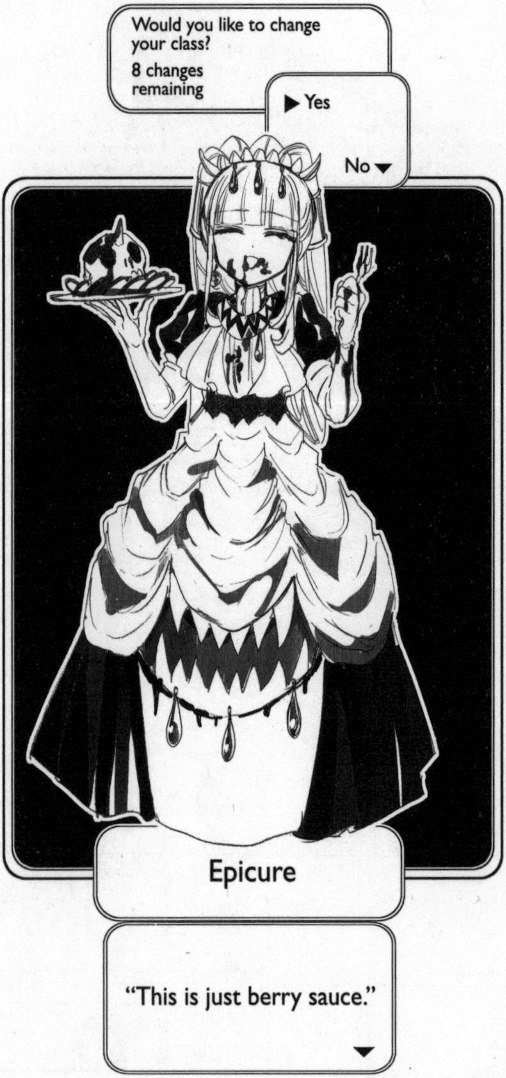
Would you like to change your class?
8 changes remaining
▶ Yes
No ▼
Epicure
"This is just berry sauce."

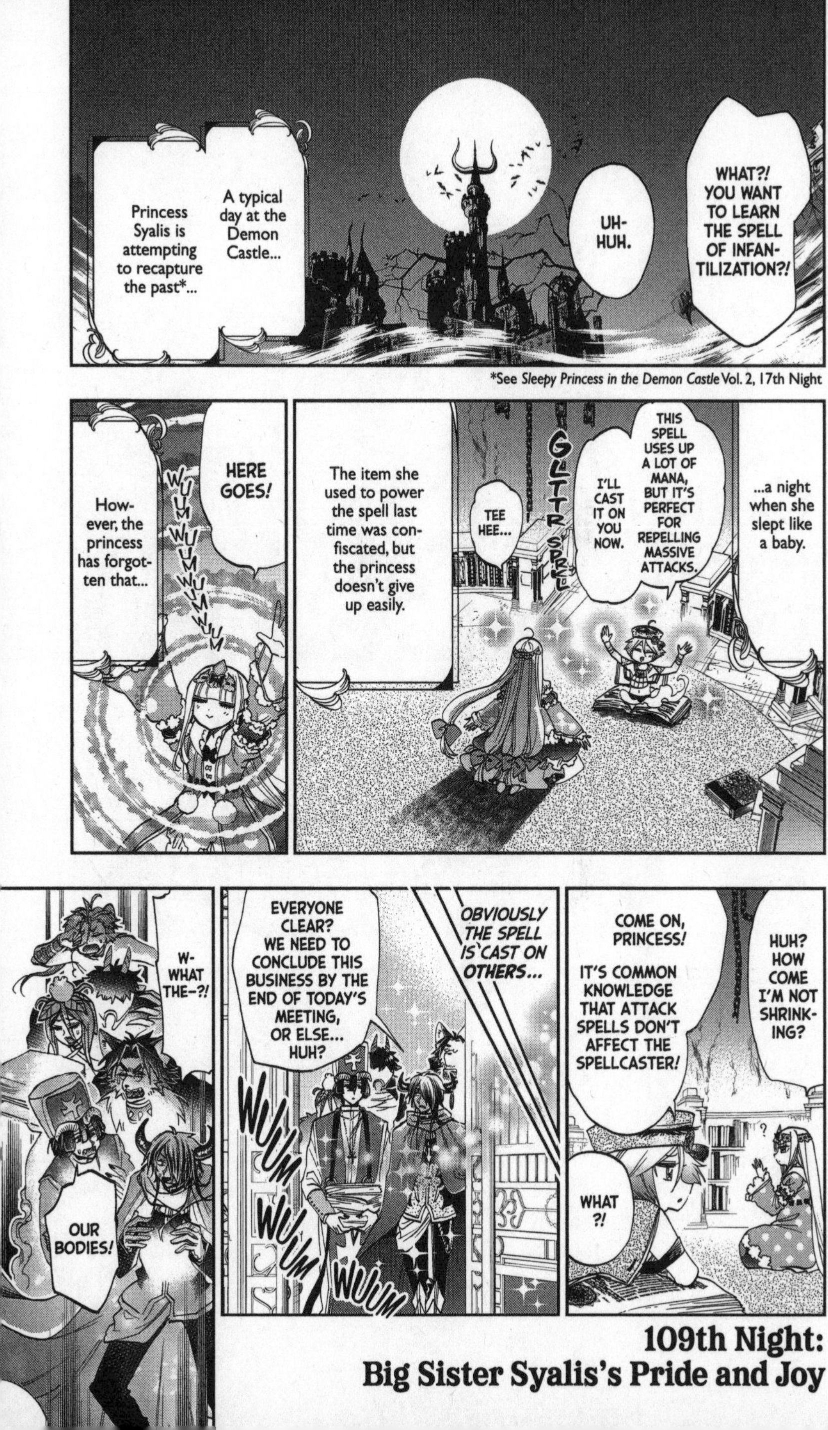

WHAT?! YOU WANT TO LEARN THE SPELL OF INFANTILIZATION?!
UH-HUH.
A typical day at the Demon Castle...
Princess Syalis is attempting to recapture the past*...
...a night when she slept like a baby.
THIS SPELL USES UP A LOT OF MANA, BUT IT'S PERFECT FOR REPELLING MASSIVE ATTACKS.
I'LL CAST IT ON YOU NOW.
GLTTR SPRL
TEE HEE...
The item she used to power the spell last time was confiscated, but the princess doesn't give up easily.
HERE GOES!
WUUMWUUMWUUMWUUMWUUM
However, the princess has forgotten that...
HUH? HOW COME I'M NOT SHRINKING?
COME ON, PRINCESS!
IT'S COMMON KNOWLEDGE THAT ATTACK SPELLS DON'T AFFECT THE SPELLCASTER!
WHAT?!
OBVIOUSLY THE SPELL IS CAST ON OTHERS...
EVERYONE CLEAR? WE NEED TO CONCLUDE THIS BUSINESS BY THE END OF TODAY'S MEETING, OR ELSE... HUH?
WUUM WUUM WUUM
W-WHAT THE-?!
OUR BODIES!

*See *Sleepy Princess in the Demon Castle* Vol. 2, 17th Night

109th Night: Big Sister Syalis's Pride and Joy

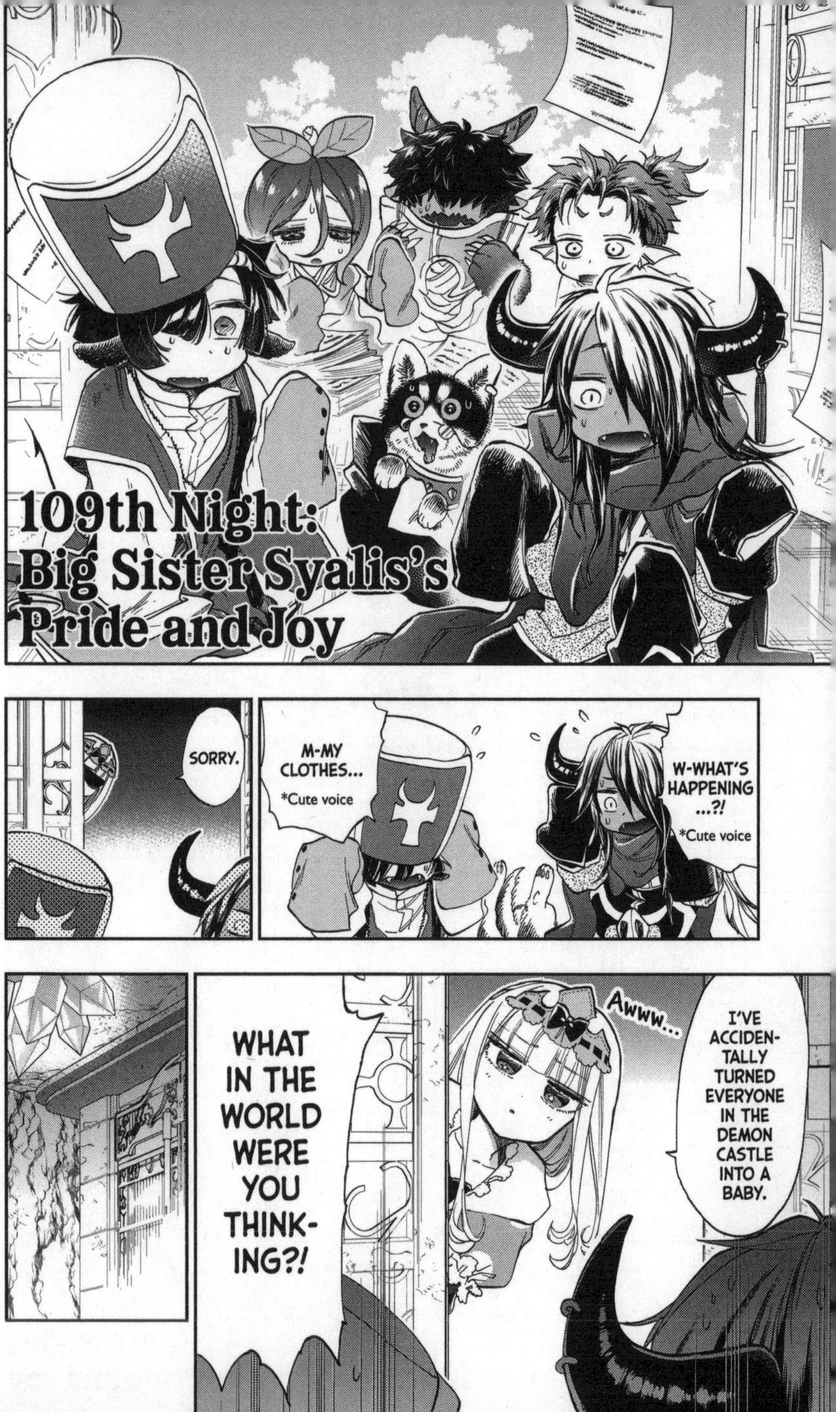
109th Night: Big Sister Syalis's Pride and Joy
W-WHAT'S HAPPENING ...?!
*Cute voice
M-MY CLOTHES...
*Cute voice
SORRY.
Awww...
I'VE ACCIDEN-TALLY TURNED EVERYONE IN THE DEMON CASTLE INTO A BABY.
WHAT IN THE WORLD WERE YOU THINK-ING?!

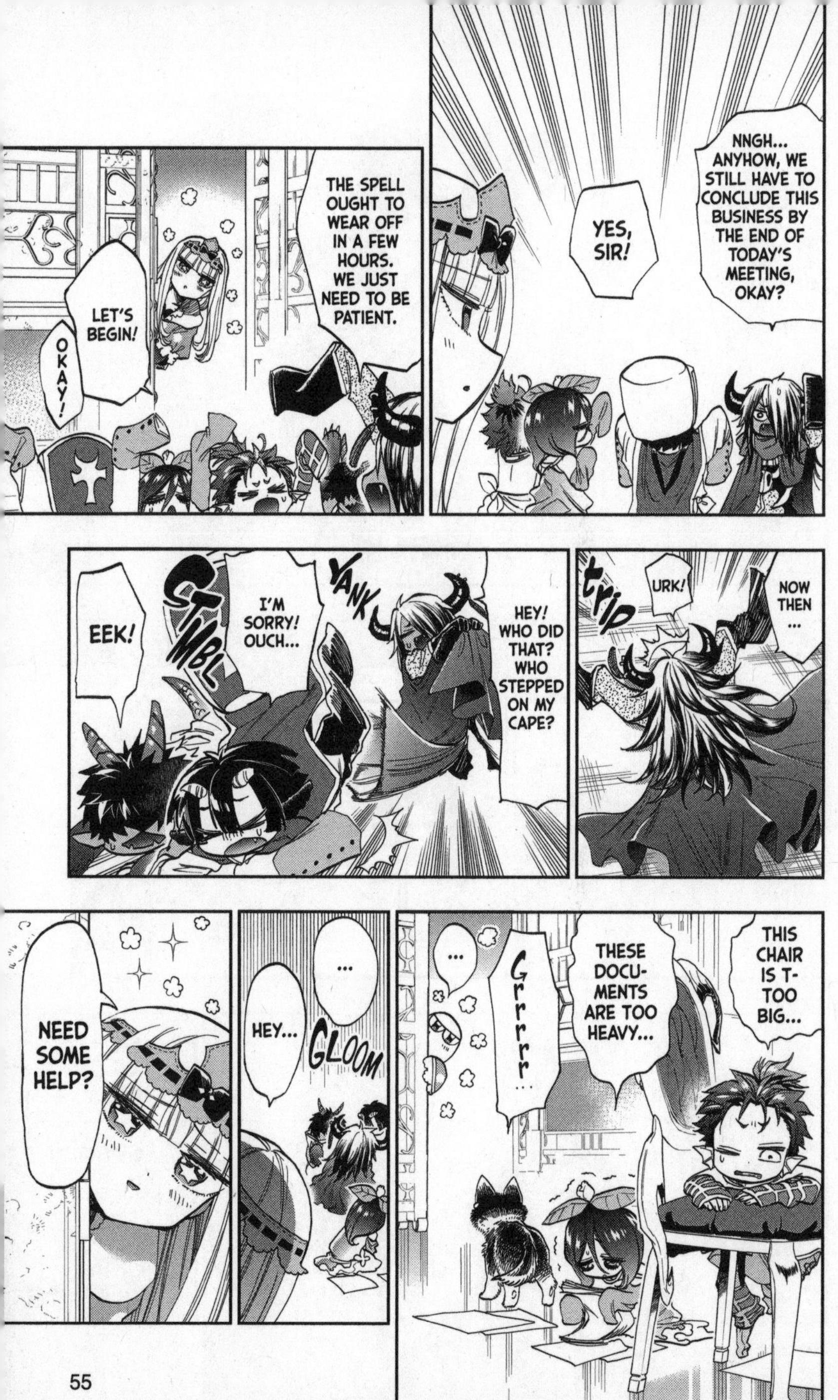
NNGH... ANYHOW, WE STILL HAVE TO CONCLUDE THIS BUSINESS BY THE END OF TODAY'S MEETING, OKAY?
YES, SIR!
THE SPELL OUGHT TO WEAR OFF IN A FEW HOURS. WE JUST NEED TO BE PATIENT.
LET'S BEGIN!
OKAY!
NOW THEN...
URK!
trip
HEY! WHO DID THAT? WHO STEPPED ON MY CAPE?
YANK
I'M SORRY! OUCH...
STMBL
EEK!
THIS CHAIR IS T-TOO BIG...
THESE DOCU-MENTS ARE TOO HEAVY...
Grrrr...
...
...
HEY...
GLOOM
NEED SOME HELP?

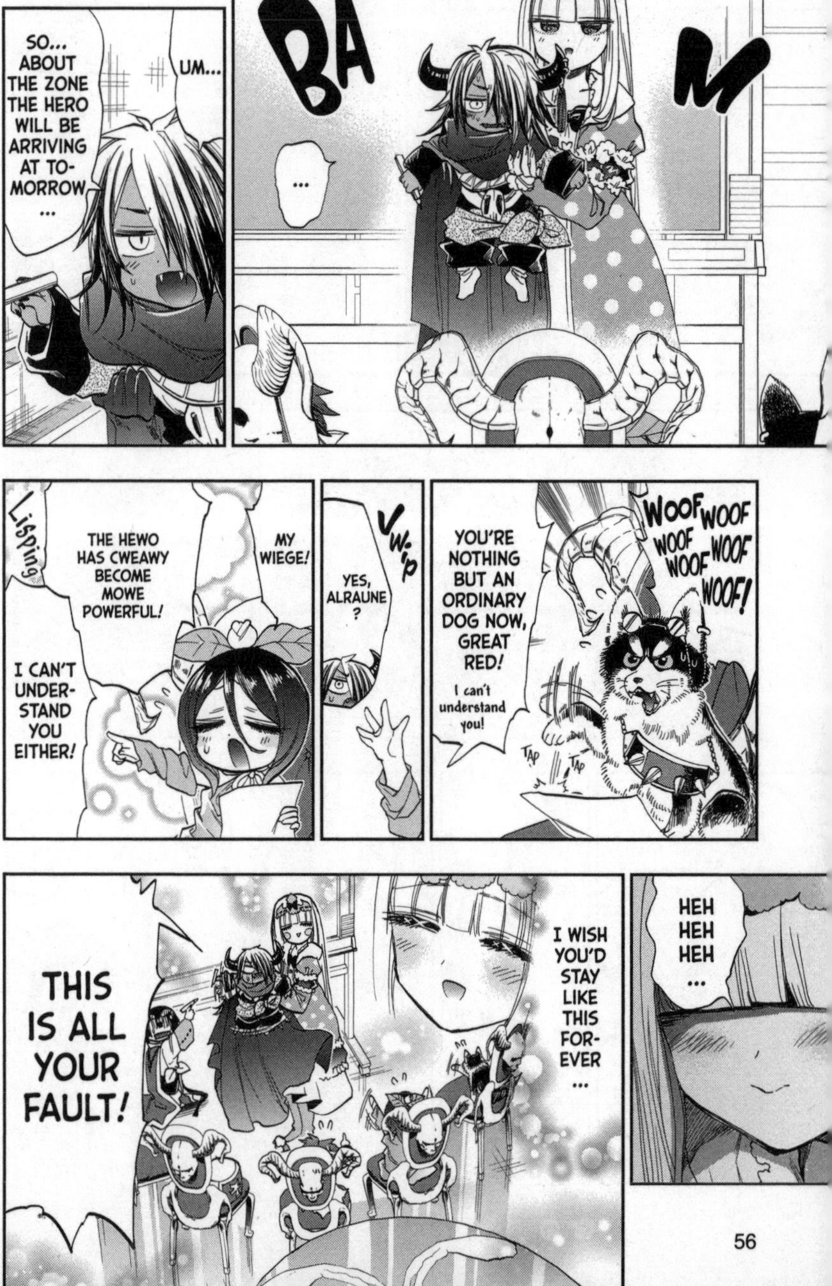
BAM
...
UM...
SO... ABOUT THE ZONE THE HERO WILL BE ARRIVING AT TOMORROW...
WOOF WOOF WOOF WOOF WOOF WOOF WOOF!
YOU'RE NOTHING BUT AN ORDINARY DOG NOW, GREAT RED!
I can't understand you!
TAP TAP
Vwip
YES, ALRAUNE?
MY WIEGE!
THE HEWO HAS CWEAWY BECOME MOWE POWERFUL!
Lisping
I CAN'T UNDERSTAND YOU EITHER!
HEH HEH HEH...
I WISH YOU'D STAY LIKE THIS FOREVER...
THIS IS ALL YOUR FAULT!

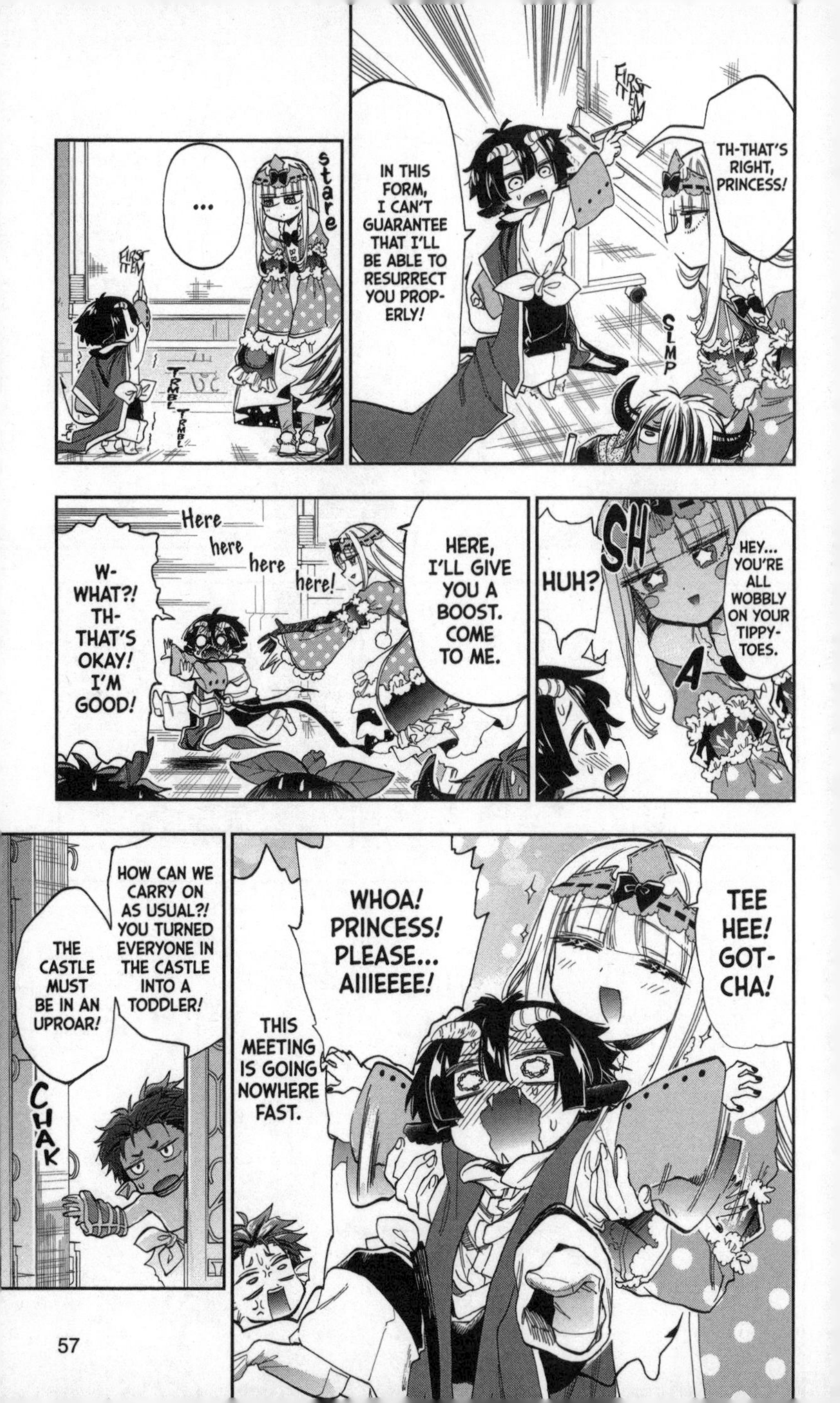
TH-THAT'S RIGHT, PRINCESS!
FIRST ITEM
IN THIS FORM, I CAN'T GUARANTEE THAT I'LL BE ABLE TO RESURRECT YOU PROP-ERLY!
SLMP
stare
...
FIRST ITEM
TRMBL TRMBL
HEY... YOU'RE ALL WOBBLY ON YOUR TIPPY-TOES.
SHA
HUH?
HERE, I'LL GIVE YOU A BOOST. COME TO ME.
Here here here here!
W-WHAT?! TH-THAT'S OKAY! I'M GOOD!
TEE HEE! GOT-CHA!
WHOA! PRINCESS! PLEASE... AIIIEEEE!
THIS MEETING IS GOING NOWHERE FAST.
HOW CAN WE CARRY ON AS USUAL?! YOU TURNED EVERYONE IN THE CASTLE INTO A TODDLER!
THE CASTLE MUST BE IN AN UPROAR!
CHAK

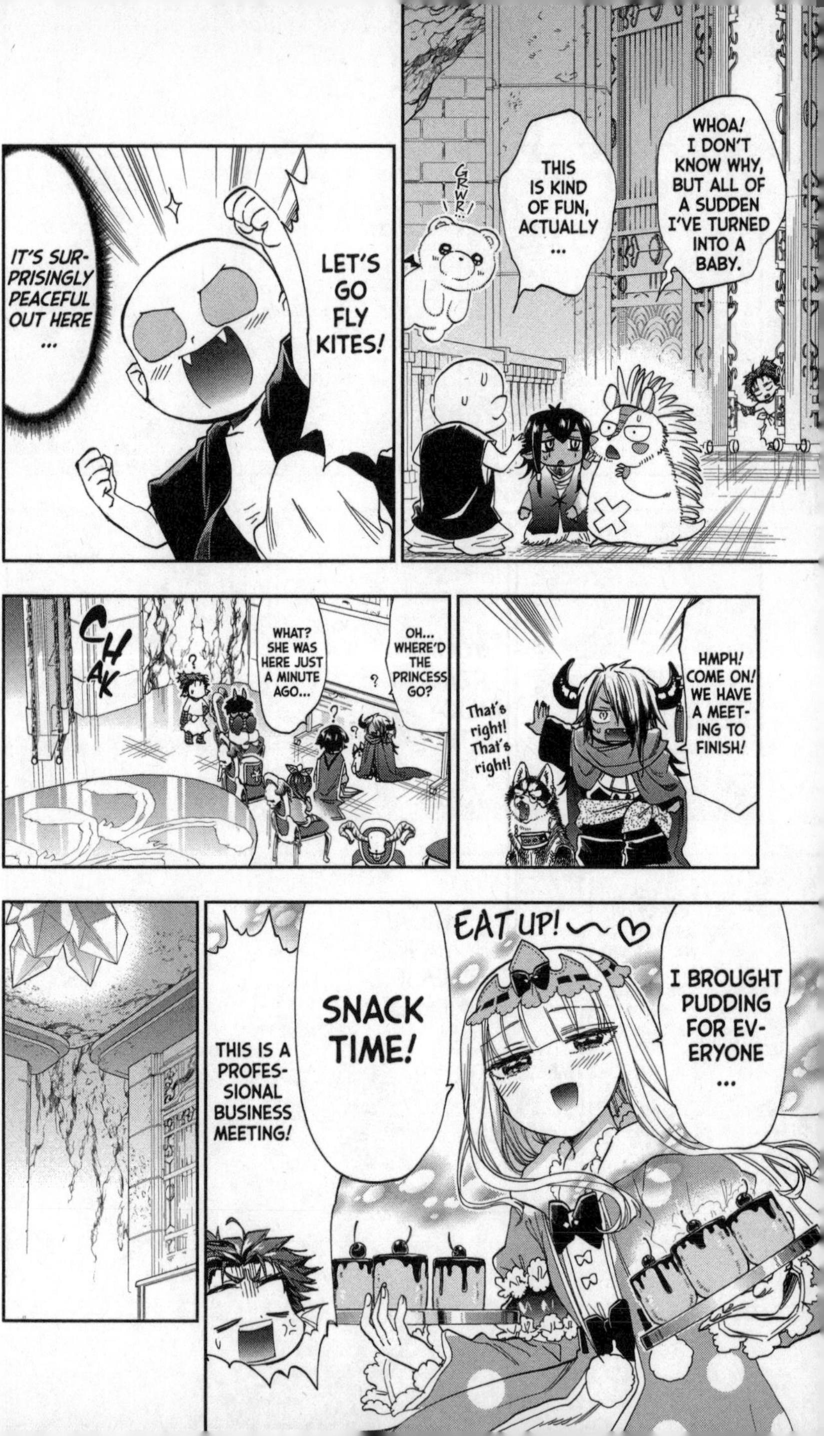
WHOA! I DON'T KNOW WHY, BUT ALL OF A SUDDEN I'VE TURNED INTO A BABY.
THIS IS KIND OF FUN, ACTUALLY ...
GRWR!...
LET'S GO FLY KITES!
IT'S SURPRISINGLY PEACEFUL OUT HERE ...
HMPH! COME ON! WE HAVE A MEETING TO FINISH!
That's right! That's right!
OH... WHERE'D THE PRINCESS GO?
WHAT? SHE WAS HERE JUST A MINUTE AGO...
CHAK
I BROUGHT PUDDING FOR EVERYONE ...
EAT UP! ~♡
SNACK TIME!
THIS IS A PROFESSIONAL BUSINESS MEETING!

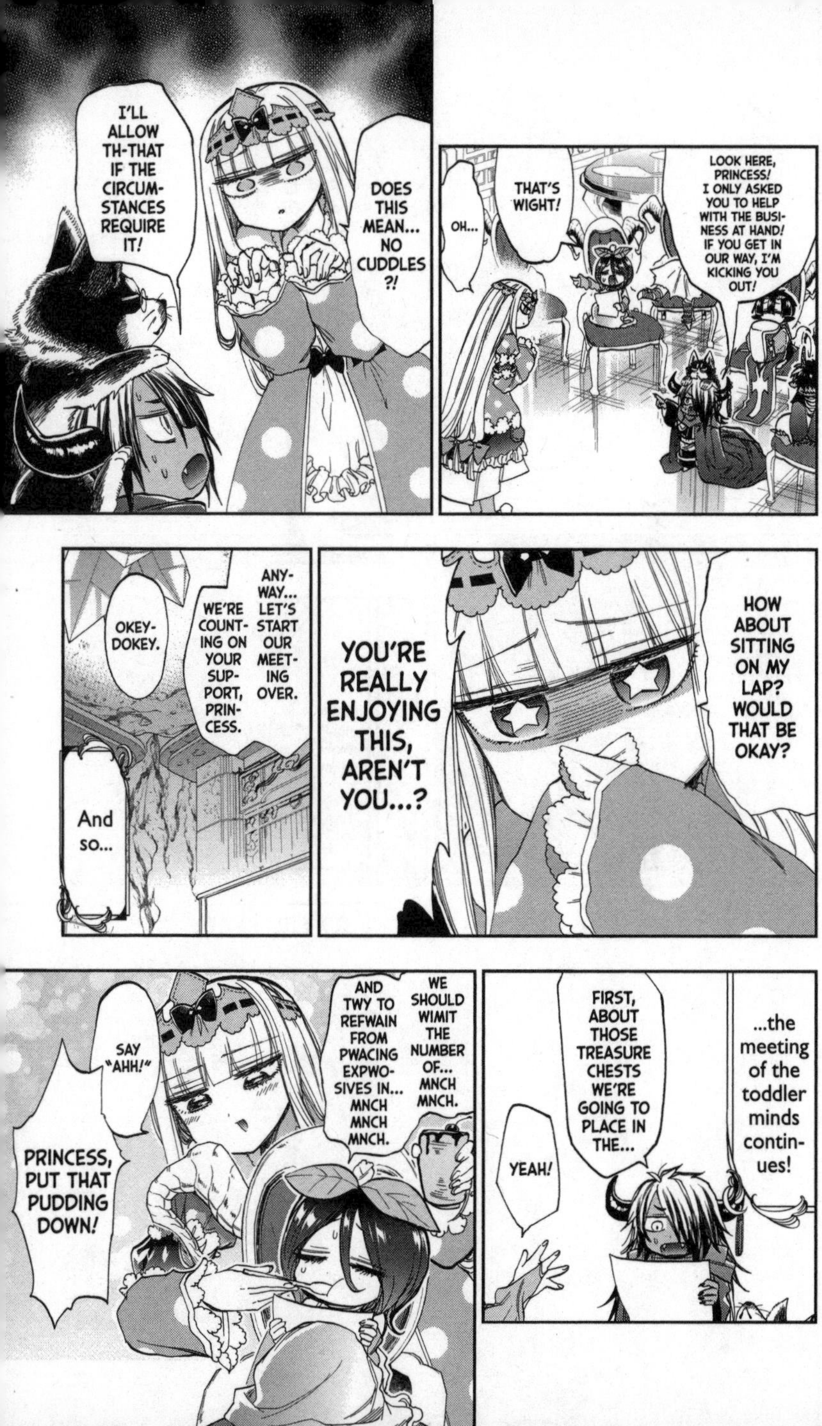
LOOK HERE, PRINCESS! I ONLY ASKED YOU TO HELP WITH THE BUSINESS AT HAND! IF YOU GET IN OUR WAY, I'M KICKING YOU OUT!
THAT'S WIGHT!
OH...
DOES THIS MEAN... NO CUDDLES?!
I'LL ALLOW TH-THAT IF THE CIRCUMSTANCES REQUIRE IT!
HOW ABOUT SITTING ON MY LAP? WOULD THAT BE OKAY?
YOU'RE REALLY ENJOYING THIS, AREN'T YOU...?
ANYWAY... LET'S START OUR MEETING OVER.
WE'RE COUNTING ON YOUR SUPPORT, PRINCESS.
OKEY-DOKEY.
And so...
...the meeting of the toddler minds continues!
FIRST, ABOUT THOSE TREASURE CHESTS WE'RE GOING TO PLACE IN THE...
YEAH!
WE SHOULD WIMIT THE NUMBER OF... MNCH MNCH.
AND TWY TO REFWAIN FROM PWACING EXPWOSIVES IN... MNCH MNCH MNCH.
SAY "AHH!"
PRINCESS, PUT THAT PUDDING DOWN!

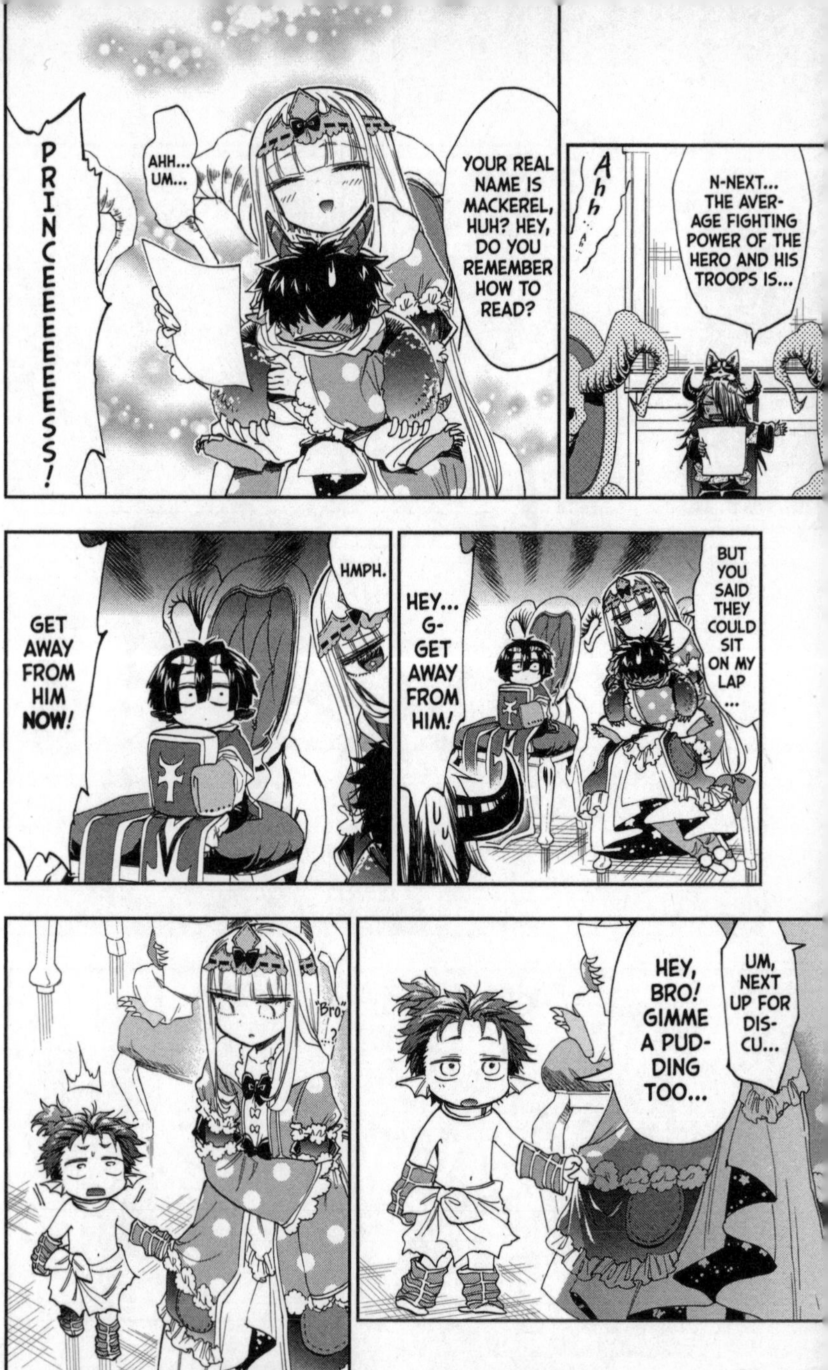
Ahh...
N-NEXT... THE AVERAGE FIGHTING POWER OF THE HERO AND HIS TROOPS IS...
YOUR REAL NAME IS MACKEREL, HUH? HEY, DO YOU REMEMBER HOW TO READ?
AHH... UM...
PRINCEEEEEESS!
BUT YOU SAID THEY COULD SIT ON MY LAP...
HEY... G-GET AWAY FROM HIM!
HMPH.
GET AWAY FROM HIM NOW!
UM, NEXT UP FOR DISCU...
HEY, BRO! GIMME A PUDDING TOO...
"Bro"!?

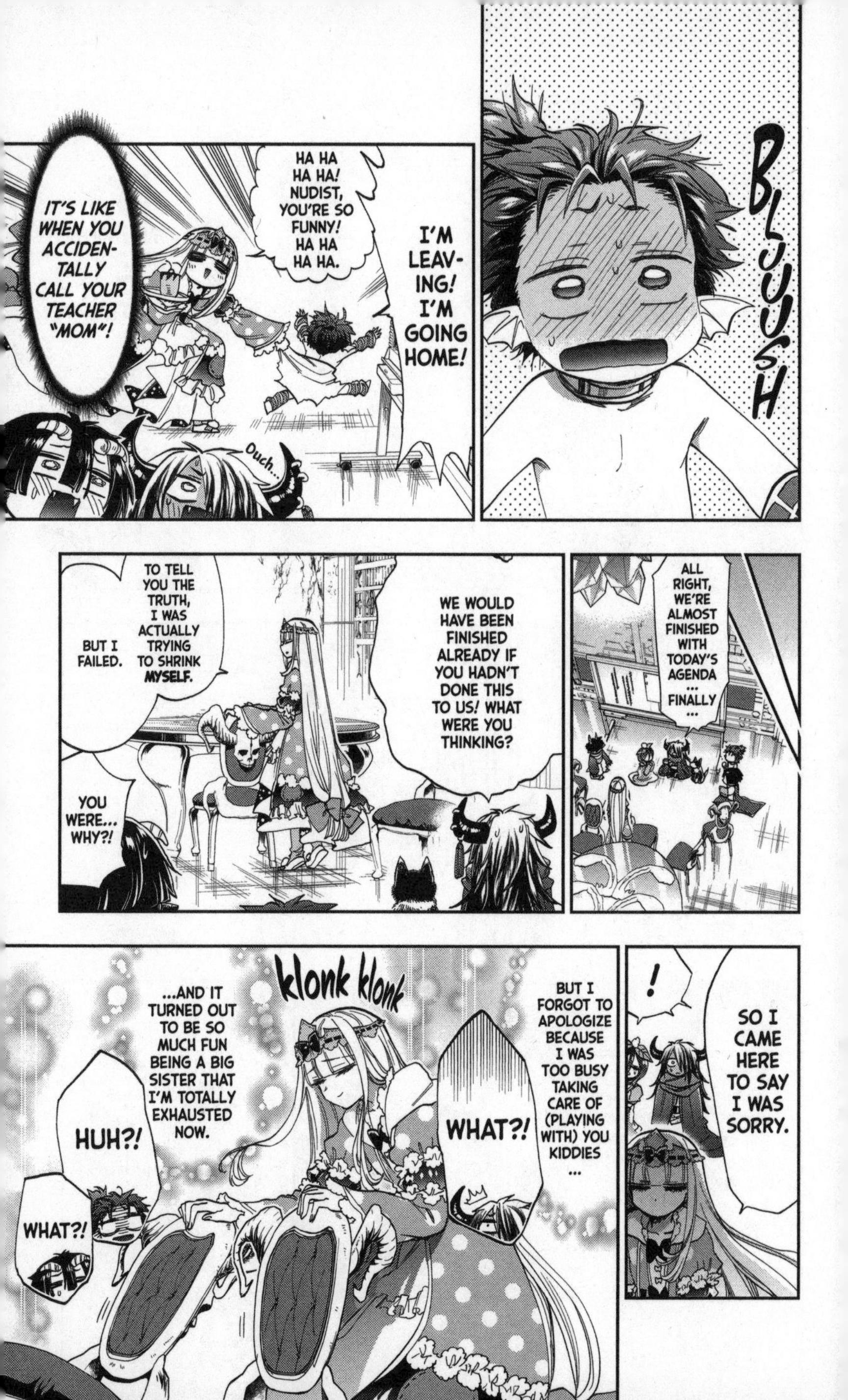
BLUUUSH
I'M LEAVING! I'M GOING HOME!
HA HA HA HA! NUDIST, YOU'RE SO FUNNY! HA HA HA HA.
IT'S LIKE WHEN YOU ACCIDENTALLY CALL YOUR TEACHER "MOM"!
Ouch...
ALL RIGHT, WE'RE ALMOST FINISHED WITH TODAY'S AGENDA... FINALLY...
WE WOULD HAVE BEEN FINISHED ALREADY IF YOU HADN'T DONE THIS TO US! WHAT WERE YOU THINKING?
TO TELL YOU THE TRUTH, I WAS ACTUALLY TRYING TO SHRINK **MYSELF**.
BUT I FAILED.
YOU WERE... WHY?!
!
SO I CAME HERE TO SAY I WAS SORRY.
BUT I FORGOT TO APOLOGIZE BECAUSE I WAS TOO BUSY TAKING CARE OF (PLAYING WITH) YOU KIDDIES...
WHAT?!
klonk klonk
...AND IT TURNED OUT TO BE SO MUCH FUN BEING A BIG SISTER THAT I'M TOTALLY EXHAUSTED NOW.
HUH?!
WHAT?!

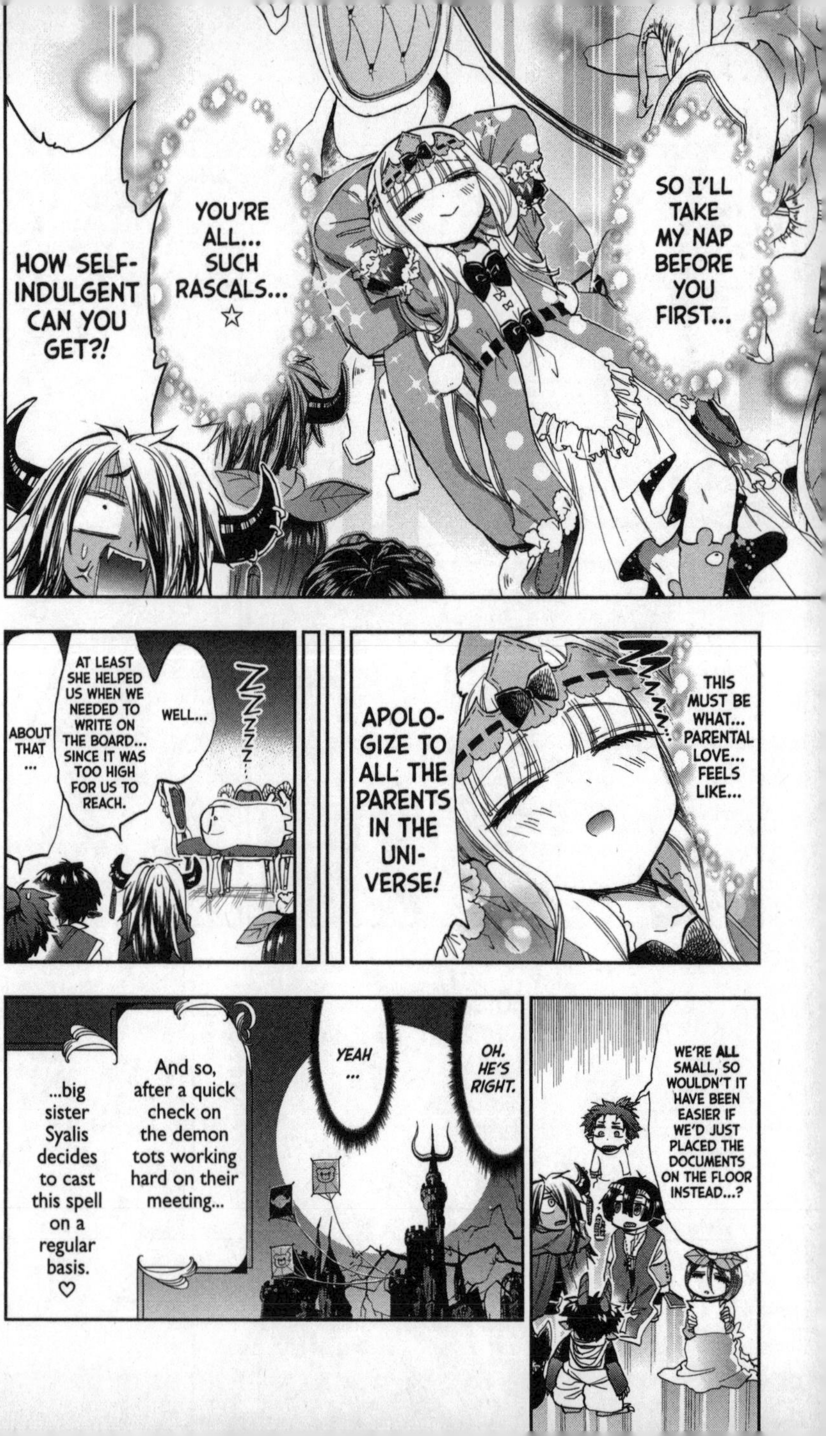
SO I'LL TAKE MY NAP BEFORE YOU FIRST...
YOU'RE ALL... SUCH RASCALS... ☆
HOW SELF-INDULGENT CAN YOU GET?!
THIS MUST BE WHAT... PARENTAL LOVE... FEELS LIKE...
ZZZZ...
APOLOGIZE TO ALL THE PARENTS IN THE UNIVERSE!
ZZZZZ...
WELL...
AT LEAST SHE HELPED US WHEN WE NEEDED TO WRITE ON THE BOARD... SINCE IT WAS TOO HIGH FOR US TO REACH.
ABOUT THAT ...
WE'RE ALL SMALL, SO WOULDN'T IT HAVE BEEN EASIER IF WE'D JUST PLACED THE DOCUMENTS ON THE FLOOR INSTEAD...?
OH. HE'S RIGHT.
YEAH ...
And so, after a quick check on the demon tots working hard on their meeting...
...big sister Syalis decides to cast this spell on a regular basis. ♡

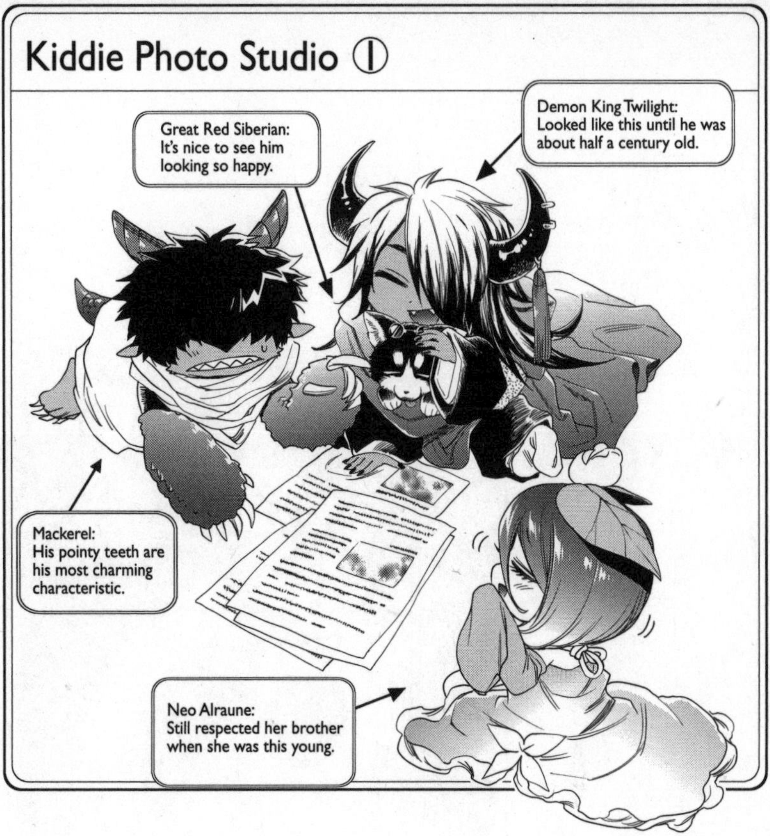
Kiddie Photo Studio ①
Demon King Twilight: Looked like this until he was about half a century old.
Great Red Siberian: It's nice to see him looking so happy.
Mackerel: His pointy teeth are his most charming characteristic.
Neo Alraune: Still respected her brother when she was this young.

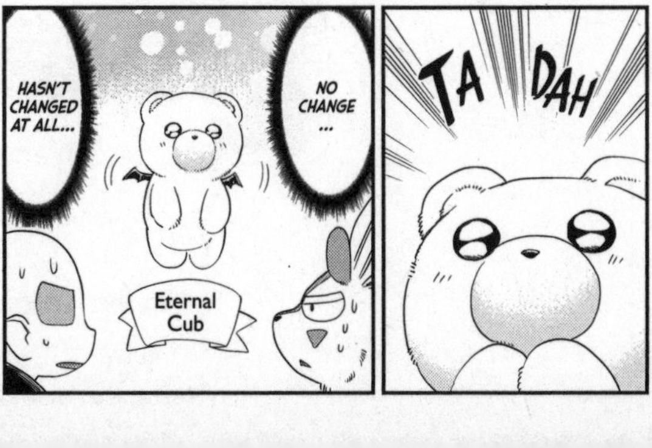
TA DAH
NO CHANGE ...
HASN'T CHANGED AT ALL...
Eternal Cub

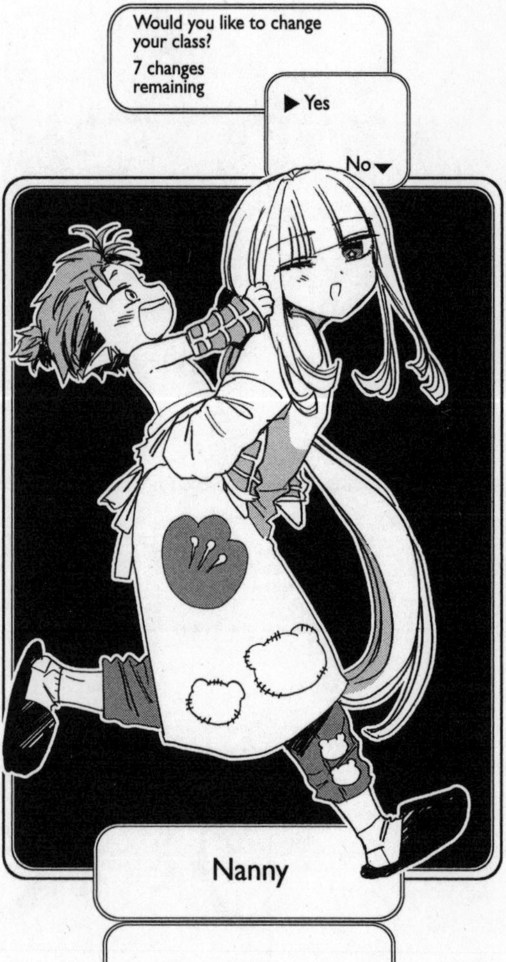

Would you like to change your class?
7 changes remaining
▶Yes
No
Nanny
"So this is parental love..."

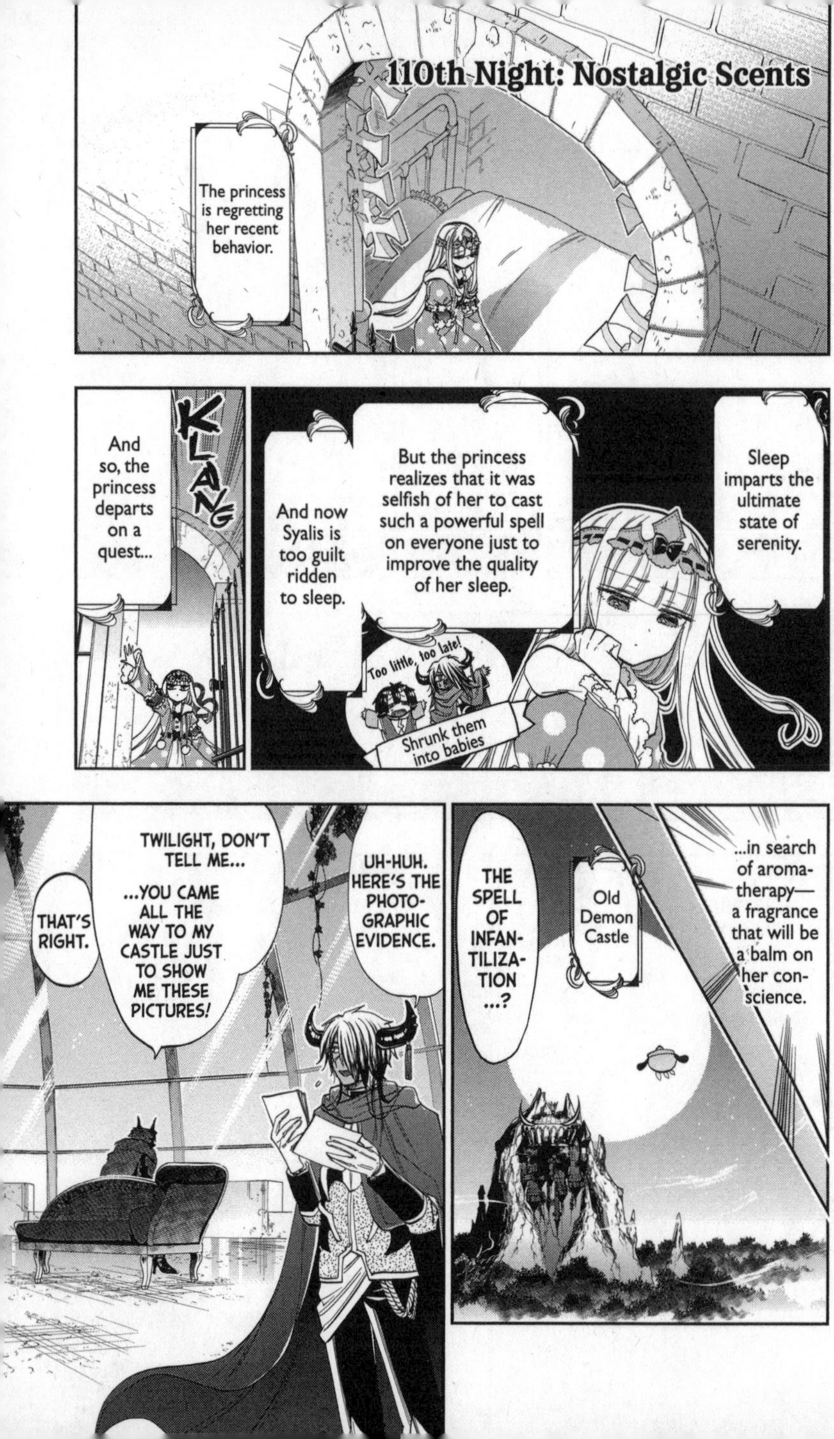
110th Night: Nostalgic Scents
The princess is regretting her recent behavior.
Sleep imparts the ultimate state of serenity.
But the princess realizes that it was selfish of her to cast such a powerful spell on everyone just to improve the quality of her sleep.
And now Syalis is too guilt ridden to sleep.
Too little, too late!
Shrunk them into babies
And so, the princess departs on a quest...
KLANG
...in search of aroma-therapy—a fragrance that will be a balm on her con-science.
Old Demon Castle
THE SPELL OF INFANTILIZATION...?
UH-HUH. HERE'S THE PHOTOGRAPHIC EVIDENCE.
TWILIGHT, DON'T TELL ME...
...YOU CAME ALL THE WAY TO MY CASTLE JUST TO SHOW ME THESE PICTURES!
THAT'S RIGHT.

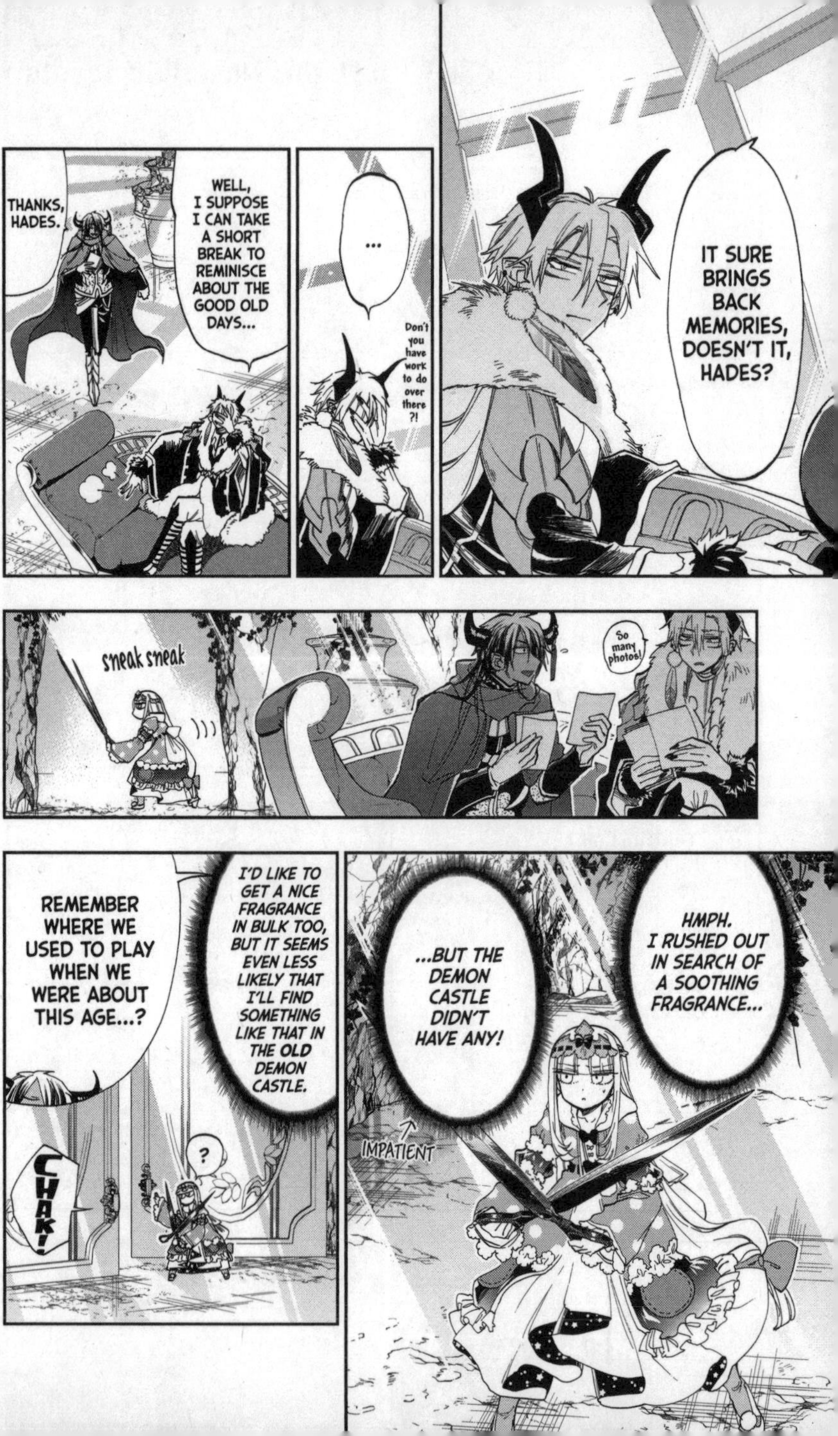
IT SURE BRINGS BACK MEMORIES, DOESN'T IT, HADES?
...
Don't you have work to do over there?!
WELL, I SUPPOSE I CAN TAKE A SHORT BREAK TO REMINISCE ABOUT THE GOOD OLD DAYS...
THANKS, HADES.
So many photos!
sneak sneak
HMPH. I RUSHED OUT IN SEARCH OF A SOOTHING FRAGRANCE...
...BUT THE DEMON CASTLE DIDN'T HAVE ANY!
IMPATIENT
I'D LIKE TO GET A NICE FRAGRANCE IN BULK TOO, BUT IT SEEMS EVEN LESS LIKELY THAT I'LL FIND SOMETHING LIKE THAT IN THE OLD DEMON CASTLE.
REMEMBER WHERE WE USED TO PLAY WHEN WE WERE ABOUT THIS AGE...?
?
CHAK!

110th Night: Nostalgic Scents

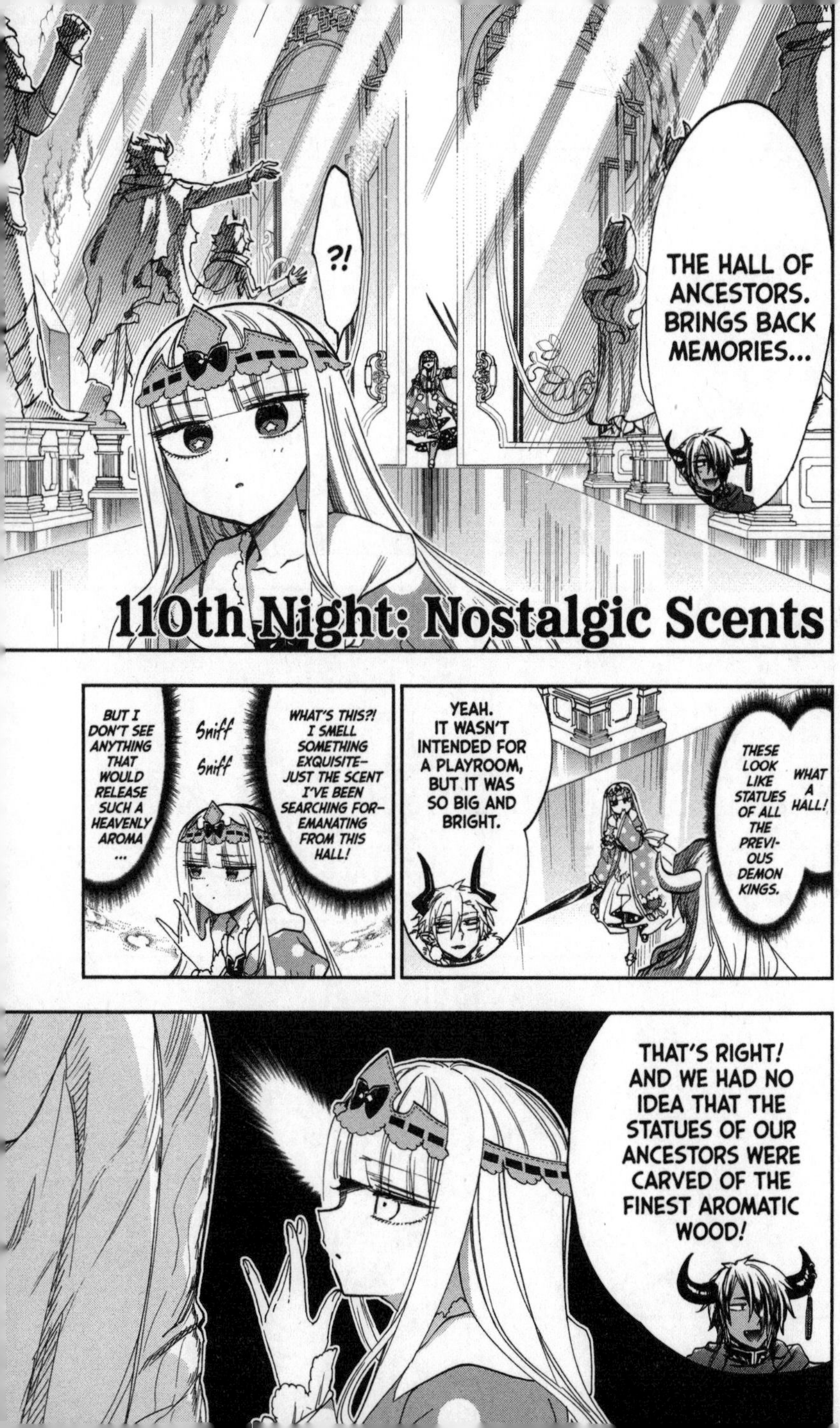
THE HALL OF ANCESTORS. BRINGS BACK MEMORIES...
?!
110th Night: Nostalgic Scents
WHAT A HALL!
THESE LOOK LIKE STATUES OF ALL THE PREVI-OUS DEMON KINGS.
YEAH. IT WASN'T INTENDED FOR A PLAYROOM, BUT IT WAS SO BIG AND BRIGHT.
WHAT'S THIS?! I SMELL SOMETHING EXQUISITE— JUST THE SCENT I'VE BEEN SEARCHING FOR— EMANATING FROM THIS HALL!
Sniff
Sniff
BUT I DON'T SEE ANYTHING THAT WOULD RELEASE SUCH A HEAVENLY AROMA ...
THAT'S RIGHT! AND WE HAD NO IDEA THAT THE STATUES OF OUR ANCESTORS WERE CARVED OF THE FINEST AROMATIC WOOD!

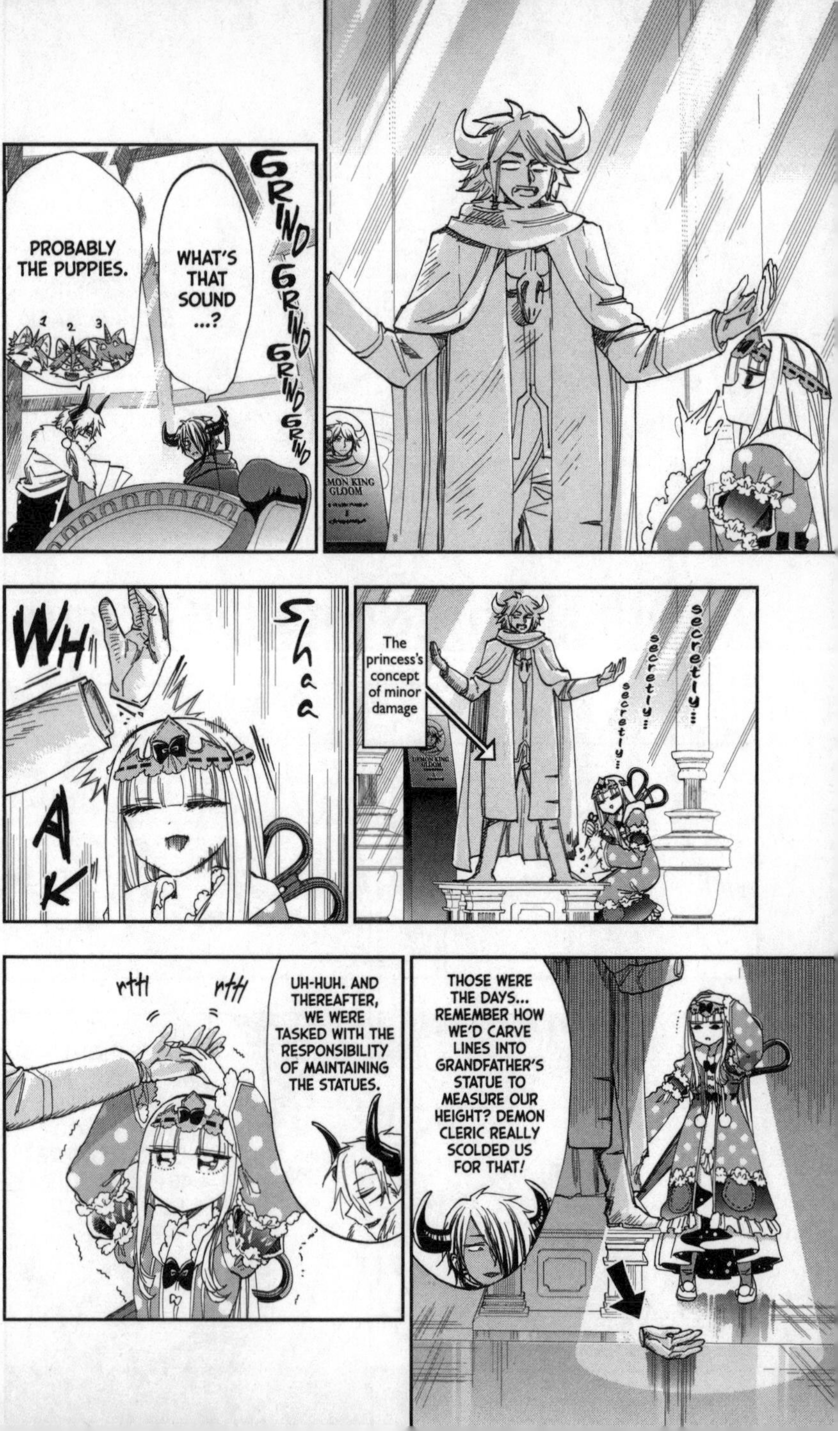
MON KING
GLOOM
GRIND GRIND GRIND GRIND
WHAT'S THAT SOUND ...?
PROBABLY THE PUPPIES.
1
2
3
The princess's concept of minor damage
secretly...
secretly...
secretly...
DEMON KING
GLOOM
Shaa
WHAK
THOSE WERE THE DAYS... REMEMBER HOW WE'D CARVE LINES INTO GRANDFATHER'S STATUE TO MEASURE OUR HEIGHT? DEMON CLERIC REALLY SCOLDED US FOR THAT!
UH-HUH. AND THEREAFTER, WE WERE TASKED WITH THE RESPONSIBILITY OF MAINTAINING THE STATUES.

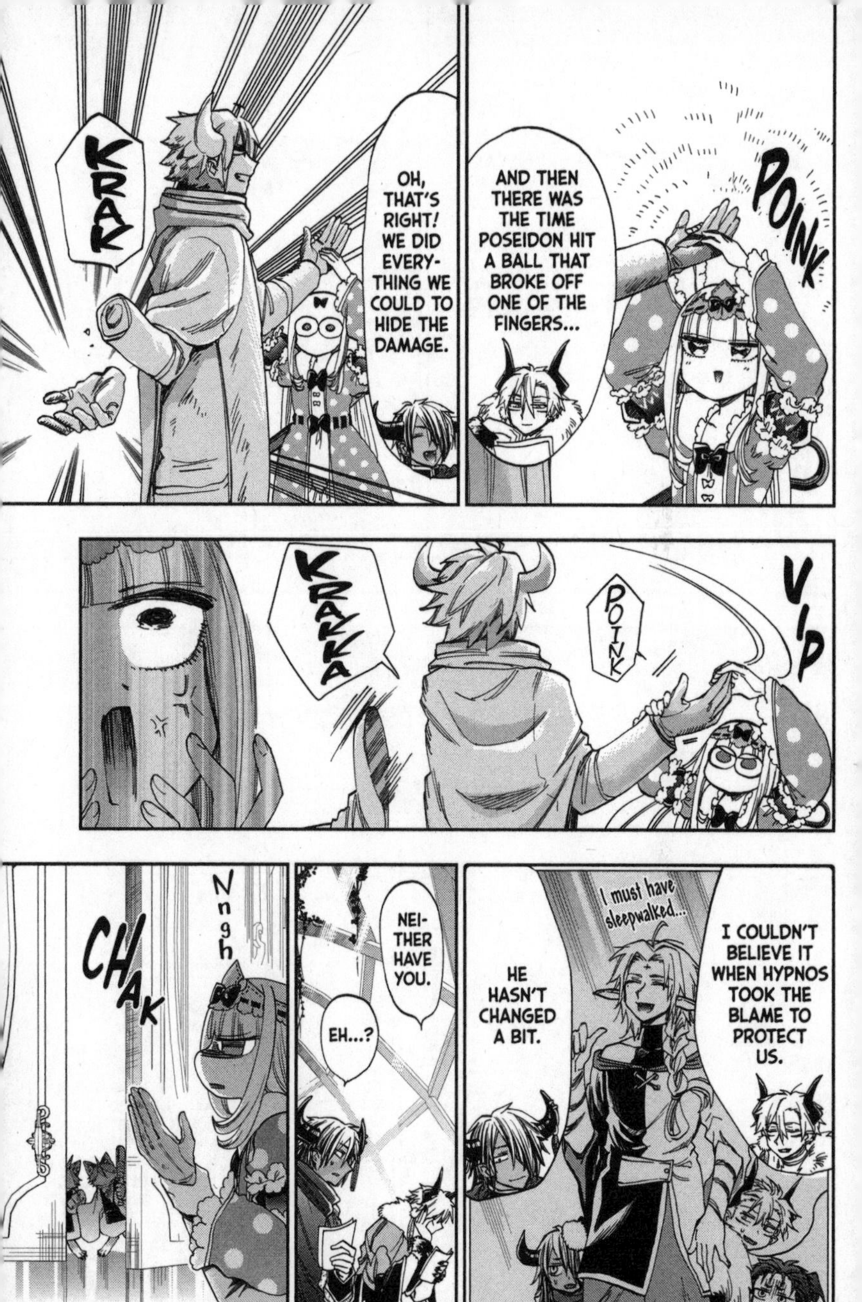
POINK
AND THEN THERE WAS THE TIME POSEIDON HIT A BALL THAT BROKE OFF ONE OF THE FINGERS...
OH, THAT'S RIGHT! WE DID EVERY-THING WE COULD TO HIDE THE DAMAGE.
KRAK
VIP
POINK
KRAKKA
I COULDN'T BELIEVE IT WHEN HYPNOS TOOK THE BLAME TO PROTECT US.
I must have sleepwalked...
HE HASN'T CHANGED A BIT.
NEI-THER HAVE YOU.
EH...?
Nngh
CHAK

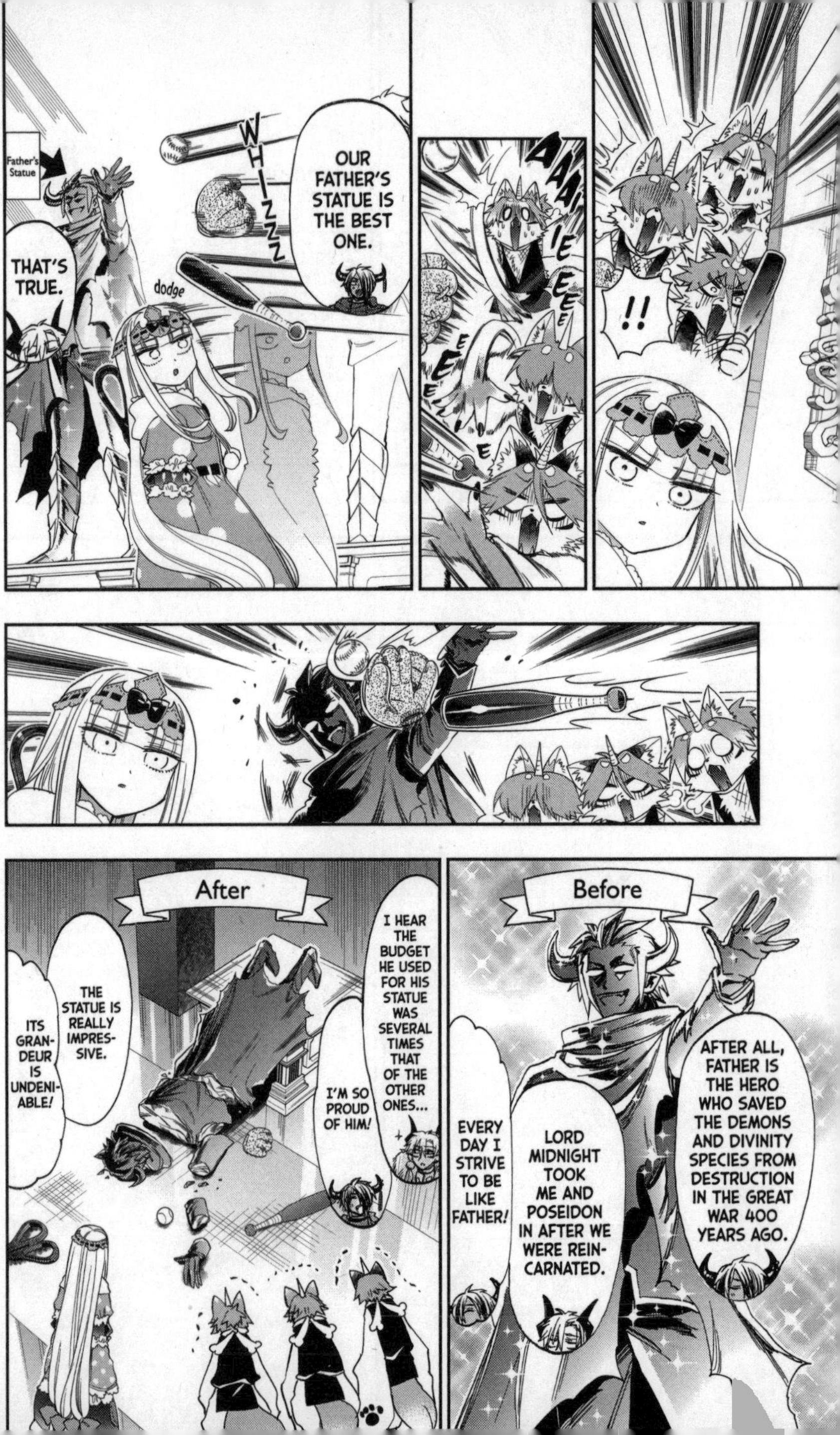
!!
AAAIIEEEE
EEEEE
OUR FATHER'S STATUE IS THE BEST ONE.
WHIZZZ
Father's Statue
THAT'S TRUE.
dodge
Before
AFTER ALL, FATHER IS THE HERO WHO SAVED THE DEMONS AND DIVINITY SPECIES FROM DESTRUCTION IN THE GREAT WAR 400 YEARS AGO.
LORD MIDNIGHT TOOK ME AND POSEIDON IN AFTER WE WERE REIN-CARNATED.
EVERY DAY I STRIVE TO BE LIKE FATHER!
After
I HEAR THE BUDGET HE USED FOR HIS STATUE WAS SEVERAL TIMES THAT OF THE OTHER ONES...
I'M SO PROUD OF HIM!
THE STATUE IS REALLY IMPRES-SIVE.
ITS GRAN-DEUR IS UNDENI-ABLE!

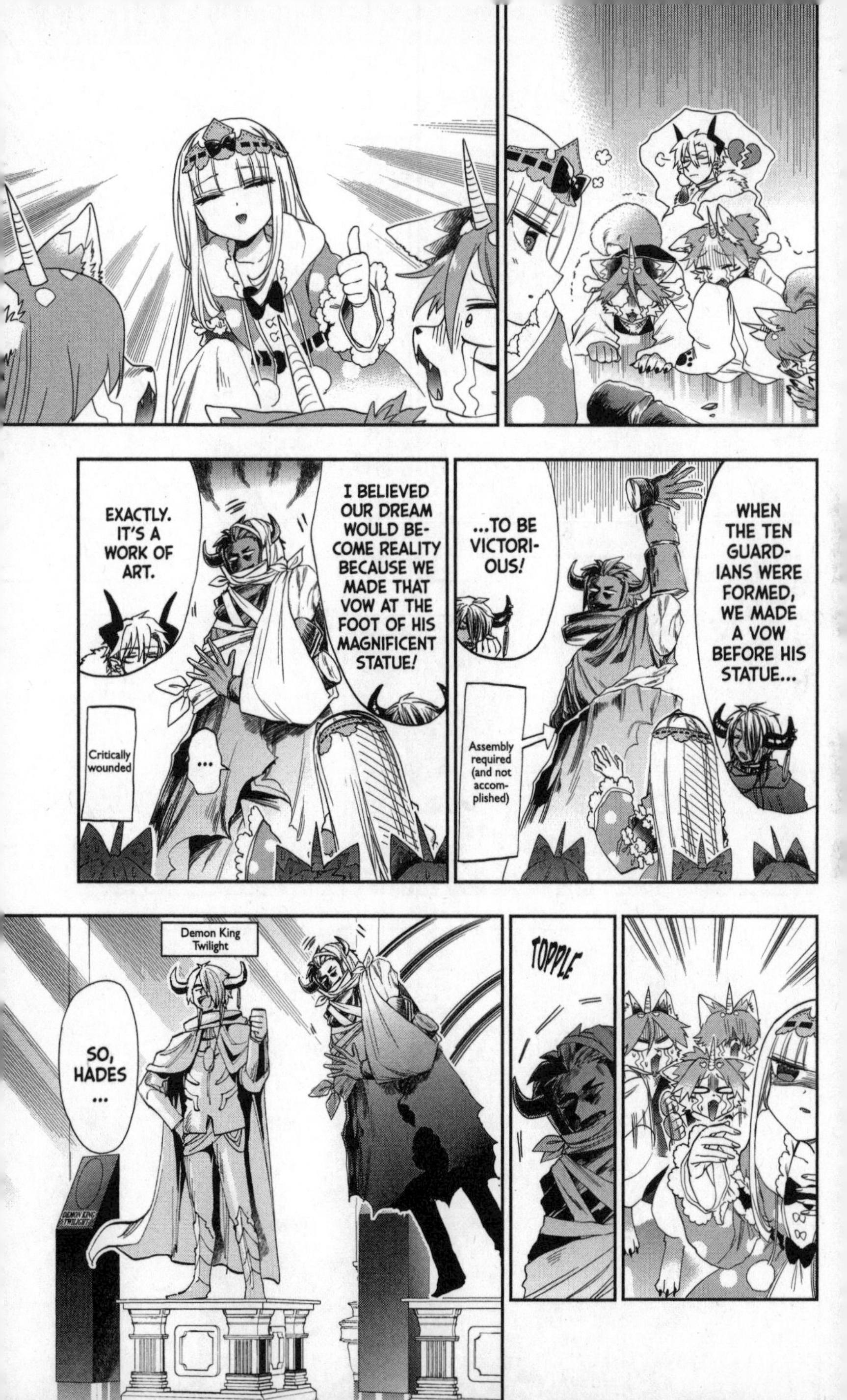
WHEN THE TEN GUARD-IANS WERE FORMED, WE MADE A VOW BEFORE HIS STATUE...
...TO BE VICTORI-OUS!
Assembly required (and not accom-plished)
I BELIEVED OUR DREAM WOULD BE-COME REALITY BECAUSE WE MADE THAT VOW AT THE FOOT OF HIS MAGNIFICENT STATUE!
EXACTLY. IT'S A WORK OF ART.
...
Critically wounded
TOPPLE
Demon King Twilight
SO, HADES ...
DEMON KING TWILIGHT

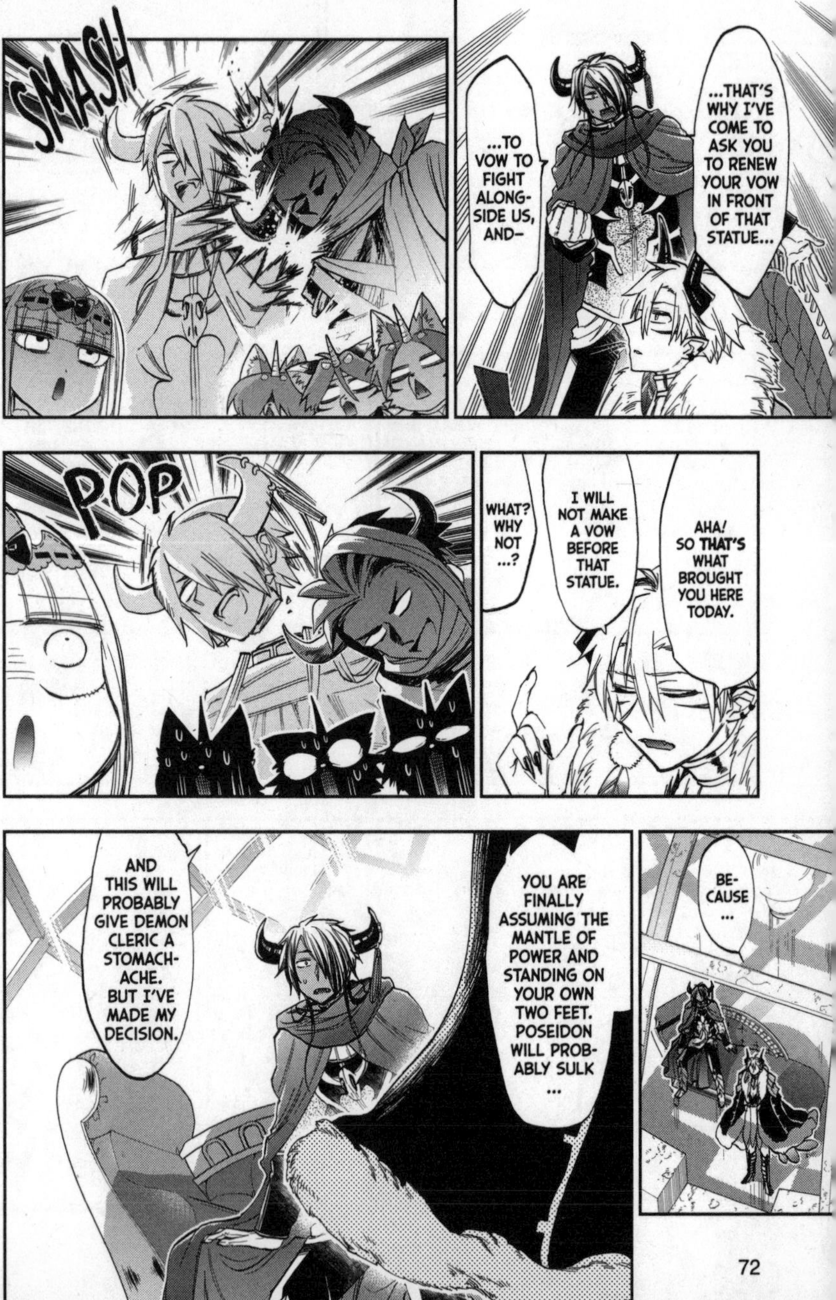
...THAT'S WHY I'VE COME TO ASK YOU TO RENEW YOUR VOW IN FRONT OF THAT STATUE...
...TO VOW TO FIGHT ALONG-SIDE US, AND—
SMASH
AHA! SO **THAT'S** WHAT BROUGHT YOU HERE TODAY.
I WILL NOT MAKE A VOW BEFORE THAT STATUE.
WHAT? WHY NOT ...?
POP
BE-CAUSE ...
YOU ARE FINALLY ASSUMING THE MANTLE OF POWER AND STANDING ON YOUR OWN TWO FEET. POSEIDON WILL PROB-ABLY SULK ...
AND THIS WILL PROBABLY GIVE DEMON CLERIC A STOMACH-ACHE. BUT I'VE MADE MY DECISION.

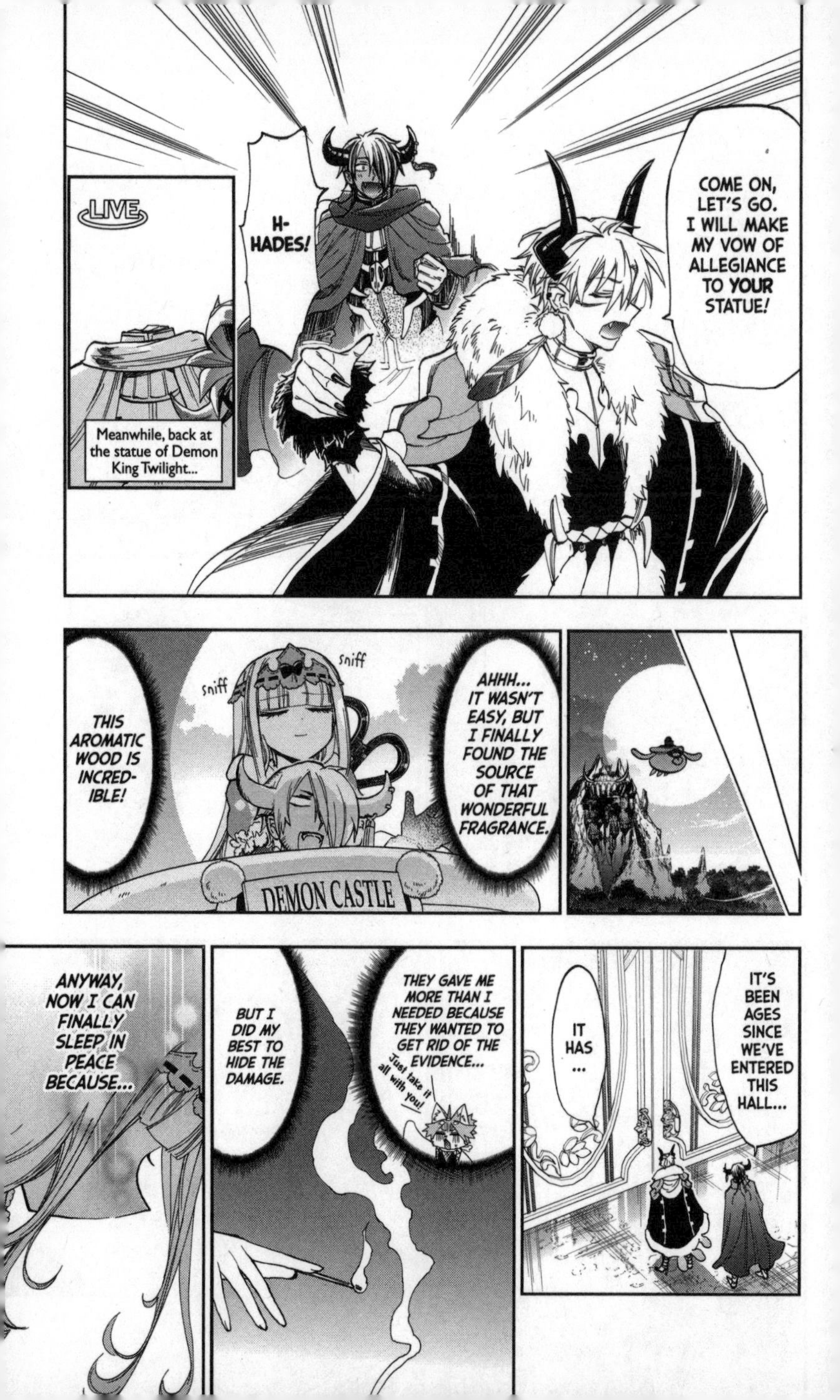
COME ON, LET'S GO. I WILL MAKE MY VOW OF ALLEGIANCE TO YOUR STATUE!
H- HADES!
LIVE
Meanwhile, back at the statue of Demon King Twilight...
AHHH... IT WASN'T EASY, BUT I FINALLY FOUND THE SOURCE OF THAT WONDERFUL FRAGRANCE.
sniff
sniff
THIS AROMATIC WOOD IS INCREDIBLE!
DEMON CASTLE
IT'S BEEN AGES SINCE WE'VE ENTERED THIS HALL...
IT HAS ...
THEY GAVE ME MORE THAN I NEEDED BECAUSE THEY WANTED TO GET RID OF THE EVIDENCE...
Just take it all with you!
BUT I DID MY BEST TO HIDE THE DAMAGE.
ANYWAY, NOW I CAN FINALLY SLEEP IN PEACE BECAUSE...

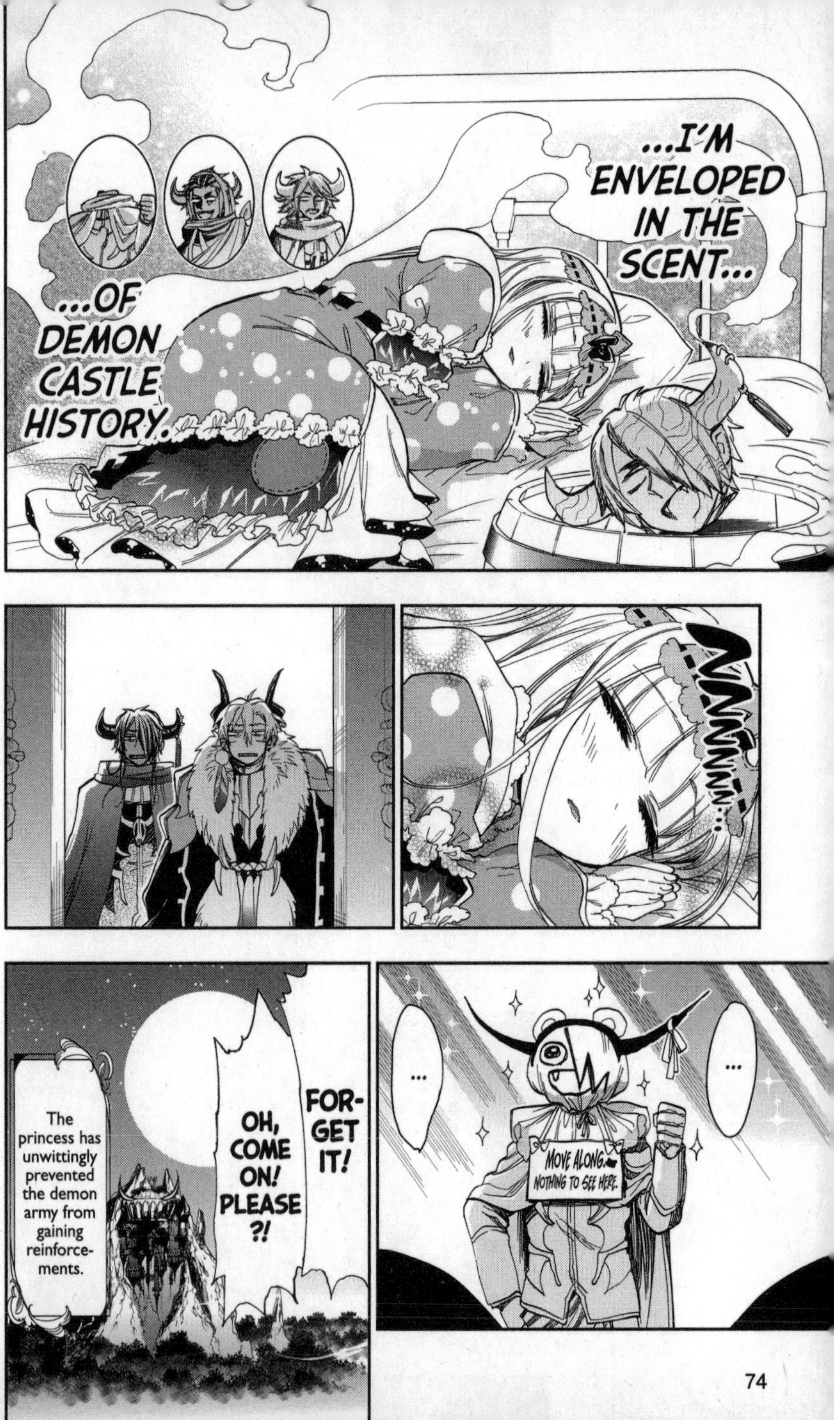
...I'M ENVELOPED IN THE SCENT...
...OF DEMON CASTLE HISTORY.
...
...
MOVE ALONG. NOTHING TO SEE HERE.
FOR-GET IT!
OH, COME ON! PLEASE?!
The princess has unwittingly prevented the demon army from gaining reinforce-ments.

Ancestor Statues

Go play somewhere else.

▼

Durability: ☆☆
Historicalness: ☆☆☆☆☆☆☆☆☆

The statues of the former demon kings are displayed in the Hall of Ancestors at the old Demon Castle. They are lavishly carved out of the finest aromatic wood and consequently lack durability. The Demon King has often wondered why his ancestors used such a delicate material, but he nevertheless had his statue created from it to keep with tradition.

The Hall of the Ancestors has long been a favorite playground for the demon children, so regardless of the material the statues are made of, they are destined to get wrecked eventually.

The illustration is of the statue of Demon King Midnight (human form), the father of the current Demon King Twilight.

Problem ten years ago:
"Why did they use such brittle wood for the statues?"

Current problem:
"Now I understand that durability isn't the problem."

▼

Evidently they got caught and scolded. ♡

What a lovely scent...

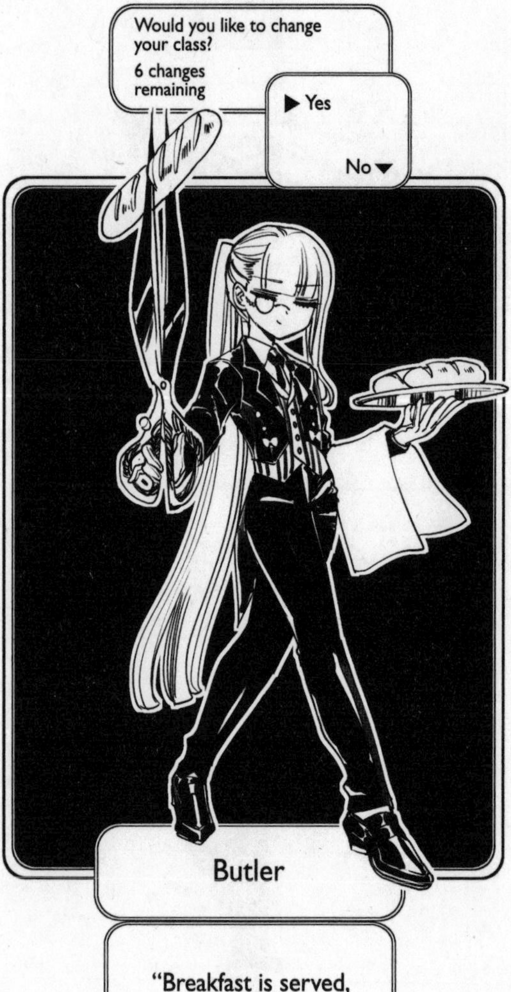
Would you like to change your class?
6 changes remaining
▶ Yes
No ▼
Butler
"Breakfast is served, my lord."

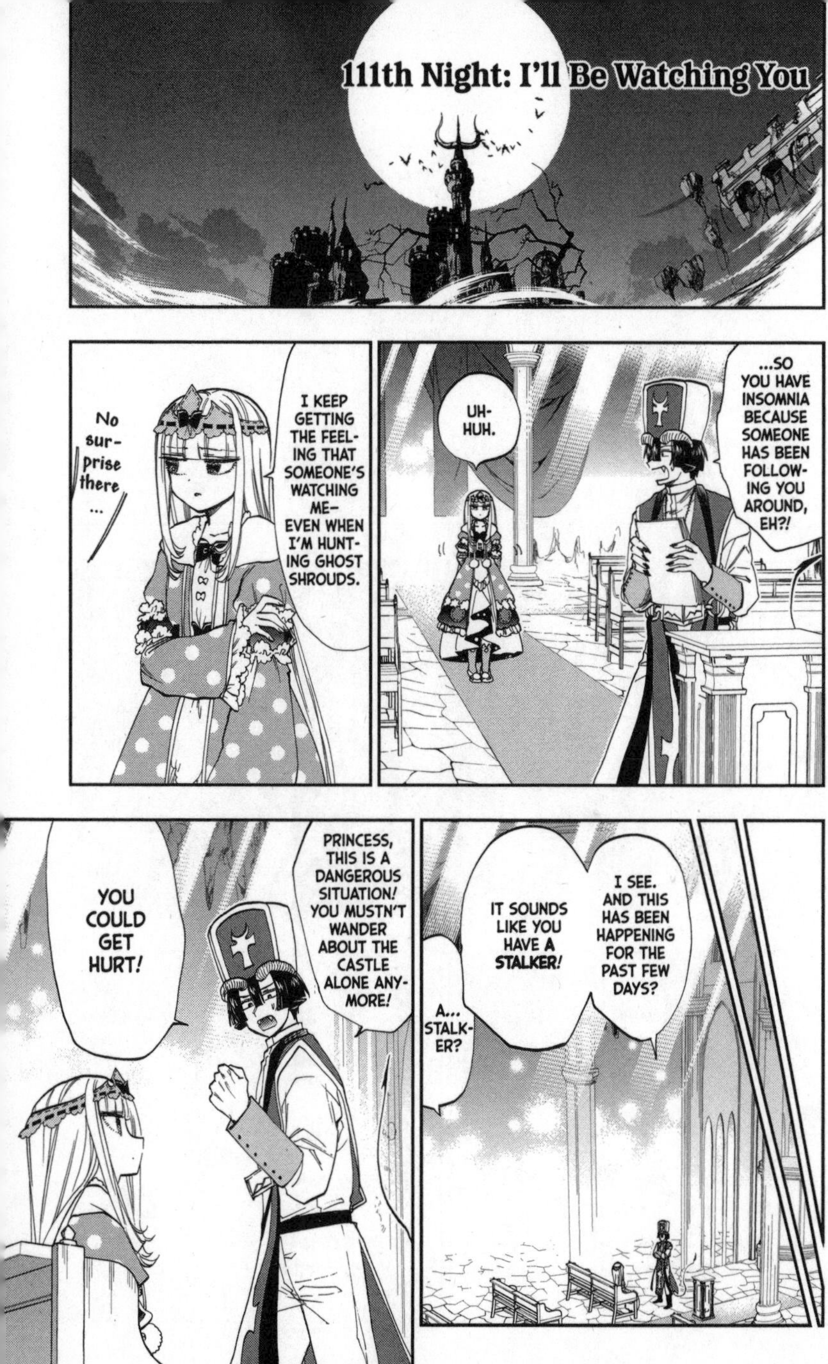
111th Night: I'll Be Watching You
...SO YOU HAVE INSOMNIA BECAUSE SOMEONE HAS BEEN FOLLOWING YOU AROUND, EH?!
UH-HUH.
I KEEP GETTING THE FEELING THAT SOMEONE'S WATCHING ME—EVEN WHEN I'M HUNTING GHOST SHROUDS.
No surprise there...
I SEE. AND THIS HAS BEEN HAPPENING FOR THE PAST FEW DAYS?
IT SOUNDS LIKE YOU HAVE A **STALKER**!
A... STALKER?
PRINCESS, THIS IS A DANGEROUS SITUATION! YOU MUSTN'T WANDER ABOUT THE CASTLE ALONE ANYMORE!
YOU COULD GET HURT!

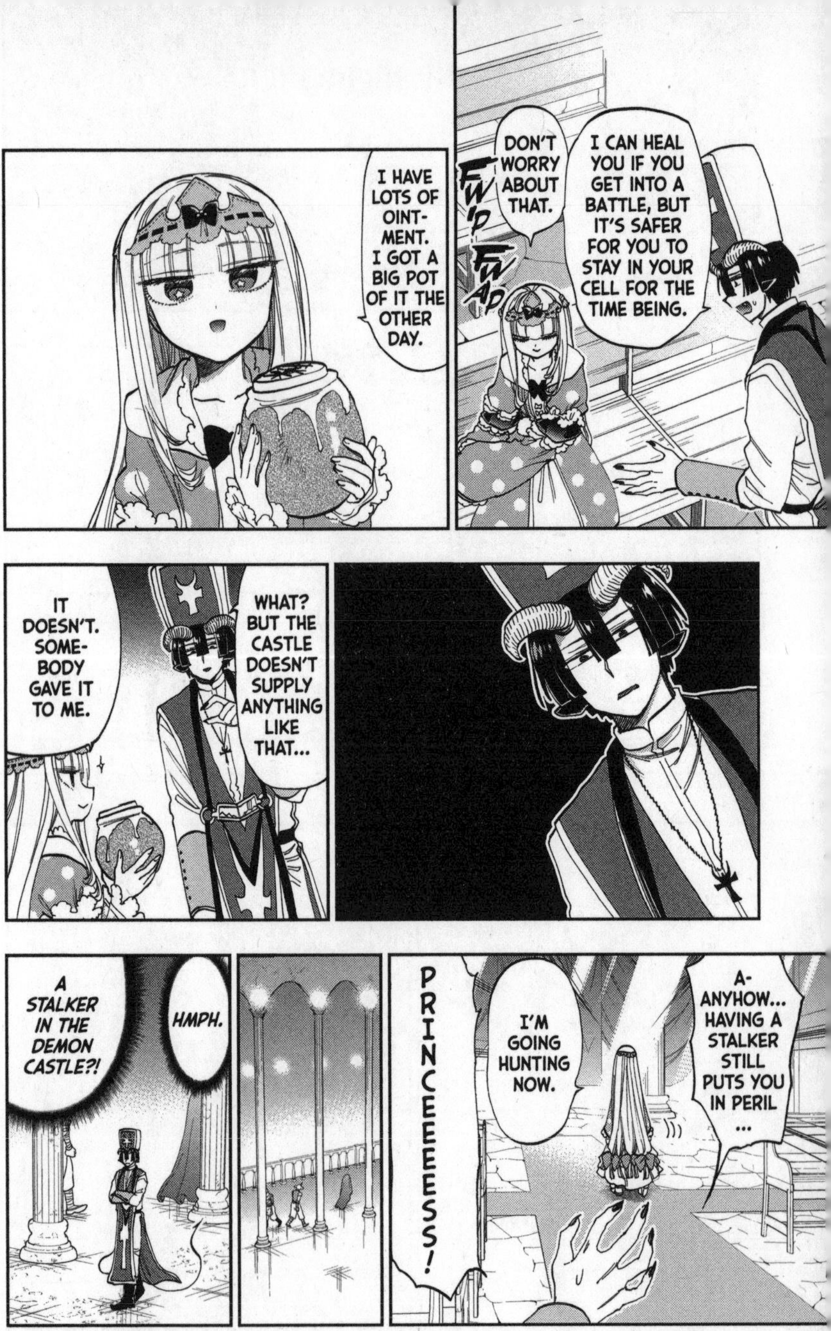
I CAN HEAL YOU IF YOU GET INTO A BATTLE, BUT IT'S SAFER FOR YOU TO STAY IN YOUR CELL FOR THE TIME BEING.
DON'T WORRY ABOUT THAT.
FWIP FWAP
I HAVE LOTS OF OINT-MENT. I GOT A BIG POT OF IT THE OTHER DAY.
WHAT? BUT THE CASTLE DOESN'T SUPPLY ANYTHING LIKE THAT...
IT DOESN'T. SOME-BODY GAVE IT TO ME.
A-ANYHOW... HAVING A STALKER STILL PUTS YOU IN PERIL ...
I'M GOING HUNTING NOW.
PRINCEEEESS!
HMPH.
A STALKER IN THE DEMON CASTLE?!

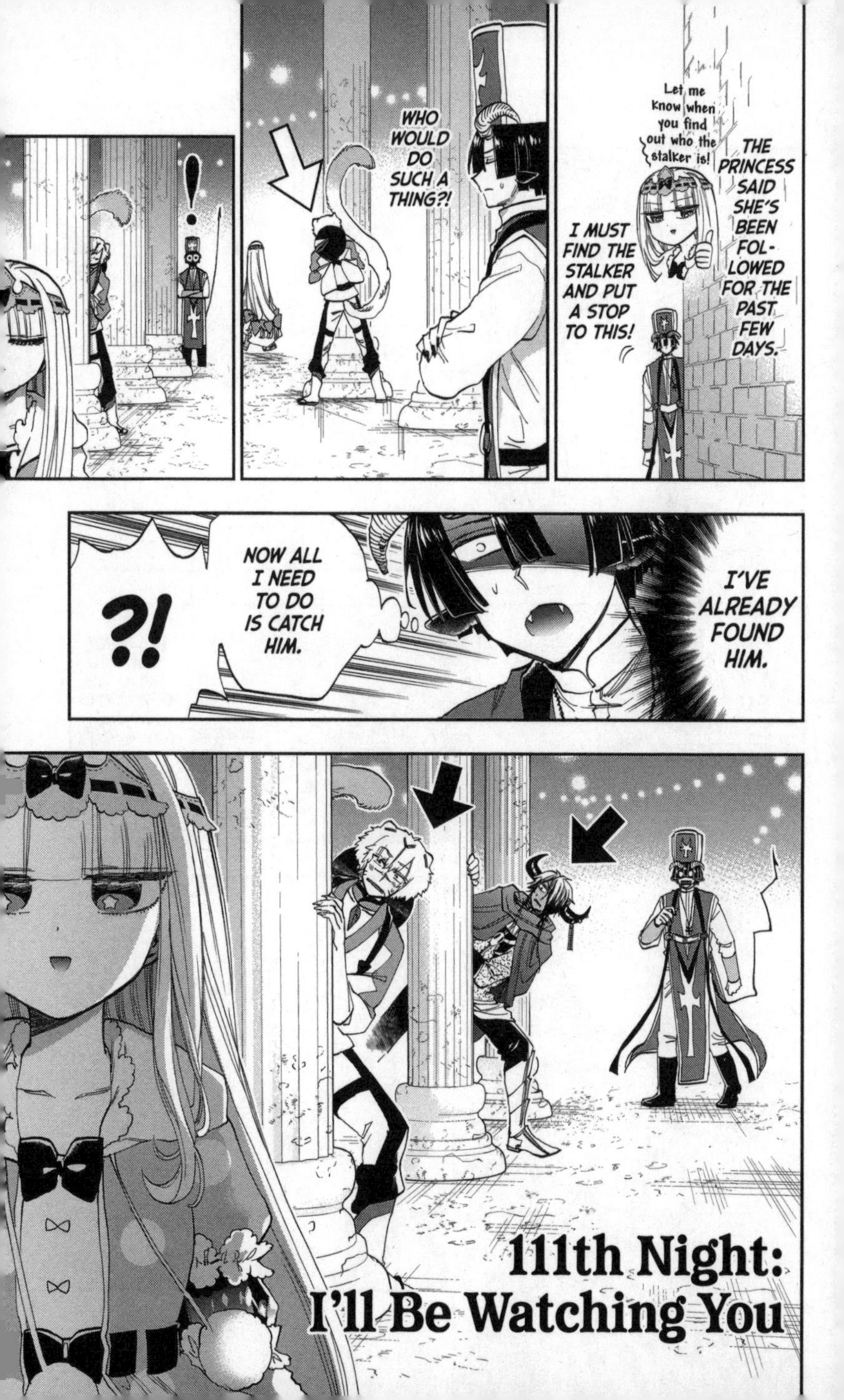
THE PRINCESS SAID SHE'S BEEN FOL-LOWED FOR THE PAST FEW DAYS.
Let me know when you find out who the stalker is!
I MUST FIND THE STALKER AND PUT A STOP TO THIS!
WHO WOULD DO SUCH A THING?!
!
I'VE ALREADY FOUND HIM.
NOW ALL I NEED TO DO IS CATCH HIM.
?!
111th Night: I'll Be Watching You

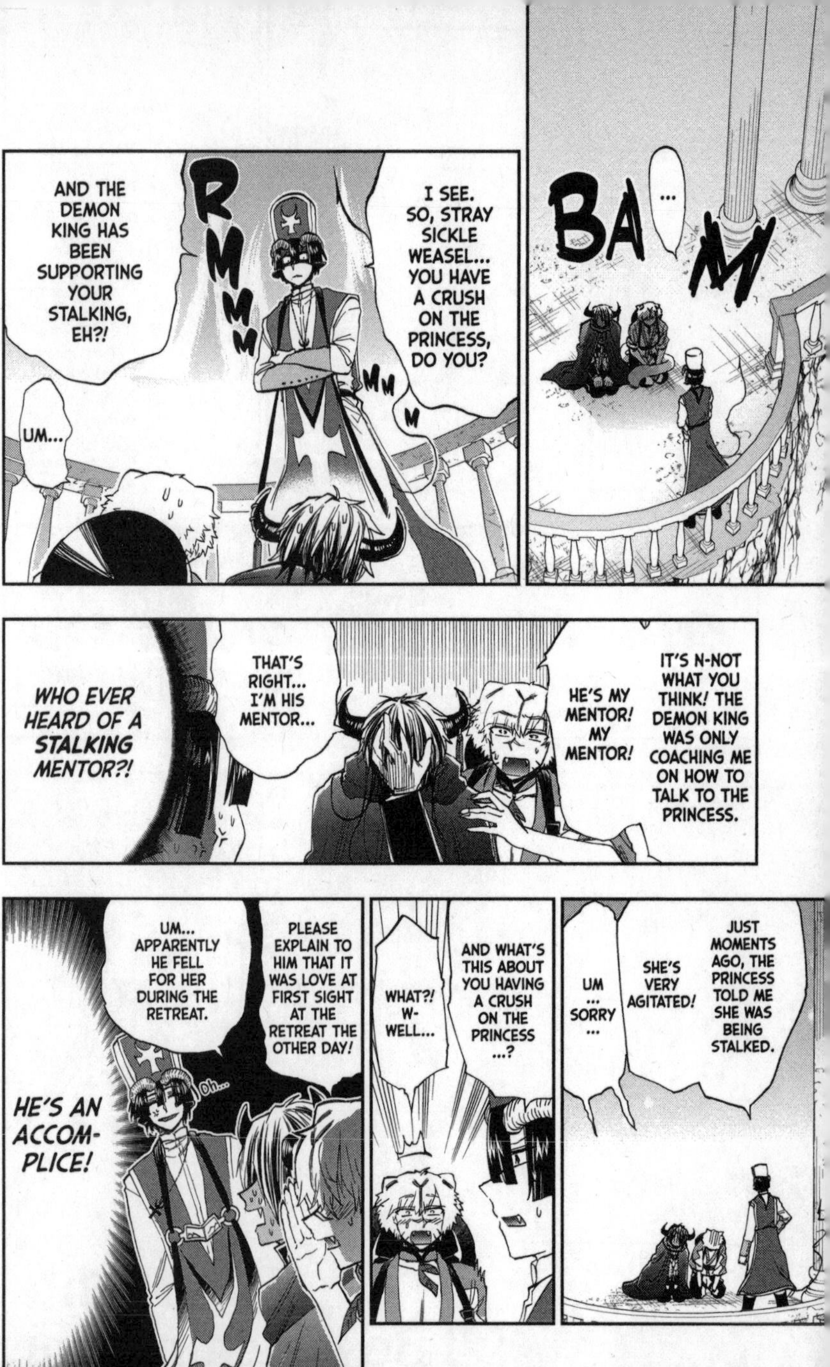
BAM
...
RMMMMMMM
I SEE. SO, STRAY SICKLE WEASEL... YOU HAVE A CRUSH ON THE PRINCESS, DO YOU?
AND THE DEMON KING HAS BEEN SUPPORTING YOUR STALKING, EH?!
UM...
IT'S N-NOT WHAT YOU THINK! THE DEMON KING WAS ONLY COACHING ME ON HOW TO TALK TO THE PRINCESS.
HE'S MY MENTOR! MY MENTOR!
THAT'S RIGHT... I'M HIS MENTOR...
WHO EVER HEARD OF A STALKING MENTOR?!
JUST MOMENTS AGO, THE PRINCESS TOLD ME SHE WAS BEING STALKED.
SHE'S VERY AGITATED!
UM ... SORRY ...
AND WHAT'S THIS ABOUT YOU HAVING A CRUSH ON THE PRINCESS ...?
WHAT?! W-WELL...
PLEASE EXPLAIN TO HIM THAT IT WAS LOVE AT FIRST SIGHT AT THE RETREAT THE OTHER DAY!
UM... APPARENTLY HE FELL FOR HER DURING THE RETREAT.
Oh...
HE'S AN ACCOM-PLICE!

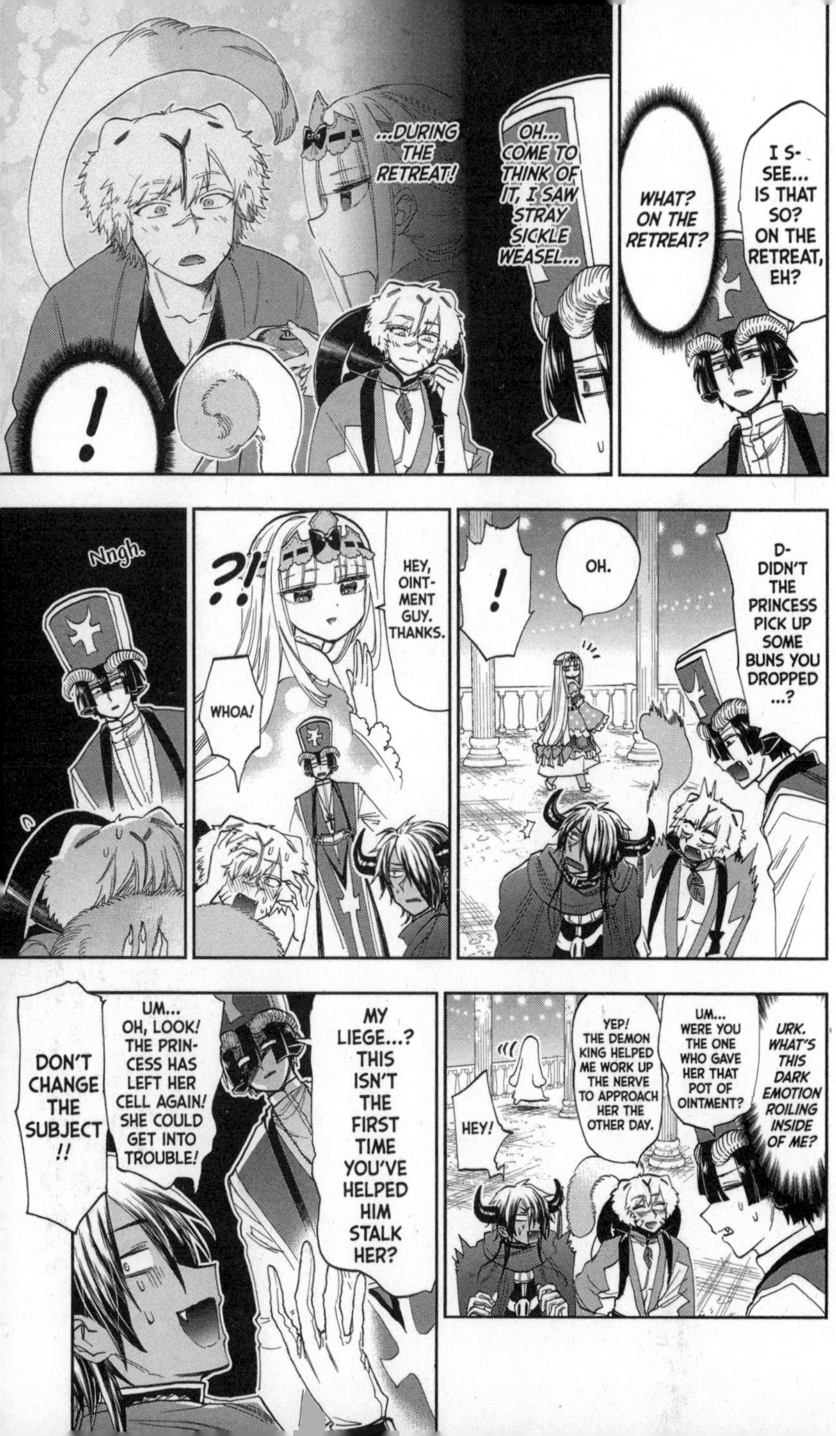
I S-SEE... IS THAT SO? ON THE RETREAT, EH?
WHAT? ON THE RETREAT?
OH... COME TO THINK OF IT, I SAW STRAY SICKLE WEASEL...
...DURING THE RETREAT!
!
D-DIDN'T THE PRINCESS PICK UP SOME BUNS YOU DROPPED...?
OH.
!
HEY, OINT-MENT GUY. THANKS.
?!
WHOA!
Nngh.
URK. WHAT'S THIS DARK EMOTION ROILING INSIDE OF ME?
UM... WERE YOU THE ONE WHO GAVE HER THAT POT OF OINTMENT?
YEP! THE DEMON KING HELPED ME WORK UP THE NERVE TO APPROACH HER THE OTHER DAY.
HEY!
MY LIEGE...? THIS ISN'T THE FIRST TIME YOU'VE HELPED HIM STALK HER?
UM... OH, LOOK! THE PRIN-CESS HAS LEFT HER CELL AGAIN! SHE COULD GET INTO TROUBLE!
DON'T CHANGE THE SUBJECT!!

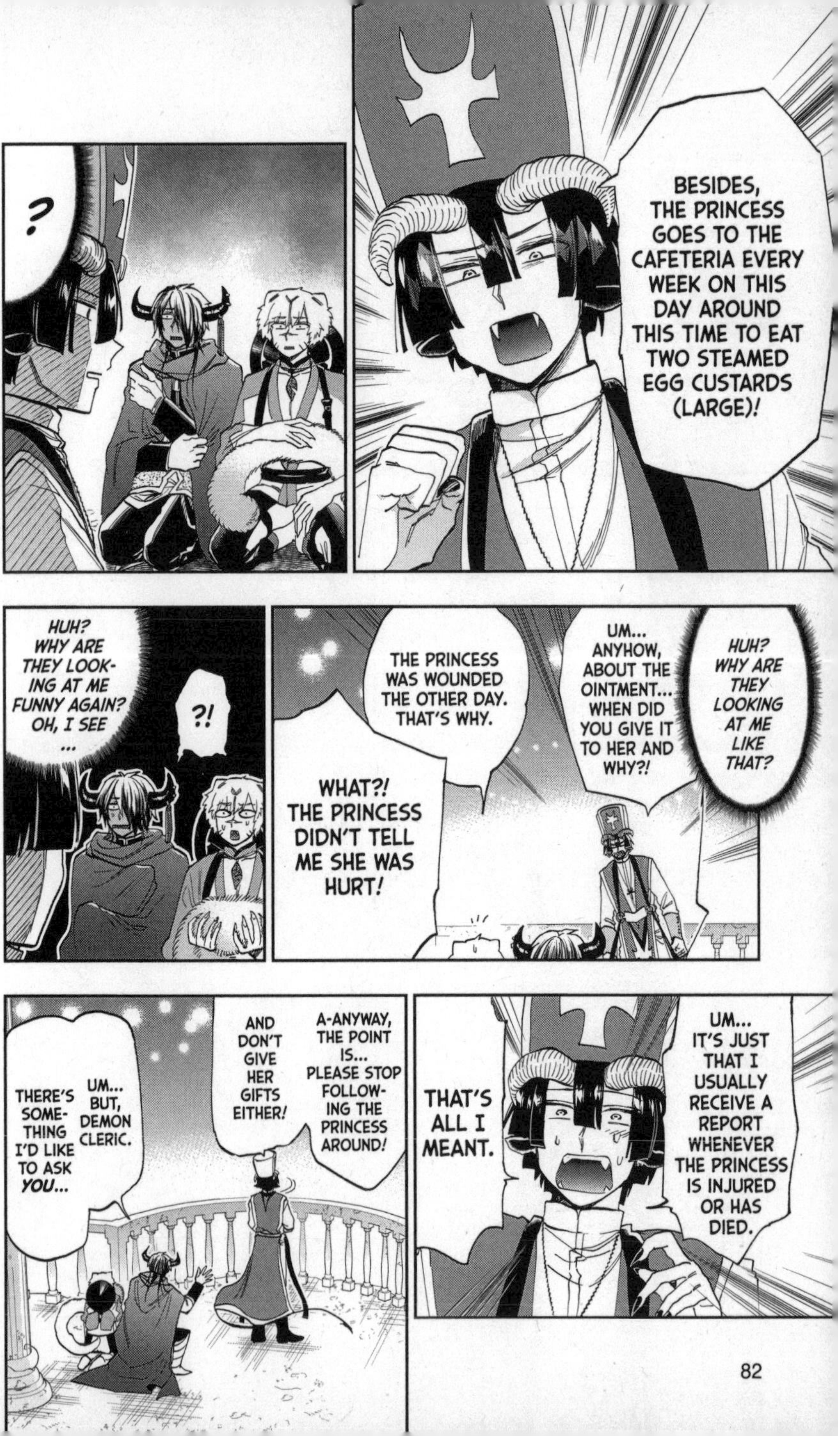
BESIDES, THE PRINCESS GOES TO THE CAFETERIA EVERY WEEK ON THIS DAY AROUND THIS TIME TO EAT TWO STEAMED EGG CUSTARDS (LARGE)!
?
HUH? WHY ARE THEY LOOKING AT ME LIKE THAT?
UM... ANYHOW, ABOUT THE OINTMENT... WHEN DID YOU GIVE IT TO HER AND WHY?!
THE PRINCESS WAS WOUNDED THE OTHER DAY. THAT'S WHY.
WHAT?! THE PRINCESS DIDN'T TELL ME SHE WAS HURT!
?!
HUH? WHY ARE THEY LOOK-ING AT ME FUNNY AGAIN? OH, I SEE ...
UM... IT'S JUST THAT I USUALLY RECEIVE A REPORT WHENEVER THE PRINCESS IS INJURED OR HAS DIED.
THAT'S ALL I MEANT.
A-ANYWAY, THE POINT IS... PLEASE STOP FOLLOW-ING THE PRINCESS AROUND!
AND DON'T GIVE HER GIFTS EITHER!
UM... BUT, DEMON CLERIC.
THERE'S SOME-THING I'D LIKE TO ASK *YOU*...

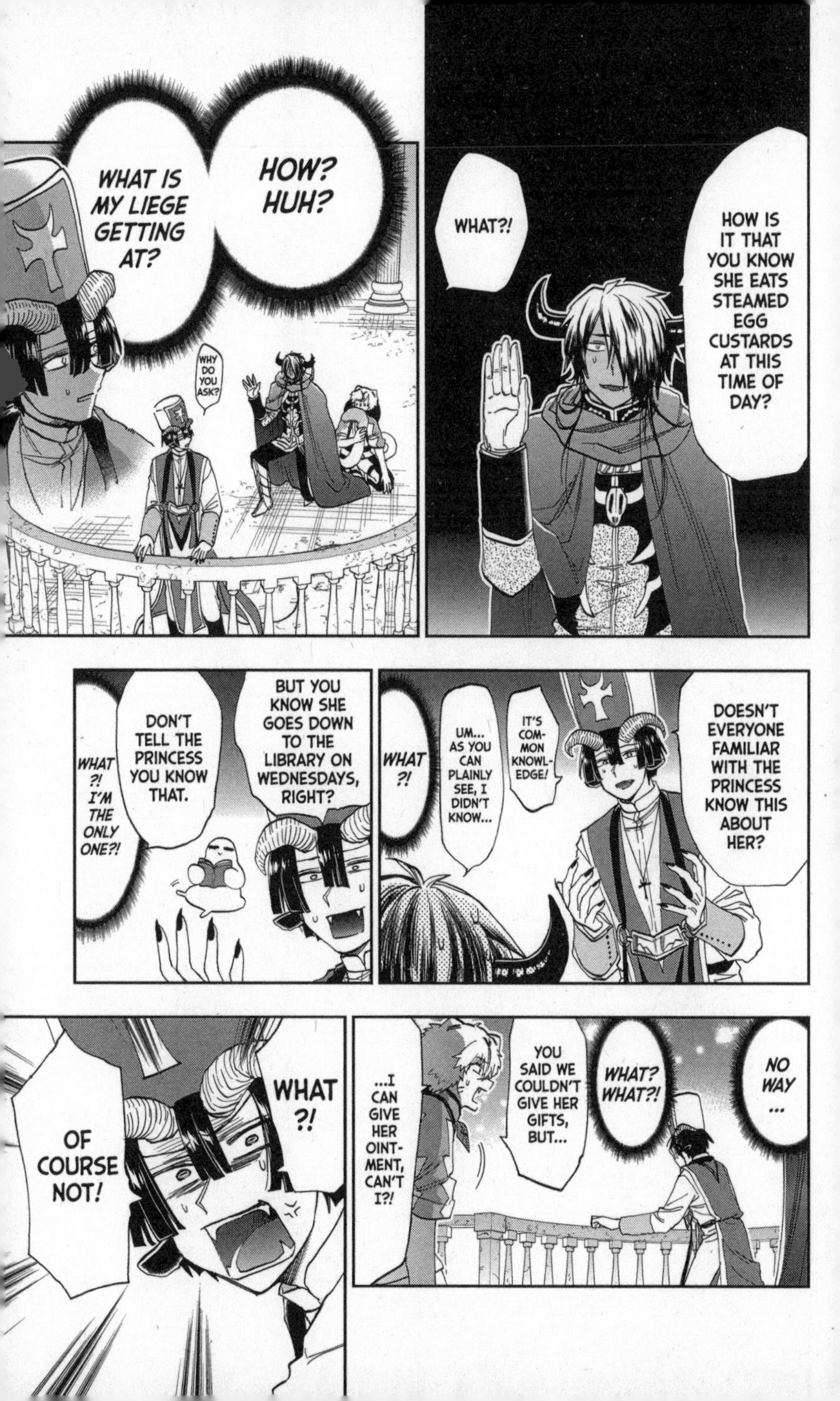
HOW IS IT THAT YOU KNOW SHE EATS STEAMED EGG CUSTARDS AT THIS TIME OF DAY?
WHAT?!
HOW? HUH?
WHAT IS MY LIEGE GETTING AT?
WHY DO YOU ASK?
DOESN'T EVERYONE FAMILIAR WITH THE PRINCESS KNOW THIS ABOUT HER?
IT'S COMMON KNOWLEDGE!
UM... AS YOU CAN PLAINLY SEE, I DIDN'T KNOW...
WHAT ?!
BUT YOU KNOW SHE GOES DOWN TO THE LIBRARY ON WEDNESDAYS, RIGHT?
DON'T TELL THE PRINCESS YOU KNOW THAT.
WHAT ?! I'M THE ONLY ONE?!
NO WAY ...
WHAT? WHAT?!
YOU SAID WE COULDN'T GIVE HER GIFTS, BUT...
...I CAN GIVE HER OINTMENT, CAN'T I?!
WHAT ?!
OF COURSE NOT!

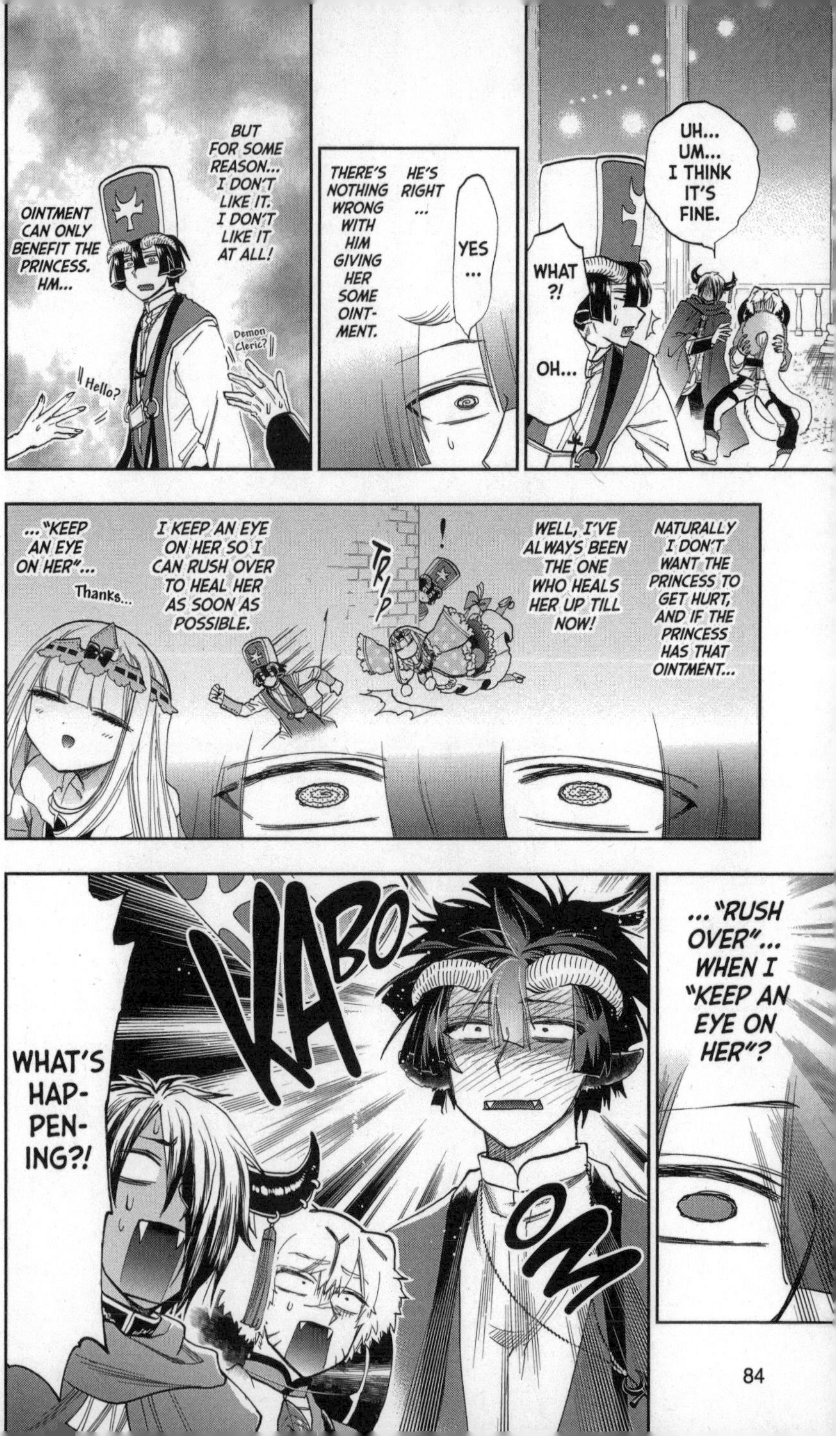
UH... UM... I THINK IT'S FINE.
WHAT ?!
OH...
HE'S RIGHT ...
THERE'S NOTHING WRONG WITH HIM GIVING HER SOME OINT-MENT.
YES ...
BUT FOR SOME REASON... I DON'T LIKE IT. I DON'T LIKE IT AT ALL!
OINTMENT CAN ONLY BENEFIT THE PRINCESS. HM...
Demon Cleric?
Hello?
NATURALLY I DON'T WANT THE PRINCESS TO GET HURT, AND IF THE PRINCESS HAS THAT OINTMENT...
WELL, I'VE ALWAYS BEEN THE ONE WHO HEALS HER UP TILL NOW!
!
TRIP
I KEEP AN EYE ON HER SO I CAN RUSH OVER TO HEAL HER AS SOON AS POSSIBLE.
..."KEEP AN EYE ON HER"...
Thanks...
..."RUSH OVER"... WHEN I "KEEP AN EYE ON HER"?
KABOOM
WHAT'S HAP-PEN-ING?!

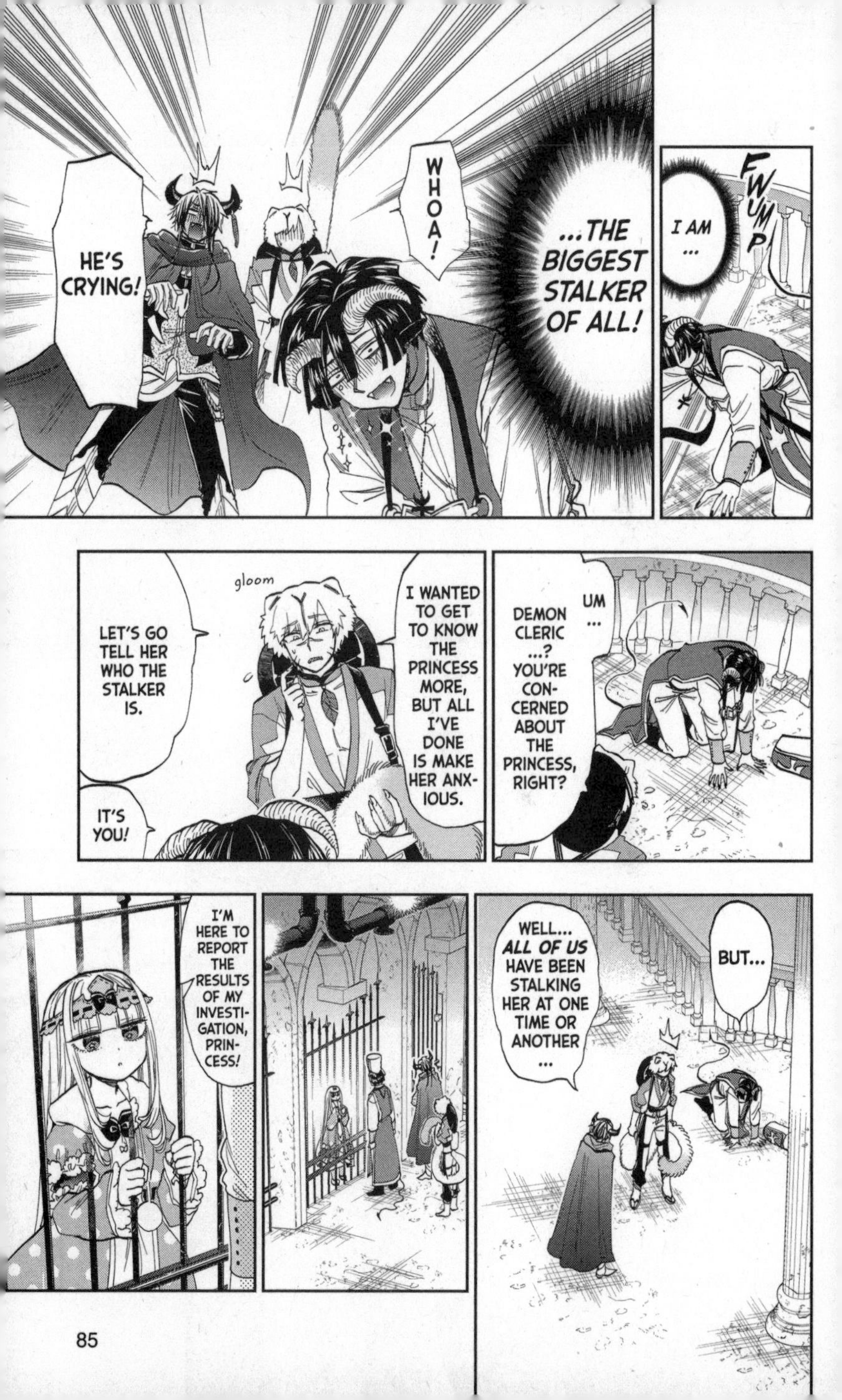
I AM ...
FWUMP
...THE BIGGEST STALKER OF ALL!
WHOA!
HE'S CRYING!
UM ...
DEMON CLERIC ...? YOU'RE CONCERNED ABOUT THE PRINCESS, RIGHT?
gloom
I WANTED TO GET TO KNOW THE PRINCESS MORE, BUT ALL I'VE DONE IS MAKE HER ANXIOUS.
LET'S GO TELL HER WHO THE STALKER IS.
IT'S YOU!
BUT...
WELL... *ALL OF US* HAVE BEEN STALKING HER AT ONE TIME OR ANOTHER ...
I'M HERE TO REPORT THE RESULTS OF MY INVESTIGATION, PRINCESS!

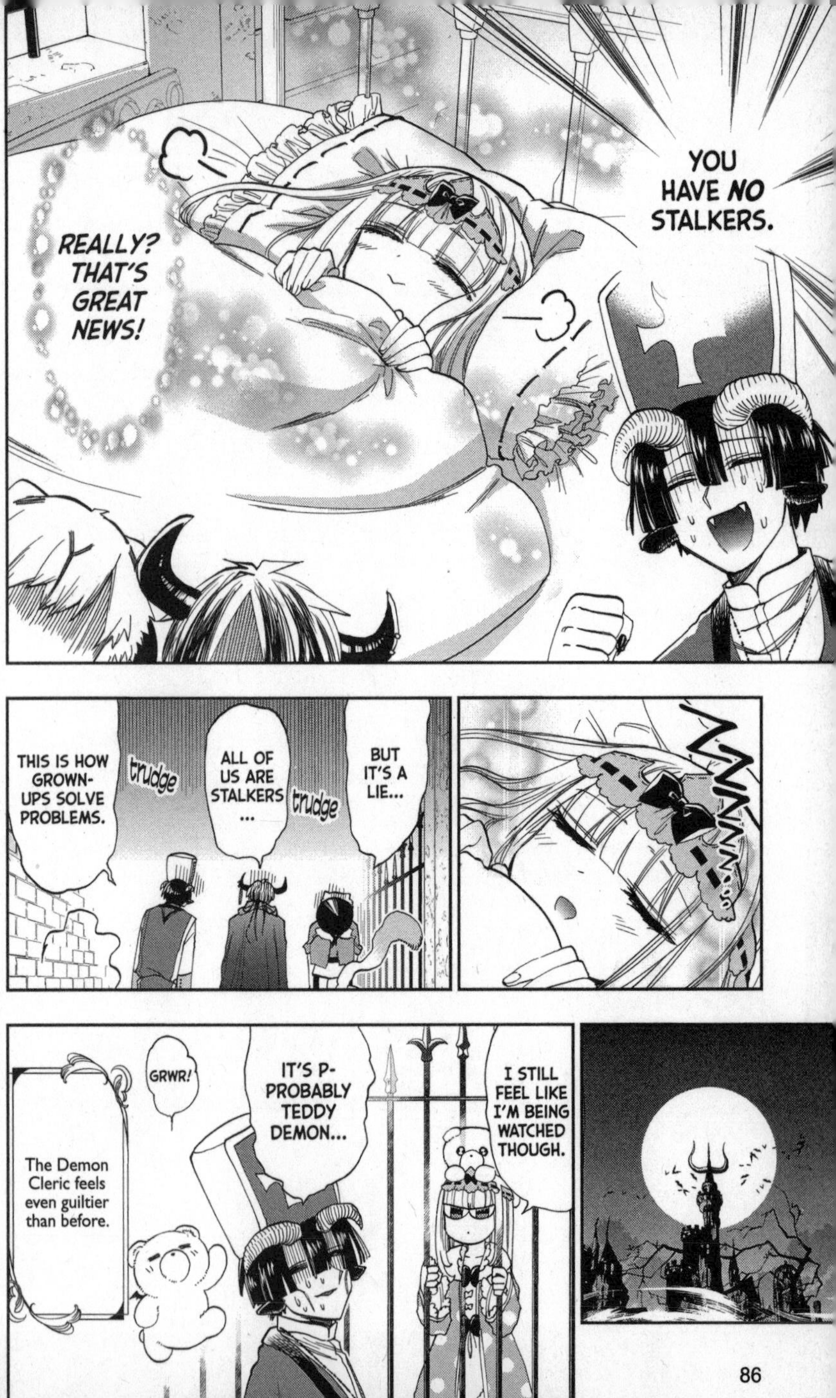
YOU HAVE NO STALKERS.
REALLY? THAT'S GREAT NEWS!
BUT IT'S A LIE...
trudge
ALL OF US ARE STALKERS ...
trudge
THIS IS HOW GROWN-UPS SOLVE PROBLEMS.
I STILL FEEL LIKE I'M BEING WATCHED THOUGH.
IT'S P-PROBABLY TEDDY DEMON...
GRWR!
The Demon Cleric feels even guiltier than before.

Kiddie Photo Studio ②

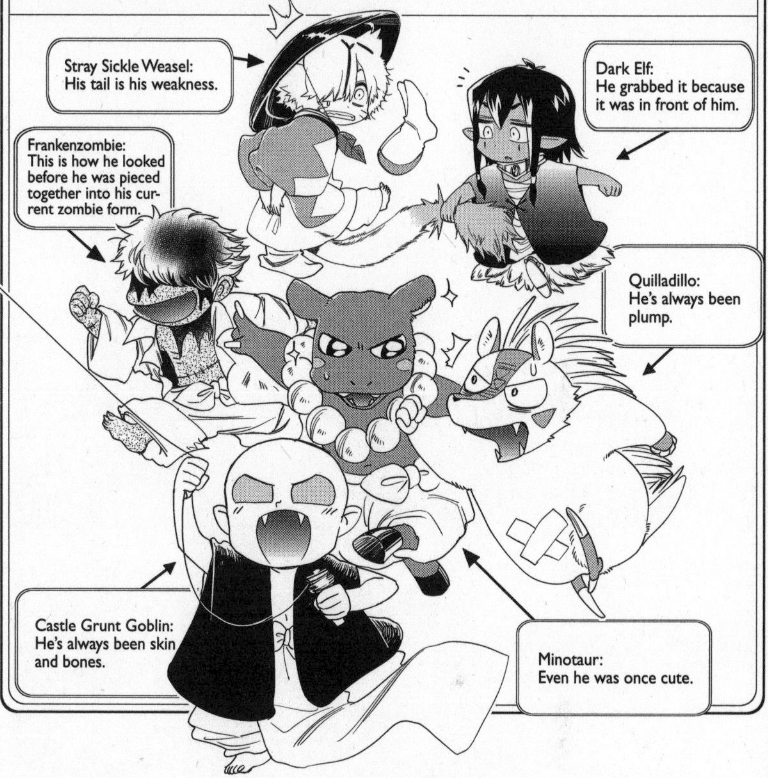
Dark Elf:
He grabbed it because it was in front of him.
Stray Sickle Weasel:
His tail is his weakness.
Frankenzombie:
This is how he looked before he was pieced together into his current zombie form.
Quilladillo:
He's always been plump.
Minotaur:
Even he was once cute.
Castle Grunt Goblin:
He's always been skin and bones.

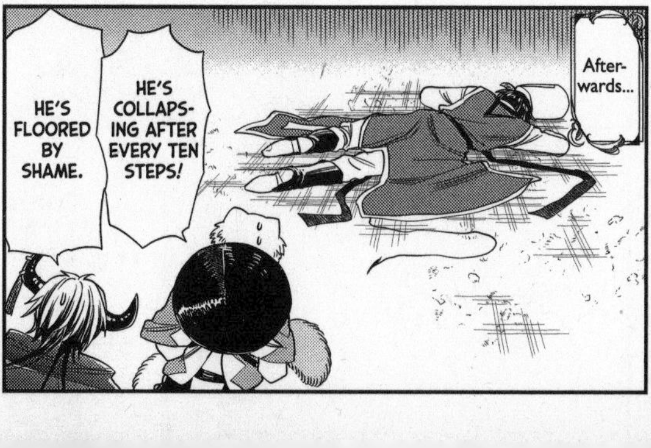
Afterwards...
HE'S COLLAPSING AFTER EVERY TEN STEPS!
HE'S FLOORED BY SHAME.

Would you like to change your class?

5 changes remaining

▶Yes

No ▼

Diver

"Nah, I'm not going to dive in."

▼

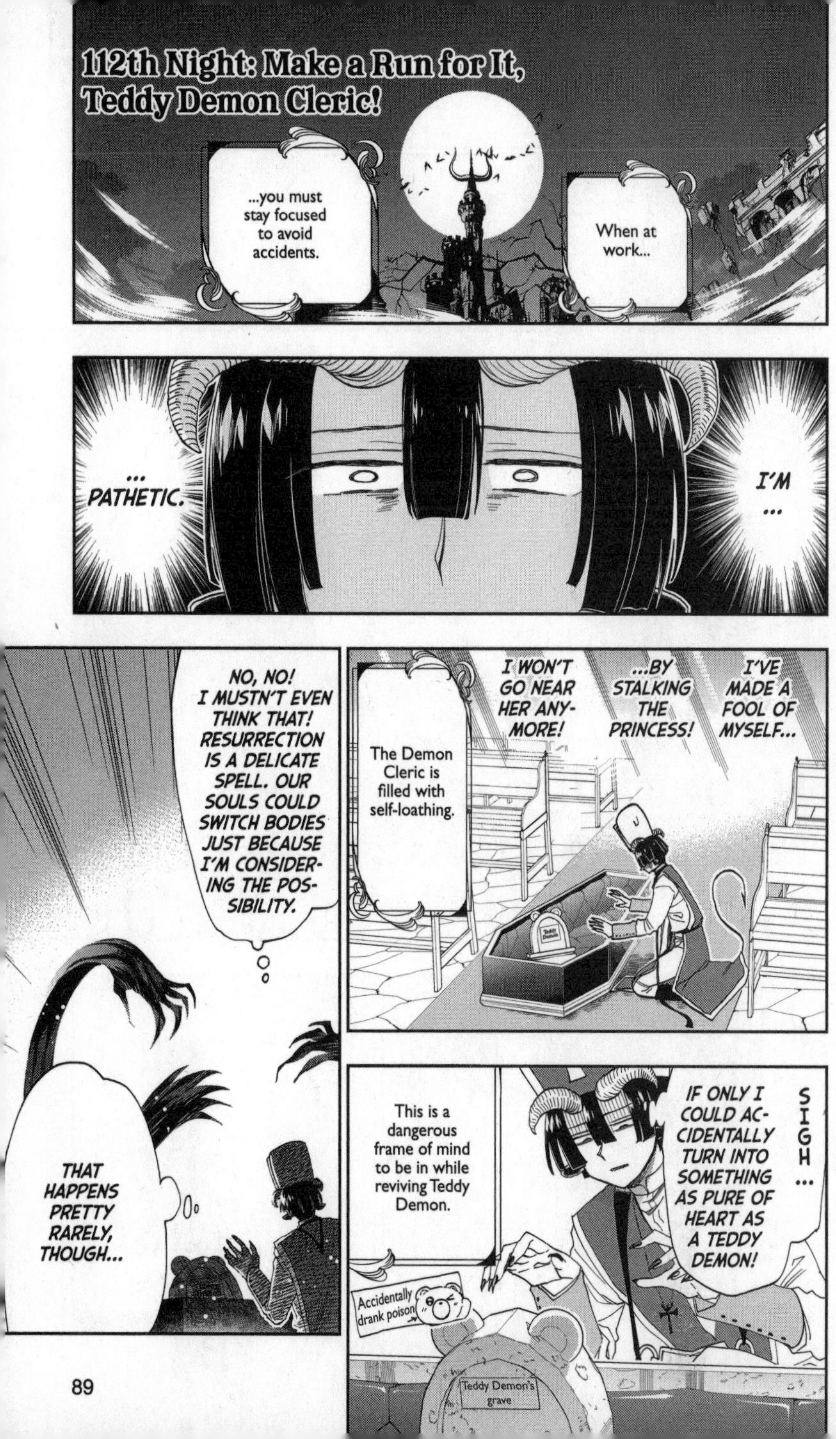
112th Night: Make a Run for It, Teddy Demon Cleric!
When at work...
...you must stay focused to avoid accidents.
I'M ...
... PATHETIC.
I'VE MADE A FOOL OF MYSELF...
...BY STALKING THE PRINCESS!
I WON'T GO NEAR HER ANYMORE!
The Demon Cleric is filled with self-loathing.
Teddy Demon
SIGH...
IF ONLY I COULD ACCIDENTALLY TURN INTO SOMETHING AS PURE OF HEART AS A TEDDY DEMON!
This is a dangerous frame of mind to be in while reviving Teddy Demon.
Accidentally drank poison
Teddy Demon's grave
NO, NO! I MUSTN'T EVEN THINK THAT! RESURRECTION IS A DELICATE SPELL. OUR SOULS COULD SWITCH BODIES JUST BECAUSE I'M CONSIDERING THE POSSIBILITY.
THAT HAPPENS PRETTY RARELY, THOUGH...

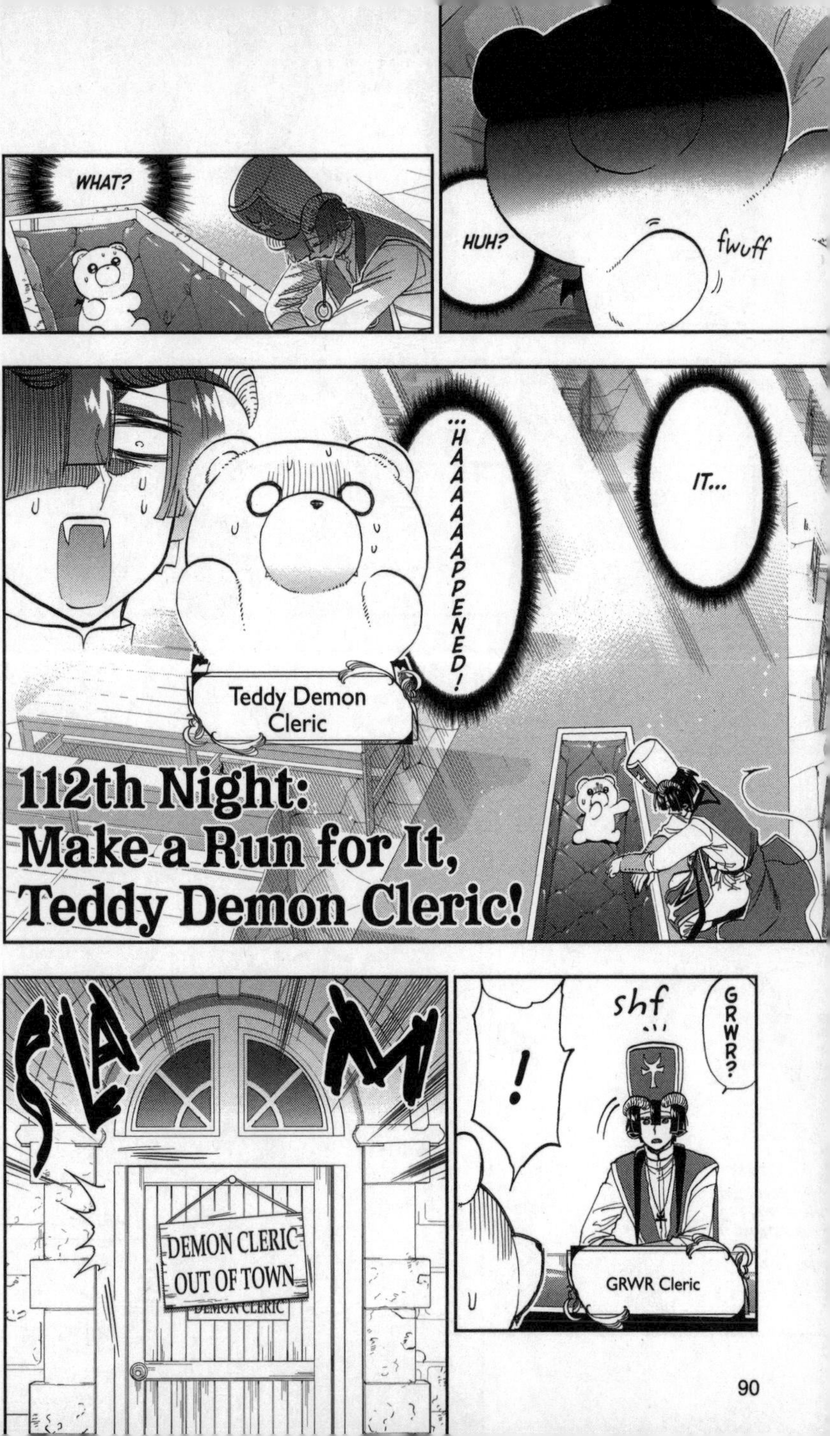
HUH?
fwuff
WHAT?
IT...
...HAAAAAAAPPENED!
Teddy Demon Cleric
112th Night: Make a Run for It, Teddy Demon Cleric!
shf
GRWR?
!
GRWR Cleric
SLAM
DEMON CLERIC OUT OF TOWN
DEMON CLERIC

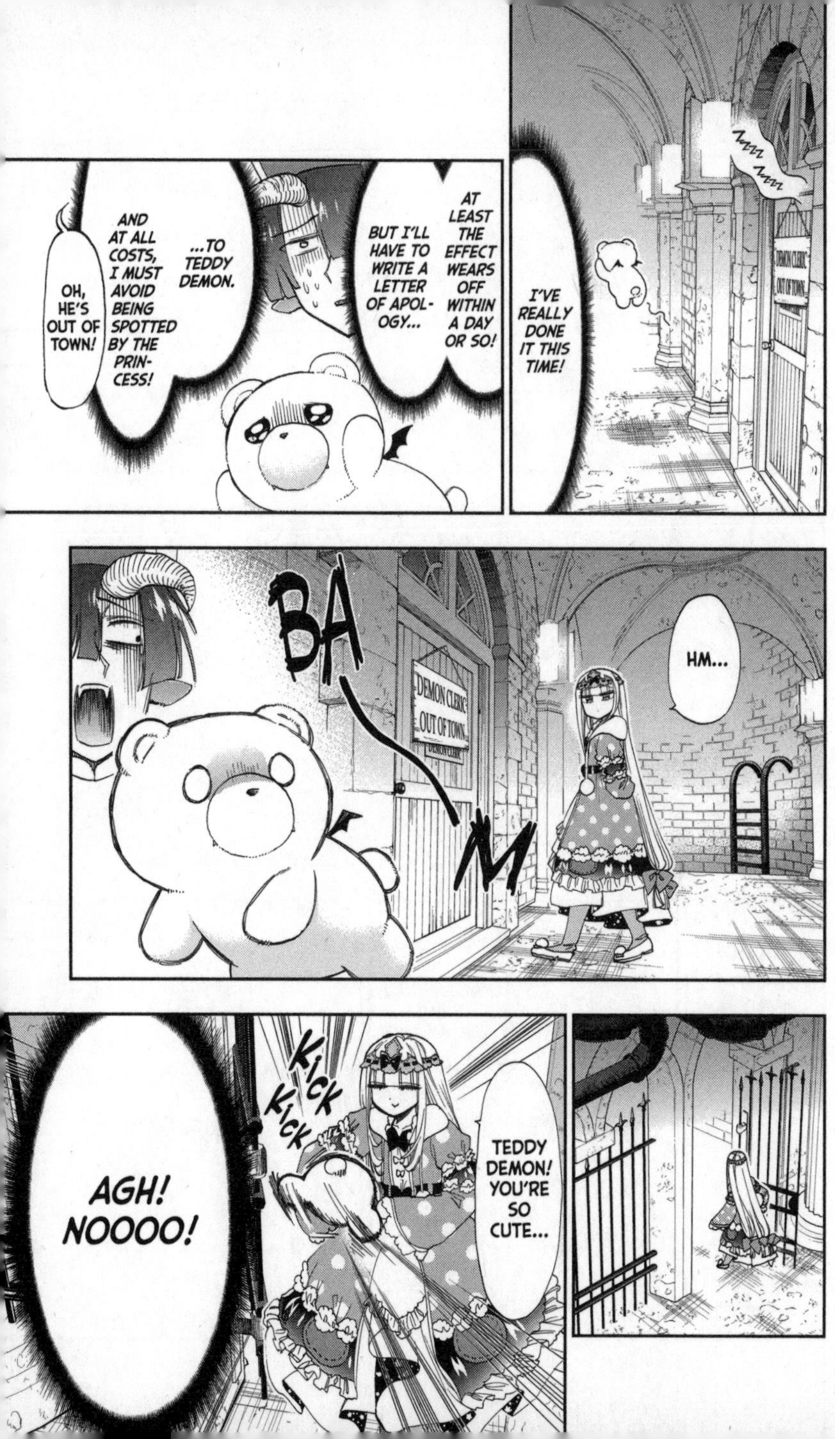
ZZZZ ZZZZ
DEMON CLERIC OUT OF TOWN
I'VE REALLY DONE IT THIS TIME!
AT LEAST THE EFFECT WEARS OFF WITHIN A DAY OR SO!
BUT I'LL HAVE TO WRITE A LETTER OF APOL- OGY...
...TO TEDDY DEMON.
AND AT ALL COSTS, I MUST AVOID BEING SPOTTED BY THE PRIN- CESS!
OH, HE'S OUT OF TOWN!
HM...
DEMON CLERIC OUT OF TOWN
DEMON CLERIC
BAM
TEDDY DEMON! YOU'RE SO CUTE...
KICK KICK
AGH! NOOOO!

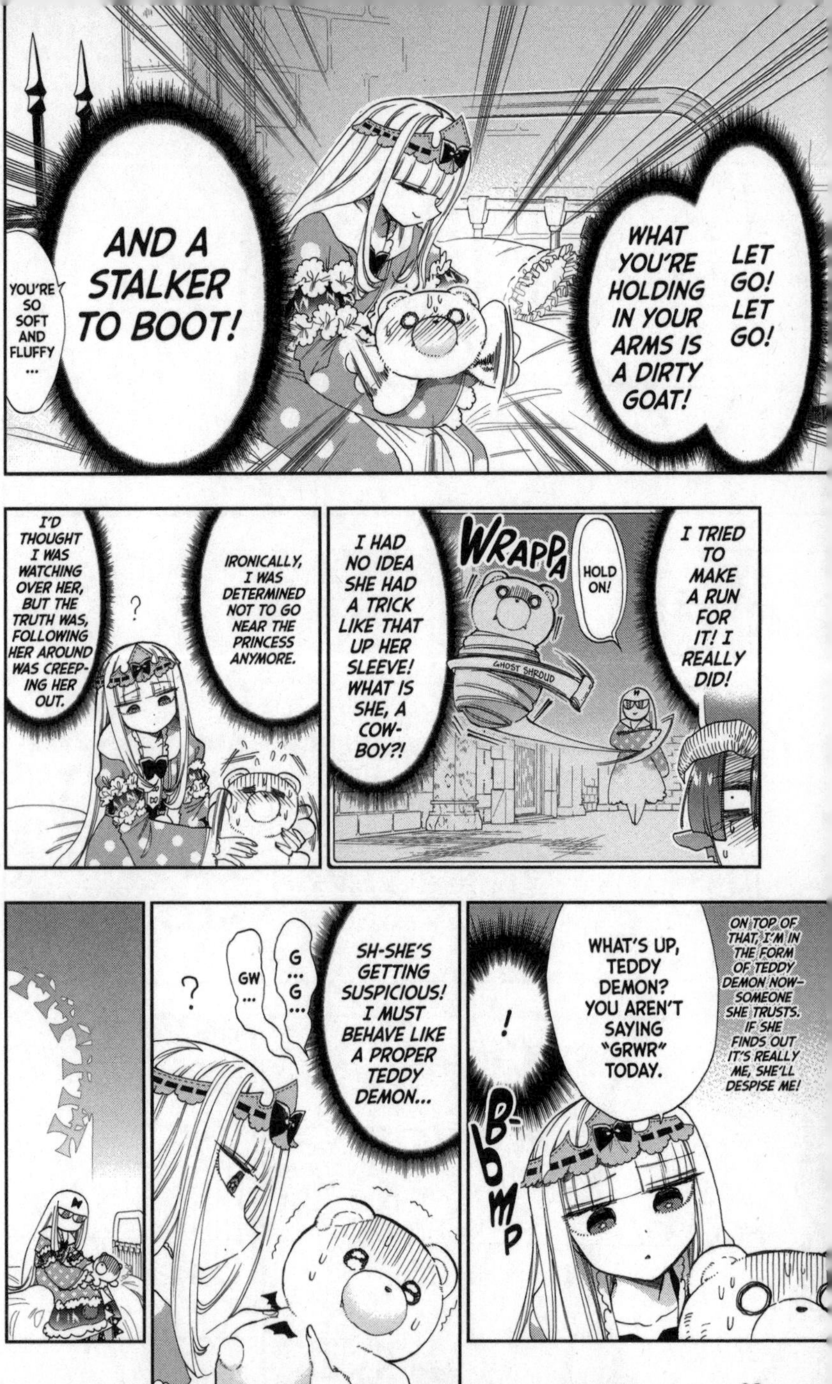
LET GO! LET GO!
WHAT YOU'RE HOLDING IN YOUR ARMS IS A DIRTY GOAT!
AND A STALKER TO BOOT!
YOU'RE SO SOFT AND FLUFFY...
I TRIED TO MAKE A RUN FOR IT! I REALLY DID!
HOLD ON!
WRAPPA
GHOST SHROUD
I HAD NO IDEA SHE HAD A TRICK LIKE THAT UP HER SLEEVE! WHAT IS SHE, A COW-BOY?!
IRONICALLY, I WAS DETERMINED NOT TO GO NEAR THE PRINCESS ANYMORE.
?
I'D THOUGHT I WAS WATCHING OVER HER, BUT THE TRUTH WAS, FOLLOWING HER AROUND WAS CREEP-ING HER OUT.
ON TOP OF THAT, I'M IN THE FORM OF TEDDY DEMON NOW— SOMEONE SHE TRUSTS. IF SHE FINDS OUT IT'S REALLY ME, SHE'LL DESPISE ME!
WHAT'S UP, TEDDY DEMON? YOU AREN'T SAYING "GRWR" TODAY.
!
B-BMP
SH-SHE'S GETTING SUSPICIOUS! I MUST BEHAVE LIKE A PROPER TEDDY DEMON...
G... G...
GW...
?

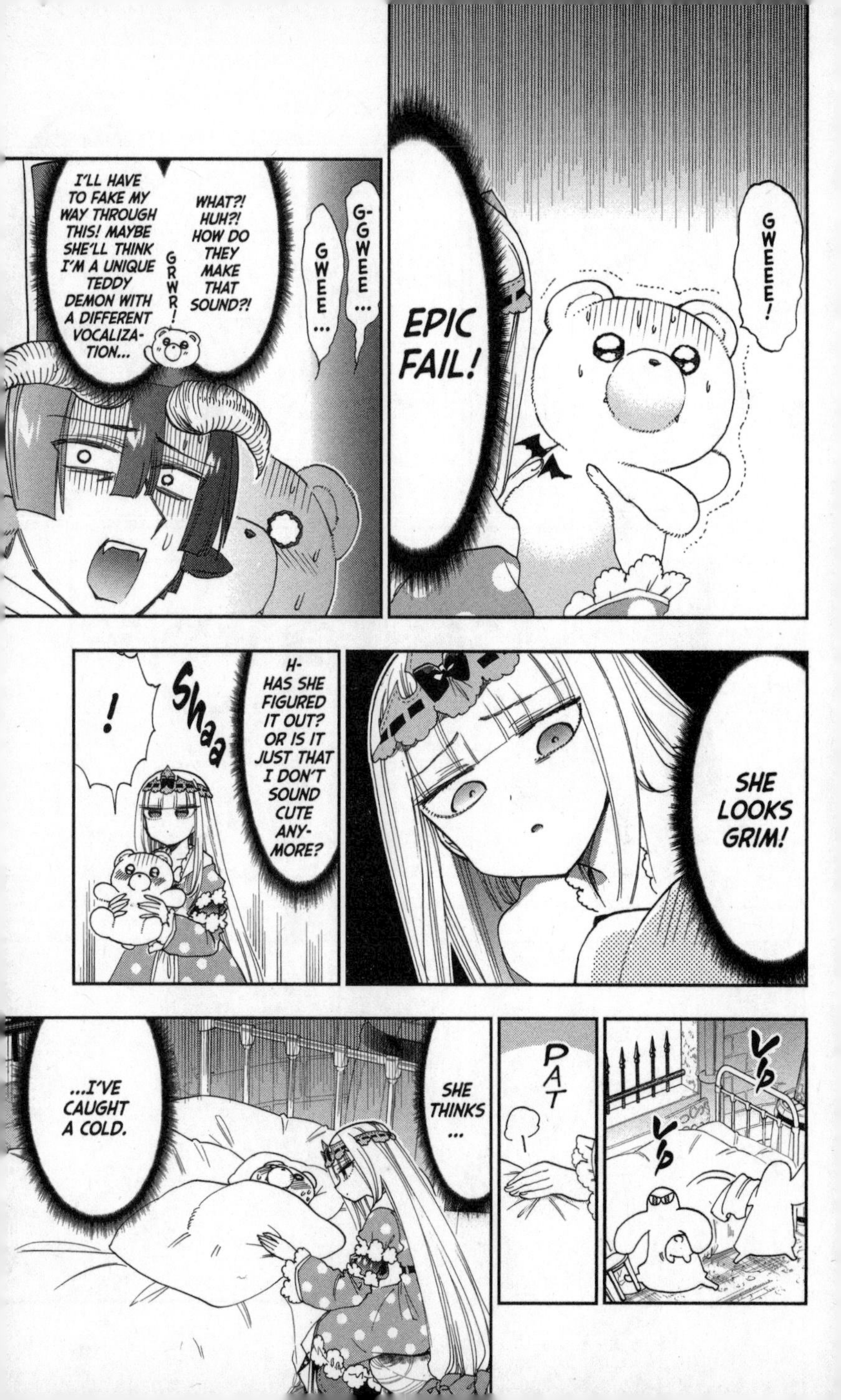
GWEEE!
EPIC FAIL!
G-GWEE...
GWEE...
WHAT?! HUH?! HOW DO THEY MAKE THAT SOUND?!
GRWR!
I'LL HAVE TO FAKE MY WAY THROUGH THIS! MAYBE SHE'LL THINK I'M A UNIQUE TEDDY DEMON WITH A DIFFERENT VOCALIZATION...
SHE LOOKS GRIM!
H- HAS SHE FIGURED IT OUT? OR IS IT JUST THAT I DON'T SOUND CUTE ANYMORE?
Shaa
!
VIP
VIP
PAT
SHE THINKS...
...I'VE CAUGHT A COLD.

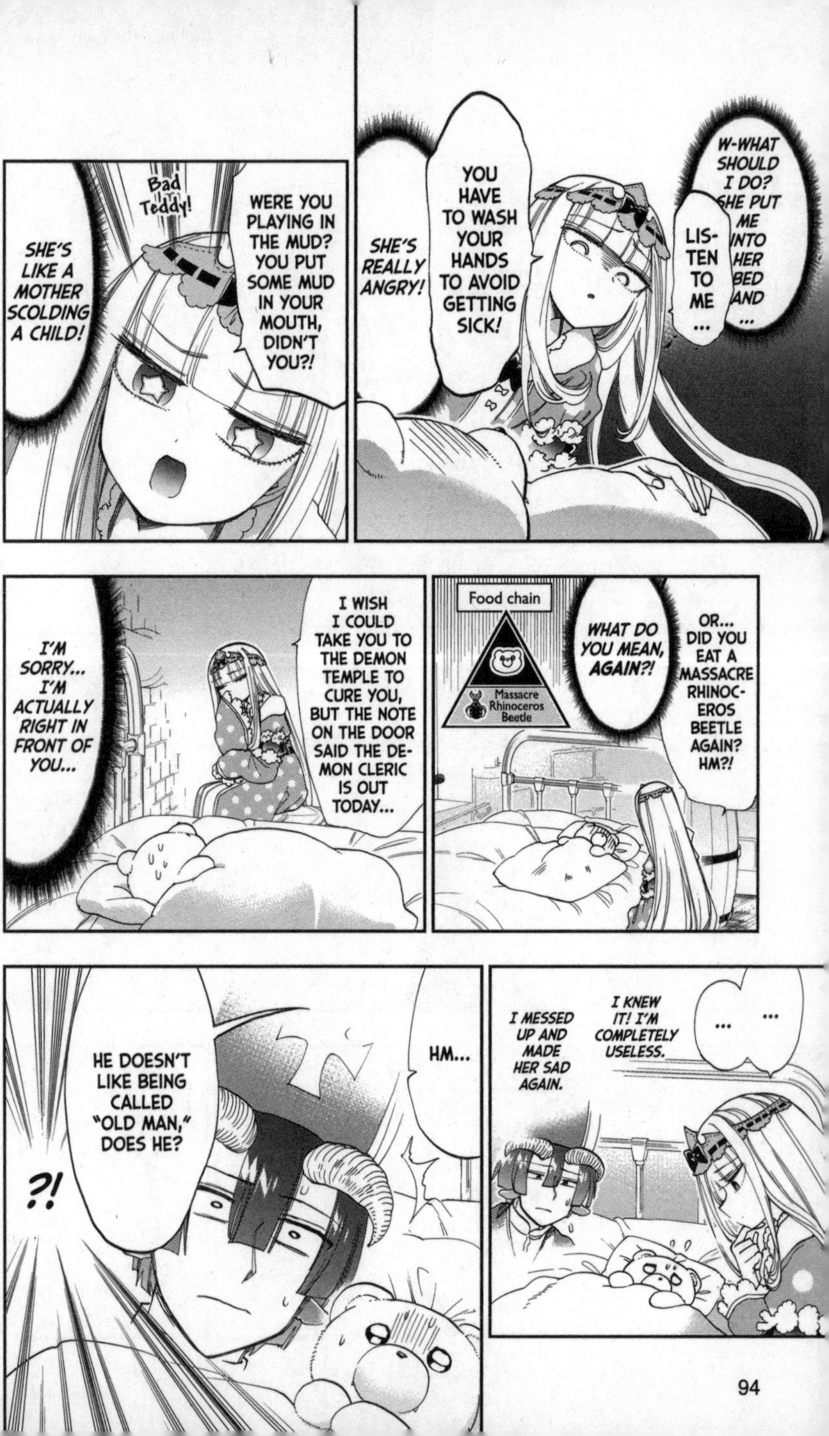
W-WHAT SHOULD I DO? SHE PUT ME INTO HER BED AND ...
LISTEN TO ME ...
YOU HAVE TO WASH YOUR HANDS TO AVOID GETTING SICK!
SHE'S REALLY ANGRY!
WERE YOU PLAYING IN THE MUD? YOU PUT SOME MUD IN YOUR MOUTH, DIDN'T YOU?!
Bad Teddy!
SHE'S LIKE A MOTHER SCOLDING A CHILD!
OR... DID YOU EAT A MASSACRE RHINOCEROS BEETLE AGAIN? HM?!
WHAT DO YOU MEAN, AGAIN?!
Food chain
Massacre Rhinoceros Beetle
I WISH I COULD TAKE YOU TO THE DEMON TEMPLE TO CURE YOU, BUT THE NOTE ON THE DOOR SAID THE DEMON CLERIC IS OUT TODAY...
I'M SORRY... I'M ACTUALLY RIGHT IN FRONT OF YOU...
...
...
I KNEW IT! I'M COMPLETELY USELESS.
I MESSED UP AND MADE HER SAD AGAIN.
HM...
HE DOESN'T LIKE BEING CALLED "OLD MAN," DOES HE?
?!

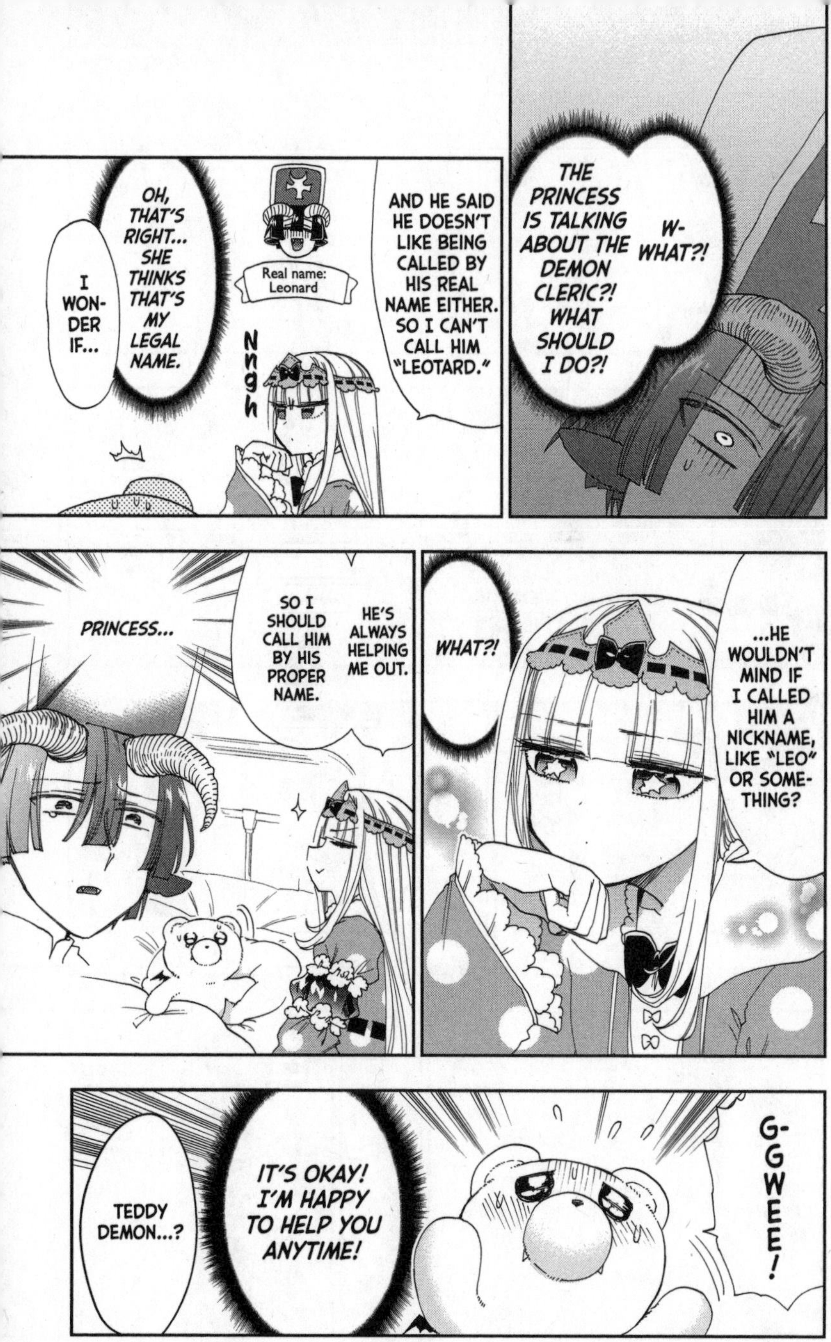
W-WHAT?!
THE PRINCESS IS TALKING ABOUT THE DEMON CLERIC?! WHAT SHOULD I DO?!
AND HE SAID HE DOESN'T LIKE BEING CALLED BY HIS REAL NAME EITHER. SO I CAN'T CALL HIM "LEOTARD."
Real name: Leonard
Nngh
OH, THAT'S RIGHT... SHE THINKS THAT'S MY LEGAL NAME.
I WONDER IF...
...HE WOULDN'T MIND IF I CALLED HIM A NICKNAME, LIKE "LEO" OR SOMETHING?
WHAT?!
HE'S ALWAYS HELPING ME OUT.
SO I SHOULD CALL HIM BY HIS PROPER NAME.
PRINCESS...
G-GWEE!
IT'S OKAY! I'M HAPPY TO HELP YOU ANYTIME!
TEDDY DEMON...?

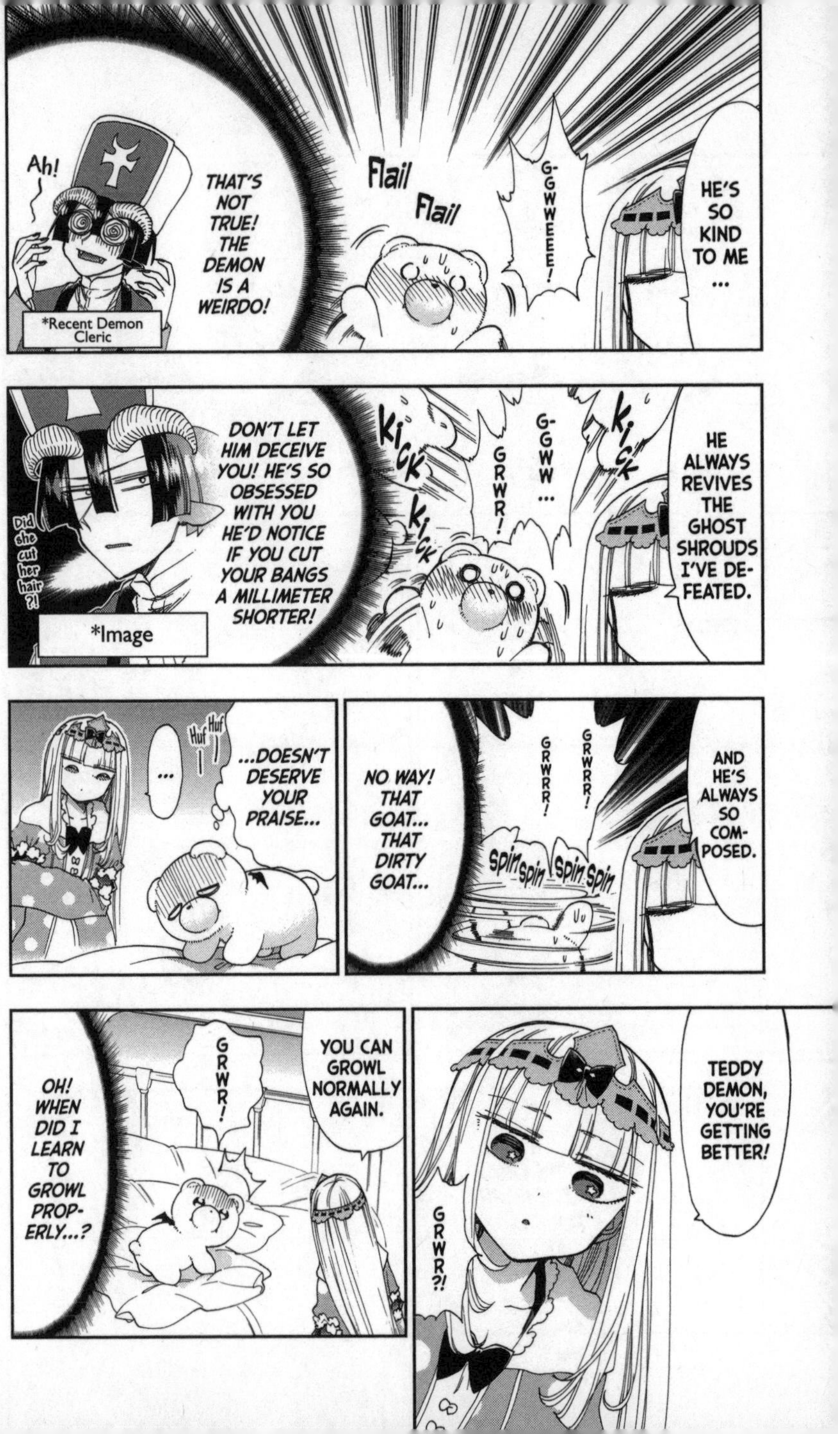
HE'S SO KIND TO ME ...
G-GWWEEEE!
Flail Flail
THAT'S NOT TRUE! THE DEMON IS A WEIRDO!
Ah!
*Recent Demon Cleric
HE ALWAYS REVIVES THE GHOST SHROUDS I'VE DE-FEATED.
kick
G-GWW ...
GRWR!
kick
DON'T LET HIM DECEIVE YOU! HE'S SO OBSESSED WITH YOU HE'D NOTICE IF YOU CUT YOUR BANGS A MILLIMETER SHORTER!
Did she cut her hair?!
*Image
AND HE'S ALWAYS SO COM-POSED.
GRWRR!
GRWRR!
spin spin spin spin
NO WAY! THAT GOAT... THAT DIRTY GOAT...
...DOESN'T DESERVE YOUR PRAISE...
Huf Huf
...
TEDDY DEMON, YOU'RE GETTING BETTER!
GRWR?!
YOU CAN GROWL NORMALLY AGAIN.
GRWR!
OH! WHEN DID I LEARN TO GROWL PROP-ERLY...?

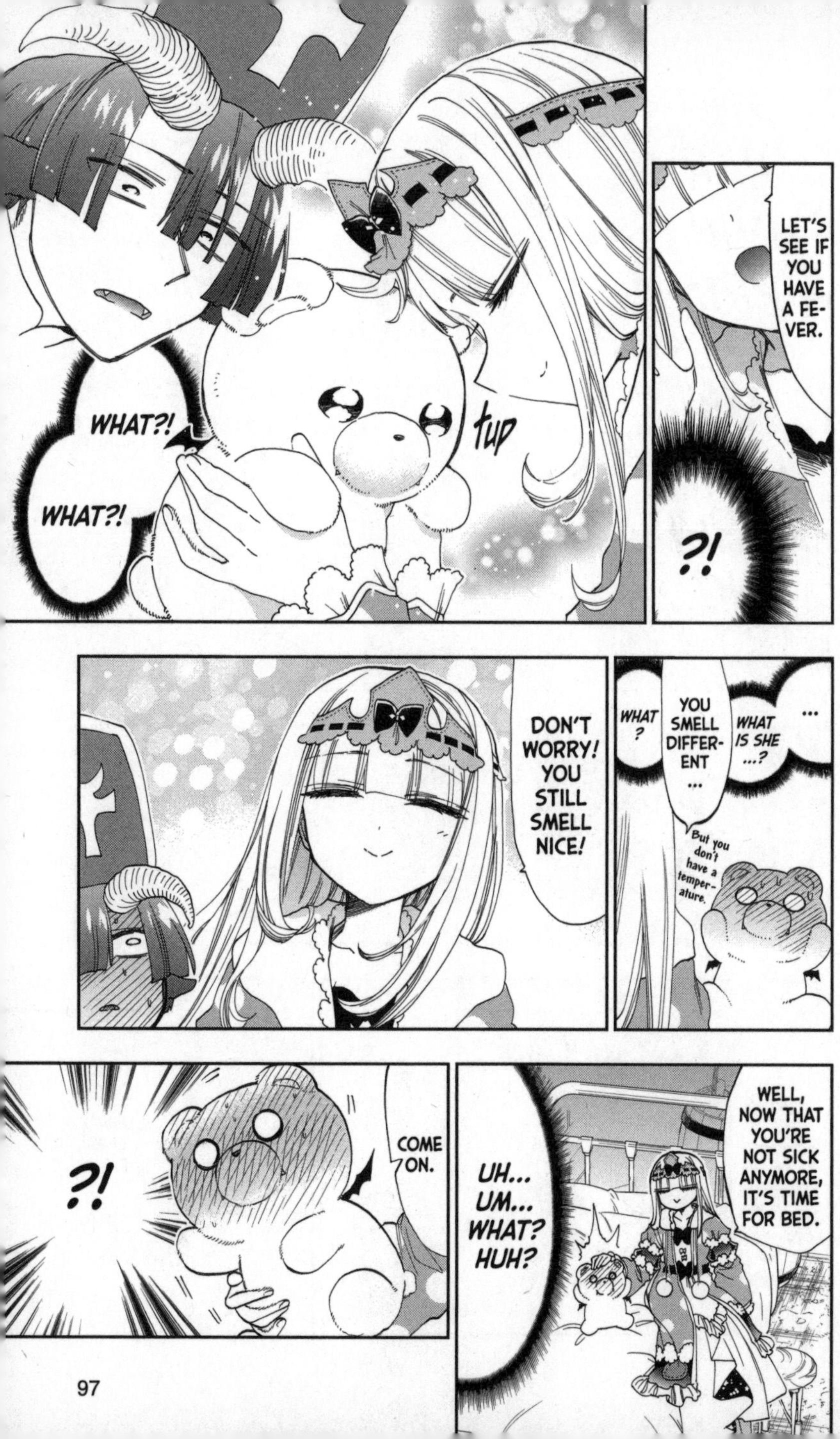
LET'S SEE IF YOU HAVE A FE-VER.
?!
tup
WHAT?!
WHAT?!
...
WHAT IS SHE ...?
YOU SMELL DIFFER-ENT ...
WHAT ?
But you don't have a temper-ature.
DON'T WORRY! YOU STILL SMELL NICE!
WELL, NOW THAT YOU'RE NOT SICK ANYMORE, IT'S TIME FOR BED.
UH... UM... WHAT? HUH?
COME ON.
?!

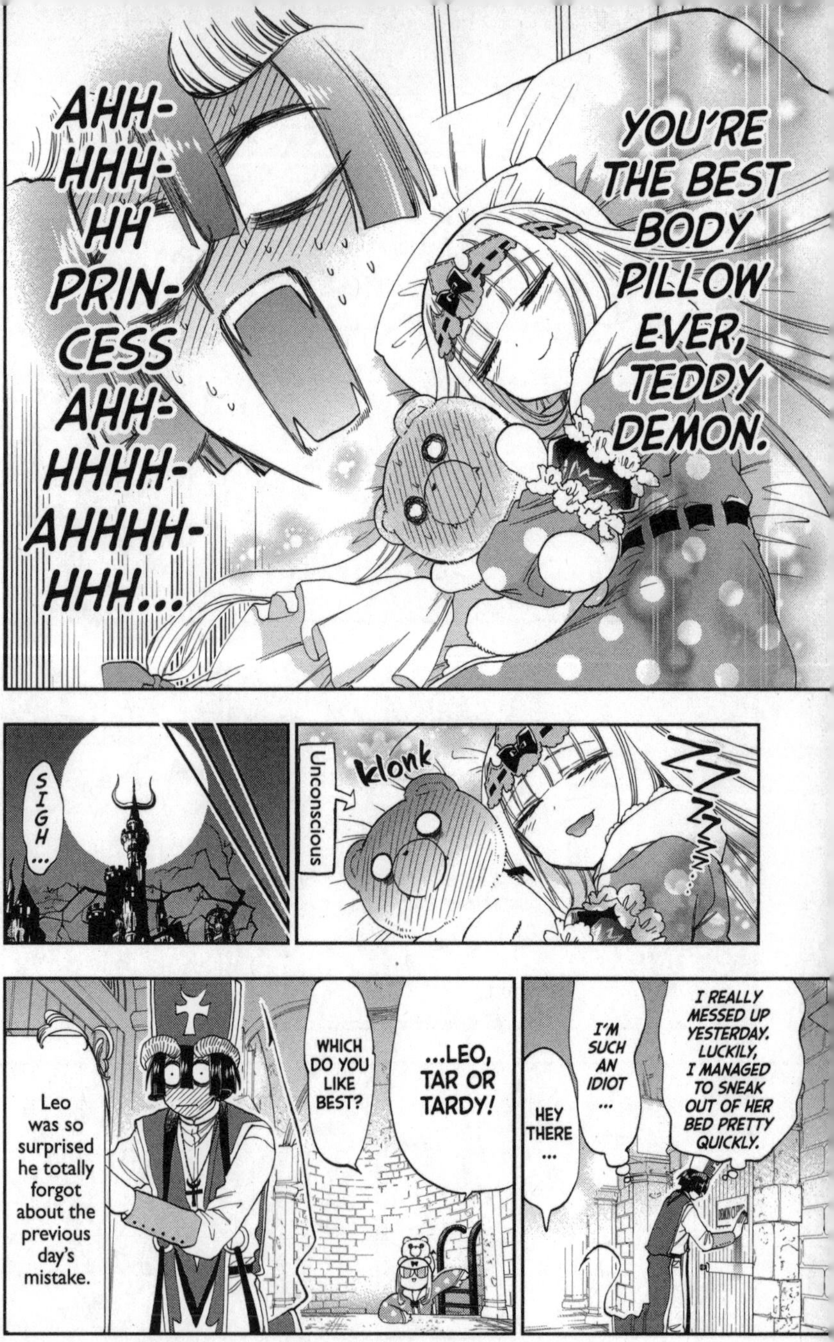
YOU'RE THE BEST BODY PILLOW EVER, TEDDY DEMON.
AHH-HHH-HH PRIN-CESS AHH-HHHH-AHHHH-HHH...
klonk
Unconscious
ZZZZZZ...
SIGH...
I REALLY MESSED UP YESTERDAY. LUCKILY, I MANAGED TO SNEAK OUT OF HER BED PRETTY QUICKLY.
I'M SUCH AN IDIOT...
HEY THERE...
...LEO, TAR OR TARDY!
WHICH DO YOU LIKE BEST?
Leo was so surprised he totally forgot about the previous day's mistake.

Teddy Demon Cleric

Cute.

Fault: ☆☆☆☆☆☆☆☆☆☆☆
Bad Acting: ☆☆☆☆☆☆☆☆

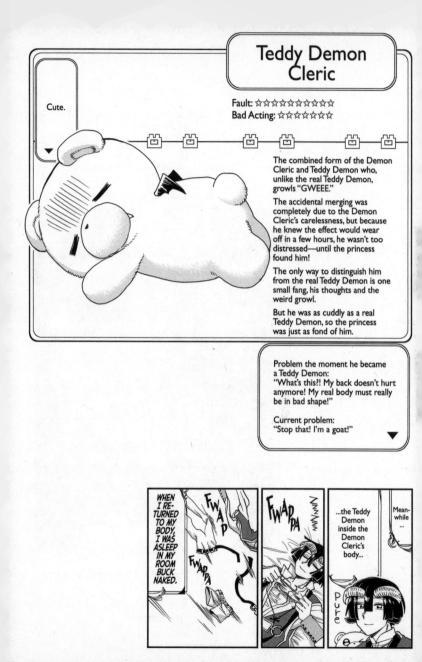

The combined form of the Demon Cleric and Teddy Demon who, unlike the real Teddy Demon, growls "GWEEE."

The accidental merging was completely due to the Demon Cleric's carelessness, but because he knew the effect would wear off in a few hours, he wasn't too distressed—until the princess found him!

The only way to distinguish him from the real Teddy Demon is one small fang, his thoughts and the weird growl.

But he was as cuddly as a real Teddy Demon, so the princess was just as fond of him.

Problem the moment he became a Teddy Demon:
"What's this?! My back doesn't hurt anymore! My real body must really be in bad shape!"

Current problem:
"Stop that! I'm a goat!"

Meanwhile...
...the Teddy Demon inside the Demon Cleric's body...
Pure
FWAPPA
WHEN I RETURNED TO MY BODY, I WAS ASLEEP IN MY ROOM BUCK NAKED.
FWAP
FWAPPA

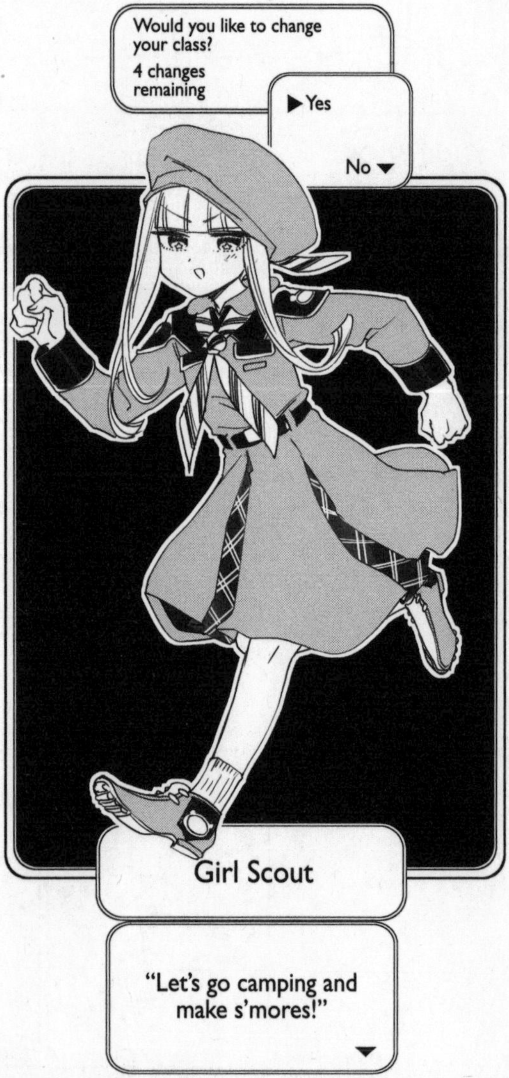
Would you like to change your class?
4 changes remaining
▶Yes
No ▼
Girl Scout
"Let's go camping and make s'mores!"

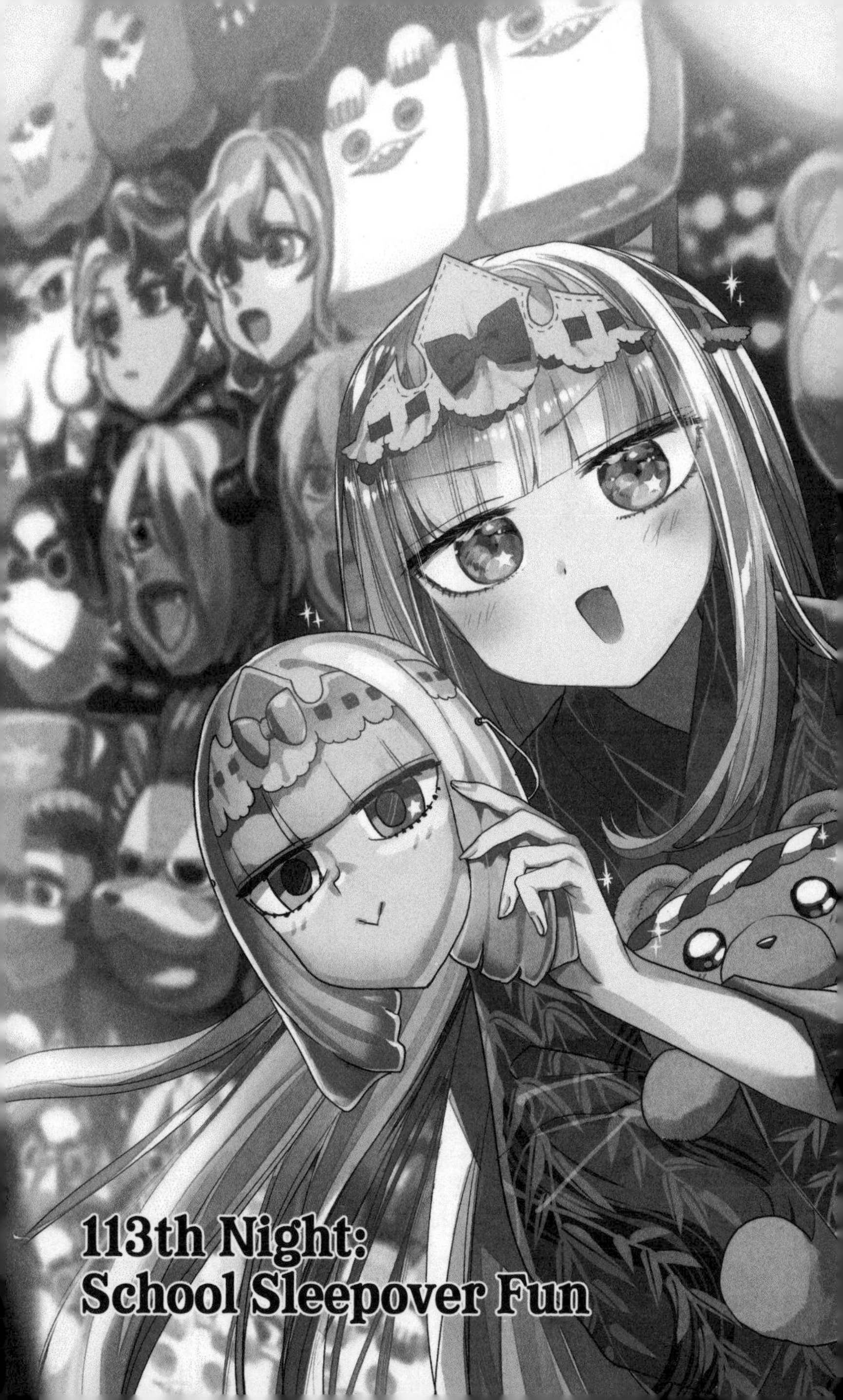
113th Night:
School Sleepover Fun

SLEEPY PRINCESS
IN THE DEMON CASTLE

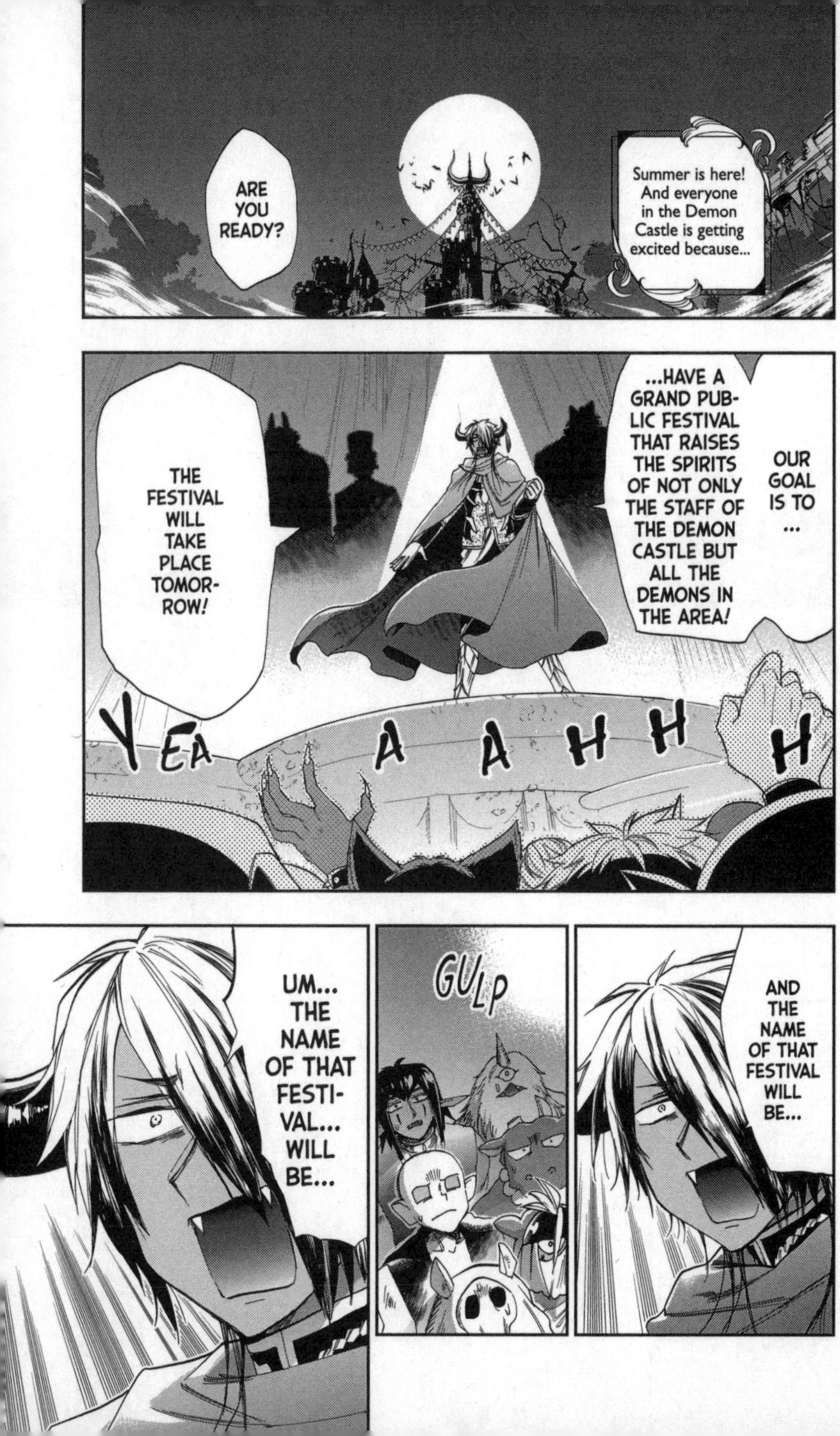
Summer is here! And everyone in the Demon Castle is getting excited because...
ARE YOU READY?
OUR GOAL IS TO ...
...HAVE A GRAND PUBLIC FESTIVAL THAT RAISES THE SPIRITS OF NOT ONLY THE STAFF OF THE DEMON CASTLE BUT ALL THE DEMONS IN THE AREA!
THE FESTIVAL WILL TAKE PLACE TOMORROW!
YEAAAHHH
AND THE NAME OF THAT FESTIVAL WILL BE...
GULP
UM... THE NAME OF THAT FESTIVAL... WILL BE...

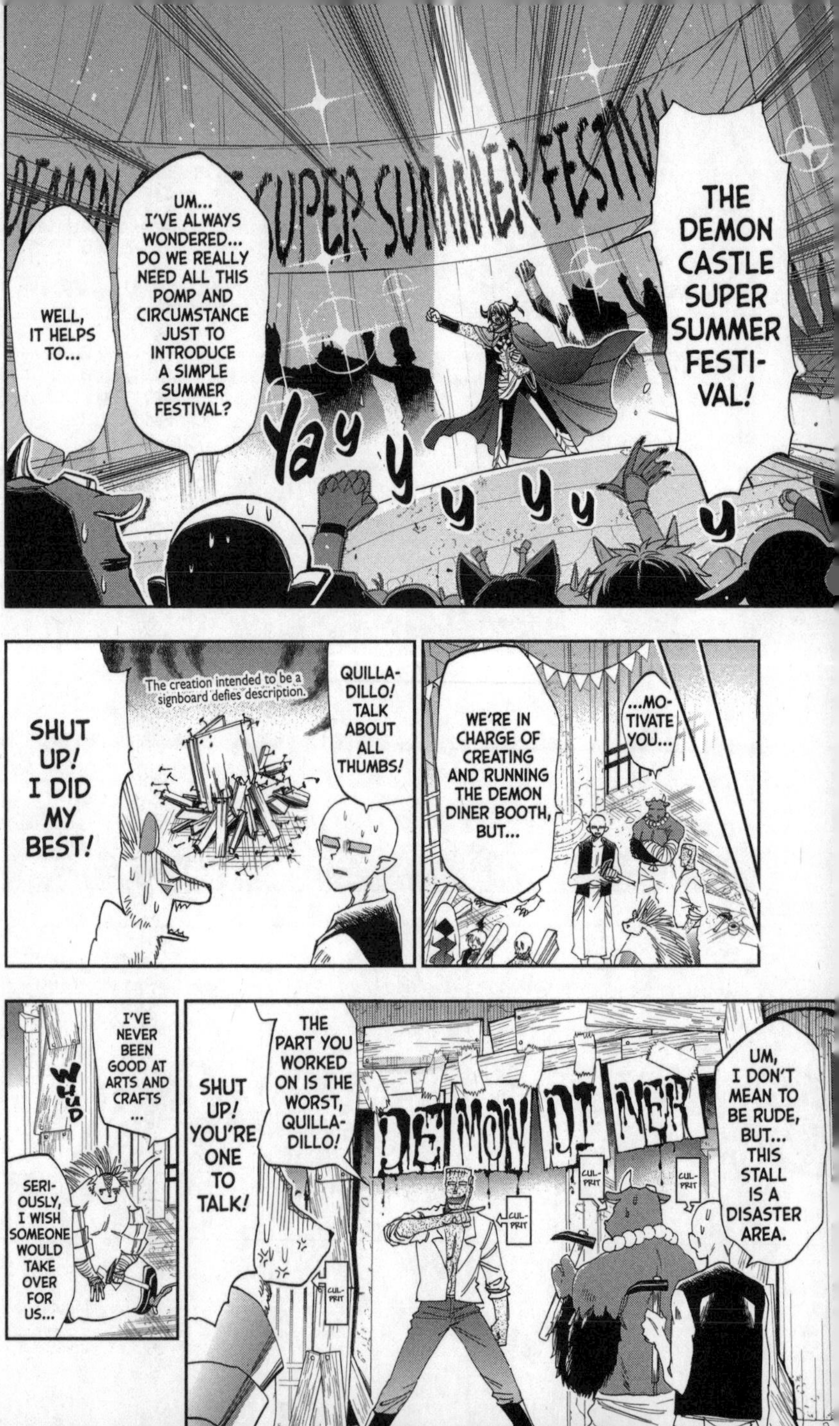
THE DEMON CASTLE SUPER SUMMER FESTIVAL!
SUPER SUMMER FESTIV
Yayyyyyyy
UM... I'VE ALWAYS WONDERED... DO WE REALLY NEED ALL THIS POMP AND CIRCUMSTANCE JUST TO INTRODUCE A SIMPLE SUMMER FESTIVAL?
WELL, IT HELPS TO...
...MOTIVATE YOU...
WE'RE IN CHARGE OF CREATING AND RUNNING THE DEMON DINER BOOTH, BUT...
QUILLADILLO! TALK ABOUT ALL THUMBS!
The creation intended to be a signboard defies description.
SHUT UP! I DID MY BEST!
UM, I DON'T MEAN TO BE RUDE, BUT... THIS STALL IS A DISASTER AREA.
DEMON DI NER
CULPRIT
CULPRIT
CULPRIT
CULPRIT
THE PART YOU WORKED ON IS THE WORST, QUILLADILLO!
SHUT UP! YOU'RE ONE TO TALK!
I'VE NEVER BEEN GOOD AT ARTS AND CRAFTS ...
WHUD
SERIOUSLY, I WISH SOMEONE WOULD TAKE OVER FOR US...

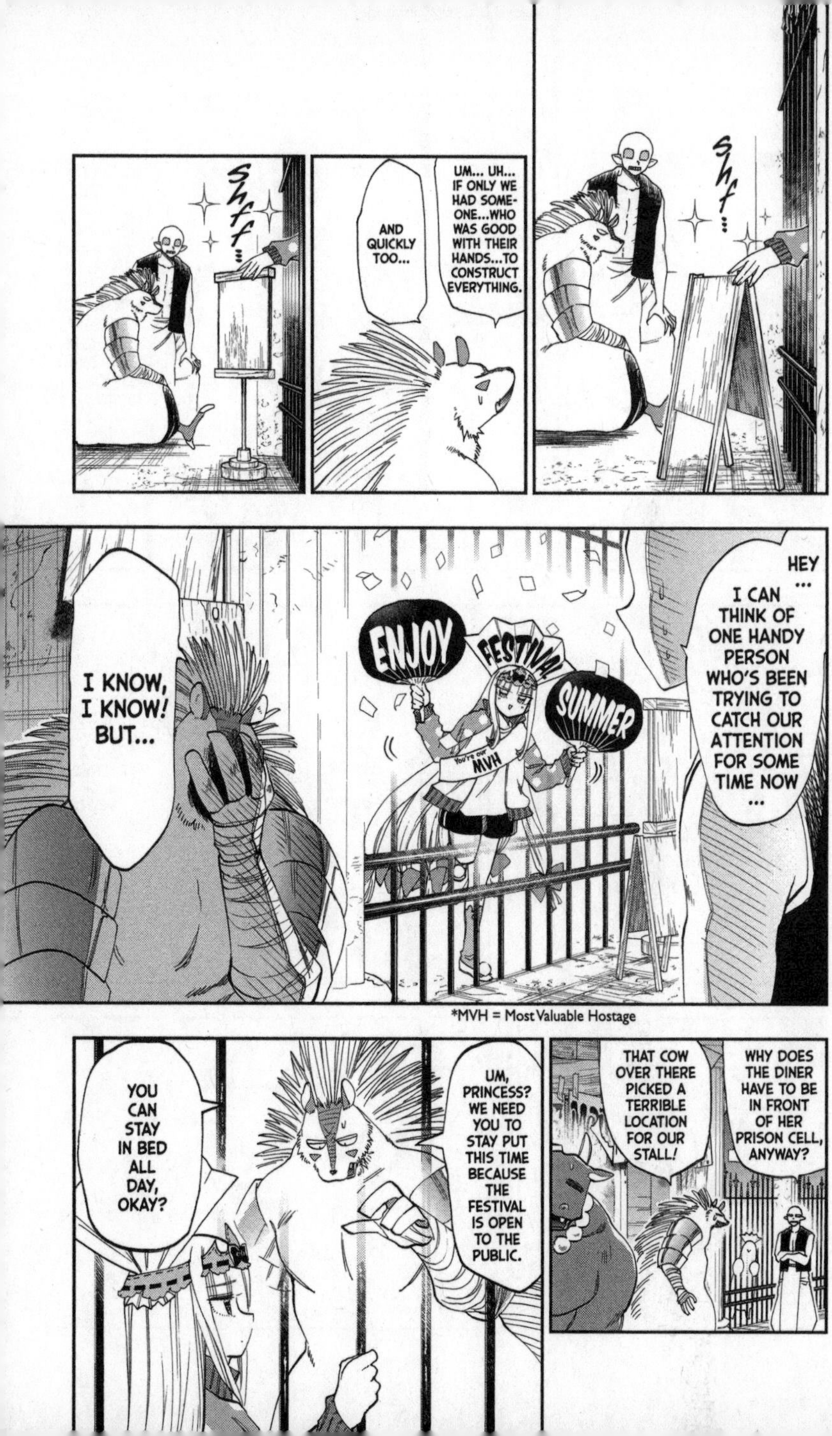
shff...
UM... UH... IF ONLY WE HAD SOME-ONE...WHO WAS GOOD WITH THEIR HANDS...TO CONSTRUCT EVERYTHING.
AND QUICKLY TOO...
shff...
HEY ... I CAN THINK OF ONE HANDY PERSON WHO'S BEEN TRYING TO CATCH OUR ATTENTION FOR SOME TIME NOW ...
ENJOY
SUMMER
FESTIVAL
You're our MVH
I KNOW, I KNOW! BUT...
WHY DOES THE DINER HAVE TO BE IN FRONT OF HER PRISON CELL, ANYWAY?
THAT COW OVER THERE PICKED A TERRIBLE LOCATION FOR OUR STALL!
UM, PRINCESS? WE NEED YOU TO STAY PUT THIS TIME BECAUSE THE FESTIVAL IS OPEN TO THE PUBLIC.
YOU CAN STAY IN BED ALL DAY, OKAY?

*MVH = Most Valuable Hostage

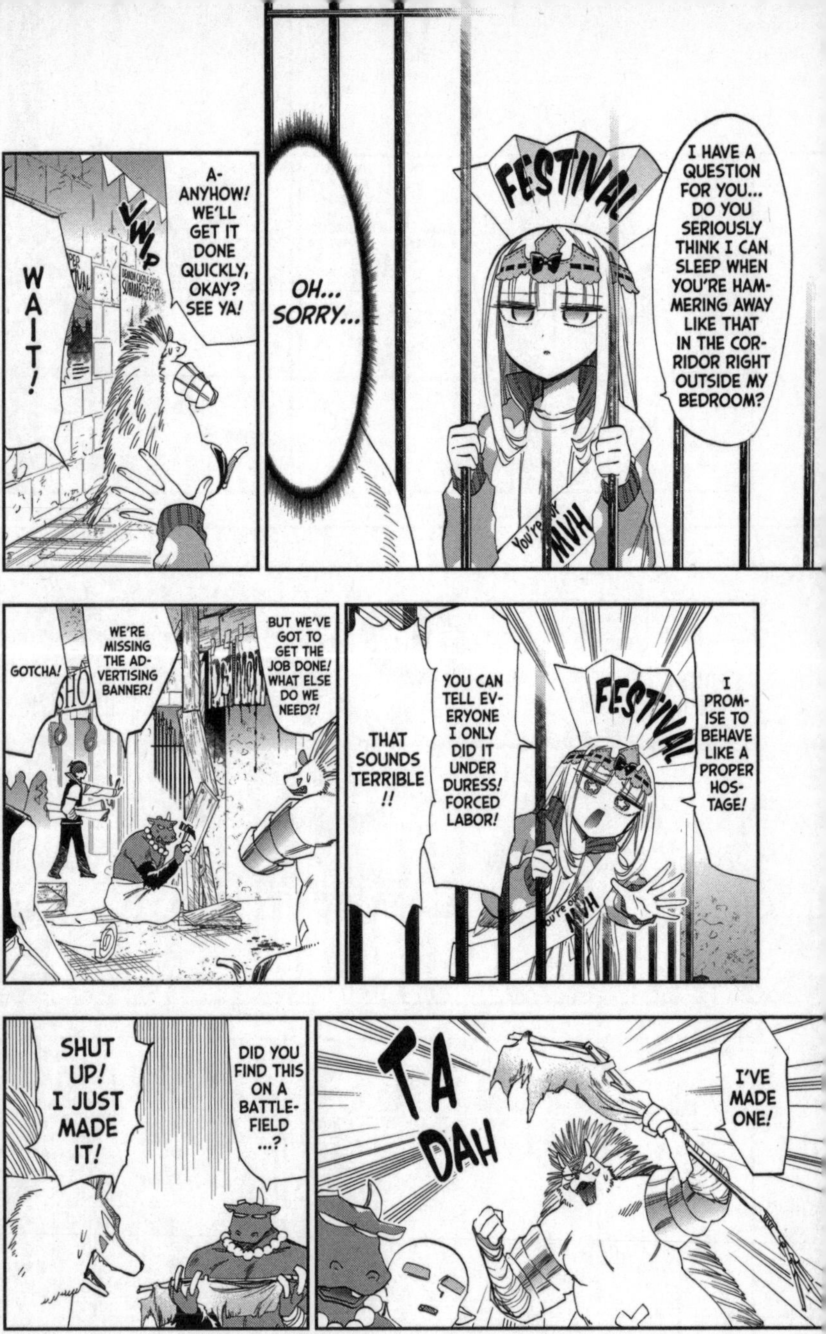
I HAVE A QUESTION FOR YOU... DO YOU SERIOUSLY THINK I CAN SLEEP WHEN YOU'RE HAMMERING AWAY LIKE THAT IN THE CORRIDOR RIGHT OUTSIDE MY BEDROOM?
FESTIVAL
You're our MVH
OH... SORRY...
A- ANYHOW! WE'LL GET IT DONE QUICKLY, OKAY? SEE YA!
VWIP
WAIT!
I PROMISE TO BEHAVE LIKE A PROPER HOSTAGE!
FESTIVAL
You're our MVH
YOU CAN TELL EVERYONE I ONLY DID IT UNDER DURESS! FORCED LABOR!
THAT SOUNDS TERRIBLE!!
BUT WE'VE GOT TO GET THE JOB DONE! WHAT ELSE DO WE NEED?!
WE'RE MISSING THE ADVERTISING BANNER!
GOTCHA!
I'VE MADE ONE!
TA DAH
DID YOU FIND THIS ON A BATTLEFIELD...?
SHUT UP! I JUST MADE IT!

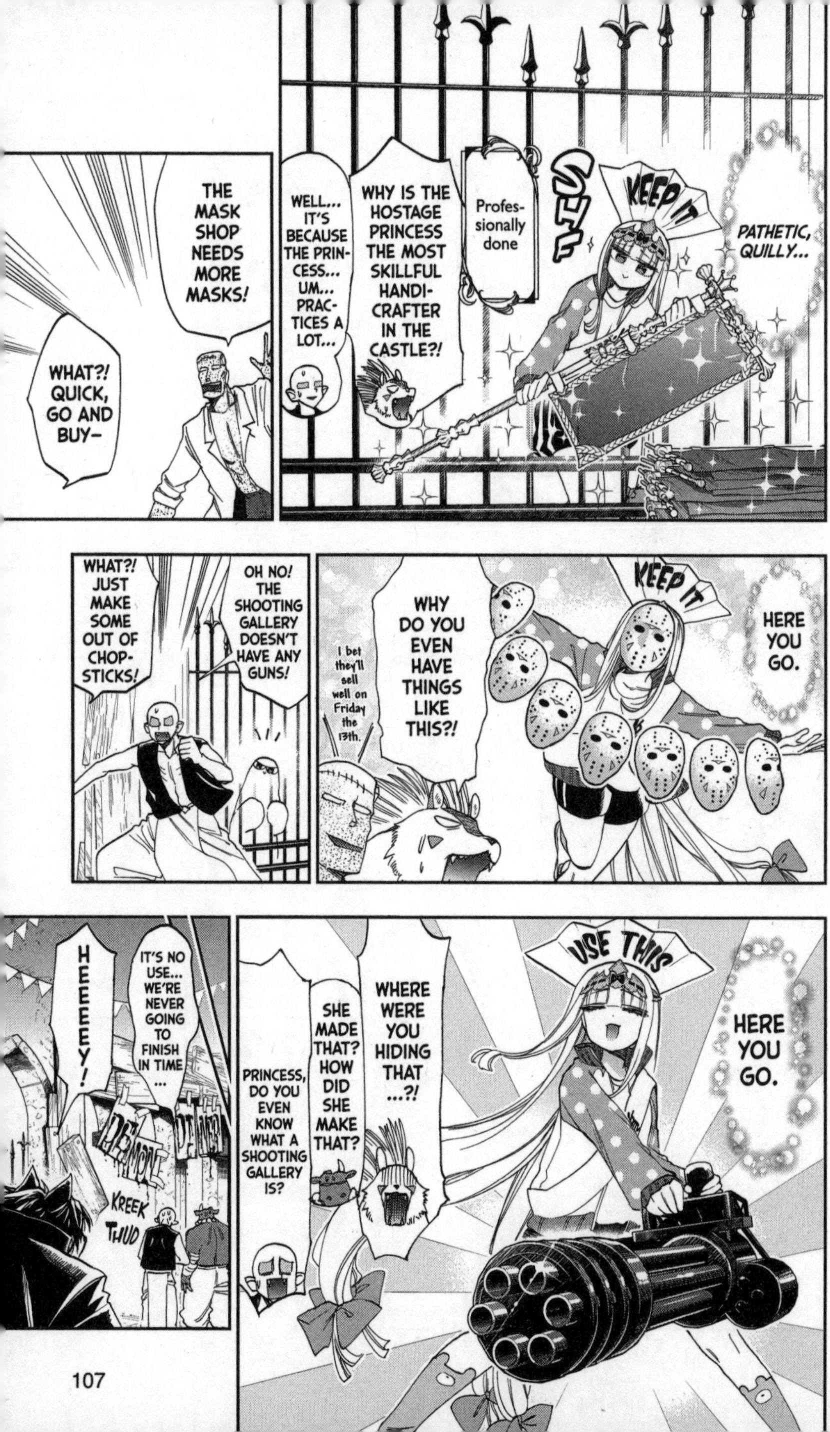
PATHETIC, QUILLY...
KEEP IT
Profes-sionally done
WHY IS THE HOSTAGE PRINCESS THE MOST SKILLFUL HANDI-CRAFTER IN THE CASTLE?!
WELL... IT'S BECAUSE THE PRIN-CESS... UM... PRAC-TICES A LOT...
THE MASK SHOP NEEDS MORE MASKS!
WHAT?! QUICK, GO AND BUY–
HERE YOU GO.
KEEP IT
WHY DO YOU EVEN HAVE THINGS LIKE THIS?!
I bet they'll sell well on Friday the 13th.
OH NO! THE SHOOTING GALLERY DOESN'T HAVE ANY GUNS!
WHAT?! JUST MAKE SOME OUT OF CHOP-STICKS!
HERE YOU GO.
USE THIS
WHERE WERE YOU HIDING THAT ...?!
SHE MADE THAT? HOW DID SHE MAKE THAT?
PRINCESS, DO YOU EVEN KNOW WHAT A SHOOTING GALLERY IS?
HEEEEEY!
IT'S NO USE... WE'RE NEVER GOING TO FINISH IN TIME ...
KREEK
THUD

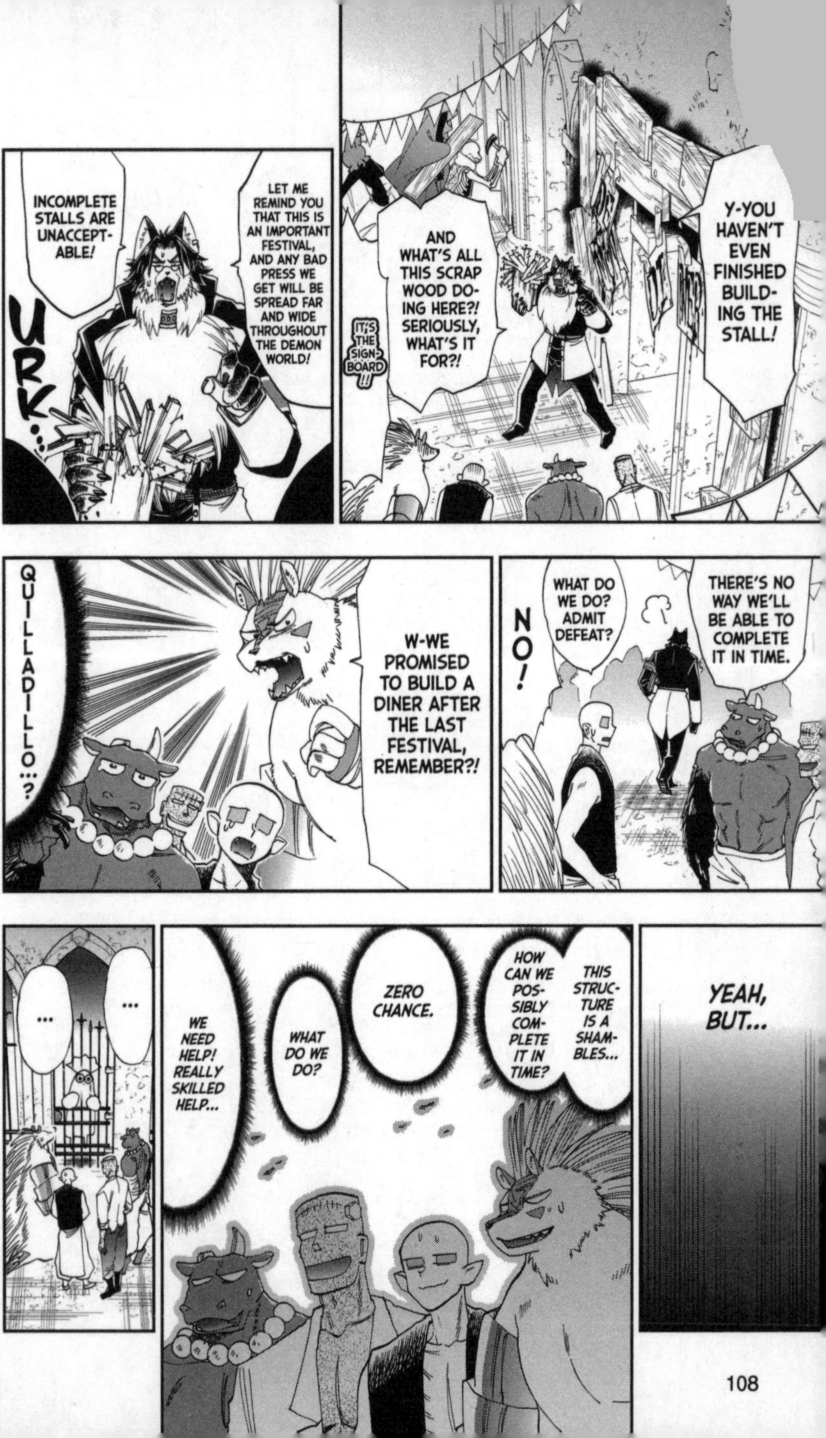
Y-YOU HAVEN'T EVEN FINISHED BUILDING THE STALL!
AND WHAT'S ALL THIS SCRAP WOOD DOING HERE?! SERIOUSLY, WHAT'S IT FOR?!
IT'S THE SIGNBOARD!!
LET ME REMIND YOU THAT THIS IS AN IMPORTANT FESTIVAL, AND ANY BAD PRESS WE GET WILL BE SPREAD FAR AND WIDE THROUGHOUT THE DEMON WORLD!
INCOMPLETE STALLS ARE UNACCEPTABLE!
URK...
THERE'S NO WAY WE'LL BE ABLE TO COMPLETE IT IN TIME.
WHAT DO WE DO? ADMIT DEFEAT?
NO!
W-WE PROMISED TO BUILD A DINER AFTER THE LAST FESTIVAL, REMEMBER?!
QUILLADILLO...?
YEAH, BUT...
THIS STRUCTURE IS A SHAMBLES...
HOW CAN WE POSSIBLY COMPLETE IT IN TIME?
ZERO CHANCE.
WHAT DO WE DO?
WE NEED HELP! REALLY SKILLED HELP...
...
...

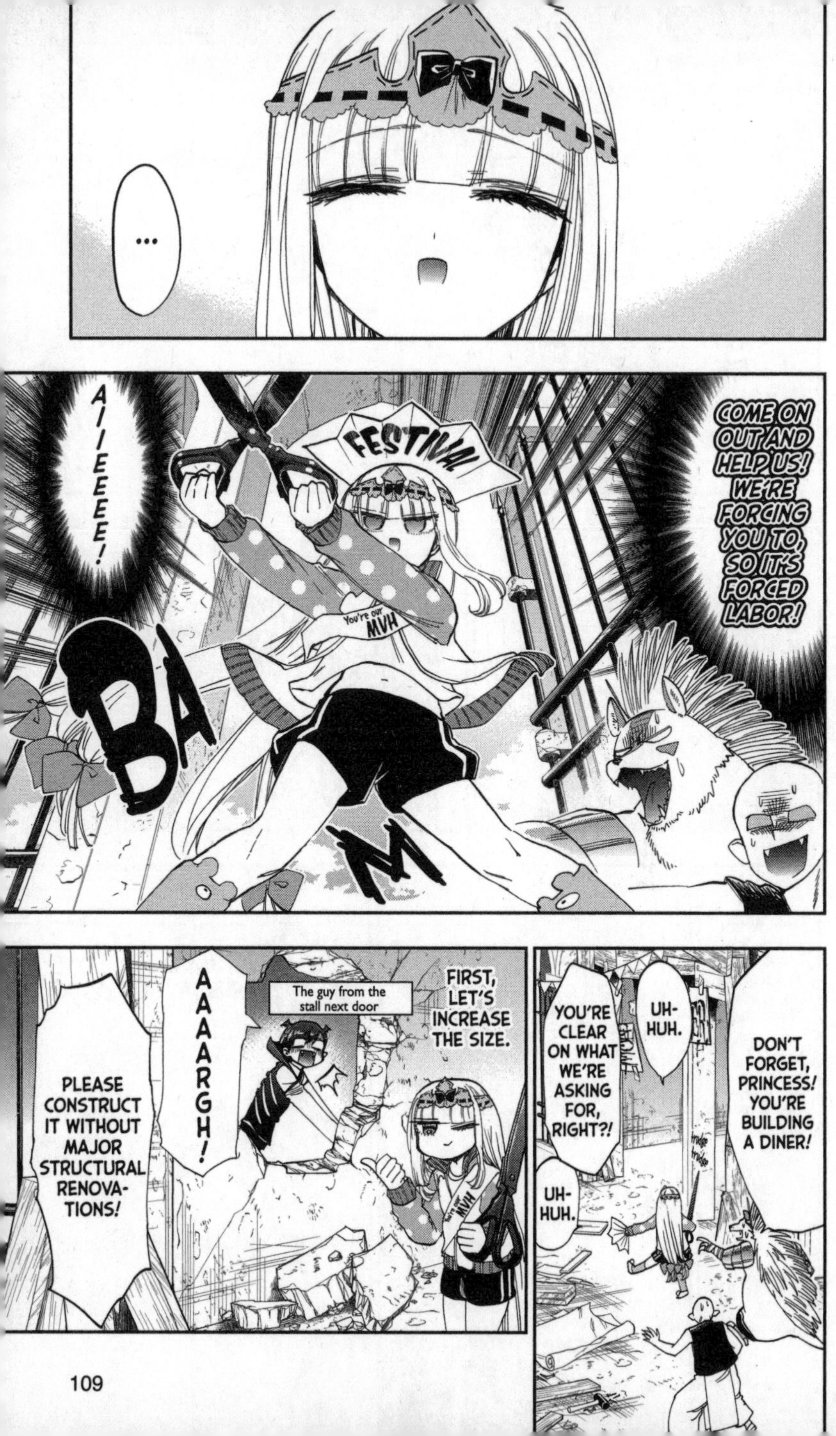
…
COME ON OUT AND HELP US! WE'RE FORCING YOU TO, SO IT'S FORCED LABOR!
FESTIVAL
AIIEEEEE!
You're our MVH
BA
M
DON'T FORGET, PRINCESS! YOU'RE BUILDING A DINER!
UH-HUH.
YOU'RE CLEAR ON WHAT WE'RE ASKING FOR, RIGHT?!
UH-HUH.
FIRST, LET'S INCREASE THE SIZE.
The guy from the stall next door
AAAAARGH!
PLEASE CONSTRUCT IT WITHOUT MAJOR STRUCTURAL RENOVATIONS!

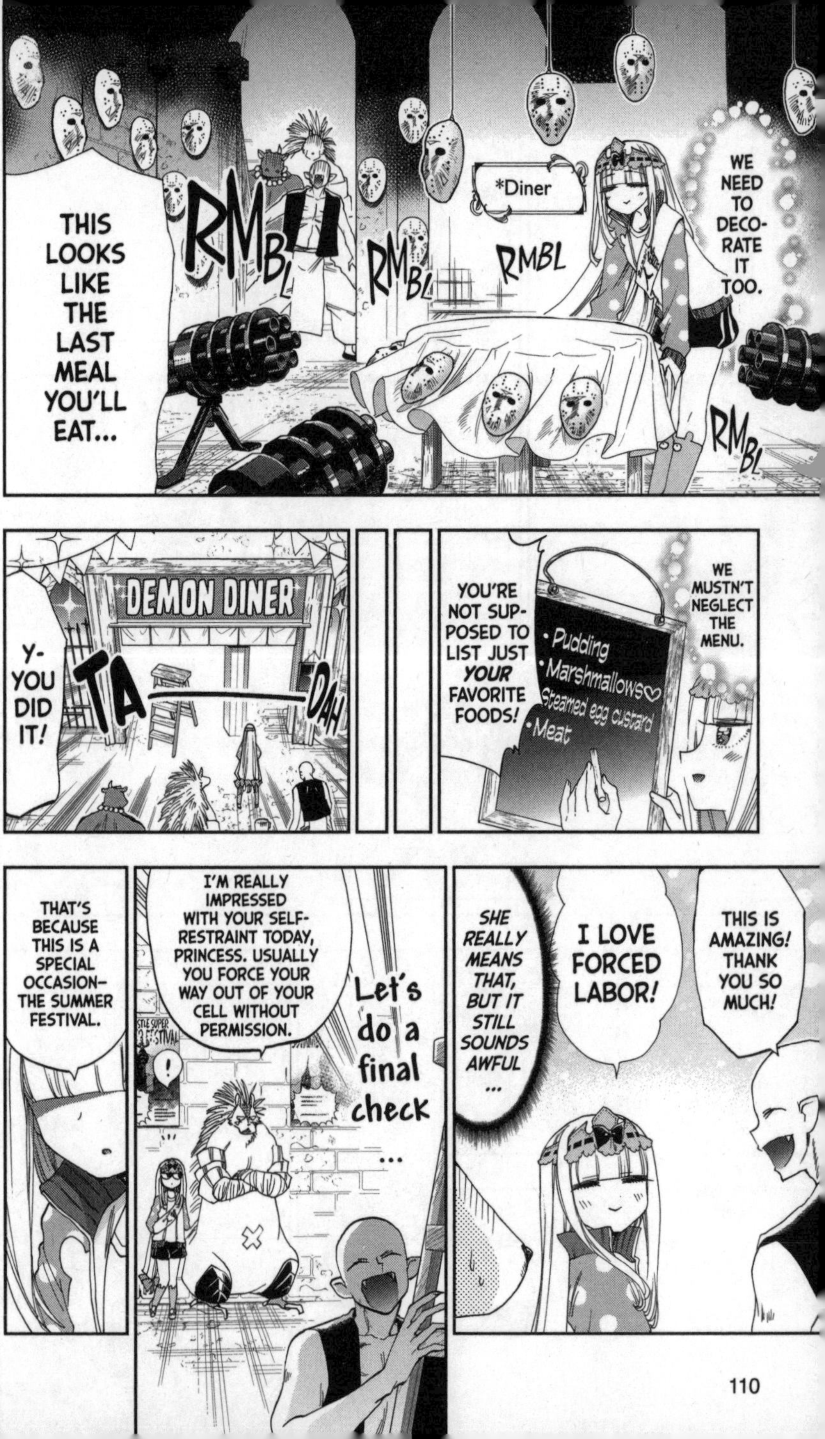
WE NEED TO DECORATE IT TOO.
*Diner
RMBL
RMBL
RMBL
RMBL
THIS LOOKS LIKE THE LAST MEAL YOU'LL EAT...
WE MUSTN'T NEGLECT THE MENU.
• Pudding
• Marshmallows♡
• Steamed egg custard
• Meat
YOU'RE NOT SUPPOSED TO LIST JUST *YOUR* FAVORITE FOODS!
DEMON DINER
TA—DAH
Y-YOU DID IT!
THIS IS AMAZING! THANK YOU SO MUCH!
I LOVE FORCED LABOR!
SHE REALLY MEANS THAT, BUT IT STILL SOUNDS AWFUL...
Let's do a final check...
I'M REALLY IMPRESSED WITH YOUR SELF-RESTRAINT TODAY, PRINCESS. USUALLY YOU FORCE YOUR WAY OUT OF YOUR CELL WITHOUT PERMISSION.
THAT'S BECAUSE THIS IS A SPECIAL OCCASION—THE SUMMER FESTIVAL.

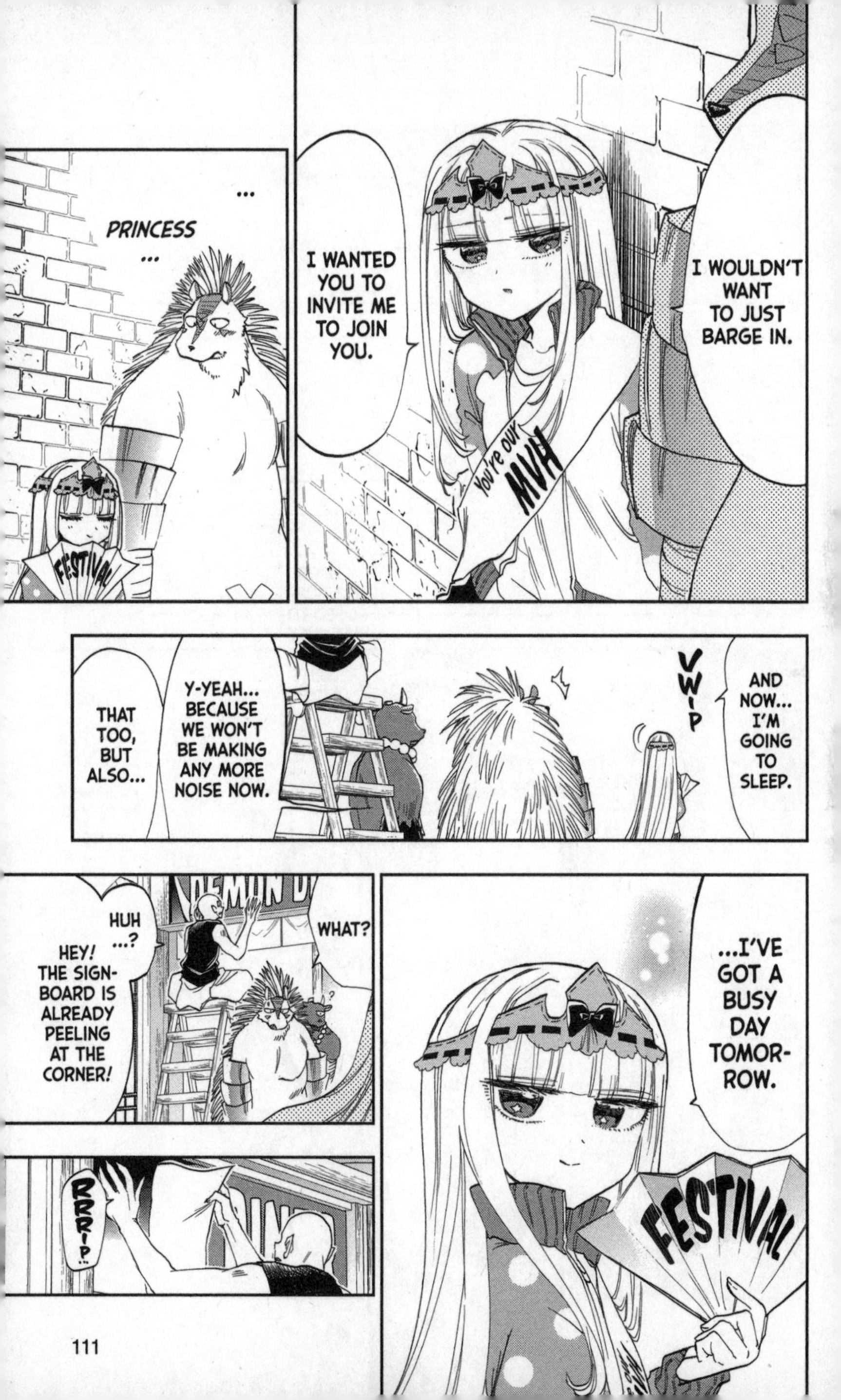
I WOULDN'T WANT TO JUST BARGE IN.
I WANTED YOU TO INVITE ME TO JOIN YOU.
You're our MVH
...
PRINCESS ...
FESTIVAL
AND NOW... I'M GOING TO SLEEP.
VWIP
Y-YEAH... BECAUSE WE WON'T BE MAKING ANY MORE NOISE NOW.
THAT TOO, BUT ALSO...
...I'VE GOT A BUSY DAY TOMORROW.
FESTIVAL
WHAT?
HUH ...?
HEY! THE SIGNBOARD IS ALREADY PEELING AT THE CORNER!
RRRIP..

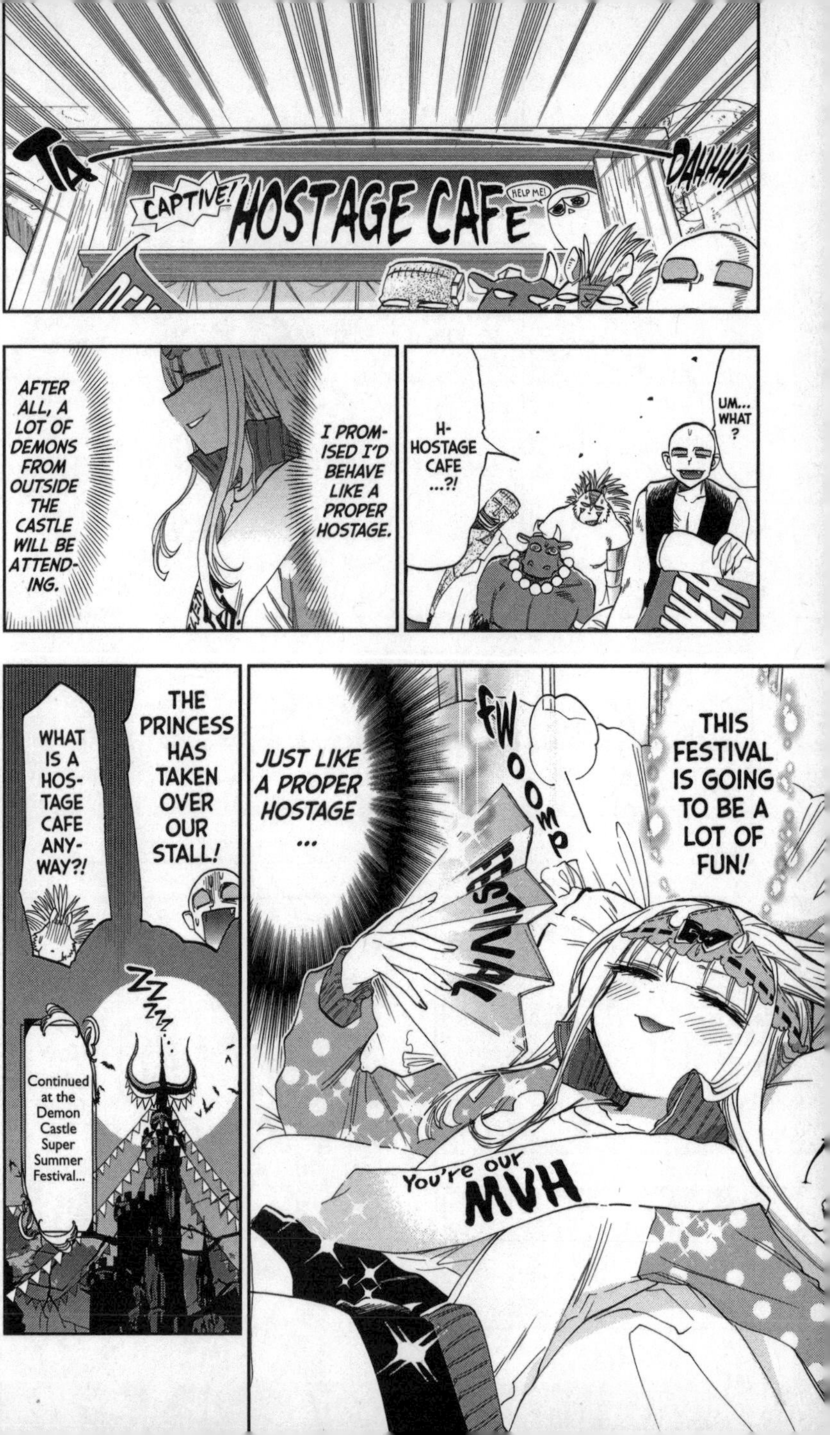
TA-DAHHH!
CAPTIVE!
HOSTAGE CAFE
HELP ME!
UM... WHAT?
H-HOSTAGE CAFE...?!
I PROMISED I'D BEHAVE LIKE A PROPER HOSTAGE.
AFTER ALL, A LOT OF DEMONS FROM OUTSIDE THE CASTLE WILL BE ATTENDING.
THIS FESTIVAL IS GOING TO BE A LOT OF FUN!
FWOOOMP
FESTIVAL
JUST LIKE A PROPER HOSTAGE...
You're our MVH
THE PRINCESS HAS TAKEN OVER OUR STALL!
WHAT IS A HOSTAGE CAFE ANYWAY?!
ZZZZ
Continued at the Demon Castle Super Summer Festival...

Demon Castle Super Summer Festival

Festi-
vaaaaaal!

Popularity: ☆☆☆☆☆☆☆☆☆

Size: ☆☆☆☆☆☆☆☆

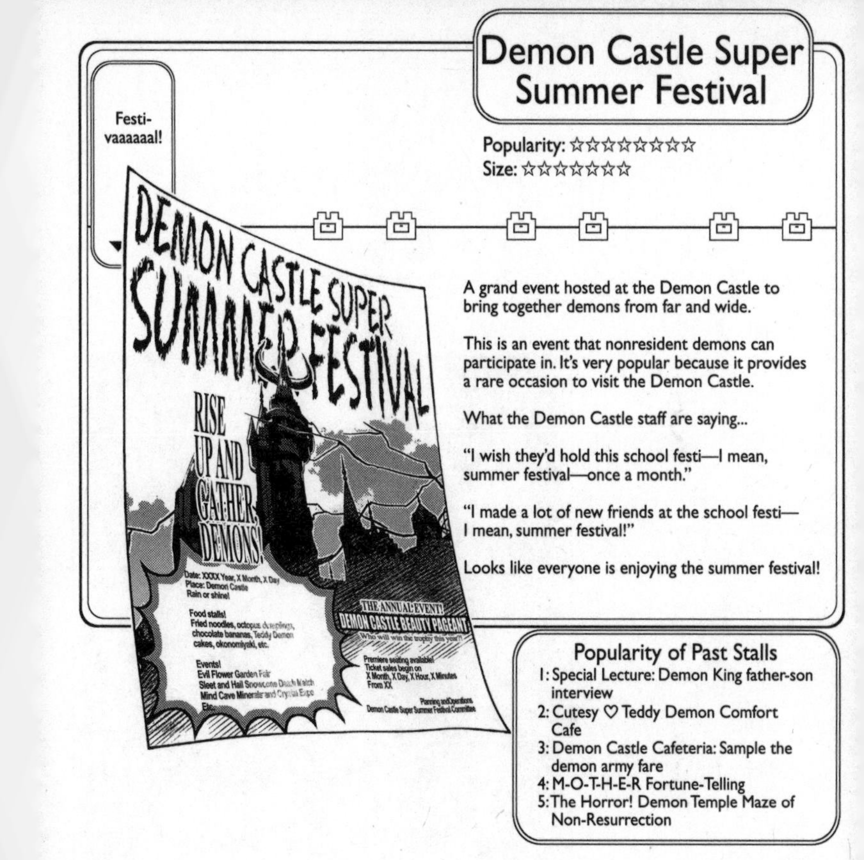
DEMON CASTLE SUPER SUMMER FESTIVAL
RISE UP AND GATHER, DEMONS!
Date: XXXX Year, X Month, X Day
Place: Demon Castle
Rain or shine!
Food stalls!
Fried noodles, octopus dumplings, chocolate bananas, Teddy Demon cakes, okonomiyaki, etc.
Events!
Evil Flower Garden Fair
Sleet and Hail Snowcone Death Match
Mind Cave Minerals and Crystals Expo
Etc.
THE ANNUAL EVENT!
DEMON CASTLE BEAUTY PAGEANT
Who will win the trophy this year?!
Premiere seating available!
Ticket sales begin on
X Month, X Day, X Hour, X Minutes
From XX
Planning and Operations
Demon Castle Super Summer Festival Committee

A grand event hosted at the Demon Castle to bring together demons from far and wide.

This is an event that nonresident demons can participate in. It's very popular because it provides a rare occasion to visit the Demon Castle.

What the Demon Castle staff are saying...

"I wish they'd hold this school festi—I mean, summer festival—once a month."

"I made a lot of new friends at the school festi—I mean, summer festival!"

Looks like everyone is enjoying the summer festival!

Popularity of Past Stalls

1: Special Lecture: Demon King father-son interview
2: Cutesy ♡ Teddy Demon Comfort Cafe
3: Demon Castle Cafeteria: Sample the demon army fare
4: M-O-T-H-E-R Fortune-Telling
5: The Horror! Demon Temple Maze of Non-Resurrection

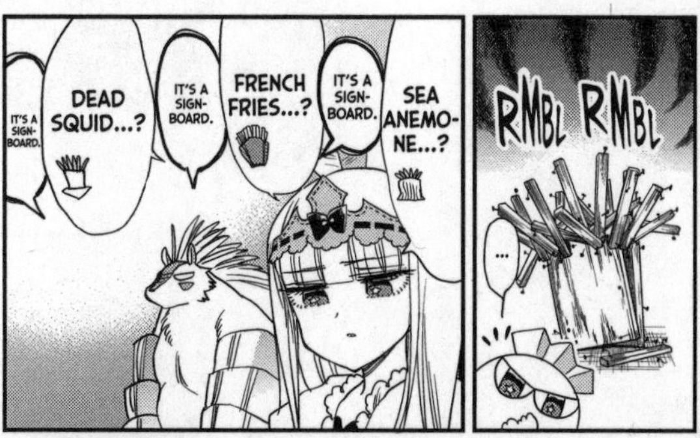
RMBL RMBL
...
SEA ANEMONE...?
IT'S A SIGNBOARD.
FRENCH FRIES...?
IT'S A SIGNBOARD.
DEAD SQUID...?
IT'S A SIGNBOARD.

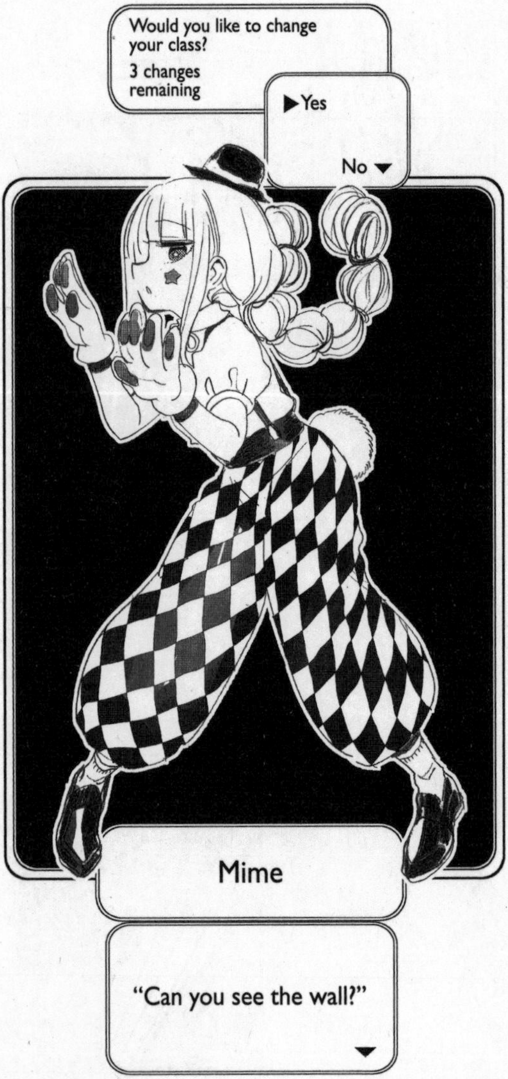
Would you like to change your class?
3 changes remaining
▶Yes
No ▼
Mime
"Can you see the wall?"

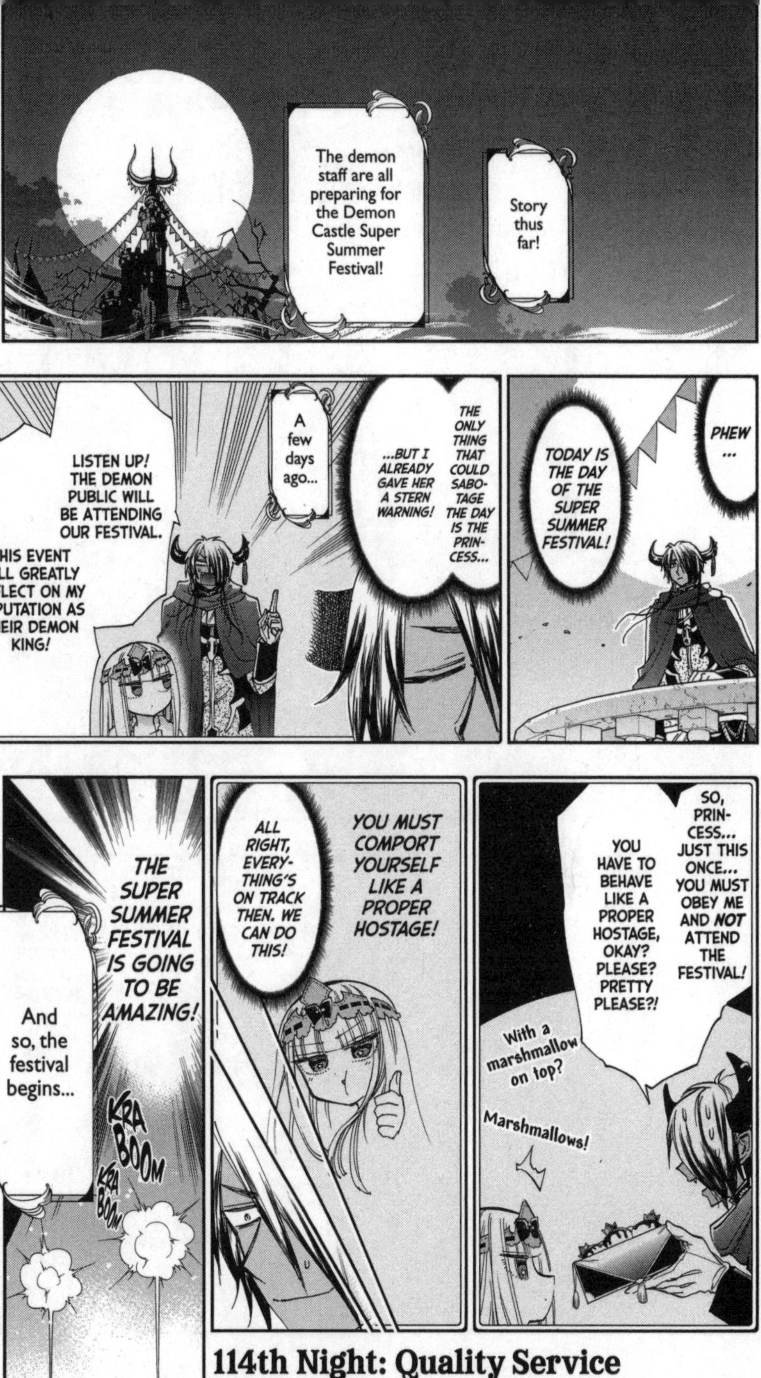
Story thus far!
The demon staff are all preparing for the Demon Castle Super Summer Festival!
PHEW...
TODAY IS THE DAY OF THE SUPER SUMMER FESTIVAL!
THE ONLY THING THAT COULD SABOTAGE THE DAY IS THE PRINCESS...
...BUT I ALREADY GAVE HER A STERN WARNING!
A few days ago...
LISTEN UP! THE DEMON PUBLIC WILL BE ATTENDING OUR FESTIVAL.
THIS EVENT WILL GREATLY REFLECT ON MY REPUTATION AS THEIR DEMON KING!
SO, PRINCESS... JUST THIS ONCE... YOU MUST OBEY ME AND NOT ATTEND THE FESTIVAL!
YOU HAVE TO BEHAVE LIKE A PROPER HOSTAGE, OKAY? PLEASE? PRETTY PLEASE?!
With a marshmallow on top?
Marshmallows!
YOU MUST COMPORT YOURSELF LIKE A PROPER HOSTAGE!
ALL RIGHT, EVERYTHING'S ON TRACK THEN. WE CAN DO THIS!
THE SUPER SUMMER FESTIVAL IS GOING TO BE AMAZING!
And so, the festival begins...
KRA BOOM
KRA BOOM

114th Night: Quality Service Provided by the Hostage

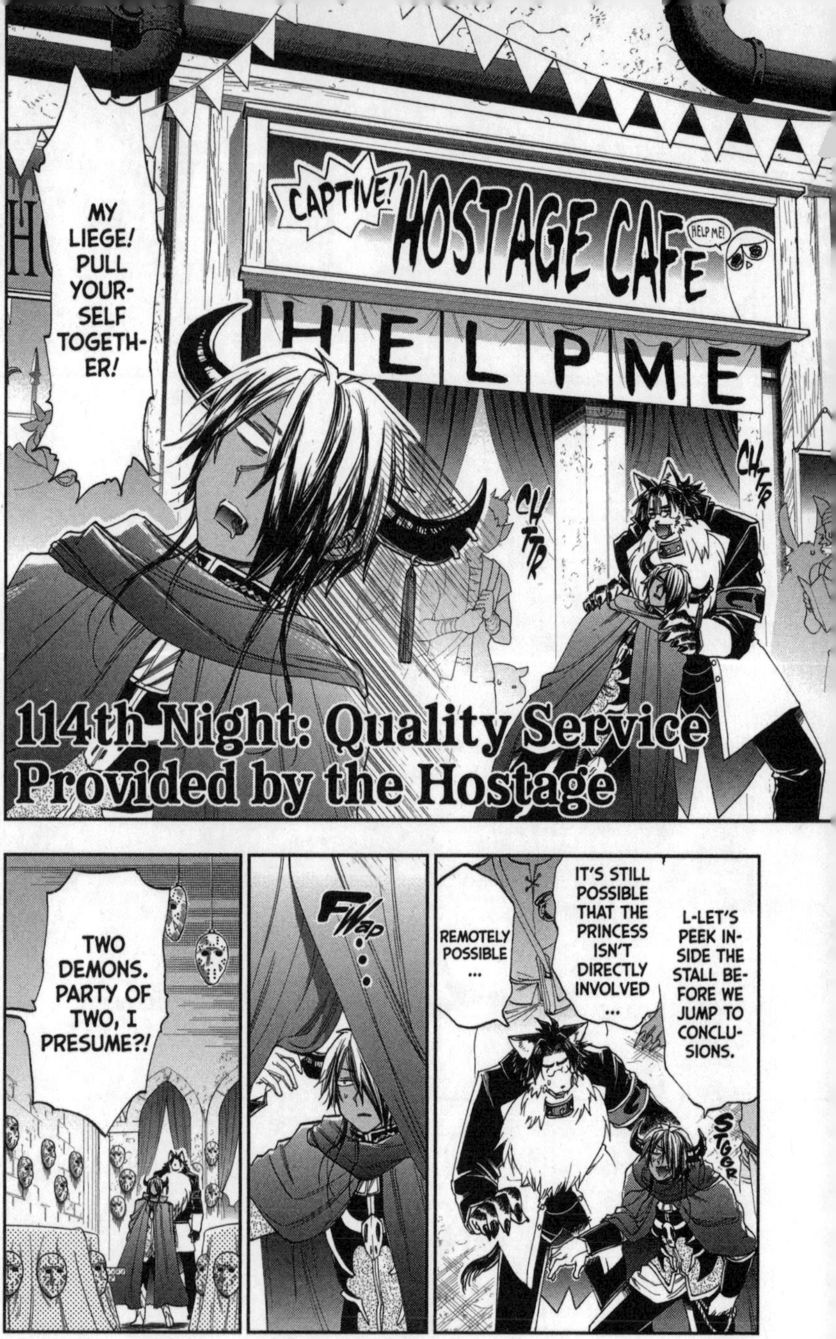
CAPTIVE! HOSTAGE CAFE
HELP ME!
HELPME
CHTTR
CHTTR
MY LIEGE! PULL YOURSELF TOGETHER!
114th Night: Quality Service Provided by the Hostage
L-LET'S PEEK INSIDE THE STALL BEFORE WE JUMP TO CONCLUSIONS.
IT'S STILL POSSIBLE THAT THE PRINCESS ISN'T DIRECTLY INVOLVED ...
REMOTELY POSSIBLE ...
STGGR
FWAP
TWO DEMONS. PARTY OF TWO, I PRESUME?!

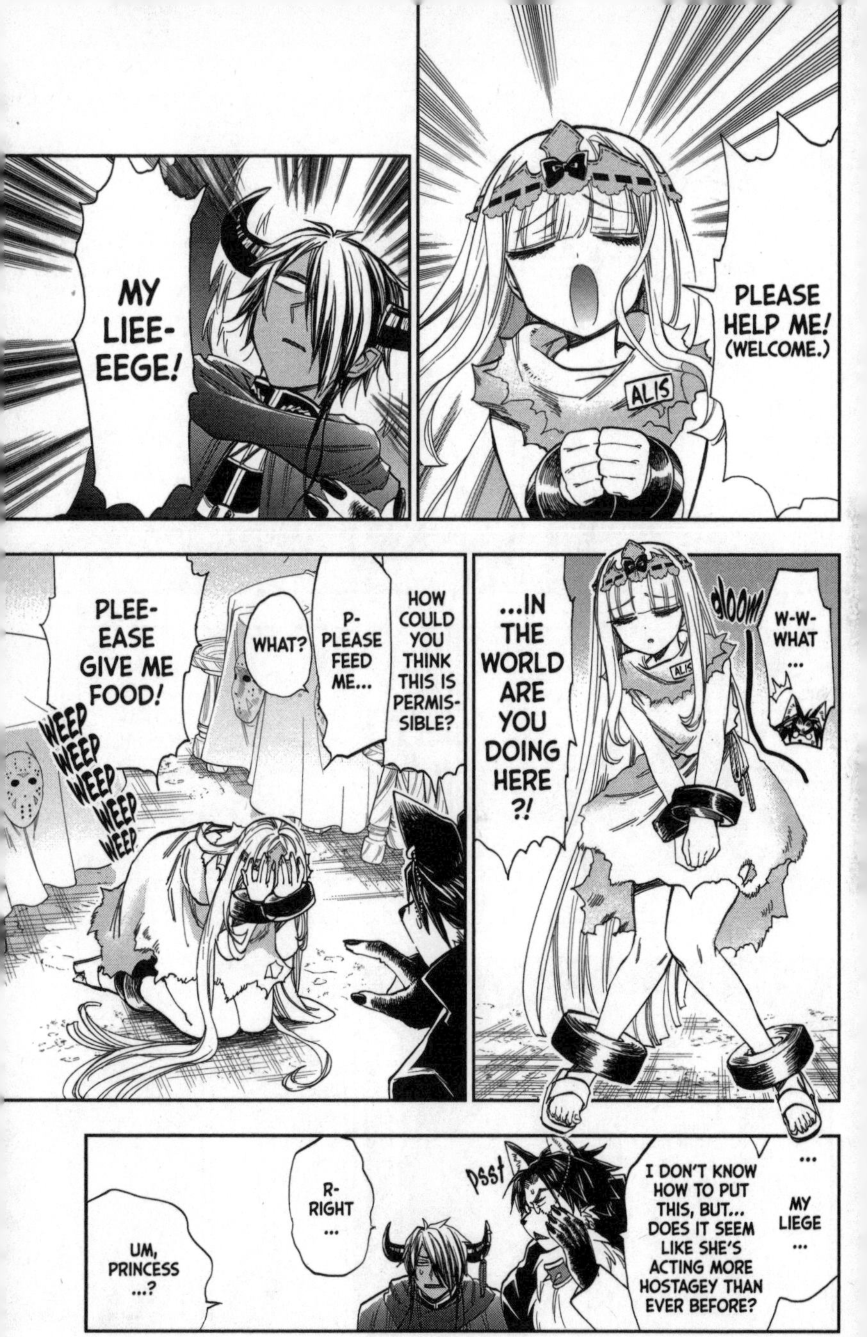

PLEASE HELP ME! (WELCOME.)
ALIS
MY LIEE-EEGE!
W-W-WHAT ...
GLOOM
ALIS
...IN THE WORLD ARE YOU DOING HERE?!
HOW COULD YOU THINK THIS IS PERMIS-SIBLE?
P-PLEASE FEED ME...
WHAT?
PLEE-EASE GIVE ME FOOD!
WEEP WEEP WEEP WEEP WEEP
... MY LIEGE ...
I DON'T KNOW HOW TO PUT THIS, BUT... DOES IT SEEM LIKE SHE'S ACTING MORE HOSTAGEY THAN EVER BEFORE?
PSST
R-RIGHT ...
UM, PRINCESS ...?

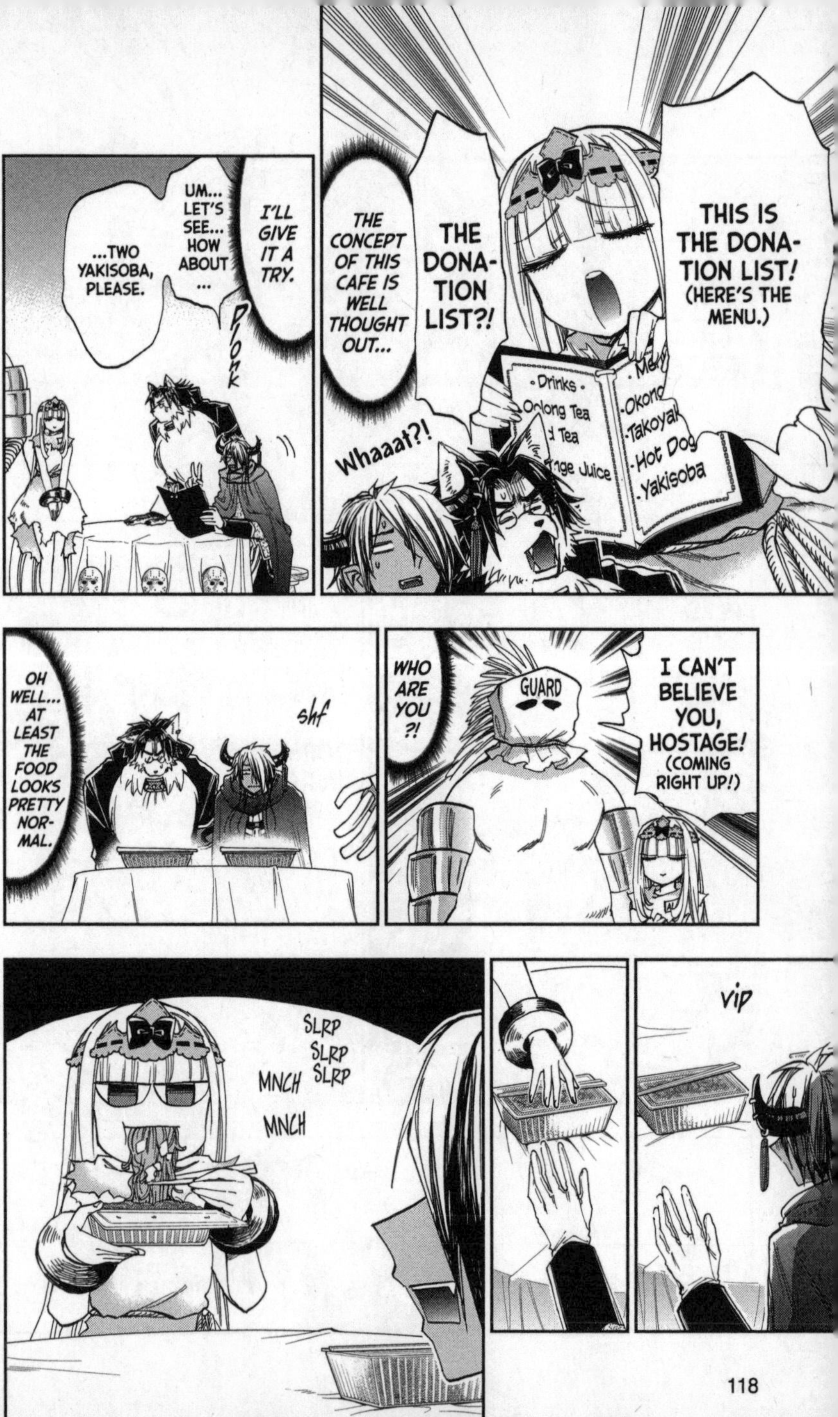
THIS IS THE DONATION LIST! (HERE'S THE MENU.)
THE DONATION LIST?!
THE CONCEPT OF THIS CAFE IS WELL THOUGHT OUT...
Whaaat?!
• Drinks •
Oolong Tea
Hot Dog
Yakisoba
I'LL GIVE IT A TRY.
Plonk
UM... LET'S SEE... HOW ABOUT ...
...TWO YAKISOBA, PLEASE.
I CAN'T BELIEVE YOU, HOSTAGE! (COMING RIGHT UP!)
GUARD
WHO ARE YOU ?!
shf
OH WELL... AT LEAST THE FOOD LOOKS PRETTY NORMAL.
vip
SLRP SLRP SLRP
MNCH MNCH

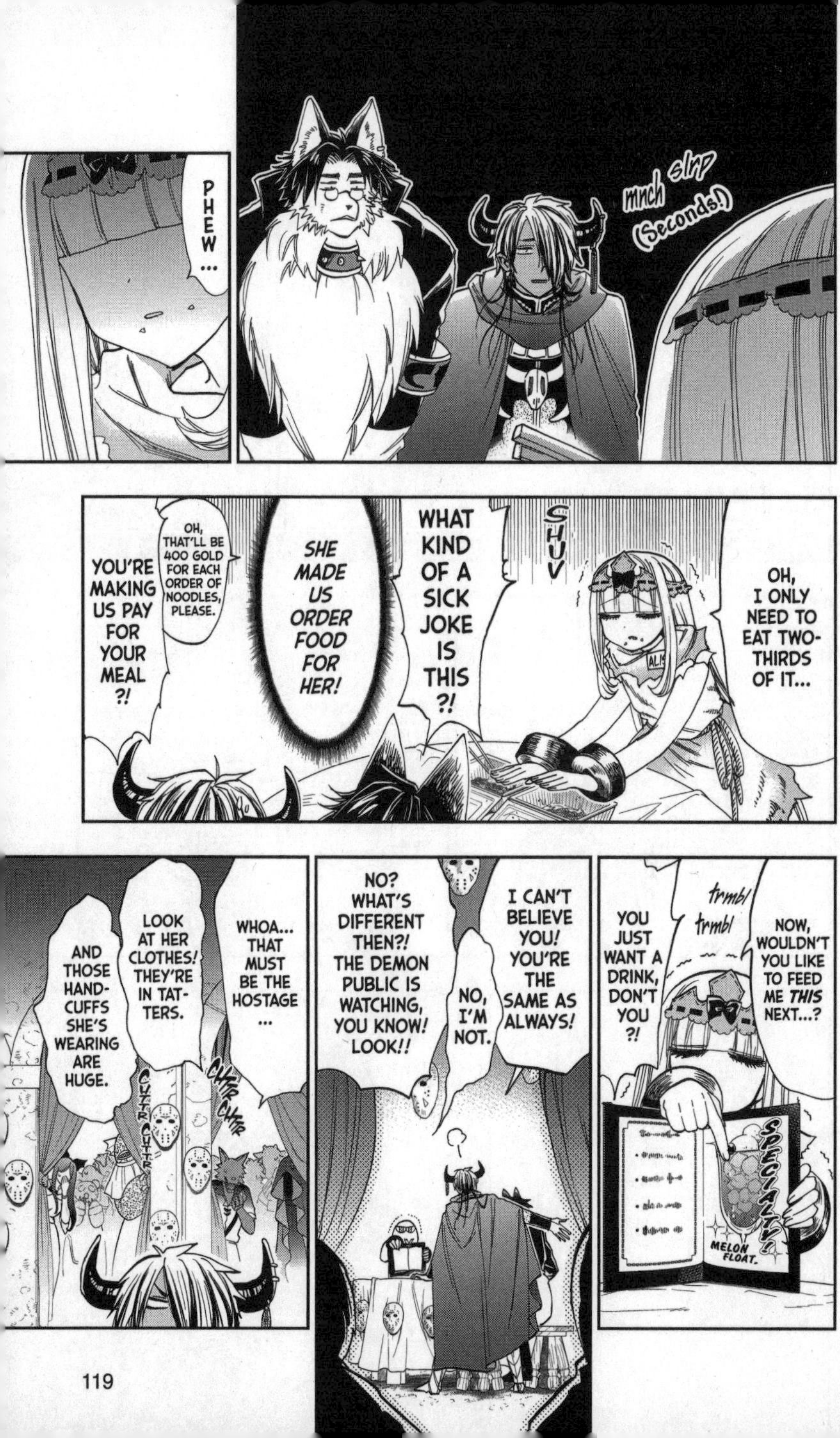
mnch slrp
(Seconds!)
PHEW...
OH, I ONLY NEED TO EAT TWO-THIRDS OF IT...
SHUV
WHAT KIND OF A SICK JOKE IS THIS?!
SHE MADE US ORDER FOOD FOR HER!
OH, THAT'LL BE 400 GOLD FOR EACH ORDER OF NOODLES, PLEASE.
YOU'RE MAKING US PAY FOR YOUR MEAL?!
NOW, WOULDN'T YOU LIKE TO FEED ME *THIS* NEXT...?
trmbl trmbl
YOU JUST WANT A DRINK, DON'T YOU?!
SPECIALTY!
MELON FLOAT.
I CAN'T BELIEVE YOU! YOU'RE THE SAME AS ALWAYS!
NO, I'M NOT.
NO? WHAT'S DIFFERENT THEN?! THE DEMON PUBLIC IS WATCHING, YOU KNOW! LOOK!!
WHOA... THAT MUST BE THE HOSTAGE...
CHTTR CHTTR
CHTTR CHTTR
LOOK AT HER CLOTHES! THEY'RE IN TATTERS.
AND THOSE HANDCUFFS SHE'S WEARING ARE HUGE.

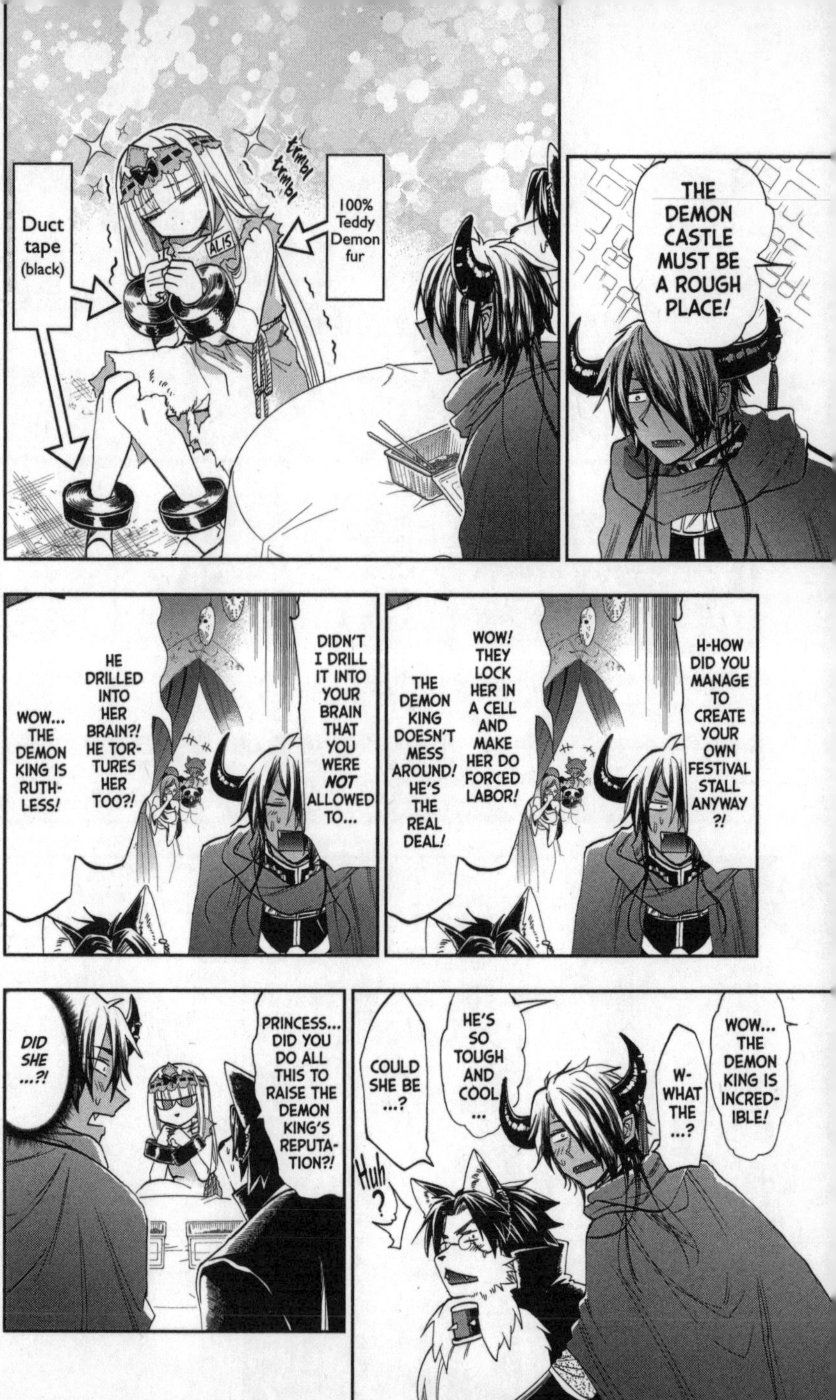
THE DEMON CASTLE MUST BE A ROUGH PLACE!
trmbl trmbl
100% Teddy Demon fur
Duct tape (black)
H-HOW DID YOU MANAGE TO CREATE YOUR OWN FESTIVAL STALL ANYWAY?!
WOW! THEY LOCK HER IN A CELL AND MAKE HER DO FORCED LABOR!
THE DEMON KING DOESN'T MESS AROUND! HE'S THE REAL DEAL!
DIDN'T I DRILL IT INTO YOUR BRAIN THAT YOU WERE *NOT* ALLOWED TO...
HE DRILLED INTO HER BRAIN?! HE TORTURES HER TOO?!
WOW... THE DEMON KING IS RUTHLESS!
WOW... THE DEMON KING IS INCREDIBLE!
W-WHAT THE ...?
HE'S SO TOUGH AND COOL ...
COULD SHE BE ...?
Huh ?
PRINCESS... DID YOU DO ALL THIS TO RAISE THE DEMON KING'S REPUTATION?!
DID SHE ...?!

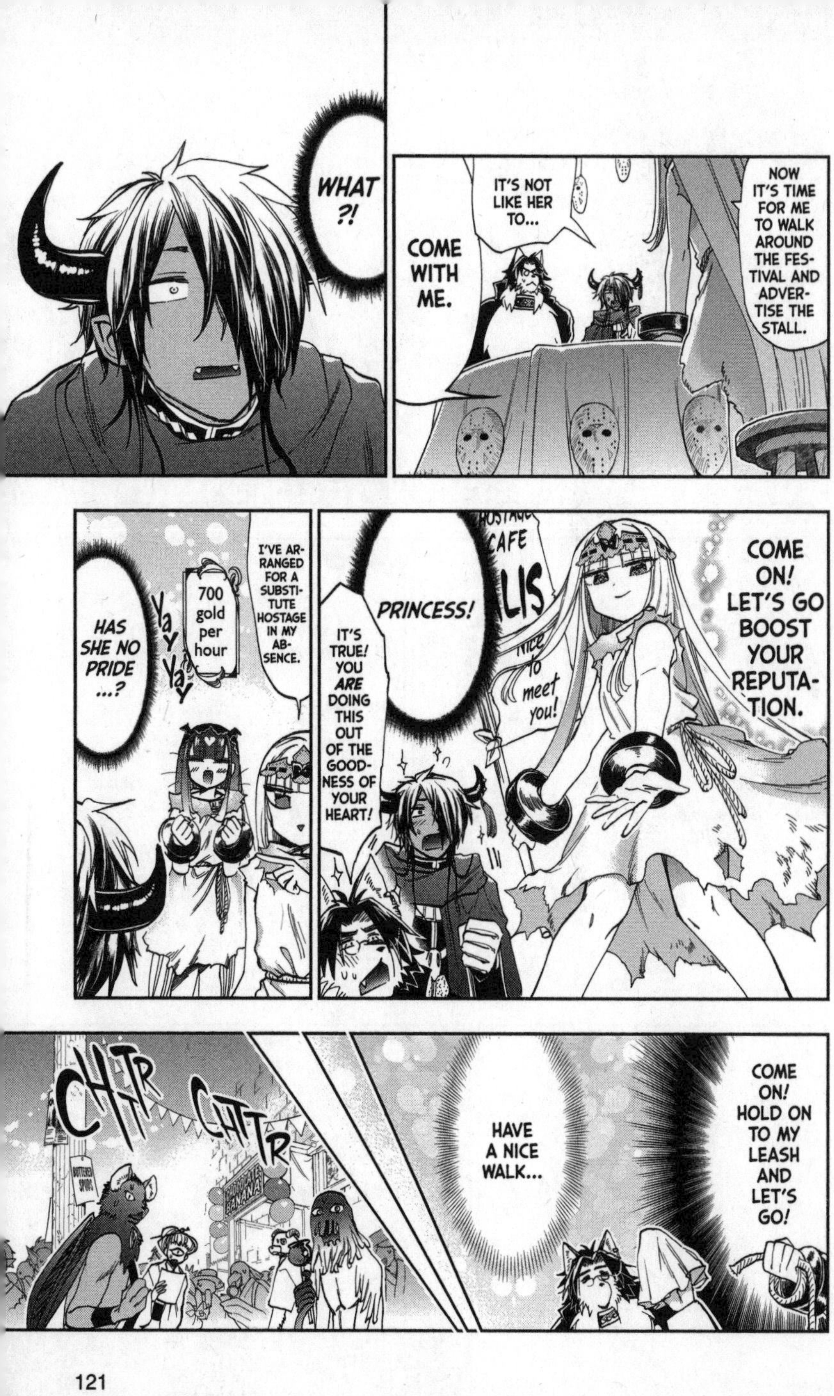
NOW IT'S TIME FOR ME TO WALK AROUND THE FESTIVAL AND ADVERTISE THE STALL.
IT'S NOT LIKE HER TO...
COME WITH ME.
WHAT?!
COME ON! LET'S GO BOOST YOUR REPUTATION.
HOSTAGE CAFE
Nice to meet you!
PRINCESS!
IT'S TRUE! YOU *ARE* DOING THIS OUT OF THE GOODNESS OF YOUR HEART!
I'VE ARRANGED FOR A SUBSTITUTE HOSTAGE IN MY ABSENCE.
700 gold per hour
Yay Yay
HAS SHE NO PRIDE...?
COME ON! HOLD ON TO MY LEASH AND LET'S GO!
HAVE A NICE WALK...
CHTR CHTR

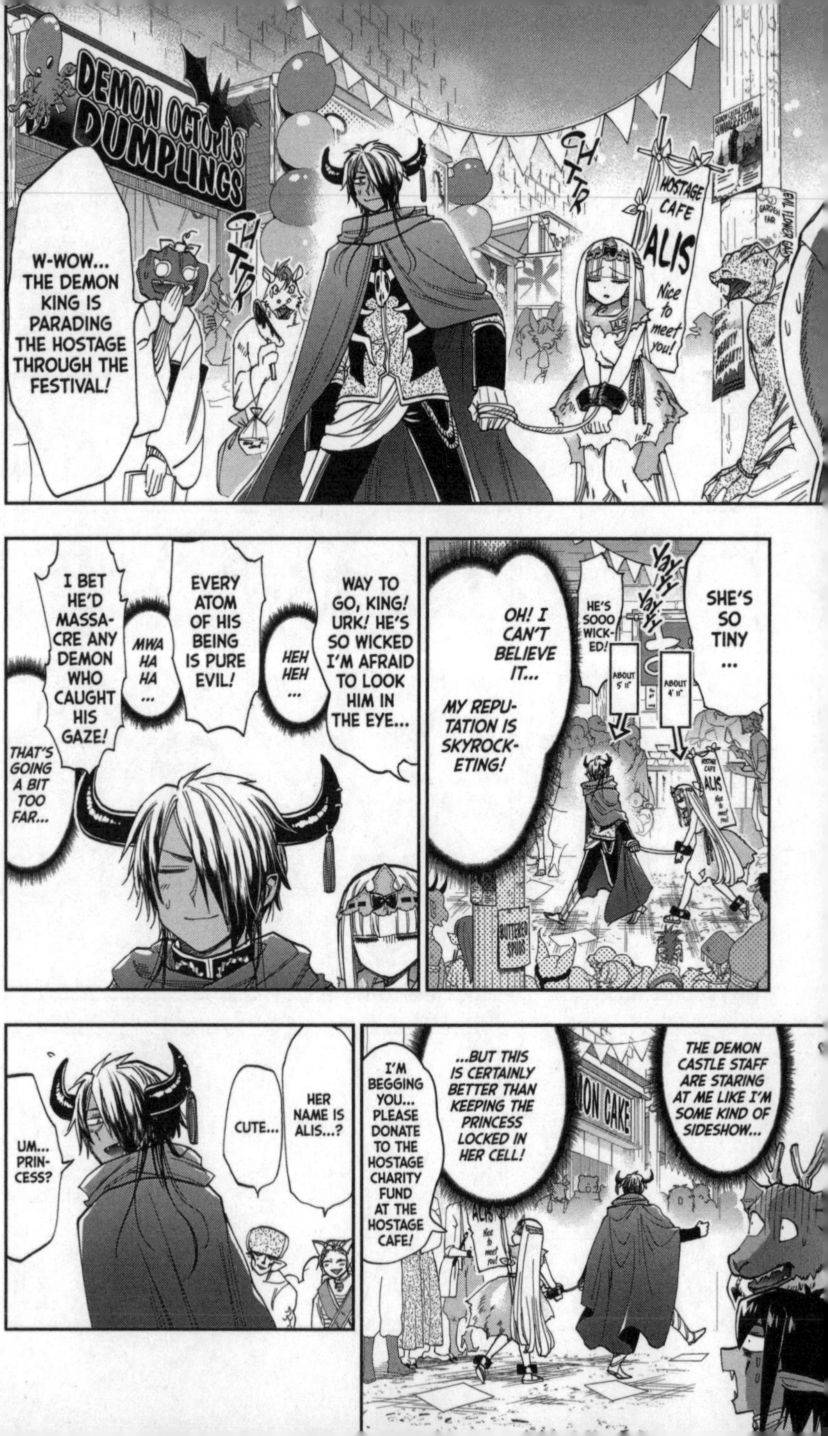
DEMON OCTOPUS DUMPLINGS
CHTTR
CHTTR
HOSTAGE CAFE
ALIS
Nice to meet you!
W-WOW... THE DEMON KING IS PARADING THE HOSTAGE THROUGH THE FESTIVAL!
SHE'S SO TINY...
YAY YAY
HE'S SOOO WICKED!
ABOUT 4' 11"
ABOUT 5' 11"
OH! I CAN'T BELIEVE IT...
MY REPUTATION IS SKYROCKETING!
BUTTERED SPURS
WAY TO GO, KING! URK! HE'S SO WICKED I'M AFRAID TO LOOK HIM IN THE EYE...
HEH HEH...
EVERY ATOM OF HIS BEING IS PURE EVIL!
MWA HA HA...
I BET HE'D MASSACRE ANY DEMON WHO CAUGHT HIS GAZE!
THAT'S GOING A BIT TOO FAR...
THE DEMON CASTLE STAFF ARE STARING AT ME LIKE I'M SOME KIND OF SIDESHOW...
...BUT THIS IS CERTAINLY BETTER THAN KEEPING THE PRINCESS LOCKED IN HER CELL!
I'M BEGGING YOU... PLEASE DONATE TO THE HOSTAGE CHARITY FUND AT THE HOSTAGE CAFE!
HER NAME IS ALIS...?
CUTE...
UM... PRINCESS?

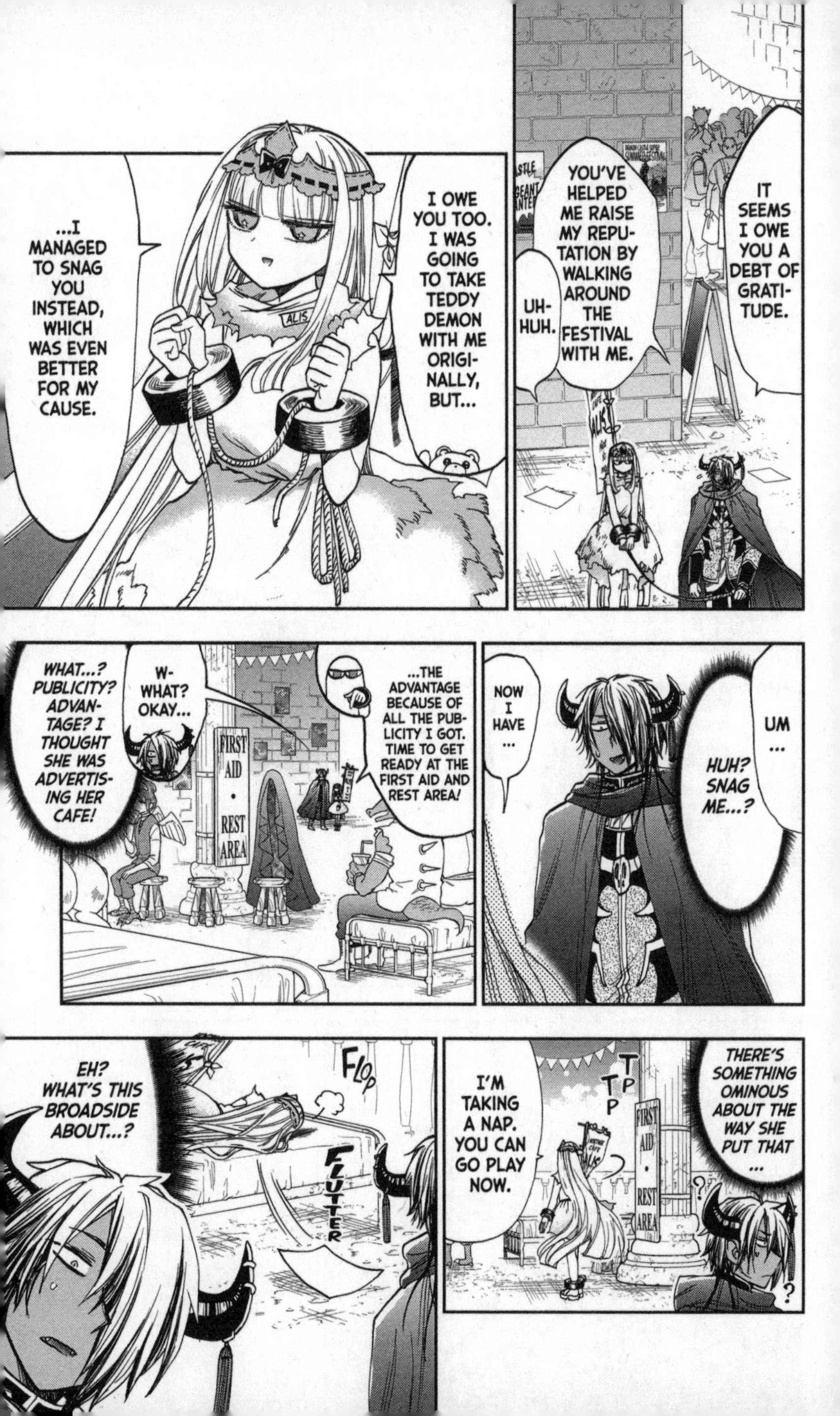
IT SEEMS I OWE YOU A DEBT OF GRATITUDE.
YOU'VE HELPED ME RAISE MY REPUTATION BY WALKING AROUND THE FESTIVAL WITH ME.
UH-HUH.
I OWE YOU TOO. I WAS GOING TO TAKE TEDDY DEMON WITH ME ORIGINALLY, BUT...
...I MANAGED TO SNAG YOU INSTEAD, WHICH WAS EVEN BETTER FOR MY CAUSE.
UM ...
HUH? SNAG ME...?
NOW I HAVE ...
...THE ADVANTAGE BECAUSE OF ALL THE PUBLICITY I GOT. TIME TO GET READY AT THE FIRST AID AND REST AREA!
FIRST AID • REST AREA
W-WHAT? OKAY...
WHAT...? PUBLICITY? ADVANTAGE? I THOUGHT SHE WAS ADVERTISING HER CAFE!
THERE'S SOMETHING OMINOUS ABOUT THE WAY SHE PUT THAT ...
TP TP TP
FIRST AID • REST AREA
I'M TAKING A NAP. YOU CAN GO PLAY NOW.
FLOP
FLUTTER
EH? WHAT'S THIS BROADSIDE ABOUT...?

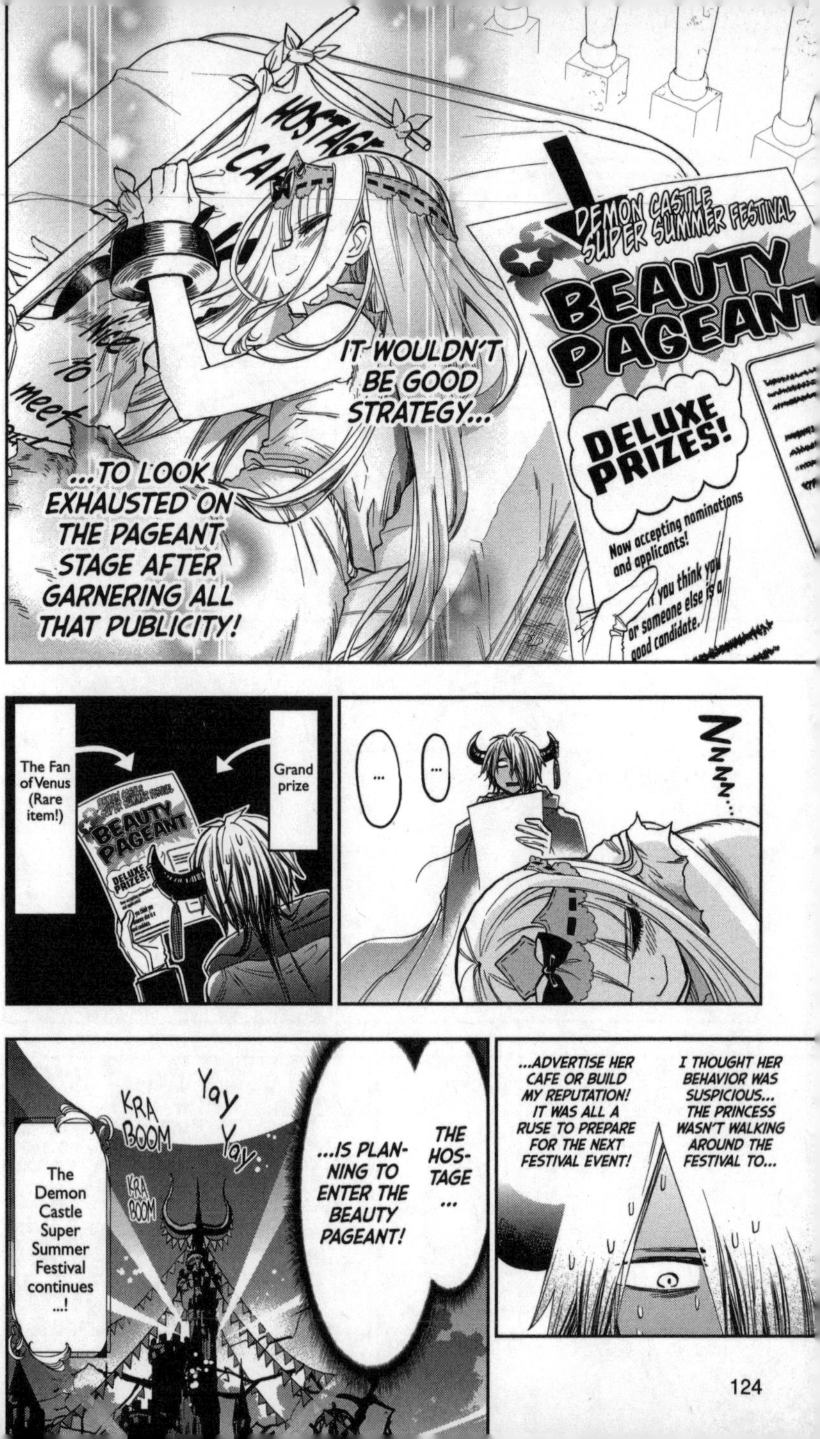
HOSTAGE
DEMON CASTLE SUPER SUMMER FESTIVAL
BEAUTY PAGEANT
DELUXE PRIZES!
Now accepting nominations and applicants!
you think you or someone else is a good candidate.
IT WOULDN'T BE GOOD STRATEGY...
...TO LOOK EXHAUSTED ON THE PAGEANT STAGE AFTER GARNERING ALL THAT PUBLICITY!
Znnn...
...
...
Grand prize
The Fan of Venus (Rare item!)
I THOUGHT HER BEHAVIOR WAS SUSPICIOUS... THE PRINCESS WASN'T WALKING AROUND THE FESTIVAL TO...
...ADVERTISE HER CAFE OR BUILD MY REPUTATION! IT WAS ALL A RUSE TO PREPARE FOR THE NEXT FESTIVAL EVENT!
THE HOS-TAGE...
...IS PLAN-NING TO ENTER THE BEAUTY PAGEANT!
Yay
Yay
KRA BOOM
KRA BOOM
The Demon Castle Super Summer Festival continues ...!

Kiddie Photo Studio ③

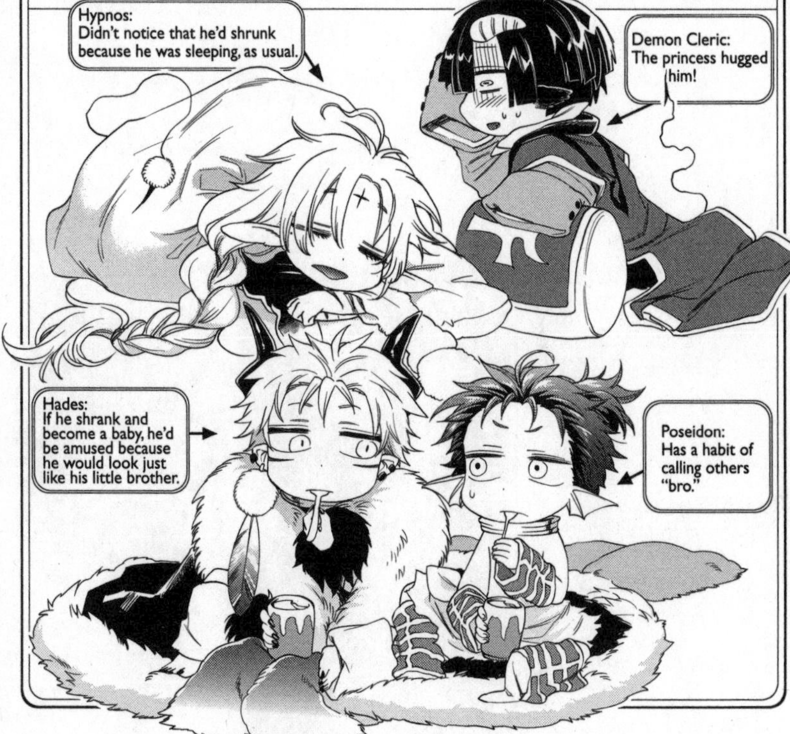
Demon Cleric:
The princess hugged him!
Hypnos:
Didn't notice that he'd shrunk because he was sleeping, as usual.
Poseidon:
Has a habit of calling others "bro."
Hades:
If he shrank and become a baby, he'd be amused because he would look just like his little brother.

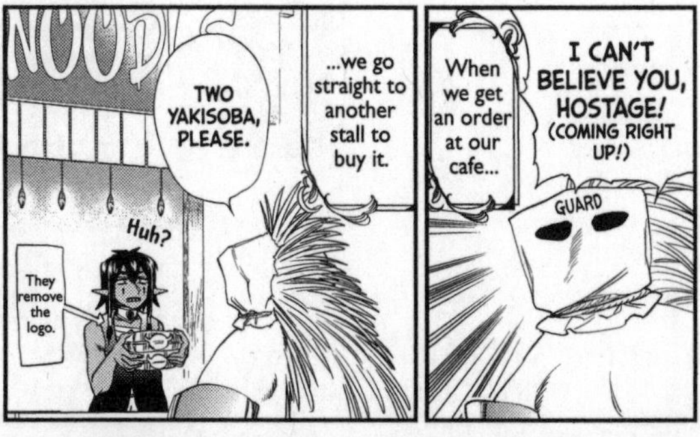
I CAN'T BELIEVE YOU, HOSTAGE! (COMING RIGHT UP!)
When we get an order at our cafe...
GUARD
...we go straight to another stall to buy it.
TWO YAKISOBA, PLEASE.
Huh?
They remove the logo.

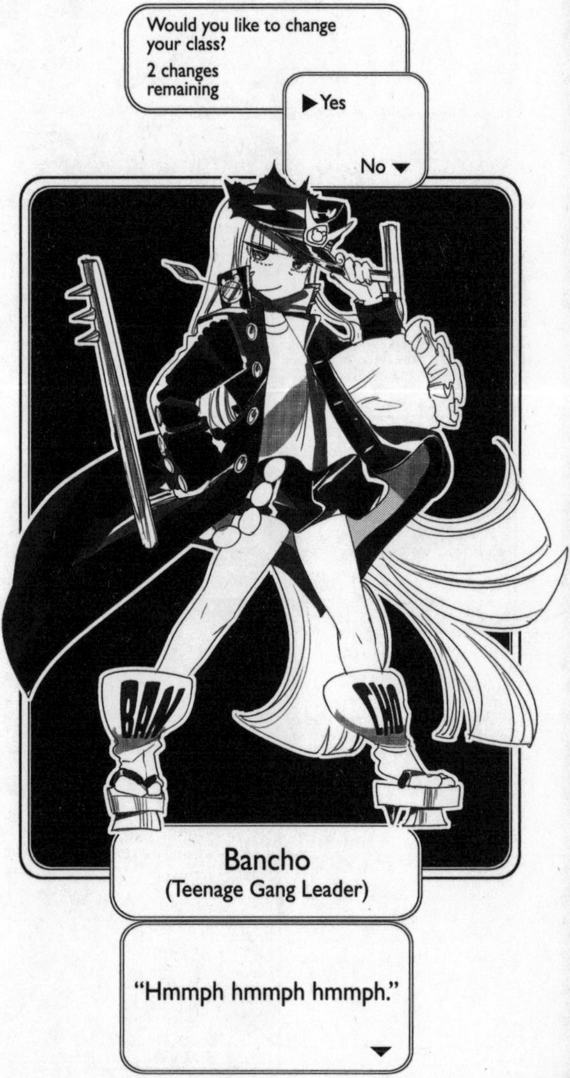
Would you like to change your class?
2 changes remaining
▶Yes
No
BAN
CHO
Bancho
(Teenage Gang Leader)
"Hmmph hmmph hmmph."

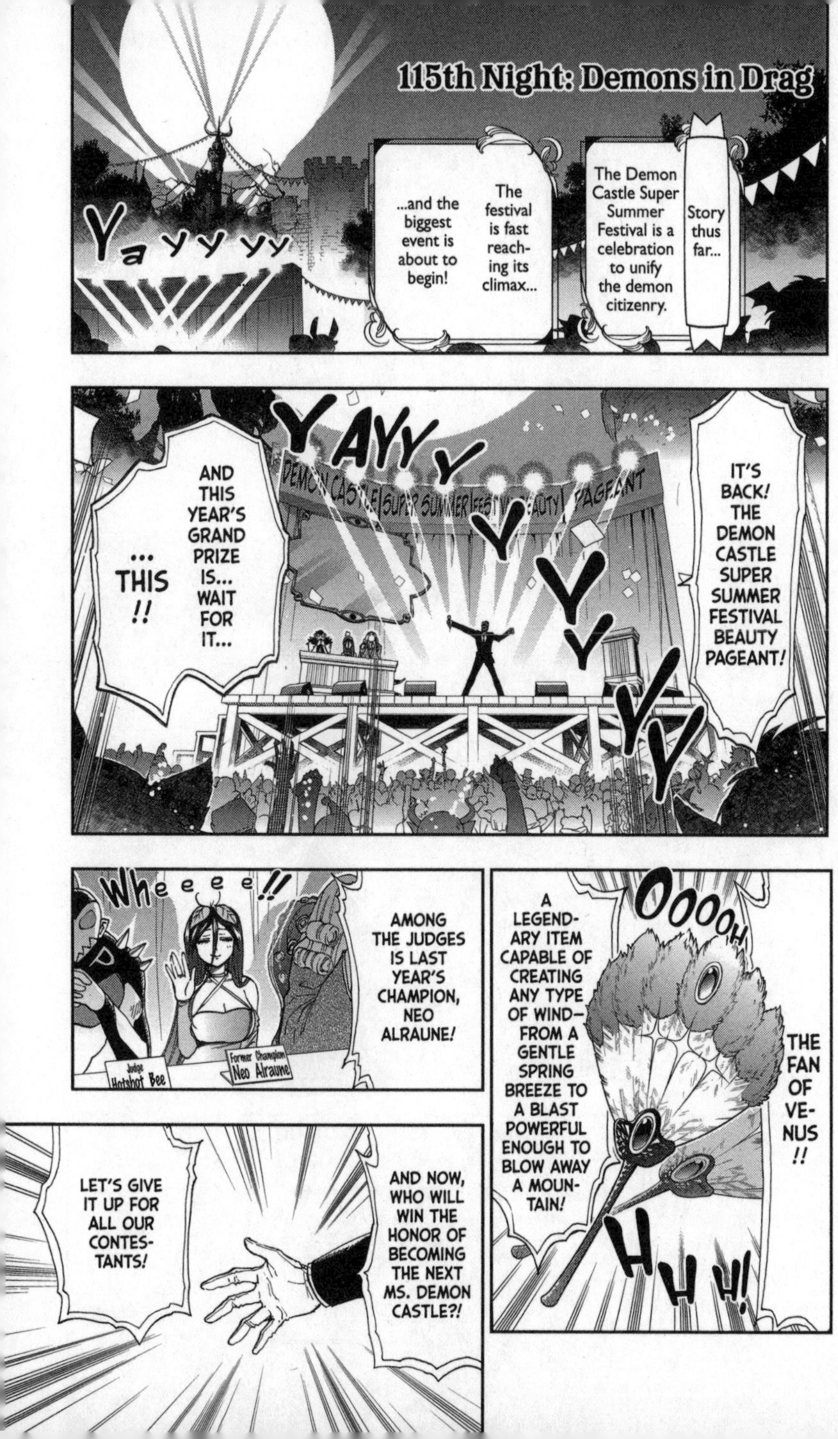
115th Night: Demons in Drag
Story thus far...
The Demon Castle Super Summer Festival is a celebration to unify the demon citizenry.
The festival is fast reaching its climax...
...and the biggest event is about to begin!
Yayyyyy
IT'S BACK! THE DEMON CASTLE SUPER SUMMER FESTIVAL BEAUTY PAGEANT!
YAYYYYYYYY
AND THIS YEAR'S GRAND PRIZE IS... WAIT FOR IT...
...THIS!!
OOOOOHHHH!
THE FAN OF VENUS!!
A LEGENDARY ITEM CAPABLE OF CREATING ANY TYPE OF WIND—FROM A GENTLE SPRING BREEZE TO A BLAST POWERFUL ENOUGH TO BLOW AWAY A MOUNTAIN!
AMONG THE JUDGES IS LAST YEAR'S CHAMPION, NEO ALRAUNE!
Wheeee!!
Former Champion Neo Alraune
Judge Hotshot Bee
AND NOW, WHO WILL WIN THE HONOR OF BECOMING THE NEXT MS. DEMON CASTLE?!
LET'S GIVE IT UP FOR ALL OUR CONTESTANTS!

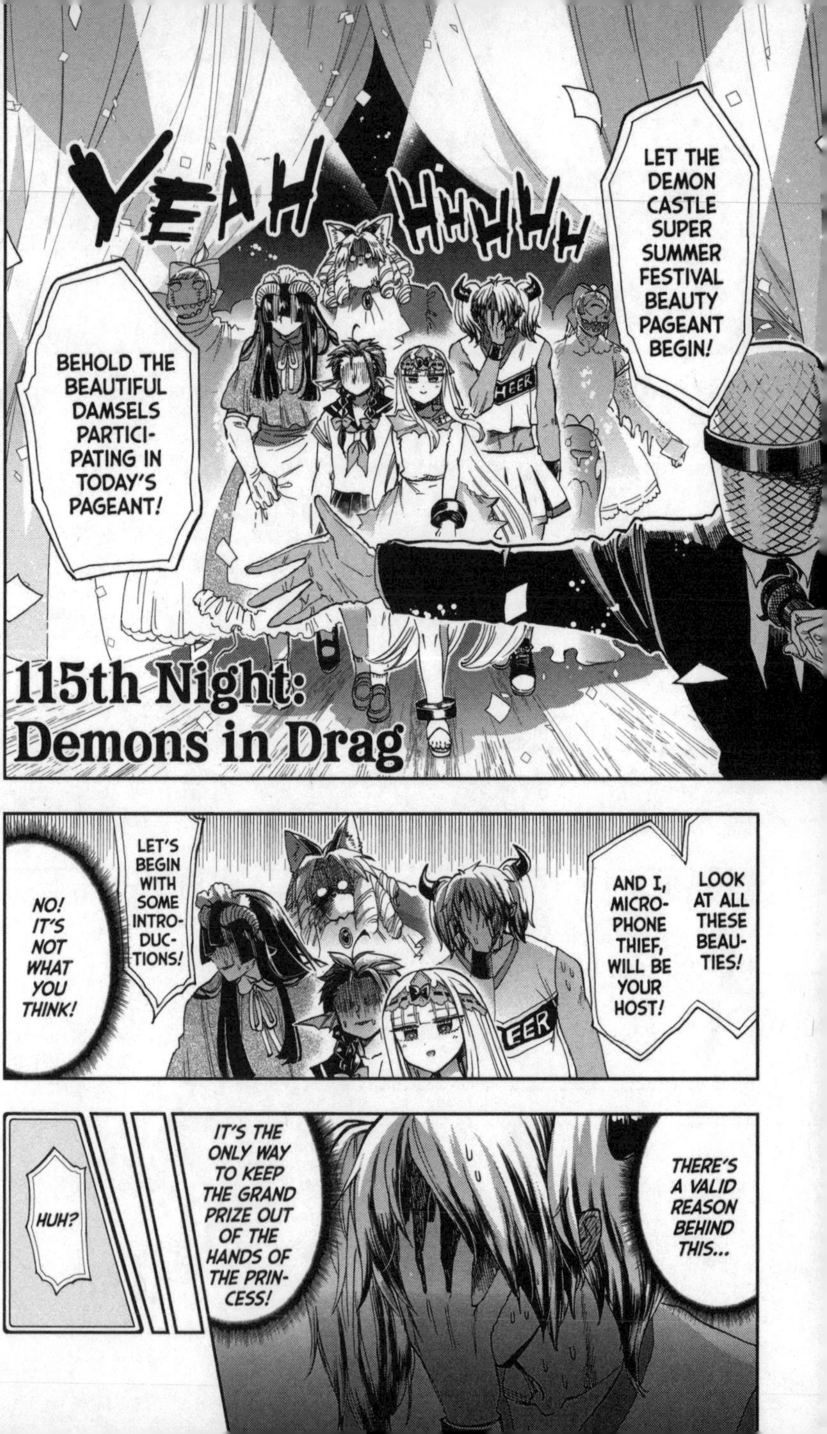
LET THE DEMON CASTLE SUPER SUMMER FESTIVAL BEAUTY PAGEANT BEGIN!
YEAHHHHHH
BEHOLD THE BEAUTIFUL DAMSELS PARTICIPATING IN TODAY'S PAGEANT!
115th Night: Demons in Drag
LOOK AT ALL THESE BEAUTIES!
AND I, MICROPHONE THIEF, WILL BE YOUR HOST!
LET'S BEGIN WITH SOME INTRODUCTIONS!
NO! IT'S NOT WHAT YOU THINK!
THERE'S A VALID REASON BEHIND THIS...
IT'S THE ONLY WAY TO KEEP THE GRAND PRIZE OUT OF THE HANDS OF THE PRINCESS!
HUH?

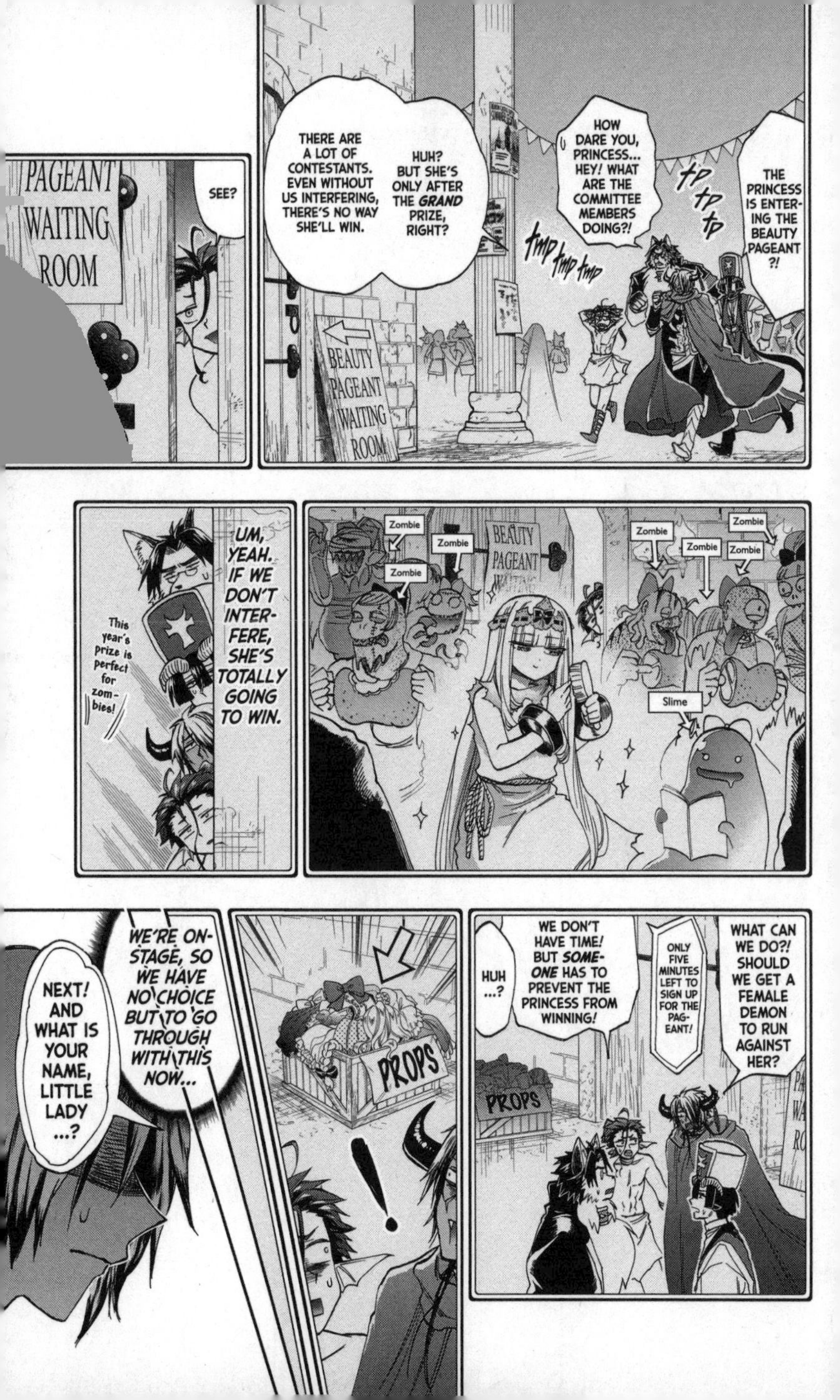
THE PRINCESS IS ENTERING THE BEAUTY PAGEANT?!
tp tp tp
HOW DARE YOU, PRINCESS... HEY! WHAT ARE THE COMMITTEE MEMBERS DOING?!
tmp tmp tmp
HUH? BUT SHE'S ONLY AFTER THE *GRAND* PRIZE, RIGHT?
THERE ARE A LOT OF CONTESTANTS. EVEN WITHOUT US INTERFERING, THERE'S NO WAY SHE'LL WIN.
BEAUTY PAGEANT WAITING ROOM
SEE?
PAGEANT WAITING ROOM
Zombie
Zombie
Zombie
Zombie
Zombie
Zombie
Zombie
Zombie
BEAUTY PAGEANT WAITING
Slime
UM, YEAH. IF WE DON'T INTERFERE, SHE'S TOTALLY GOING TO WIN.
This year's prize is perfect for zombies!
WHAT CAN WE DO?! SHOULD WE GET A FEMALE DEMON TO RUN AGAINST HER?
ONLY FIVE MINUTES LEFT TO SIGN UP FOR THE PAGEANT!
WE DON'T HAVE TIME! BUT *SOMEONE* HAS TO PREVENT THE PRINCESS FROM WINNING!
HUH ...?
PROPS
PROPS
!
WE'RE ONSTAGE, SO WE HAVE NO CHOICE BUT TO GO THROUGH WITH THIS NOW...
NEXT! AND WHAT IS YOUR NAME, LITTLE LADY ...?

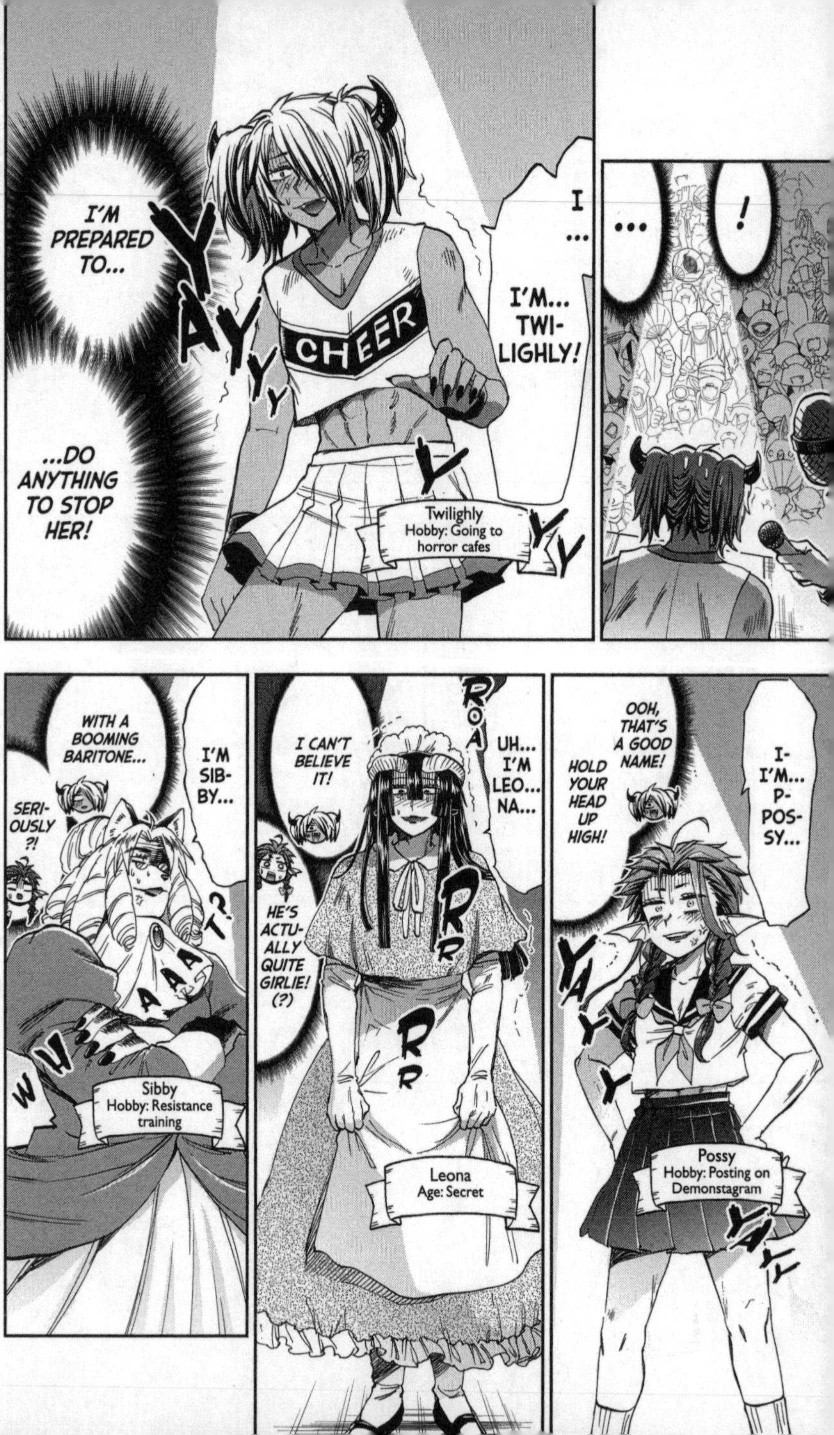
...
!
I
...
I'M... TWI-LIGHLY!
YAYYYY
I'M PREPARED TO...
...DO ANYTHING TO STOP HER!
Twilighly
Hobby: Going to horror cafes
I-
I'M... P-POS-SY...
OOH, THAT'S A GOOD NAME!
HOLD YOUR HEAD UP HIGH!
YAYYY
Possy
Hobby: Posting on Demonstagram
YAYY
UH... I'M LEO... NA...
ROARRRRR
I CAN'T BELIEVE IT!
HE'S ACTU-ALLY QUITE GIRLIE! (?)
Leona
Age: Secret
I'M SIB-BY...
WITH A BOOMING BARITONE...
SERI-OUSLY ?!
WHAAAAT?
Sibby
Hobby: Resistance training

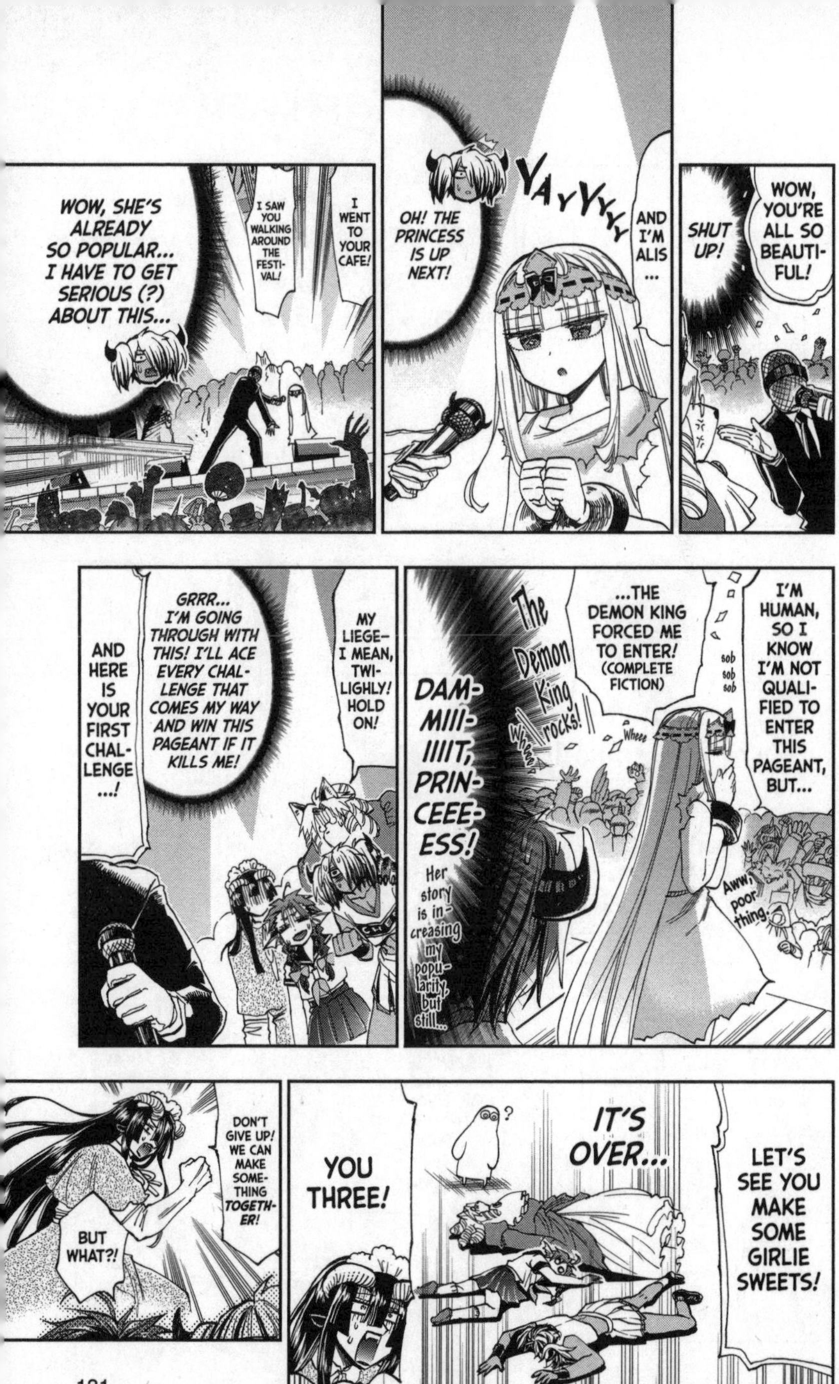
WOW, YOU'RE ALL SO BEAUTIFUL!
SHUT UP!
AND I'M ALIS...
YAYYYYY
OH! THE PRINCESS IS UP NEXT!
I WENT TO YOUR CAFE!
I SAW YOU WALKING AROUND THE FESTIVAL!
WOW, SHE'S ALREADY SO POPULAR... I HAVE TO GET SERIOUS (?) ABOUT THIS...
I'M HUMAN, SO I KNOW I'M NOT QUALIFIED TO ENTER THIS PAGEANT, BUT...
sob sob sob
...THE DEMON KING FORCED ME TO ENTER! (COMPLETE FICTION)
The Demon King rocks!
Wheee
Wheee
Aww, poor thing.
DAMMIIIIIIT, PRINCEEEESS!
Her story is increasing my popularity, but still...
MY LIEGE— I MEAN, TWILIGHLY! HOLD ON!
GRRR... I'M GOING THROUGH WITH THIS! I'LL ACE EVERY CHALLENGE THAT COMES MY WAY AND WIN THIS PAGEANT IF IT KILLS ME!
AND HERE IS YOUR FIRST CHALLENGE...!
LET'S SEE YOU MAKE SOME GIRLIE SWEETS!
IT'S OVER...
?
YOU THREE!
DON'T GIVE UP! WE CAN MAKE SOMETHING TOGETHER!
BUT WHAT?!

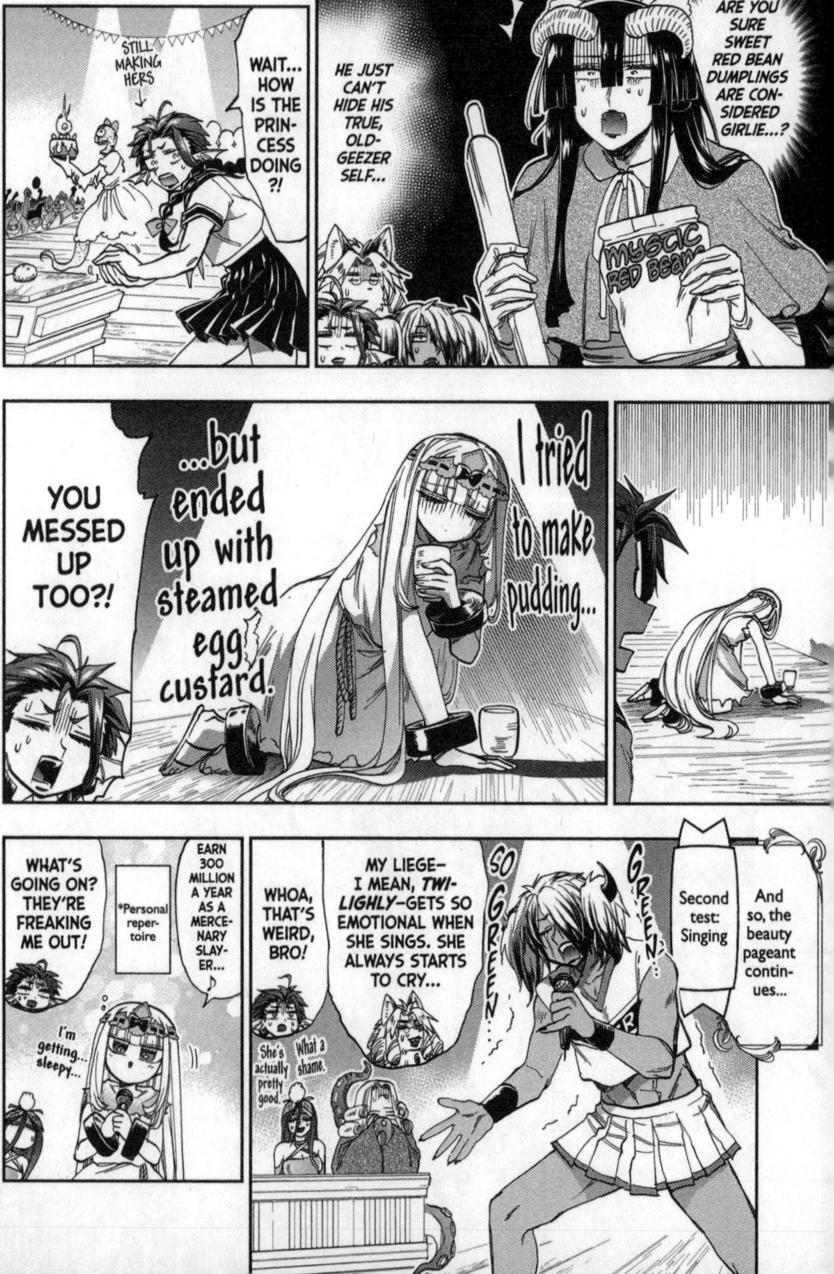
ARE YOU SURE SWEET RED BEAN DUMPLINGS ARE CONSIDERED GIRLIE...?
MYSTIC
HE JUST CAN'T HIDE HIS TRUE, OLD-GEEZER SELF...
WAIT... HOW IS THE PRINCESS DOING?!
STILL MAKING HERS
I tried to make pudding...
...but ended up with steamed egg custard.
YOU MESSED UP TOO?!
And so, the beauty pageant continues...
Second test: Singing
GREEN...
SO GREEN...
MY LIEGE— I MEAN, *TWILIGHLY*—GETS SO EMOTIONAL WHEN SHE SINGS. SHE ALWAYS STARTS TO CRY...
WHOA, THAT'S WEIRD, BRO!
What a shame.
She's actually pretty good.
EARN 300 MILLION A YEAR AS A MERCENARY SLAYER... ♪
*Personal repertoire
WHAT'S GOING ON? THEY'RE FREAKING ME OUT!
I'm getting... sleepy...

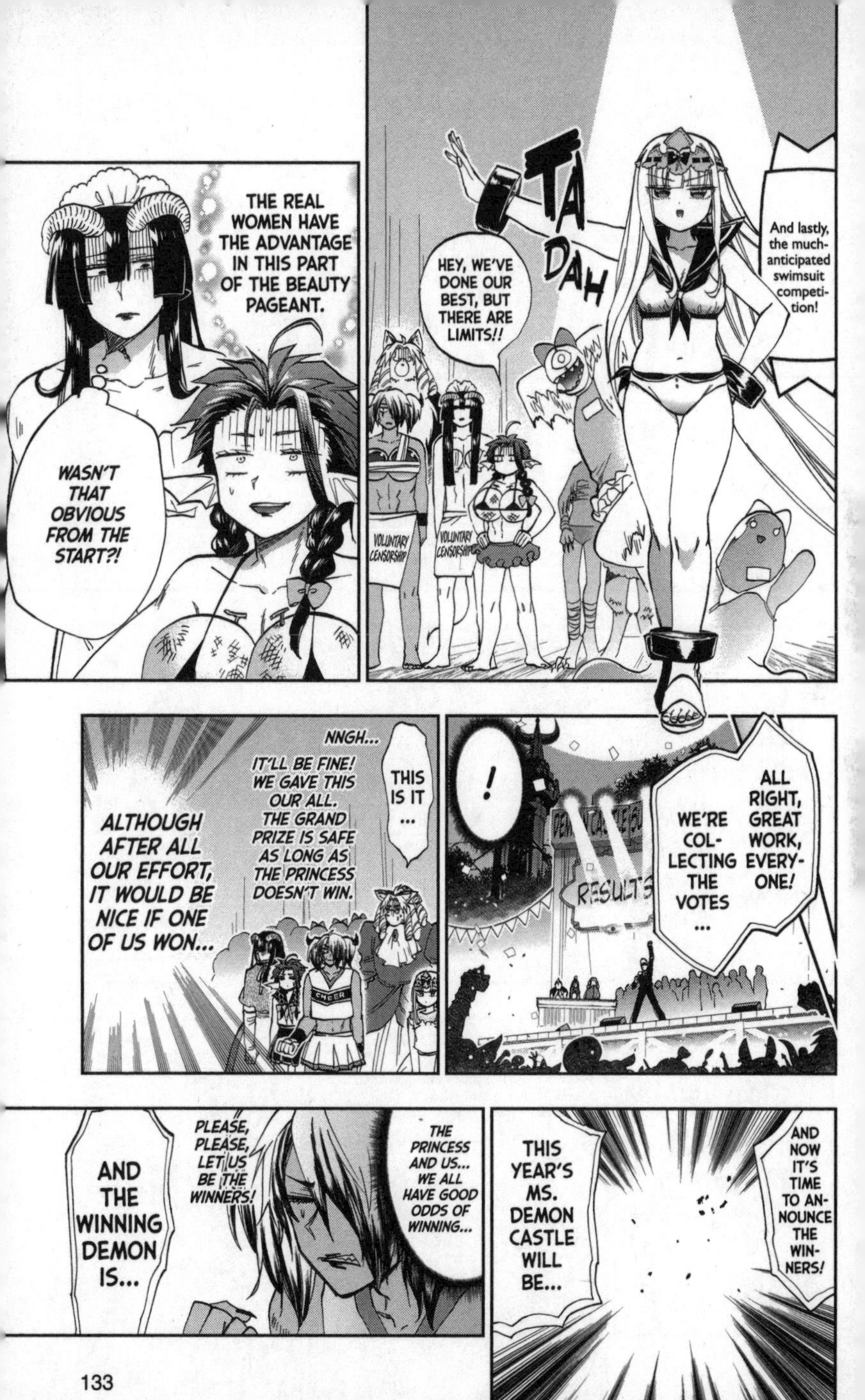
And lastly, the much-anticipated swimsuit competition!
TA DAH
HEY, WE'VE DONE OUR BEST, BUT THERE ARE LIMITS!!
VOLUNTARY CENSORSHIP
VOLUNTARY CENSORSHIP
THE REAL WOMEN HAVE THE ADVANTAGE IN THIS PART OF THE BEAUTY PAGEANT.
WASN'T THAT OBVIOUS FROM THE START?!
ALL RIGHT, GREAT WORK, EVERYONE!
WE'RE COLLECTING THE VOTES...
!
RESULTS
THIS IS IT...
NNGH...
IT'LL BE FINE! WE GAVE THIS OUR ALL. THE GRAND PRIZE IS SAFE AS LONG AS THE PRINCESS DOESN'T WIN.
ALTHOUGH AFTER ALL OUR EFFORT, IT WOULD BE NICE IF ONE OF US WON...
CHEER
AND NOW IT'S TIME TO ANNOUNCE THE WINNERS!
THIS YEAR'S MS. DEMON CASTLE WILL BE...
THE PRINCESS AND US... WE ALL HAVE GOOD ODDS OF WINNING...
PLEASE, PLEASE, LET US BE THE WINNERS!
AND THE WINNING DEMON IS...

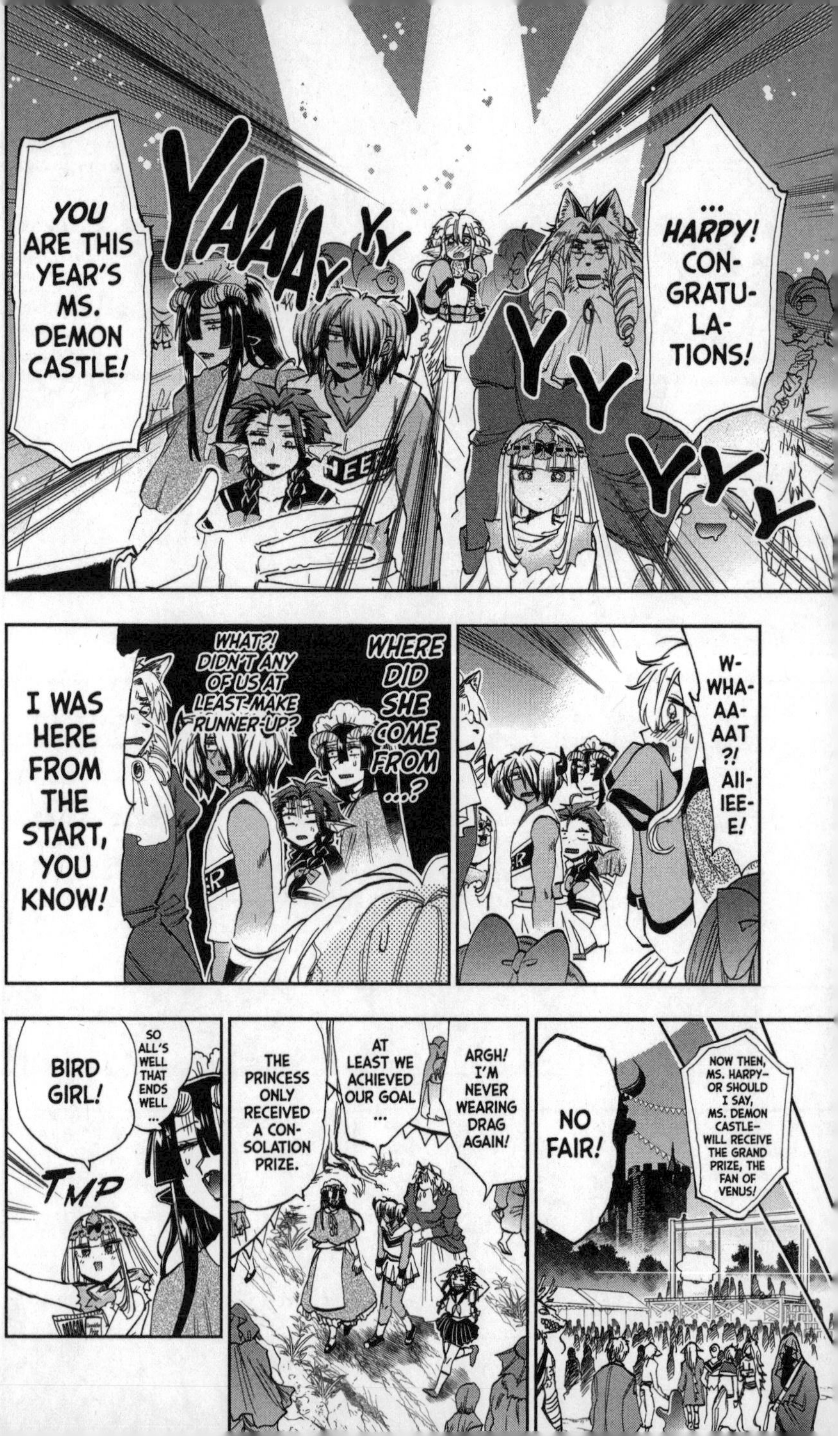
...HARPY! CONGRATULATIONS!
YAAAYYYYYYYYY
YOU ARE THIS YEAR'S MS. DEMON CASTLE!
W-WHAAAAAT?! AIIIEEE-E!
WHERE DID SHE COME FROM...?
WHAT?! DIDN'T ANY OF US AT LEAST MAKE RUNNER-UP?
I WAS HERE FROM THE START, YOU KNOW!
NOW THEN, MS. HARPY— OR SHOULD I SAY, MS. DEMON CASTLE— WILL RECEIVE THE GRAND PRIZE, THE FAN OF VENUS!
NO FAIR!
ARGH! I'M NEVER WEARING DRAG AGAIN!
AT LEAST WE ACHIEVED OUR GOAL...
THE PRINCESS ONLY RECEIVED A CONSOLATION PRIZE.
SO ALL'S WELL THAT ENDS WELL...
BIRD GIRL!
TMP

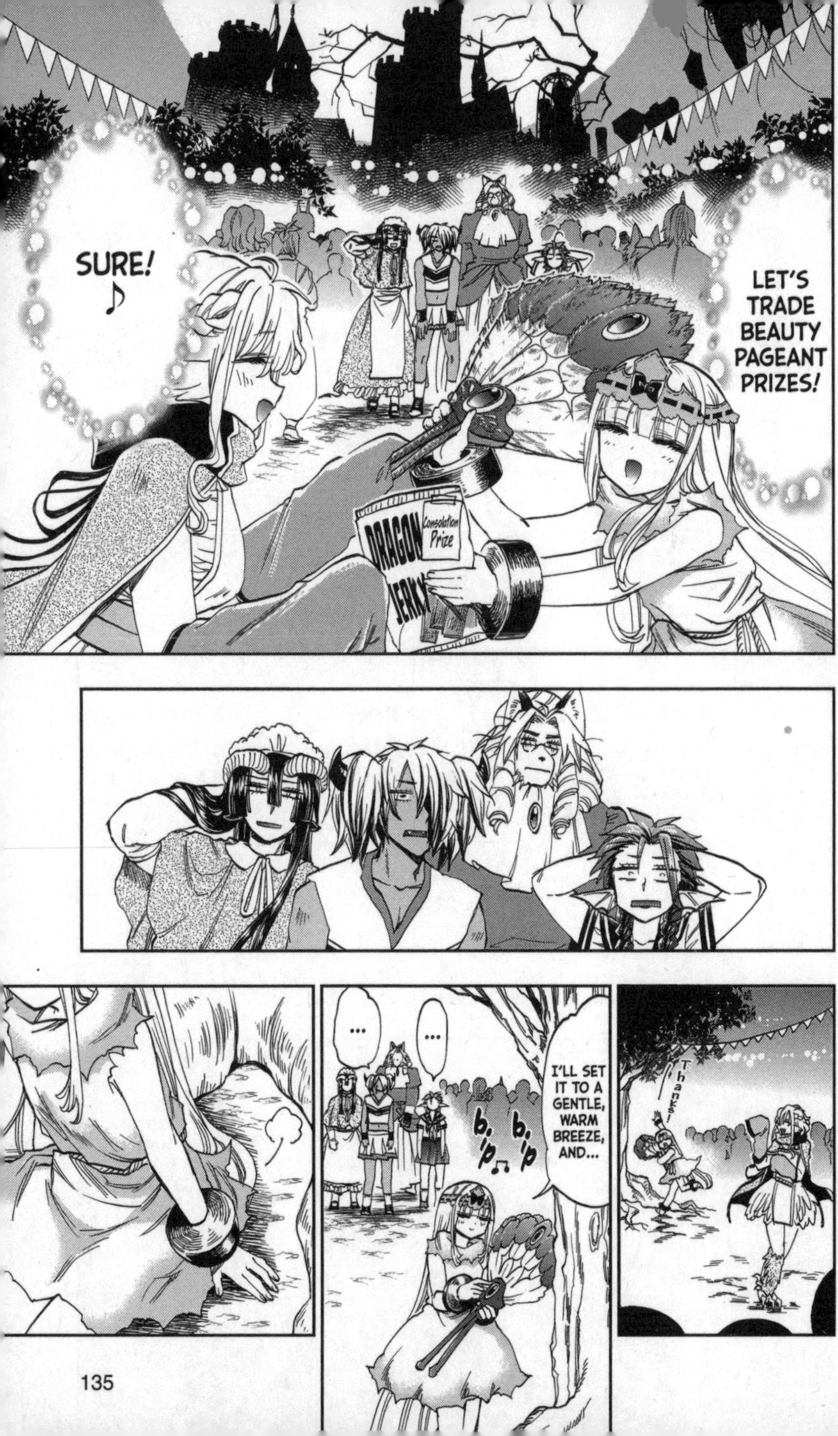
LET'S TRADE BEAUTY PAGEANT PRIZES!
SURE! ♪
DRAGON JERKY
Consolation Prize
Thanks!
I'LL SET IT TO A GENTLE, WARM BREEZE, AND...
bip bip
...
...

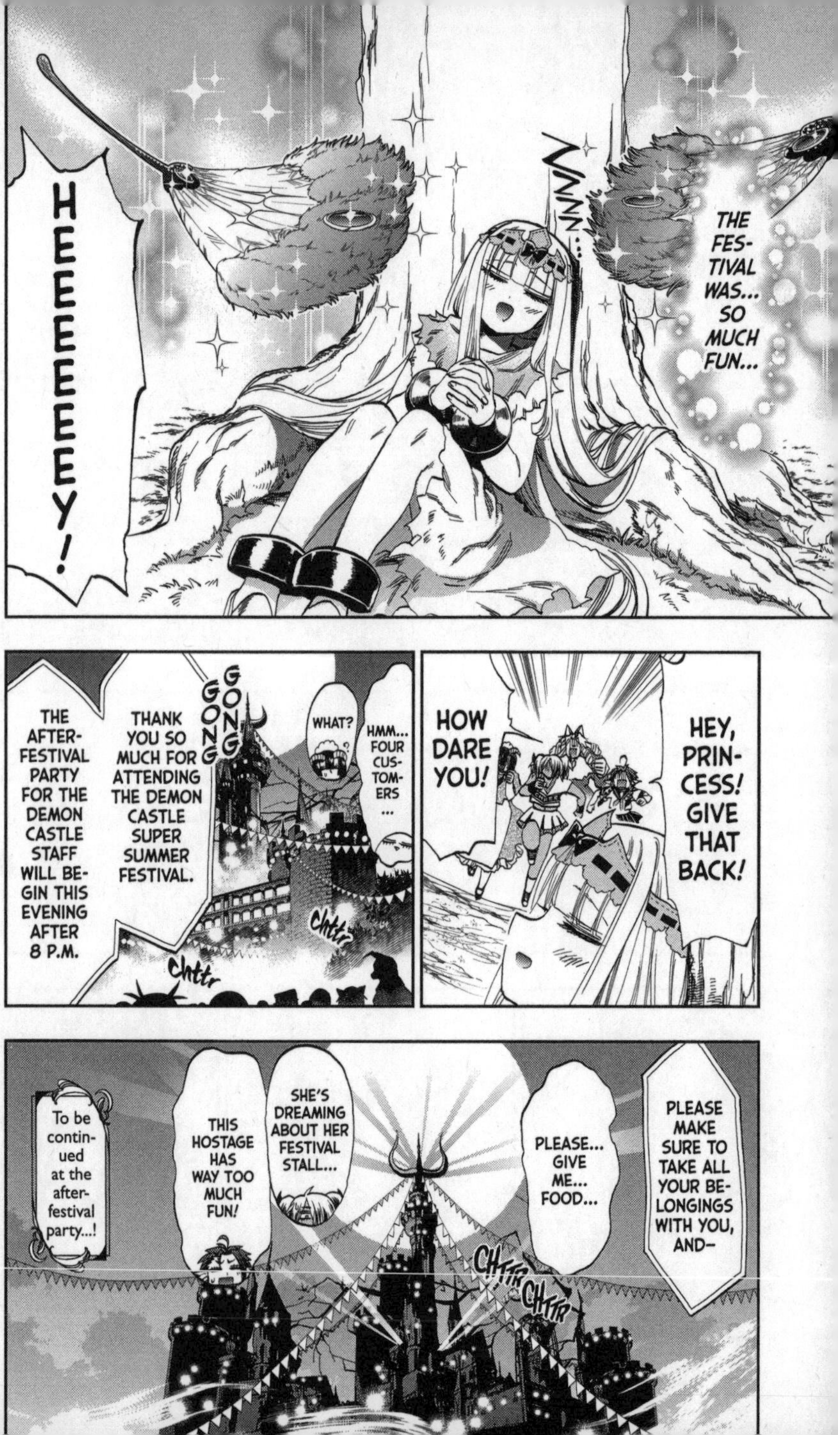
THE FES-TIVAL WAS... SO MUCH FUN...
ZZZ...
HEEEEEEEEY!
HEY, PRIN-CESS! GIVE THAT BACK!
HOW DARE YOU!
HMM... FOUR CUS-TOM-ERS ...
WHAT?
THANK YOU SO MUCH FOR ATTENDING THE DEMON CASTLE SUPER SUMMER FESTIVAL.
GONG GONG
THE AFTER-FESTIVAL PARTY FOR THE DEMON CASTLE STAFF WILL BE-GIN THIS EVENING AFTER 8 P.M.
Chttr
Chttr
PLEASE MAKE SURE TO TAKE ALL YOUR BE-LONGINGS WITH YOU, AND—
PLEASE... GIVE ME... FOOD...
CHTTR CHTTR
SHE'S DREAMING ABOUT HER FESTIVAL STALL...
THIS HOSTAGE HAS WAY TOO MUCH FUN!
To be contin-ued at the after-festival party...!

Mysterious Beauties

Mysteriousness: ☆☆☆☆☆☆☆☆☆☆
Manliness: ☆☆☆☆☆☆☆

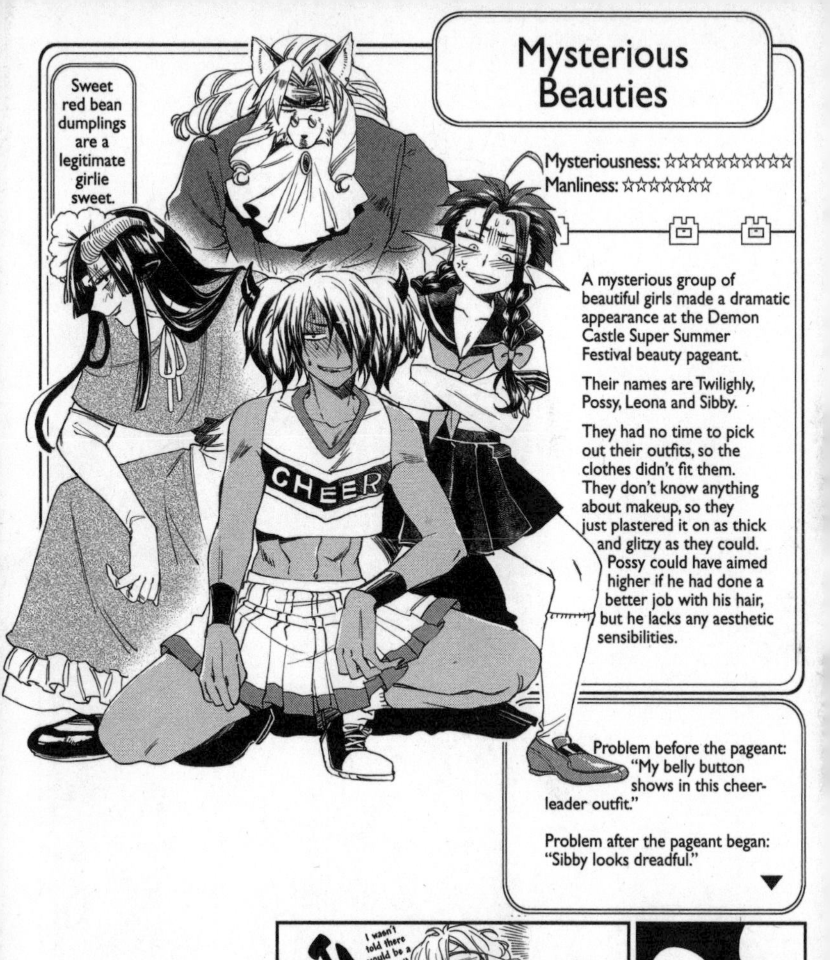

Sweet red bean dumplings are a legitimate girlie sweet.
CHEER

A mysterious group of beautiful girls made a dramatic appearance at the Demon Castle Super Summer Festival beauty pageant.

Their names are Twilighly, Possy, Leona and Sibby.

They had no time to pick out their outfits, so the clothes didn't fit them. They don't know anything about makeup, so they just plastered it on as thick and glitzy as they could. Possy could have aimed higher if he had done a better job with his hair, but he lacks any aesthetic sensibilities.

Problem before the pageant: "My belly button shows in this cheerleader outfit."

Problem after the pageant began: "Sibby looks dreadful."

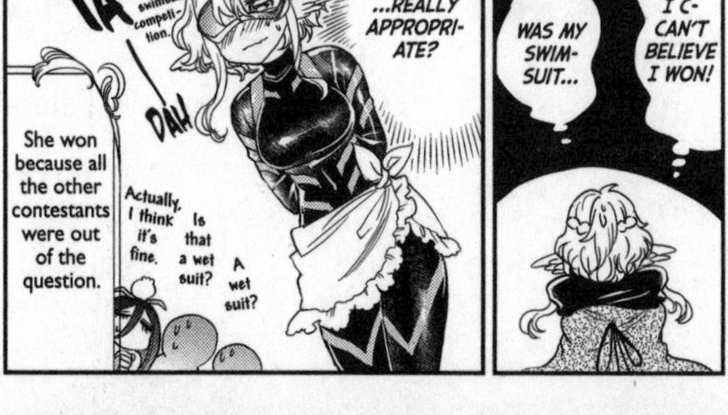

I C-CAN'T BELIEVE I WON!
WAS MY SWIM-SUIT...
...REALLY APPROPRI-ATE?
TA
I wasn't told there would be a swimsuit competition.
DAH
She won because all the other contestants were out of the question.
A wet suit?
Is that a wet suit?
Actually, I think it's fine.

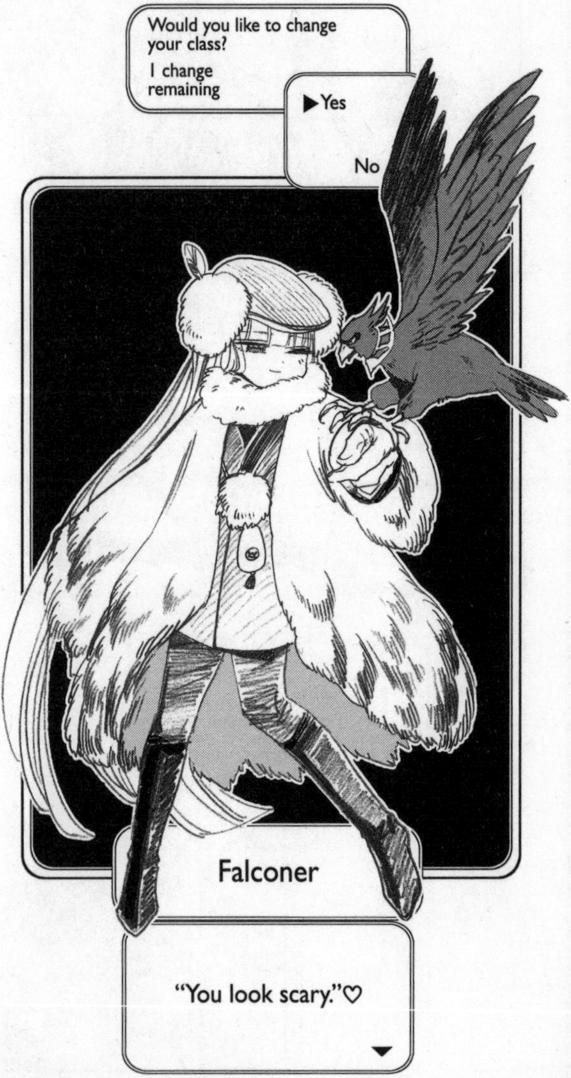
Would you like to change your class?
1 change remaining
▶Yes
No
Falconer
"You look scary."♡

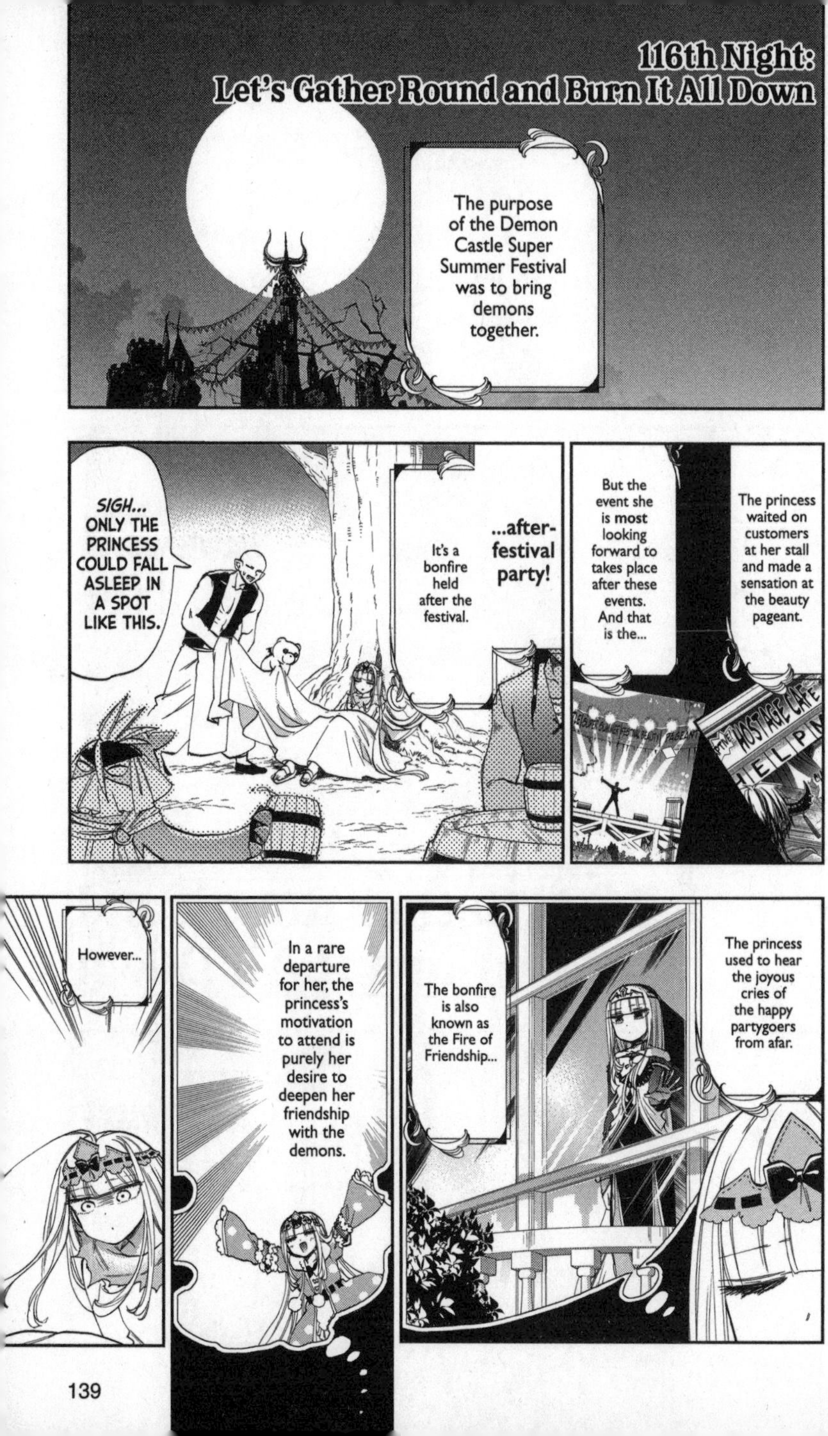

116th Night:
Let's Gather Round and Burn It All Down
The purpose of the Demon Castle Super Summer Festival was to bring demons together.
The princess waited on customers at her stall and made a sensation at the beauty pageant.
HOSTAGE CAFE
But the event she is most looking forward to takes place after these events. And that is the...
...after-festival party!
It's a bonfire held after the festival.
SIGH... ONLY THE PRINCESS COULD FALL ASLEEP IN A SPOT LIKE THIS.
The princess used to hear the joyous cries of the happy partygoers from afar.
The bonfire is also known as the Fire of Friendship...
In a rare departure for her, the princess's motivation to attend is purely her desire to deepen her friendship with the demons.
However...

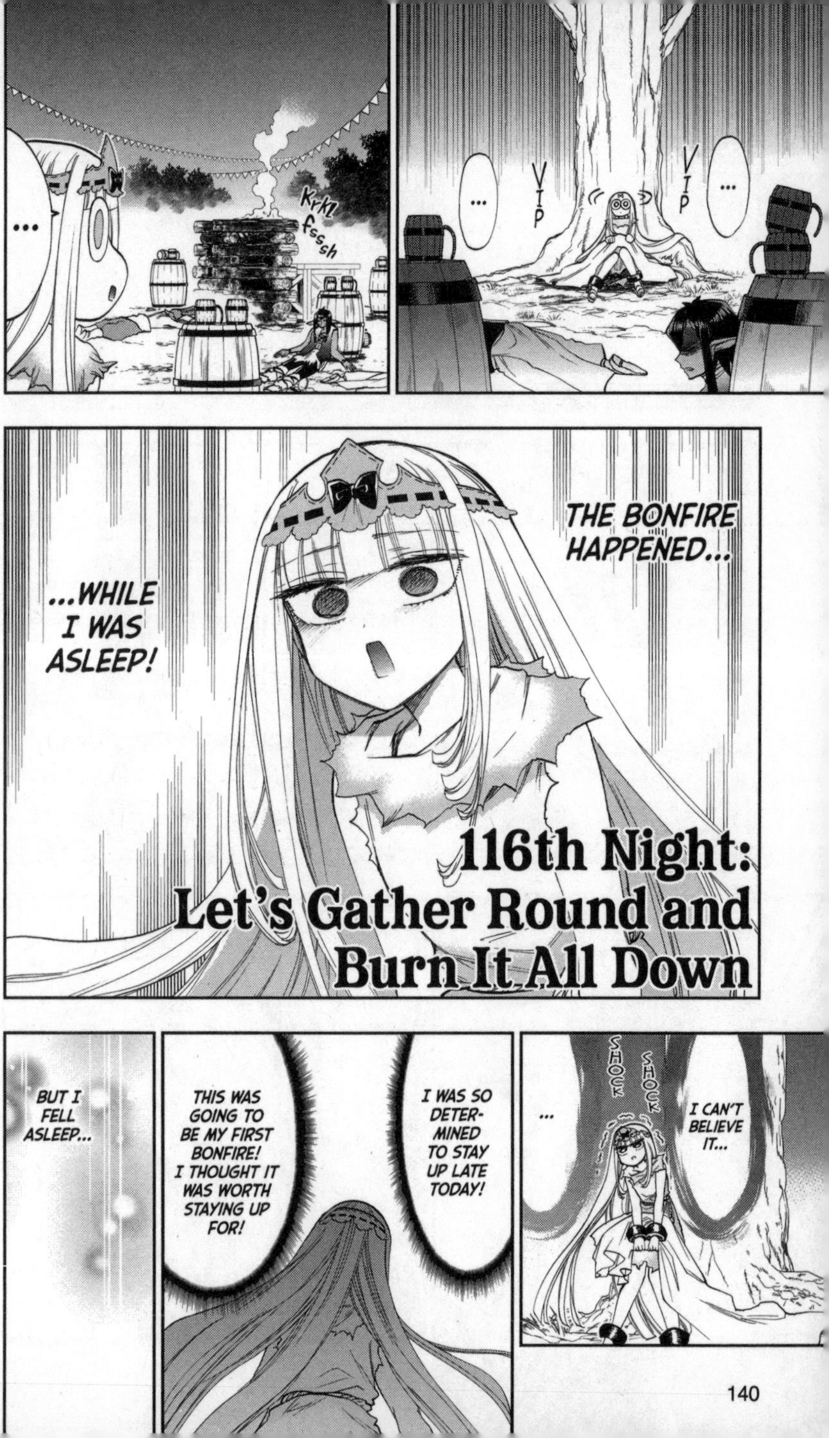

...
VIP
VIP
...
Krkl fsssh
...
THE BONFIRE HAPPENED...
...WHILE I WAS ASLEEP!
116th Night: Let's Gather Round and Burn It All Down
SHOCK
SHOCK
I CAN'T BELIEVE IT...
...
I WAS SO DETERMINED TO STAY UP LATE TODAY!
THIS WAS GOING TO BE MY FIRST BONFIRE! I THOUGHT IT WAS WORTH STAYING UP FOR!
BUT I FELL ASLEEP...

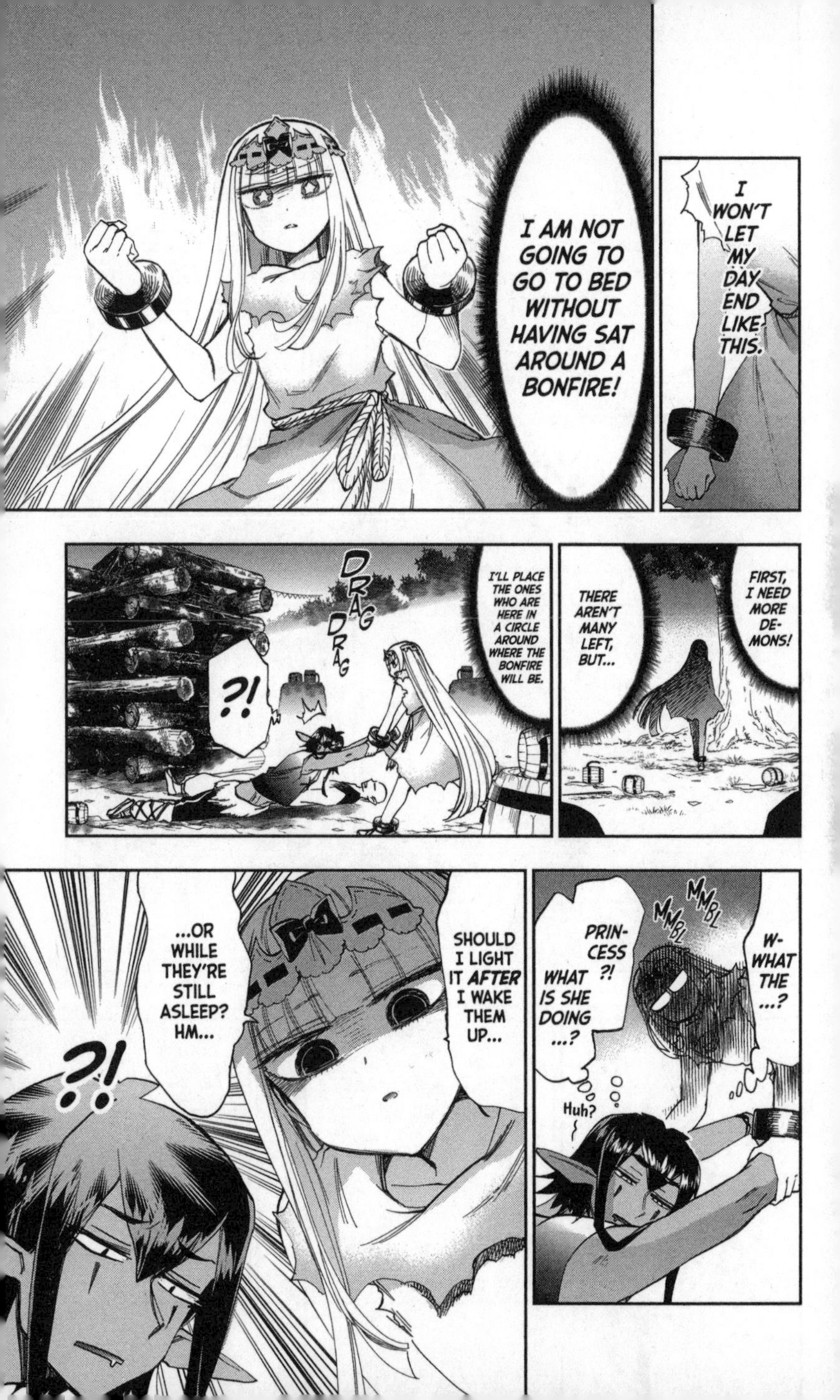
I WON'T LET MY DAY END LIKE THIS.
I AM NOT GOING TO GO TO BED WITHOUT HAVING SAT AROUND A BONFIRE!
FIRST, I NEED MORE DE-MONS!
THERE AREN'T MANY LEFT, BUT...
I'LL PLACE THE ONES WHO ARE HERE IN A CIRCLE AROUND WHERE THE BONFIRE WILL BE.
DRAG DRAG
?!
MMBL MMBL
W-WHAT THE ...?
PRIN-CESS ?!
WHAT IS SHE DOING ...?
Huh?
SHOULD I LIGHT IT *AFTER* I WAKE THEM UP...
...OR WHILE THEY'RE STILL ASLEEP? HM...
?!

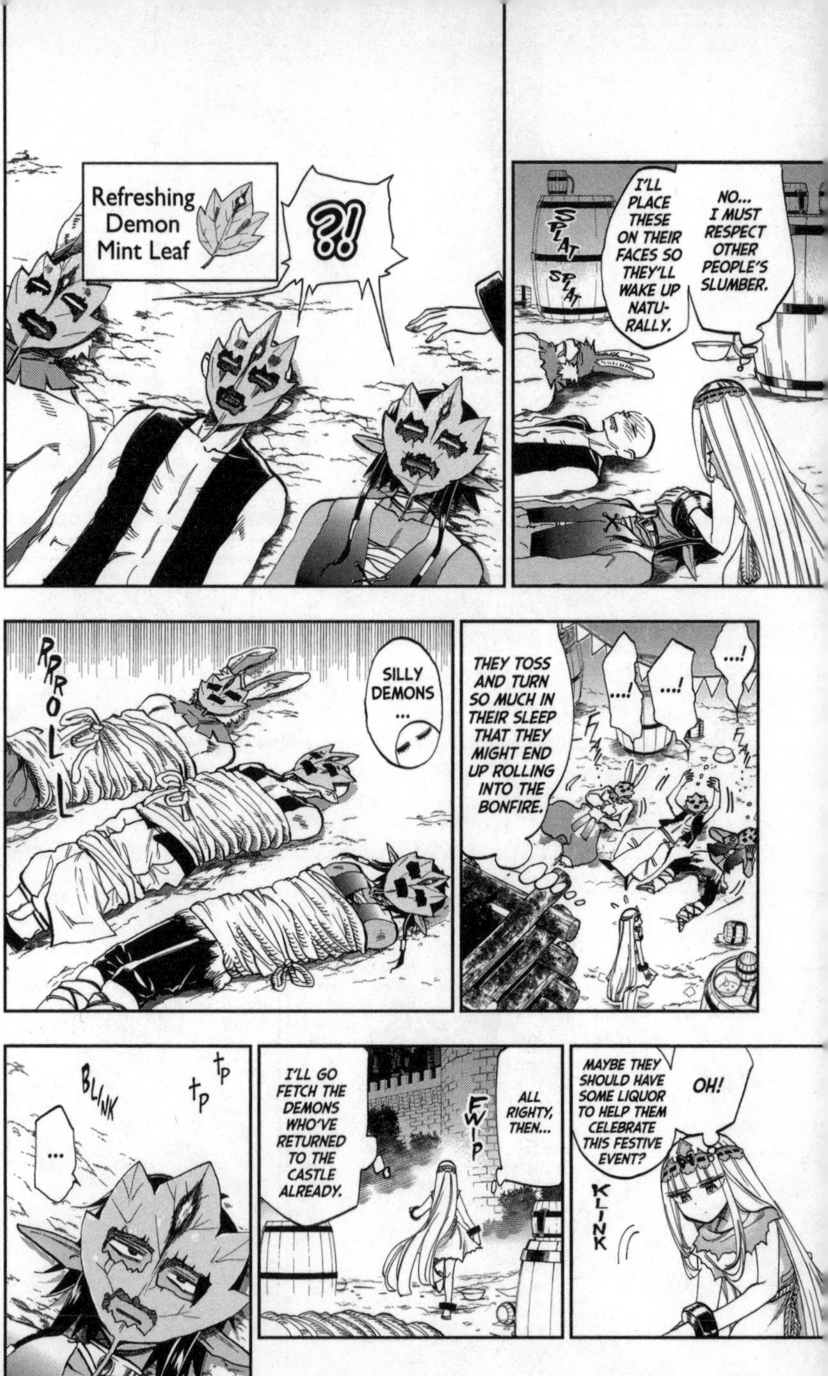

NO... I MUST RESPECT OTHER PEOPLE'S SLUMBER.
I'LL PLACE THESE ON THEIR FACES SO THEY'LL WAKE UP NATU-RALLY.
SPLAT
SPLAT
Refreshing Demon Mint Leaf
?!
...!
...!
...!
FLAIL
FLAIL
THEY TOSS AND TURN SO MUCH IN THEIR SLEEP THAT THEY MIGHT END UP ROLLING INTO THE BONFIRE.
SILLY DEMONS...
RRROLL
OH!
MAYBE THEY SHOULD HAVE SOME LIQUOR TO HELP THEM CELEBRATE THIS FESTIVE EVENT?
KLINK
ALL RIGHTY, THEN...
FWIP
I'LL GO FETCH THE DEMONS WHO'VE RETURNED TO THE CASTLE ALREADY.
tp
tp
BLINK
...

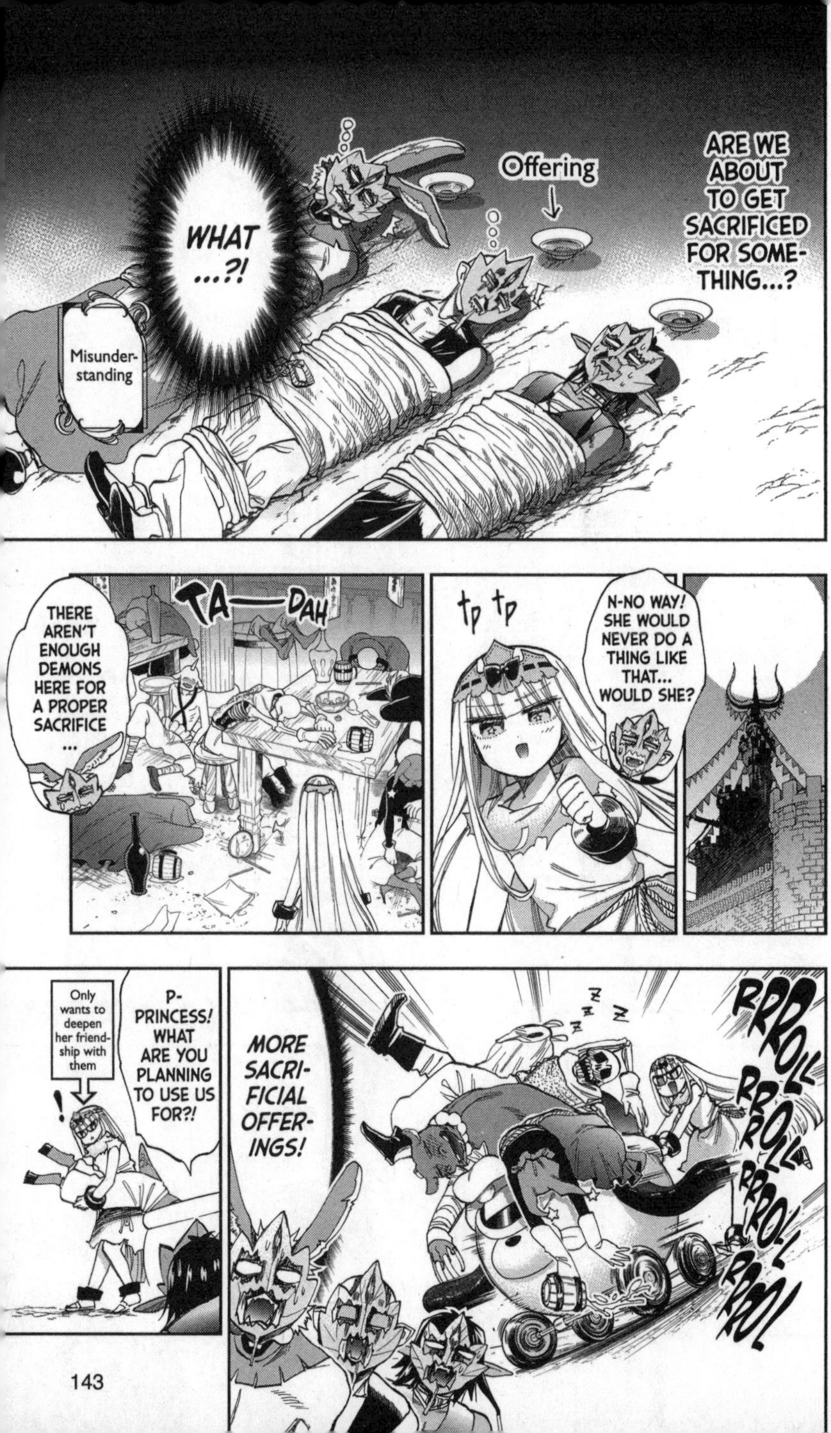

ARE WE ABOUT TO GET SACRIFICED FOR SOME-THING...?
Offering
WHAT ...?!
Misunder-standing
tp tp
N-NO WAY! SHE WOULD NEVER DO A THING LIKE THAT... WOULD SHE?
TA—DAH
THERE AREN'T ENOUGH DEMONS HERE FOR A PROPER SACRIFICE ...
RRROLL RRROLL RRROLL RRROLL RRROLL!
Z Z Z
MORE SACRI-FICIAL OFFER-INGS!
P-PRINCESS! WHAT ARE YOU PLANNING TO USE US FOR?!
Only wants to deepen her friend-ship with them
!

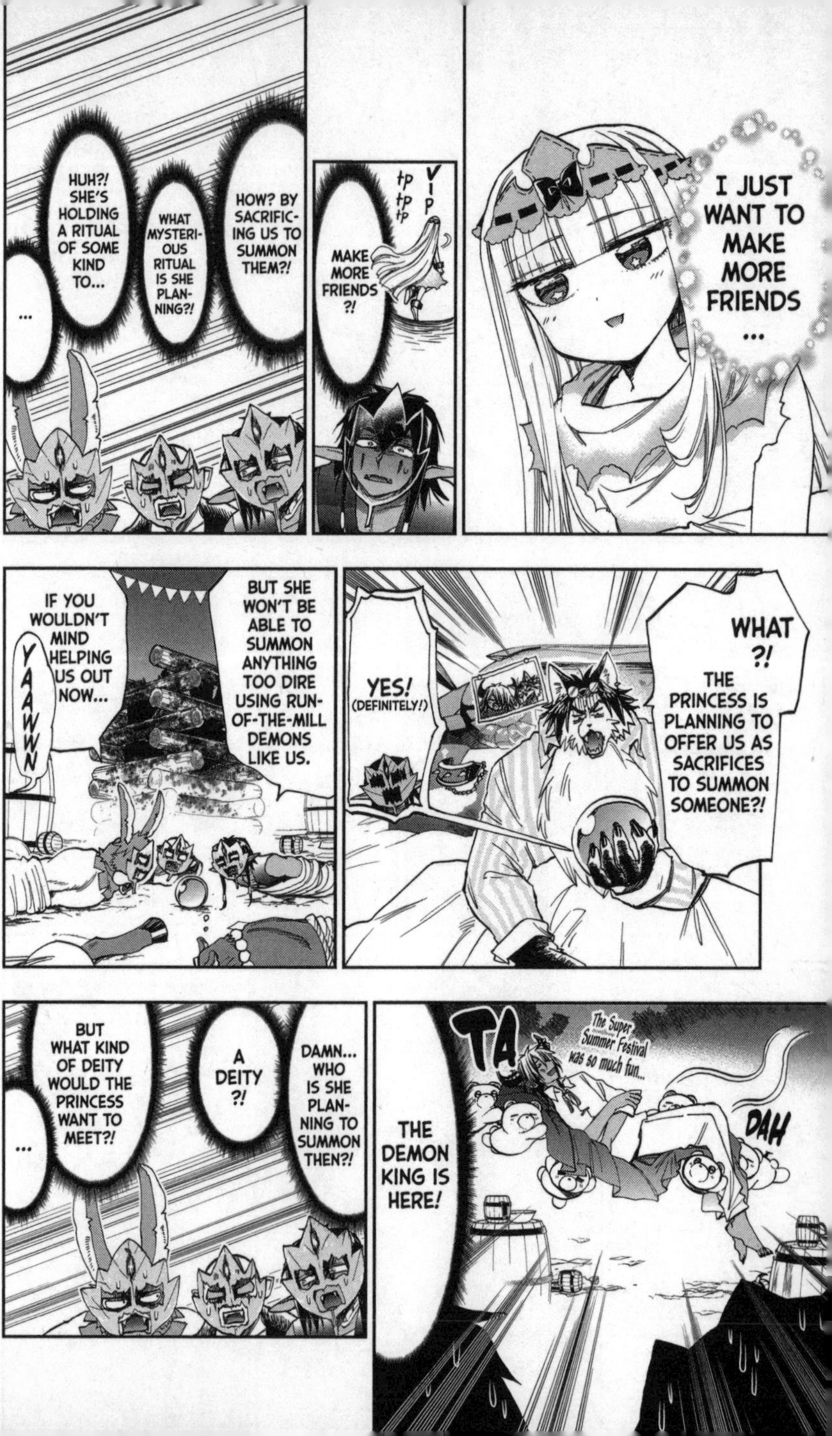
I JUST WANT TO MAKE MORE FRIENDS ...
VIP
tp tp tp
MAKE MORE FRIENDS ?!
HOW? BY SACRIFICING US TO SUMMON THEM?!
WHAT MYSTERIOUS RITUAL IS SHE PLANNING?!
HUH?! SHE'S HOLDING A RITUAL OF SOME KIND TO...
...
WHAT ?!
THE PRINCESS IS PLANNING TO OFFER US AS SACRIFICES TO SUMMON SOMEONE?!
YES! (DEFINITELY!)
BUT SHE WON'T BE ABLE TO SUMMON ANYTHING TOO DIRE USING RUN-OF-THE-MILL DEMONS LIKE US.
IF YOU WOULDN'T MIND HELPING US OUT NOW...
YAAWWN
TA
The Super Summer Festival was so much fun...
DAH
THE DEMON KING IS HERE!
DAMN... WHO IS SHE PLANNING TO SUMMON THEN?!
A DEITY ?!
BUT WHAT KIND OF DEITY WOULD THE PRINCESS WANT TO MEET?!
...

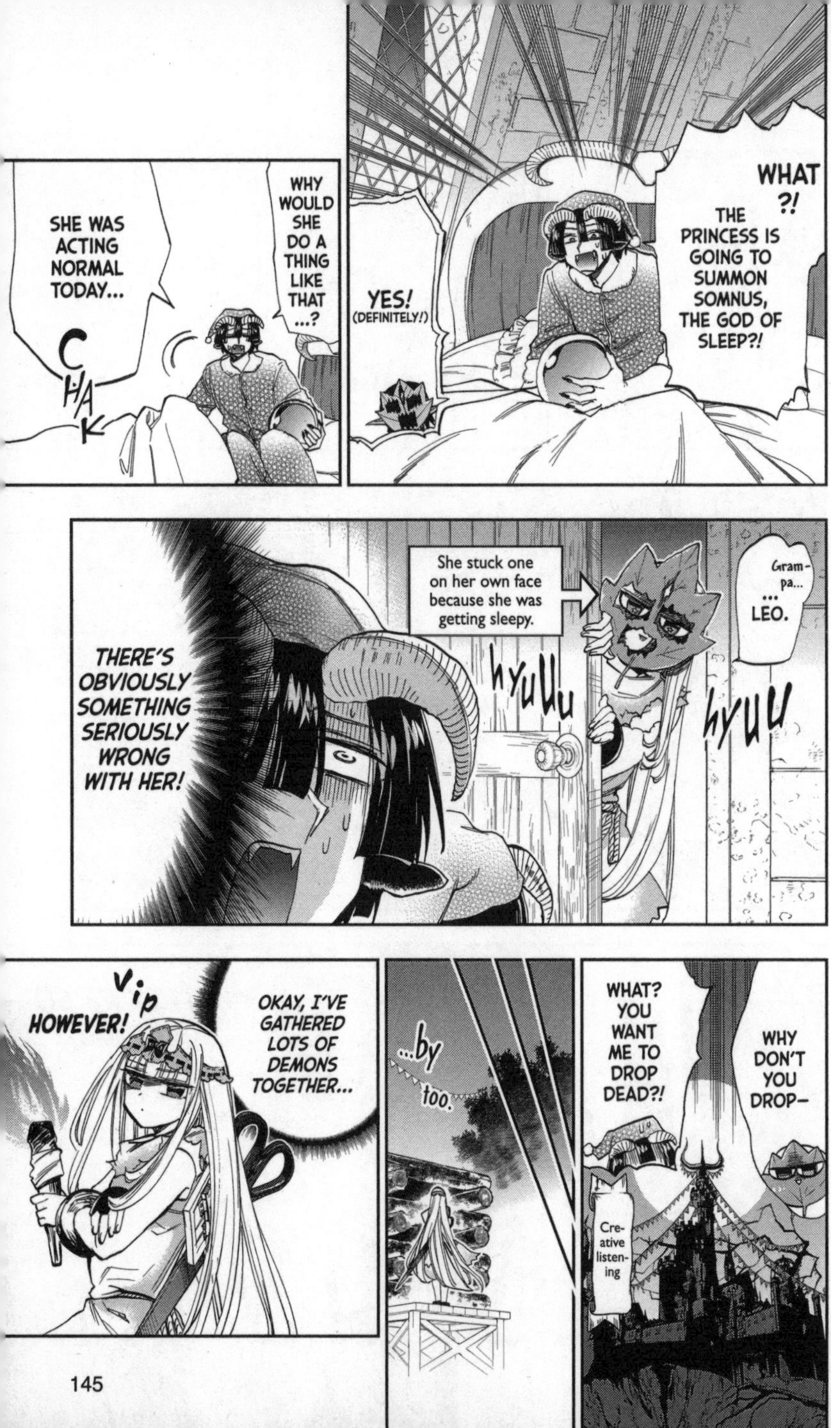
WHAT ?!
THE PRINCESS IS GOING TO SUMMON SOMNUS, THE GOD OF SLEEP?!
YES! (DEFINITELY!)
WHY WOULD SHE DO A THING LIKE THAT ...?
SHE WAS ACTING NORMAL TODAY...
CHAK
Gram-pa... ... LEO.
hyuU
She stuck one on her own face because she was getting sleepy.
hyuUu
THERE'S OBVIOUSLY SOMETHING SERIOUSLY WRONG WITH HER!
WHY DON'T YOU DROP—
WHAT? YOU WANT ME TO DROP DEAD?!
Cre-ative listen-ing
...by too.
OKAY, I'VE GATHERED LOTS OF DEMONS TOGETHER...
vip
HOWEVER!

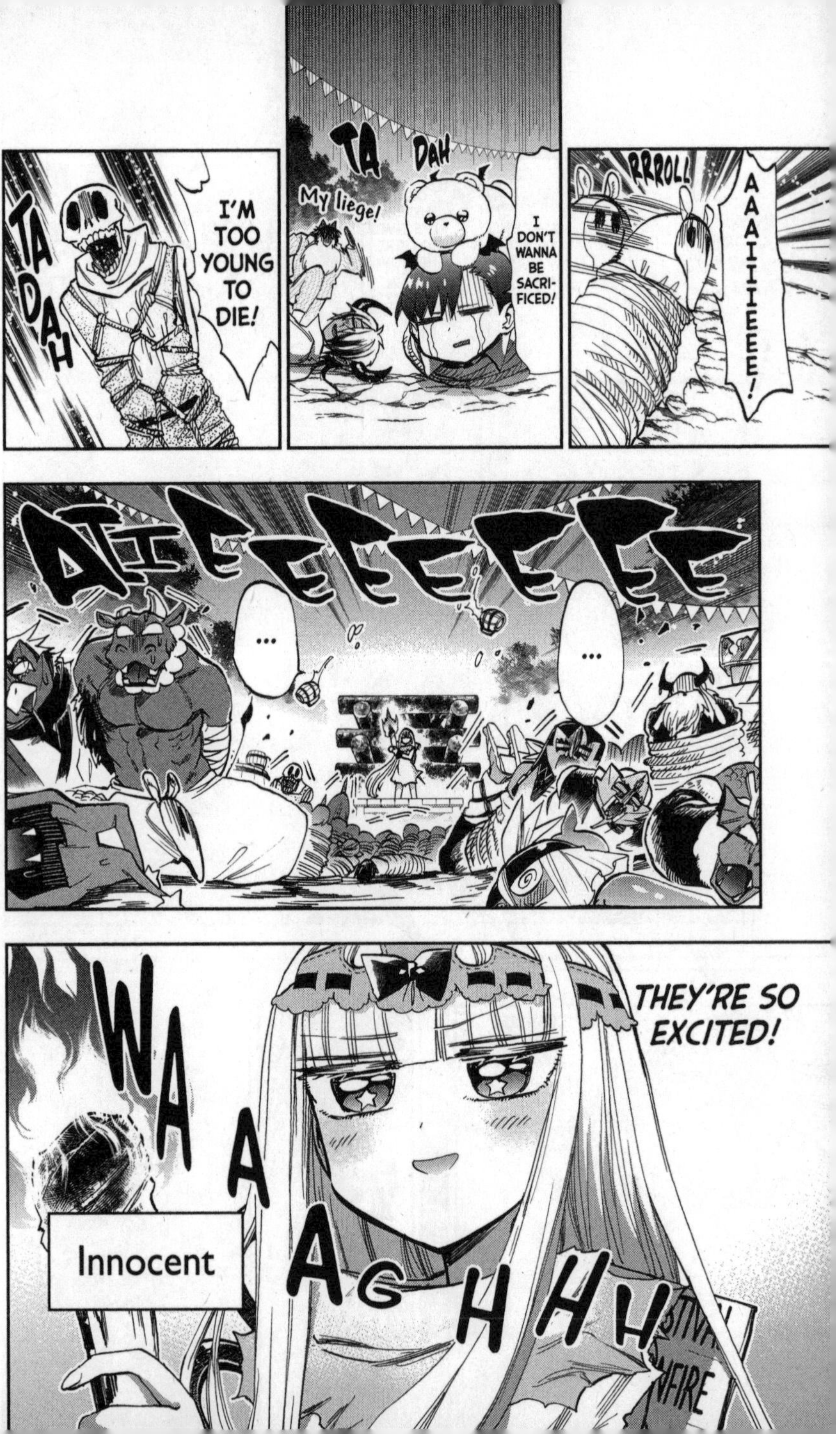
RRROLL
AAAIIIEEEE!
TA DAH
My liege!
I DON'T WANNA BE SACRIFICED!
TA DAH
I'M TOO YOUNG TO DIE!
AIIEEEEEEE
...
...
THEY'RE SO EXCITED!
WAAAGHHH
Innocent

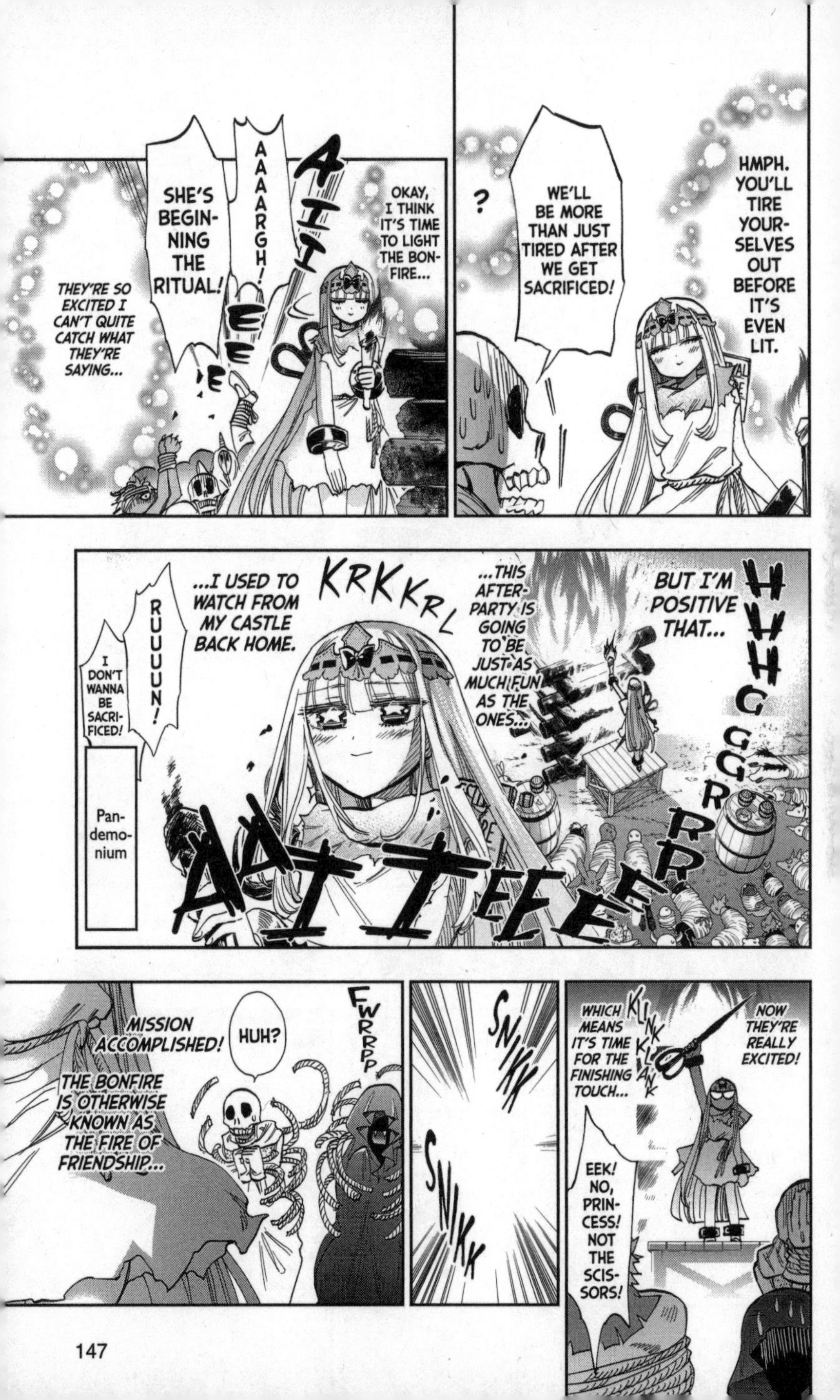
HMPH. YOU'LL TIRE YOURSELVES OUT BEFORE IT'S EVEN LIT.
?
WE'LL BE MORE THAN JUST TIRED AFTER WE GET SACRIFICED!
OKAY, I THINK IT'S TIME TO LIGHT THE BONFIRE...
AAAAARGH!
AIIIEEE
SHE'S BEGINNING THE RITUAL!
THEY'RE SO EXCITED I CAN'T QUITE CATCH WHAT THEY'RE SAYING...
BUT I'M POSITIVE THAT...
HHHHGGGRRRR
...THIS AFTER-PARTY IS GOING TO BE JUST AS MUCH FUN AS THE ONES...
KRKKRL
...I USED TO WATCH FROM MY CASTLE BACK HOME.
RUUUUUN!
I DON'T WANNA BE SACRIFICED!
Pandemonium
AAIIEEE
NOW THEY'RE REALLY EXCITED!
WHICH MEANS IT'S TIME FOR THE FINISHING TOUCH...
KLINK KLANK
EEK! NO, PRINCESS! NOT THE SCISSORS!
SNIKK
SNIKK
FWRRPP
HUH?
MISSION ACCOMPLISHED!
THE BONFIRE IS OTHERWISE KNOWN AS THE FIRE OF FRIENDSHIP...

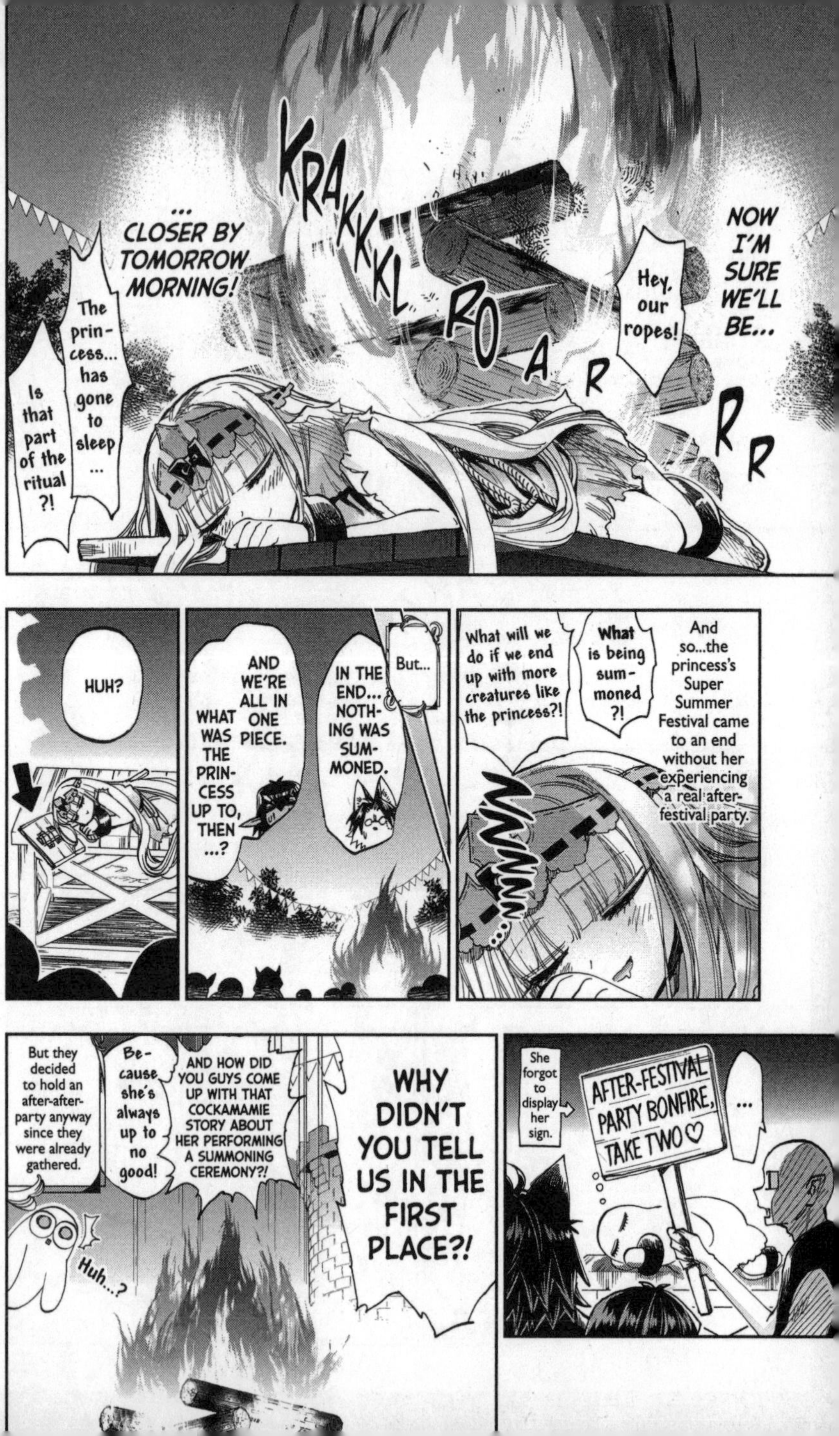
NOW I'M SURE WE'LL BE...
Hey, our ropes!
KRAKKKL
ROARRR
...CLOSER BY TOMORROW MORNING!
The princess... has gone to sleep...
Is that part of the ritual?!
And so...the princess's Super Summer Festival came to an end without her experiencing a real after-festival party.
What is being summoned?!
What will we do if we end up with more creatures like the princess?!
But...
IN THE END... NOTHING WAS SUMMONED.
AND WE'RE ALL IN ONE PIECE.
WHAT WAS THE PRINCESS UP TO, THEN...?
HUH?
She forgot to display her sign.
AFTER-FESTIVAL PARTY BONFIRE, TAKE TWO ♡
...
WHY DIDN'T YOU TELL US IN THE FIRST PLACE?!
AND HOW DID YOU GUYS COME UP WITH THAT COCKAMAMIE STORY ABOUT HER PERFORMING A SUMMONING CEREMONY?!
Because she's always up to no good!
But they decided to hold an after-after-party anyway since they were already gathered.
Huh...?

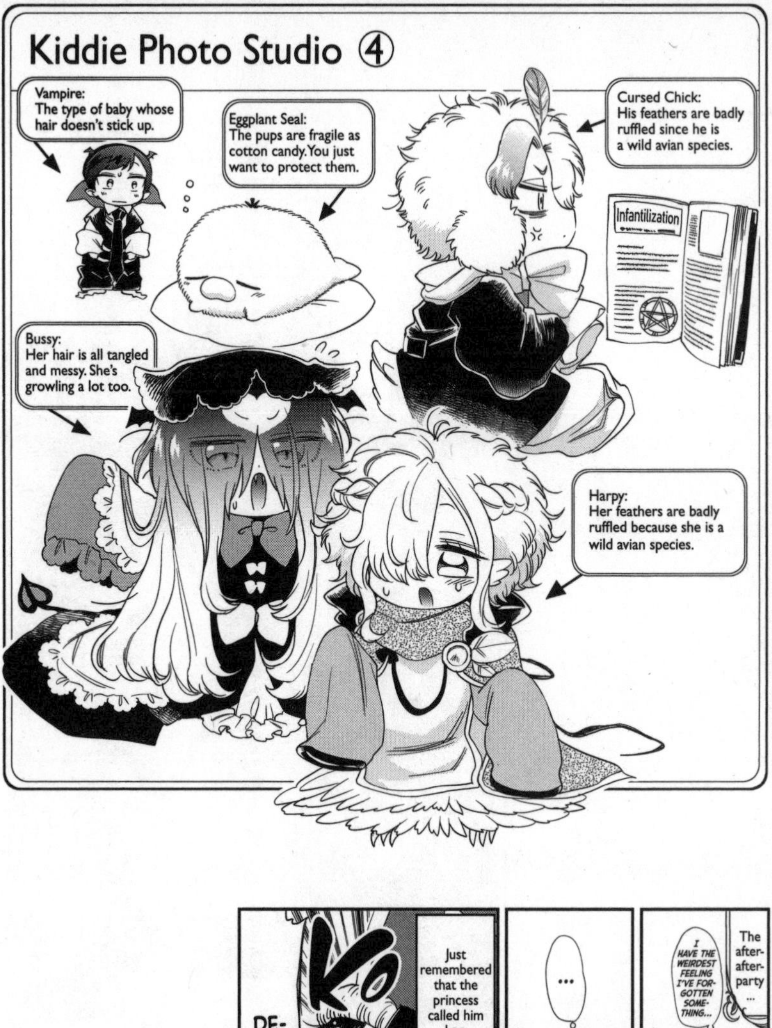
Kiddie Photo Studio ④
Cursed Chick: His feathers are badly ruffled since he is a wild avian species.
Infantilization
Eggplant Seal: The pups are fragile as cotton candy. You just want to protect them.
Vampire: The type of baby whose hair doesn't stick up.
Harpy: Her feathers are badly ruffled because she is a wild avian species.
Bussy: Her hair is all tangled and messy. She's growling a lot too.

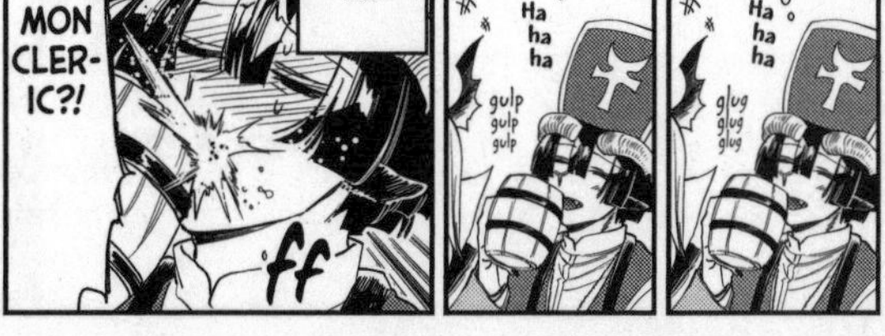
The after-after-party ...
I HAVE THE WEIRDEST FEELING I'VE FORGOTTEN SOMETHING...
Ha ha ha
glug glug glug
...
Ha ha ha
gulp gulp gulp
Just remembered that the princess called him Leo.
KO
DEMON CLERIC?!
ff

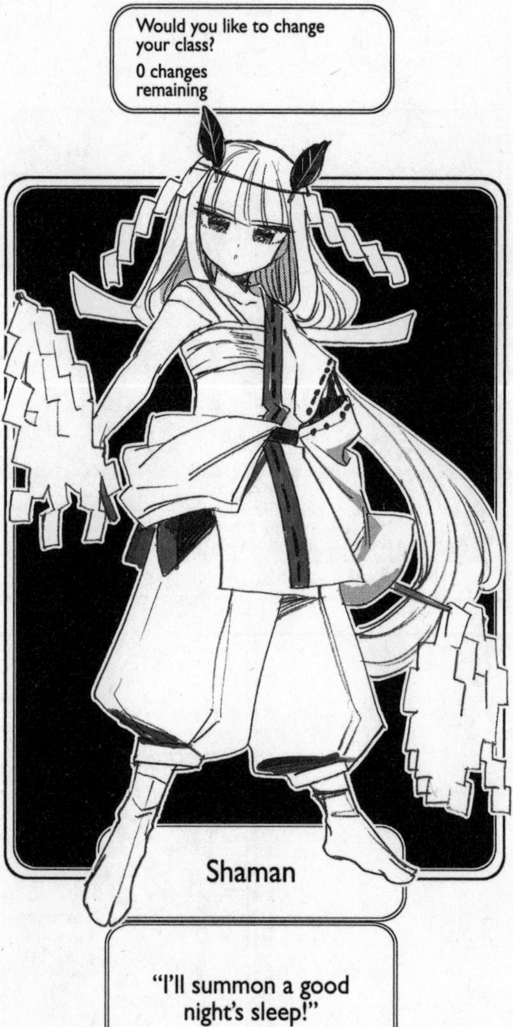
Would you like to change your class?
0 changes remaining
Shaman
"I'll summon a good night's sleep!"

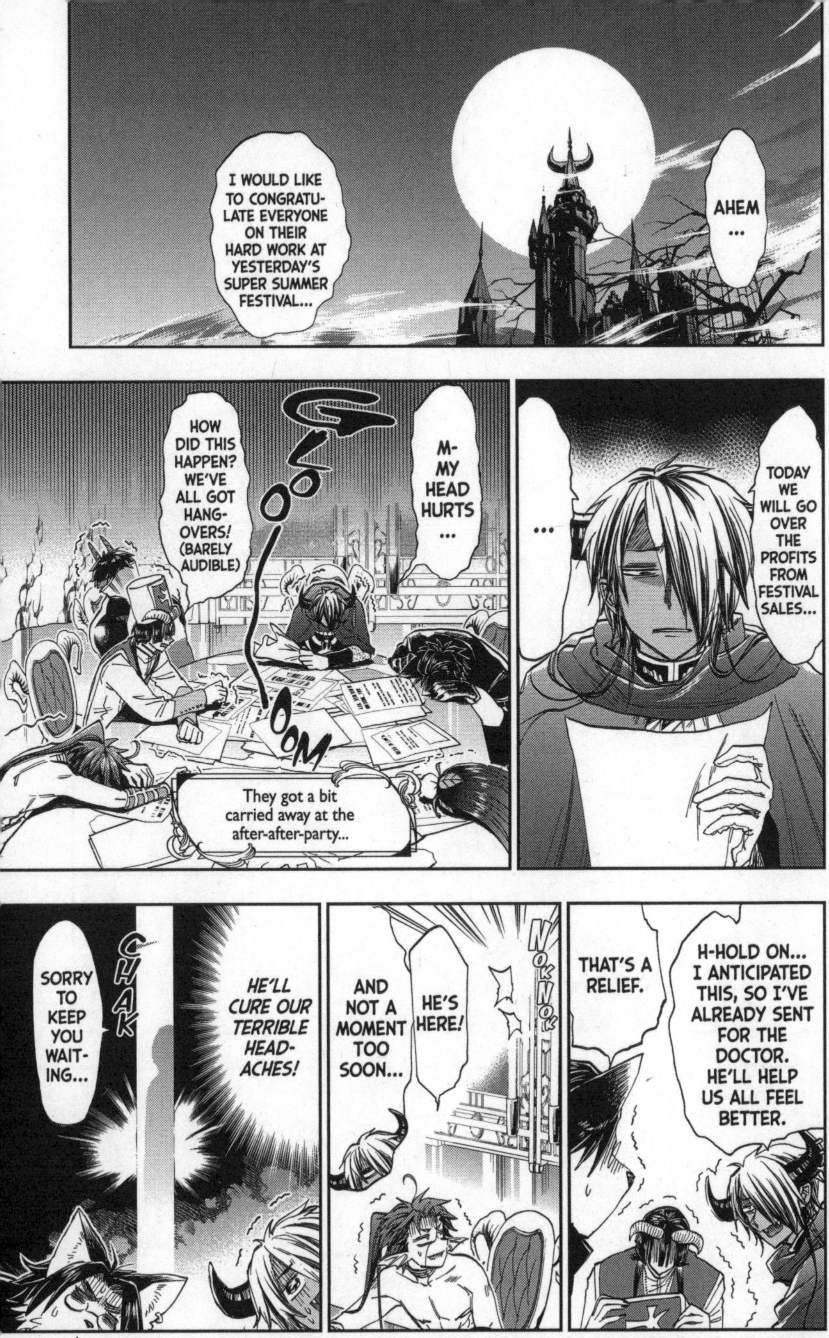
AHEM ...
I WOULD LIKE TO CONGRATU-LATE EVERYONE ON THEIR HARD WORK AT YESTERDAY'S SUPER SUMMER FESTIVAL...
TODAY WE WILL GO OVER THE PROFITS FROM FESTIVAL SALES...
...
M-MY HEAD HURTS ...
GLOOM
HOW DID THIS HAPPEN? WE'VE ALL GOT HANG-OVERS! (BARELY AUDIBLE)
They got a bit carried away at the after-after-party...
H-HOLD ON... I ANTICIPATED THIS, SO I'VE ALREADY SENT FOR THE DOCTOR. HE'LL HELP US ALL FEEL BETTER.
THAT'S A RELIEF.
NOKNOK
HE'S HERE!
AND NOT A MOMENT TOO SOON...
HE'LL CURE OUR TERRIBLE HEAD-ACHES!
CHAK
SORRY TO KEEP YOU WAIT-ING...

117th Night: It's Your Own Fault for Drinking Too Much

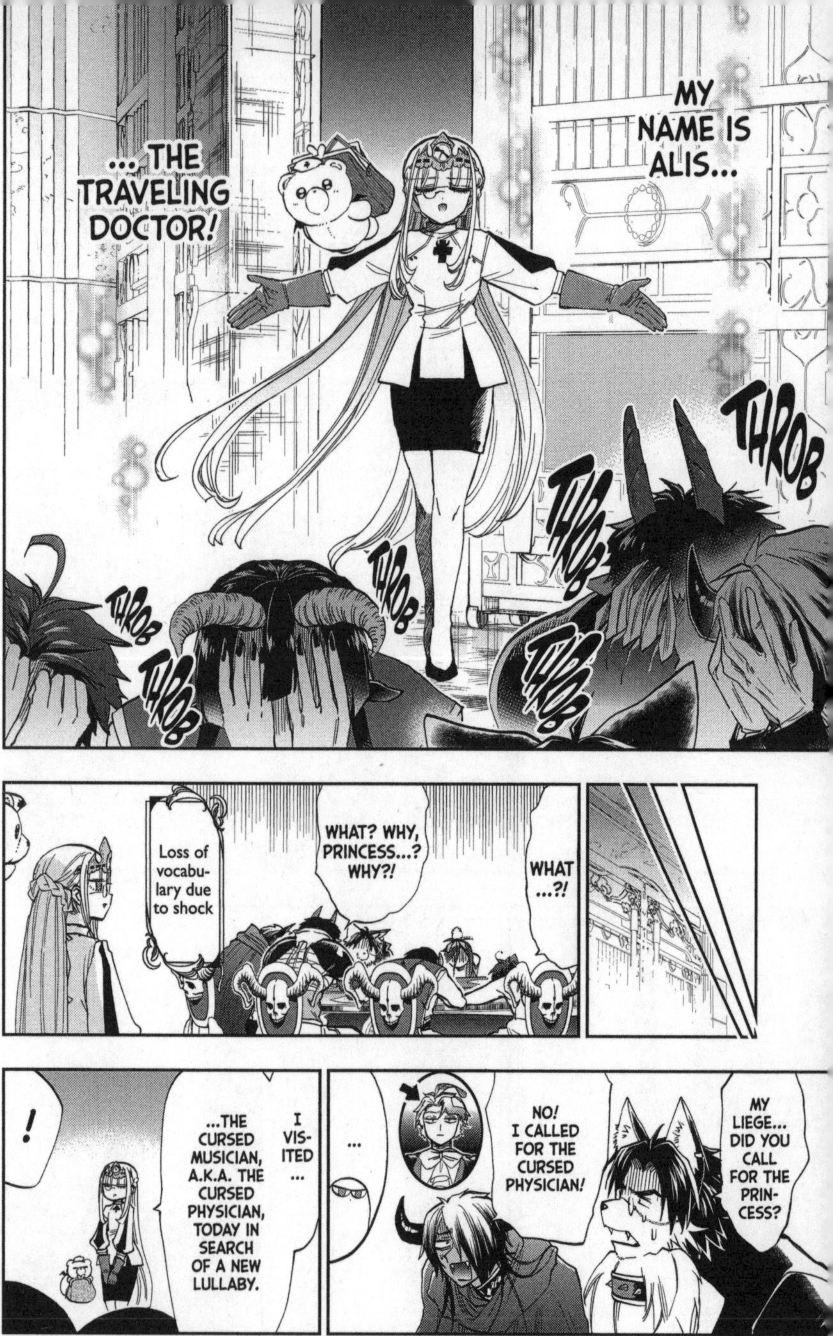
MY NAME IS ALIS...
... THE TRAVELING DOCTOR!
THROB
THROB
THROB
THROB
THROB
THROB
THROB
WHAT ...?!
WHAT? WHY, PRINCESS...? WHY?!
Loss of vocabulary due to shock
MY LIEGE... DID YOU CALL FOR THE PRINCESS?
NO! I CALLED FOR THE CURSED PHYSICIAN!
...
I VISITED ...
...THE CURSED MUSICIAN, A.K.A. THE CURSED PHYSICIAN, TODAY IN SEARCH OF A NEW LULLABY.
!

117th Night:
It's Your Own Fault for Drinking Too Much

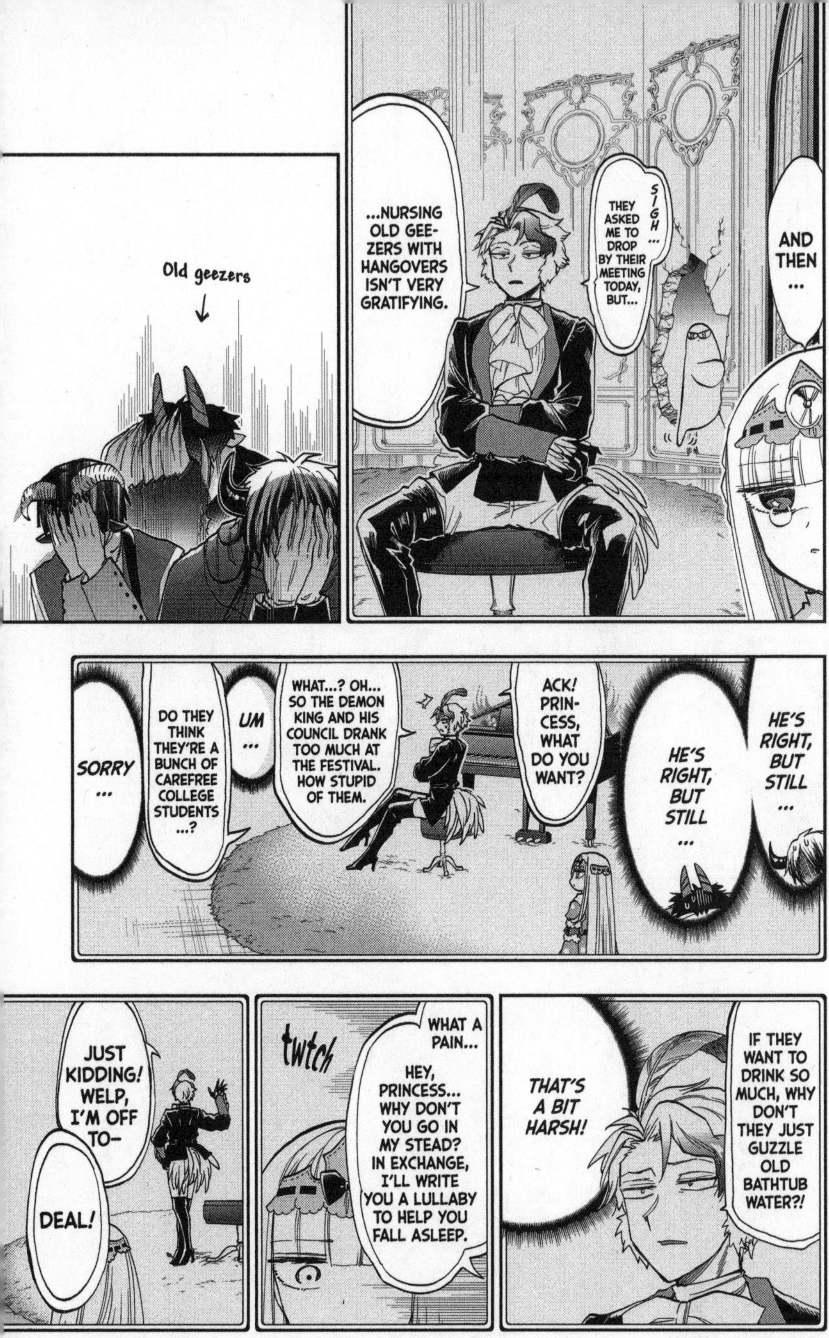
AND THEN...
SIGH...
THEY ASKED ME TO DROP BY THEIR MEETING TODAY, BUT...
...NURSING OLD GEE-ZERS WITH HANGOVERS ISN'T VERY GRATIFYING.
Old geezers
HE'S RIGHT, BUT STILL...
HE'S RIGHT, BUT STILL...
ACK! PRIN-CESS, WHAT DO YOU WANT?
WHAT...? OH... SO THE DEMON KING AND HIS COUNCIL DRANK TOO MUCH AT THE FESTIVAL. HOW STUPID OF THEM.
UM...
DO THEY THINK THEY'RE A BUNCH OF CAREFREE COLLEGE STUDENTS...?
SORRY...
IF THEY WANT TO DRINK SO MUCH, WHY DON'T THEY JUST GUZZLE OLD BATHTUB WATER?!
THAT'S A BIT HARSH!
WHAT A PAIN...
HEY, PRINCESS... WHY DON'T YOU GO IN MY STEAD? IN EXCHANGE, I'LL WRITE YOU A LULLABY TO HELP YOU FALL ASLEEP.
twtch
JUST KIDDING! WELP, I'M OFF TO–
DEAL!

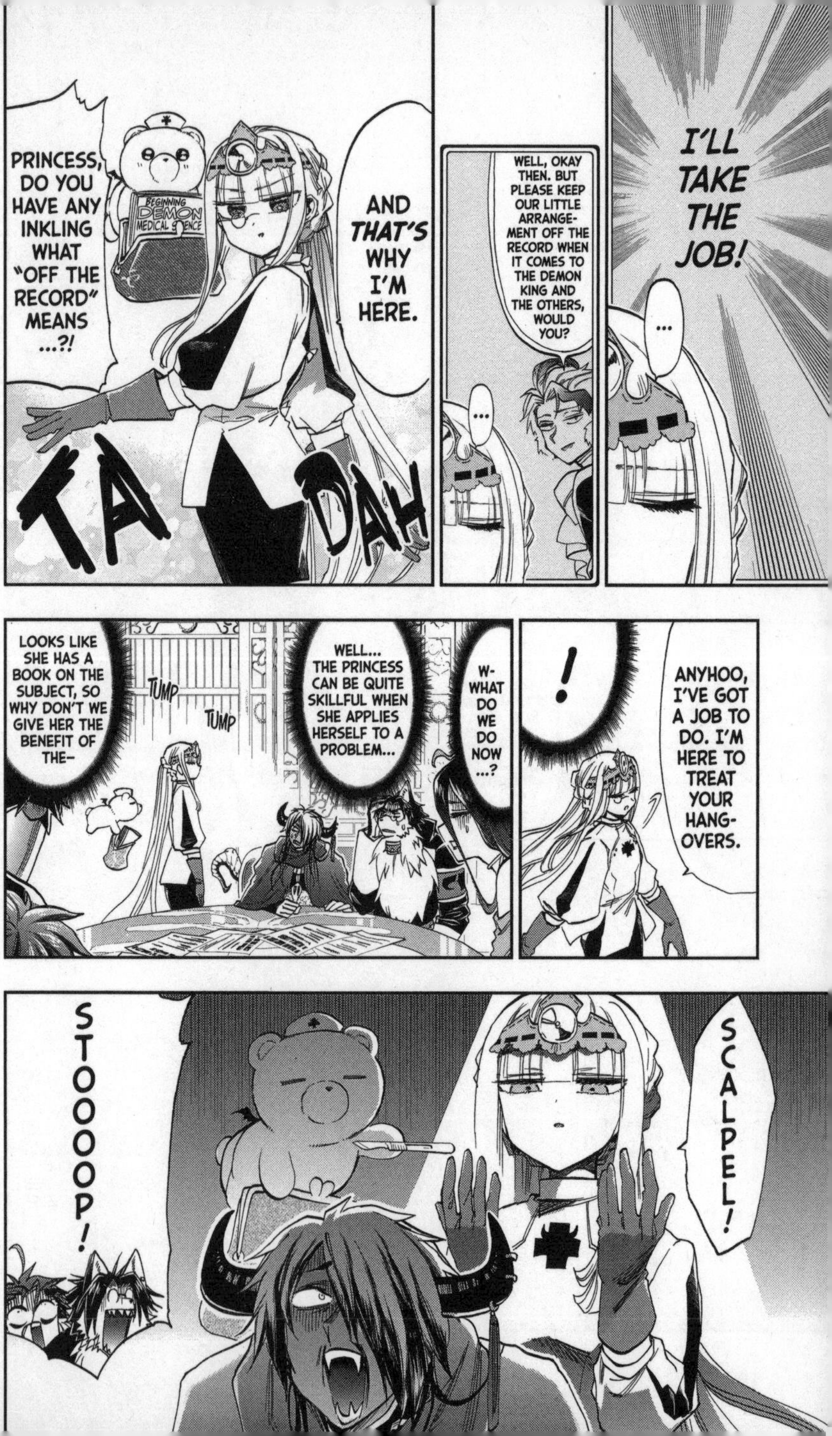

I'LL TAKE THE JOB!
...
WELL, OKAY THEN. BUT PLEASE KEEP OUR LITTLE ARRANGE-MENT OFF THE RECORD WHEN IT COMES TO THE DEMON KING AND THE OTHERS, WOULD YOU?
...
AND *THAT'S* WHY I'M HERE.
BEGINNING DEMON MEDICAL SCIENCE
PRINCESS, DO YOU HAVE ANY INKLING WHAT "OFF THE RECORD" MEANS ...?!
TA DAH
ANYHOO, I'VE GOT A JOB TO DO. I'M HERE TO TREAT YOUR HANG-OVERS.
!
W-WHAT DO WE DO NOW ...?
WELL... THE PRINCESS CAN BE QUITE SKILLFUL WHEN SHE APPLIES HERSELF TO A PROBLEM...
TUMP
TUMP
LOOKS LIKE SHE HAS A BOOK ON THE SUBJECT, SO WHY DON'T WE GIVE HER THE BENEFIT OF THE–
SCALPEL!
STOOOOOP!

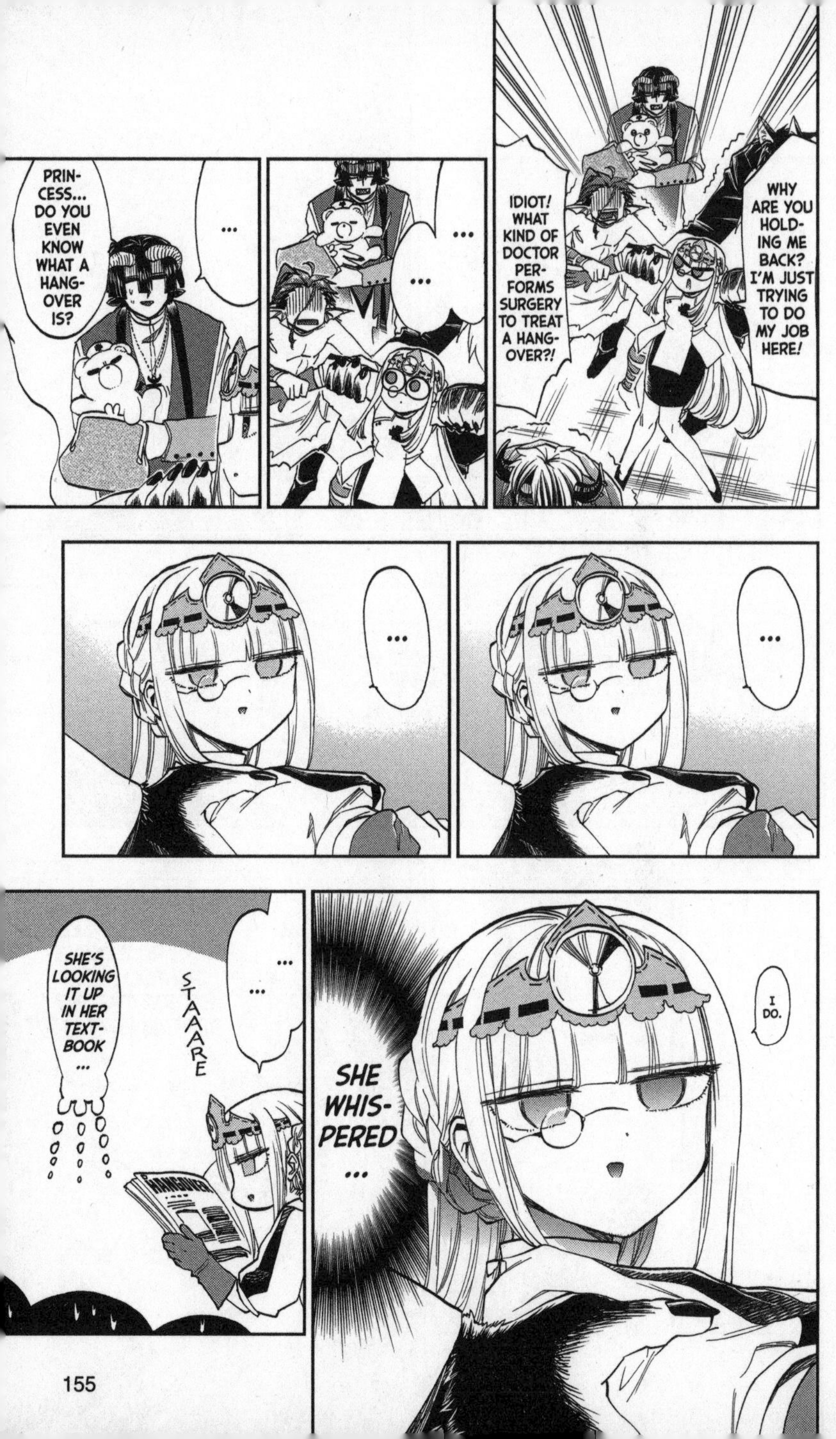
WHY ARE YOU HOLDING ME BACK? I'M JUST TRYING TO DO MY JOB HERE!
IDIOT! WHAT KIND OF DOCTOR PERFORMS SURGERY TO TREAT A HANGOVER?!
...
...
...
PRINCESS... DO YOU EVEN KNOW WHAT A HANGOVER IS?
...
...
I DO.
SHE WHISPERED...
...
...
STAAAARE
SHE'S LOOKING IT UP IN HER TEXTBOOK...

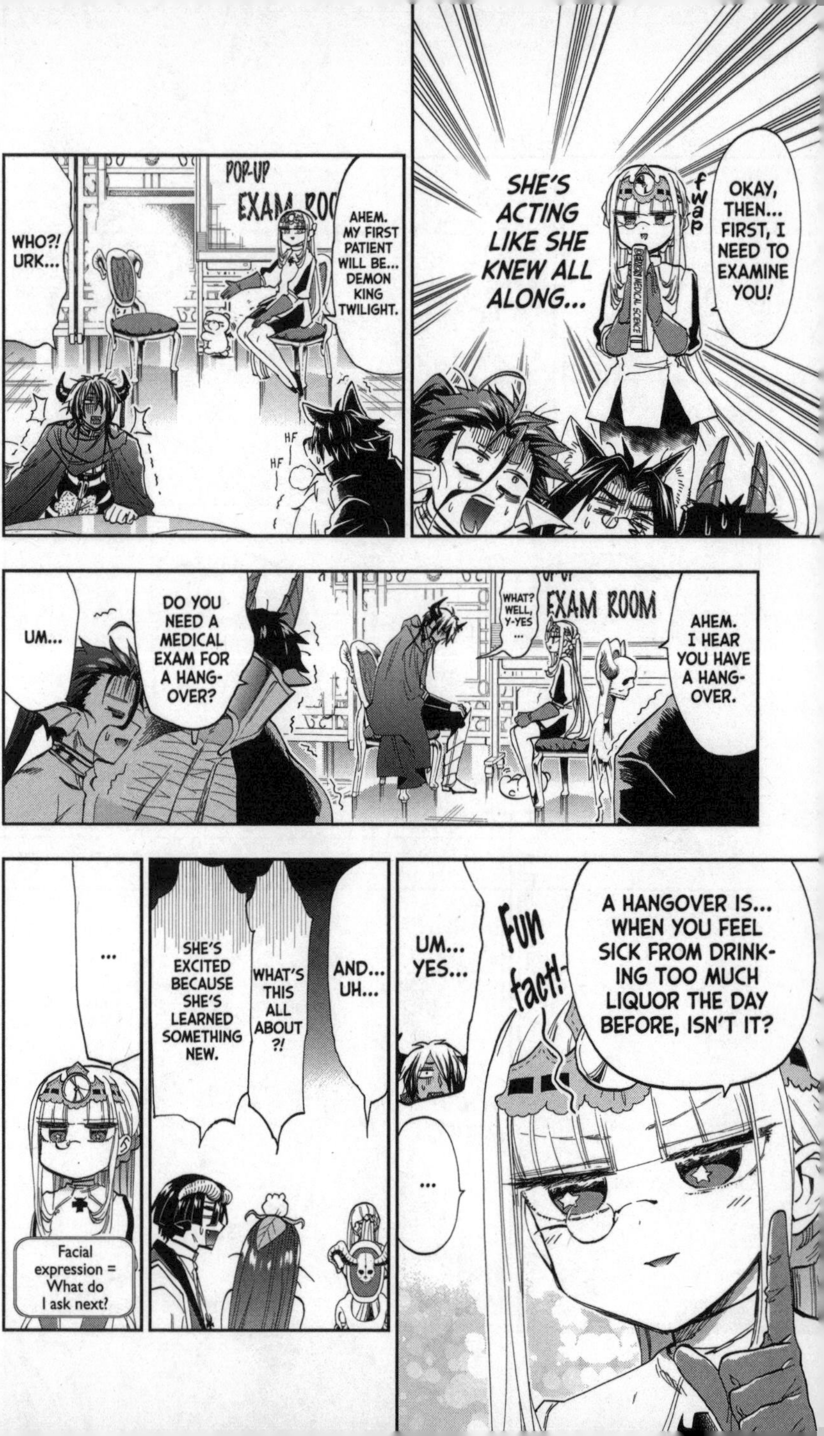

OKAY, THEN... FIRST, I NEED TO EXAMINE YOU!
fwap
DEMON MEDICAL SCIENCE
SHE'S ACTING LIKE SHE KNEW ALL ALONG...
POP-UP EXAM ROO
AHEM. MY FIRST PATIENT WILL BE... DEMON KING TWILIGHT.
WHO?! URK...
HF HF
AHEM. I HEAR YOU HAVE A HANG-OVER.
EXAM ROOM
WHAT? WELL, Y-YES...
DO YOU NEED A MEDICAL EXAM FOR A HANG-OVER?
UM...
A HANGOVER IS... WHEN YOU FEEL SICK FROM DRINK-ING TOO MUCH LIQUOR THE DAY BEFORE, ISN'T IT?
Fun fact!
UM... YES...
...
AND... UH...
WHAT'S THIS ALL ABOUT?!
SHE'S EXCITED BECAUSE SHE'S LEARNED SOMETHING NEW.
...
Facial expression = What do I ask next?

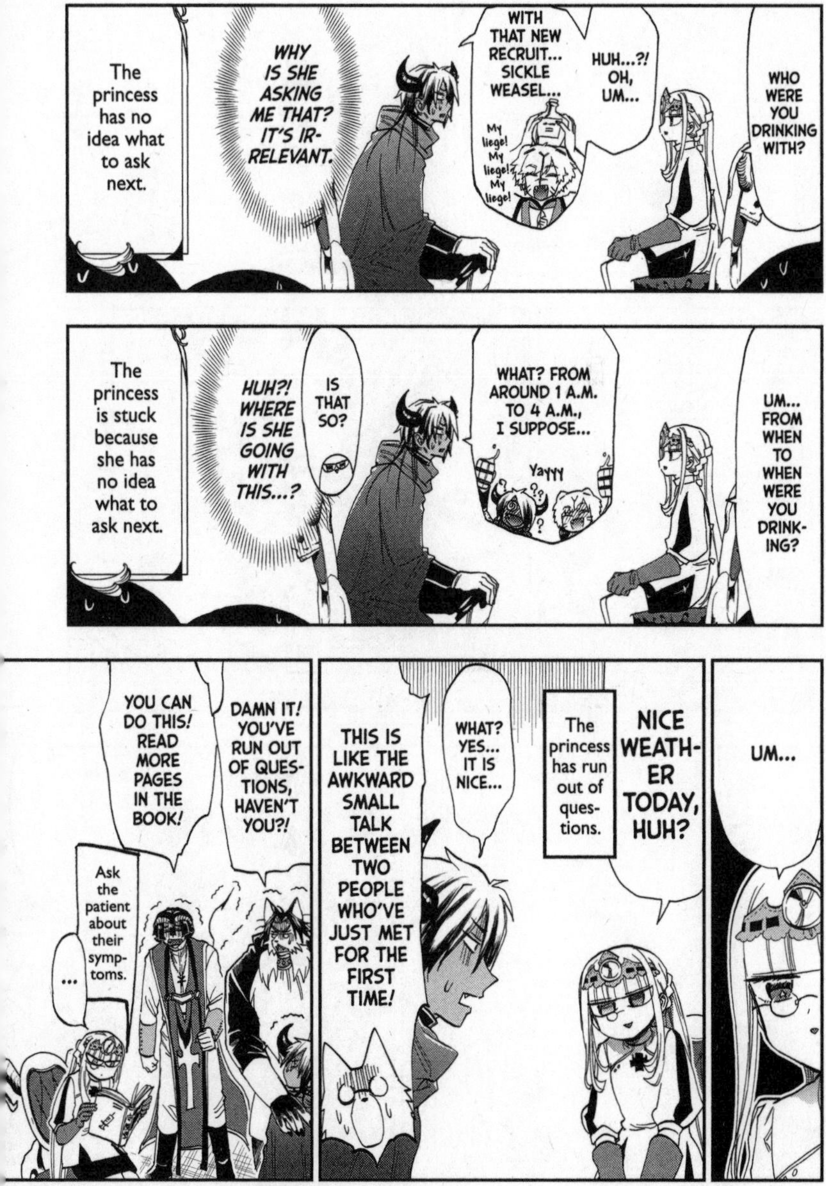
WHO WERE YOU DRINKING WITH?
HUH...?! OH, UM...
WITH THAT NEW RECRUIT... SICKLE WEASEL...
My liege! My liege! My liege!
WHY IS SHE ASKING ME THAT? IT'S IR-RELEVANT.
The princess has no idea what to ask next.
UM... FROM WHEN TO WHEN WERE YOU DRINK-ING?
WHAT? FROM AROUND 1 A.M. TO 4 A.M., I SUPPOSE...
Yayyy
IS THAT SO?
HUH?! WHERE IS SHE GOING WITH THIS...?
The princess is stuck because she has no idea what to ask next.
UM...
NICE WEATH-ER TODAY, HUH?
The princess has run out of ques-tions.
WHAT? YES... IT IS NICE...
THIS IS LIKE THE AWKWARD SMALL TALK BETWEEN TWO PEOPLE WHO'VE JUST MET FOR THE FIRST TIME!
DAMN IT! YOU'VE RUN OUT OF QUES-TIONS, HAVEN'T YOU?!
YOU CAN DO THIS! READ MORE PAGES IN THE BOOK!
Ask the patient about their symp-toms.
...

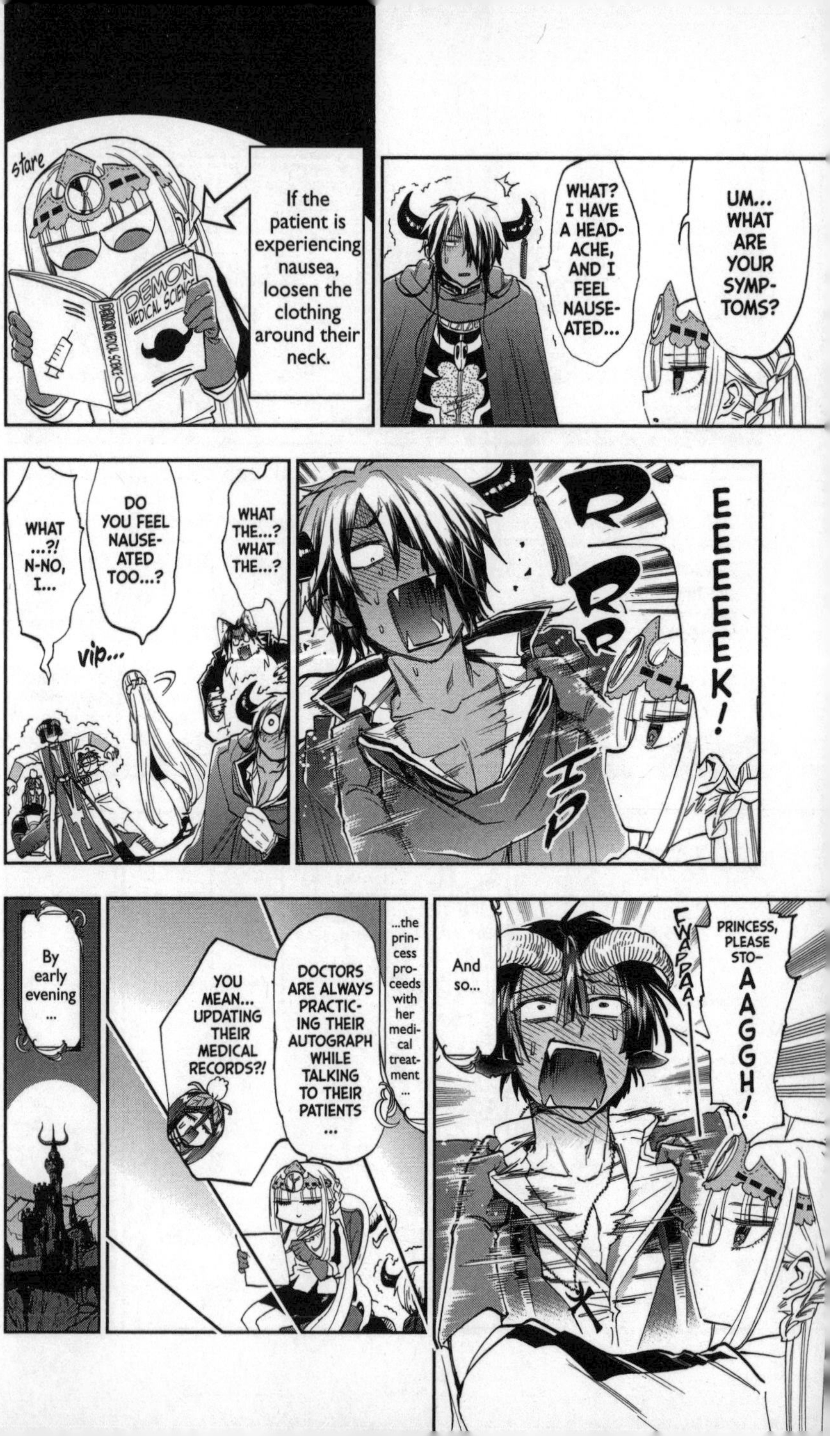
UM... WHAT ARE YOUR SYMPTOMS?
WHAT? I HAVE A HEADACHE, AND I FEEL NAUSEATED...
stare
If the patient is experiencing nausea, loosen the clothing around their neck.
DEMON MEDICAL SCIENCE
EEEEEEK!
WHAT THE...? WHAT THE...?
DO YOU FEEL NAUSEATED TOO...?
WHAT...?! N-NO, I...
vip...
PRINCESS, PLEASE STO-AAGGH!
FWAPPA
And so...
...the princess proceeds with her medical treatment...
DOCTORS ARE ALWAYS PRACTICING THEIR AUTOGRAPH WHILE TALKING TO THEIR PATIENTS...
YOU MEAN... UPDATING THEIR MEDICAL RECORDS?!
By early evening...

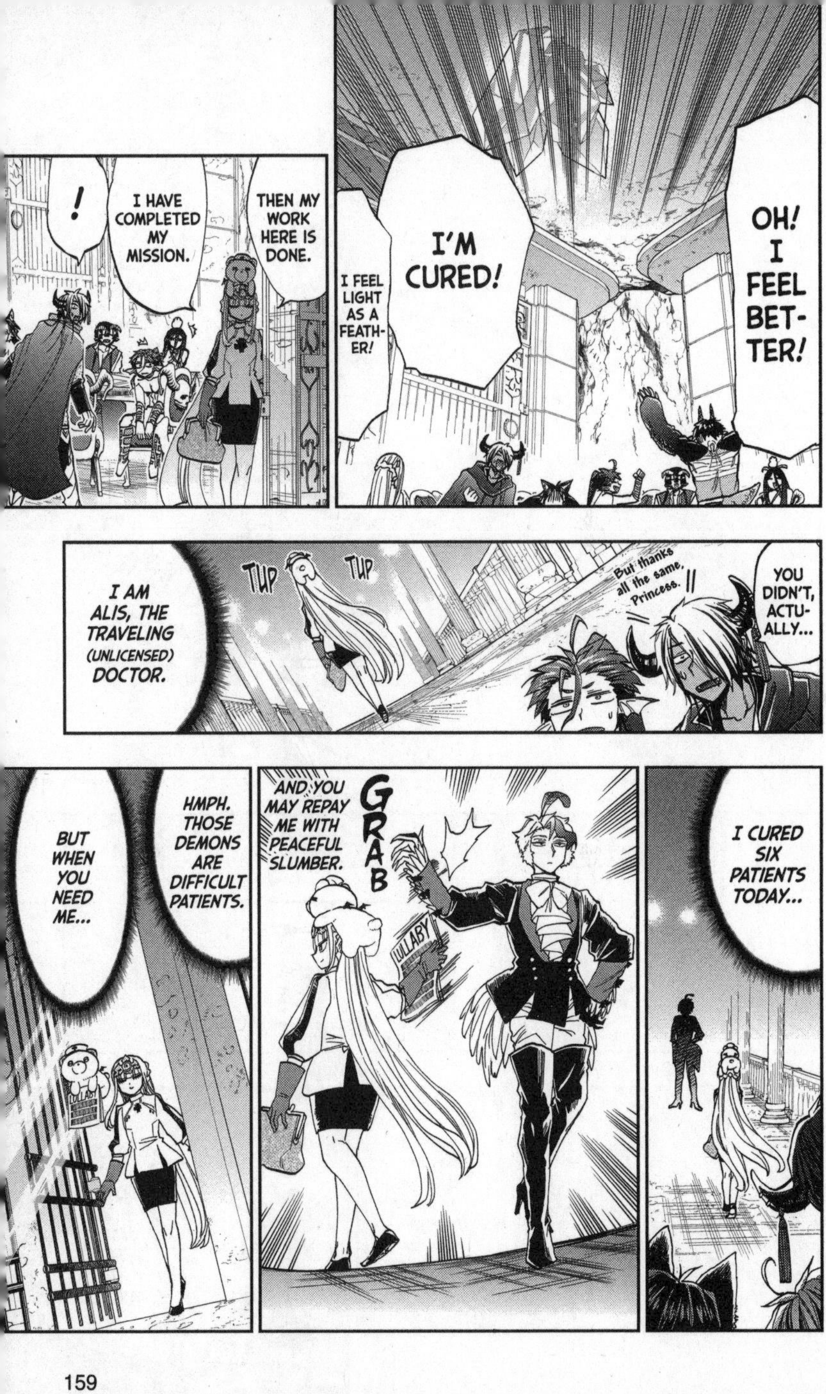
OH! I FEEL BET-TER!
I'M CURED!
I FEEL LIGHT AS A FEATH-ER!
THEN MY WORK HERE IS DONE.
I HAVE COMPLETED MY MISSION.
!
YOU DIDN'T, ACTU-ALLY...
But thanks all the same, Princess.
TUP
TUP
I AM ALIS, THE TRAVELING (UNLICENSED) DOCTOR.
I CURED SIX PATIENTS TODAY...
GRAB
AND YOU MAY REPAY ME WITH PEACEFUL SLUMBER.
LULLABY
HMPH. THOSE DEMONS ARE DIFFICULT PATIENTS.
BUT WHEN YOU NEED ME...

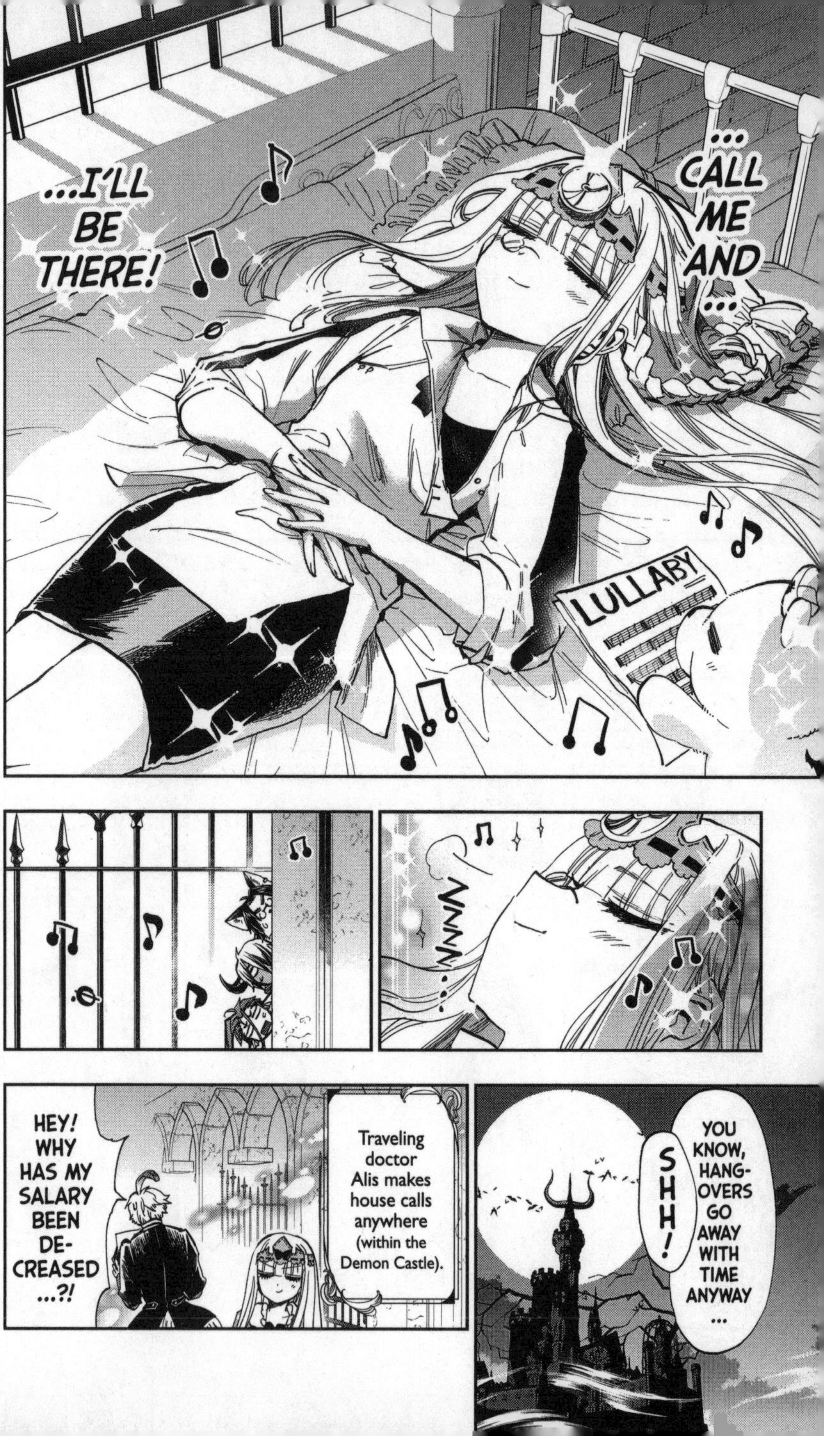
...CALL ME AND ...
...I'LL BE THERE!
LULLABY
...NNNN
YOU KNOW, HANG-OVERS GO AWAY WITH TIME ANYWAY ...
SHH!
Traveling doctor Alis makes house calls anywhere (within the Demon Castle).
HEY! WHY HAS MY SALARY BEEN DE-CREASED ...?!

Bonus: 117.9th Night

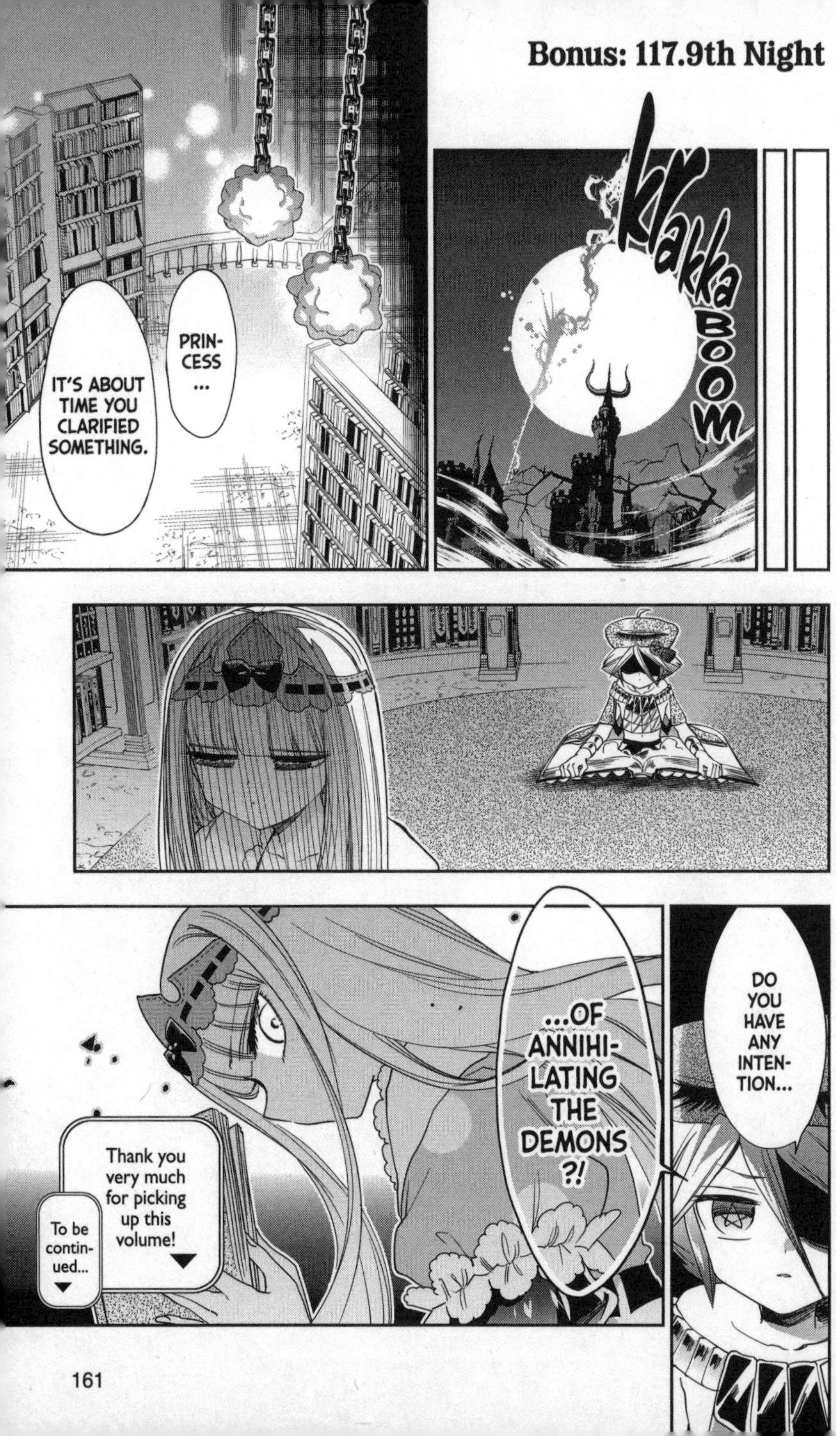

KLAKKA BOOM
PRINCESS...
IT'S ABOUT TIME YOU CLARIFIED SOMETHING.
DO YOU HAVE ANY INTENTION...
...OF ANNIHILATING THE DEMONS?!
Thank you very much for picking up this volume!
To be continued...

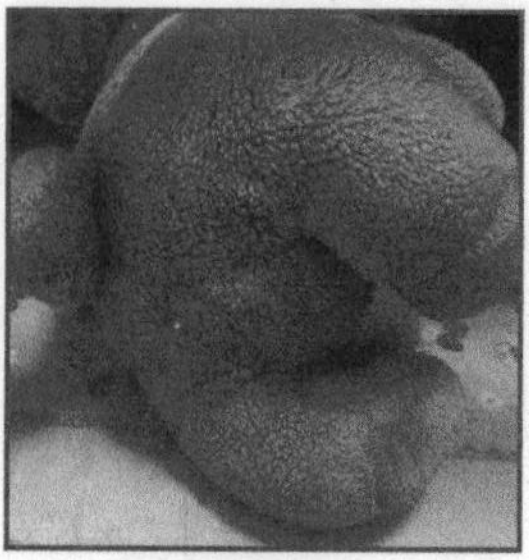

Wow...
Nine volumes published already!

– KAGIJI KUMANOMATA

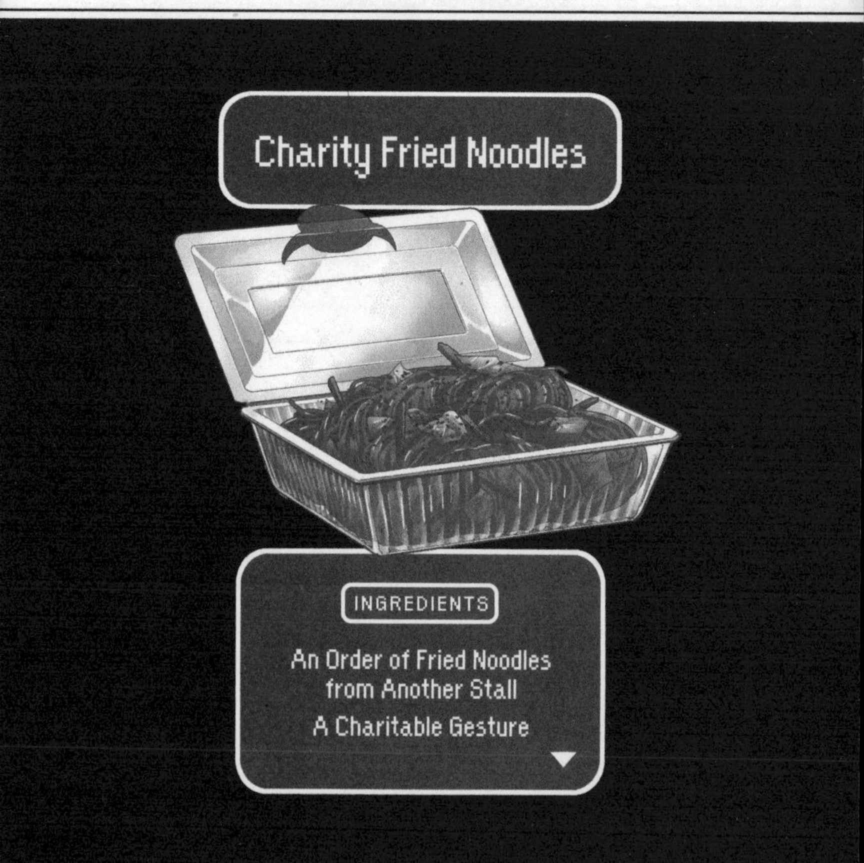
Charity Fried Noodles
INGREDIENTS
An Order of Fried Noodles
from Another Stall
A Charitable Gesture

Those who lurk beneath the cover...

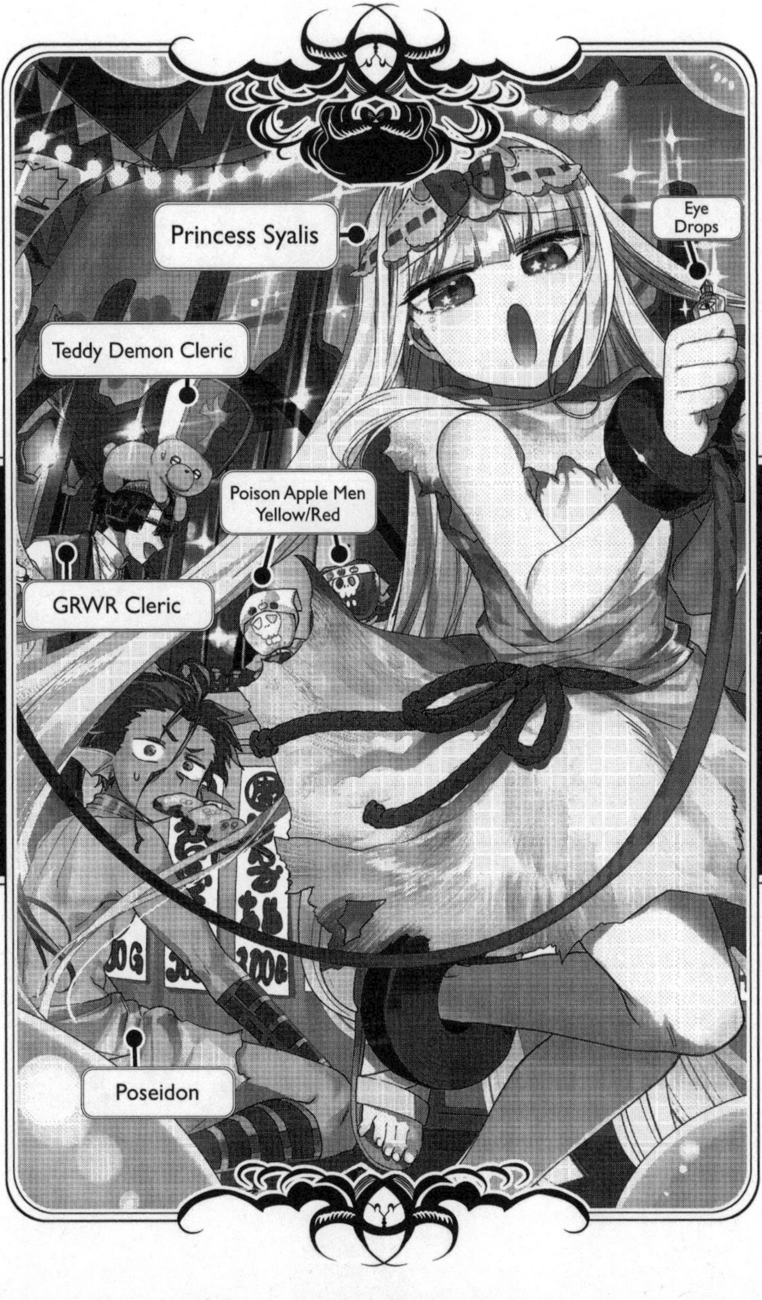
Princess Syalis
Eye Drops
Teddy Demon Cleric
Poison Apple Men Yellow/Red
GRWR Cleric
Poseidon

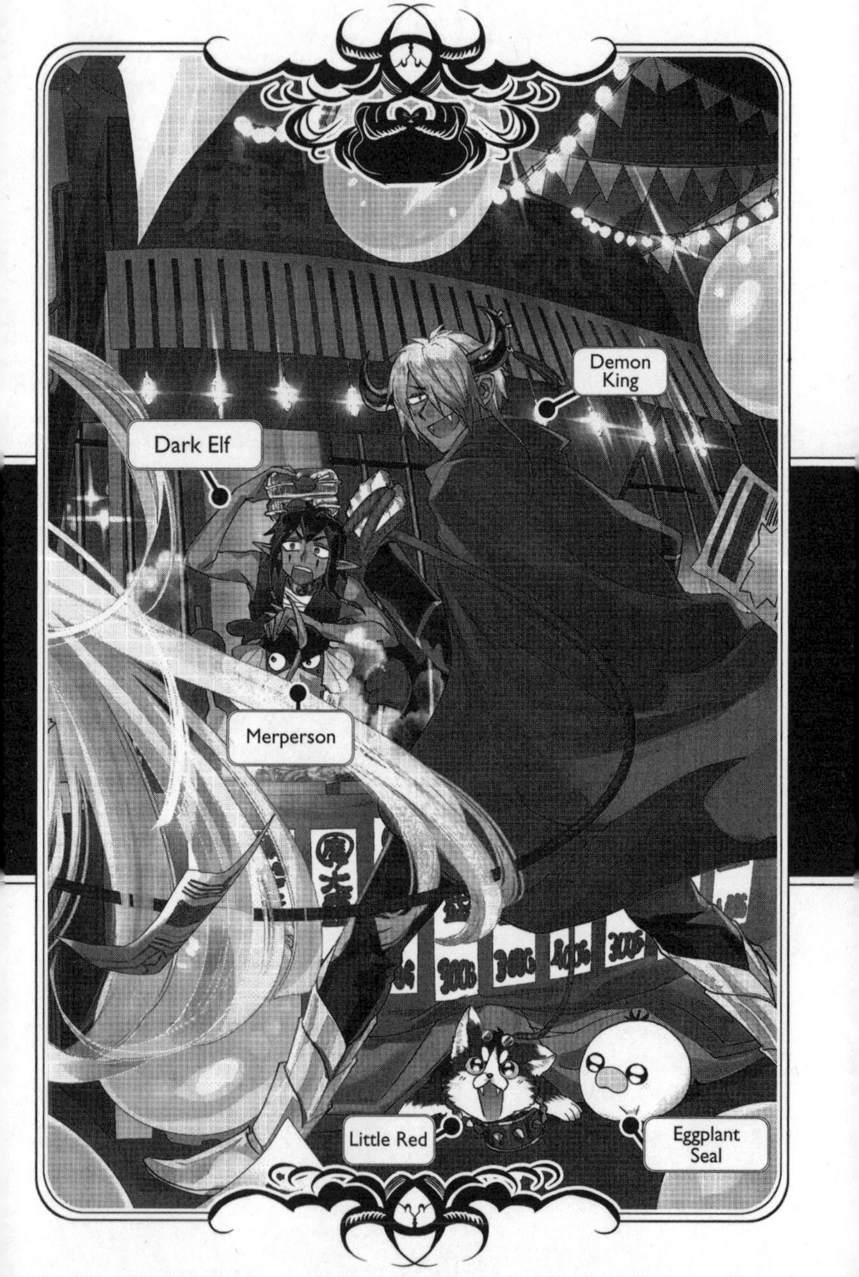
Demon King
Dark Elf
Merperson
Little Red
Eggplant Seal

Sleepy Princess in the Demon Castle

9

Shonen Sunday Edition

STORY AND ART BY

KAGIJI KUMANOMATA

MAOUJO DE OYASUMI Vol. 9
by Kagiji KUMANOMATA
© 2016 Kagiji KUMANOMATA
All rights reserved.
Original Japanese edition published by SHOGAKUKAN.
English translation rights in the United States of America, Canada,
the United Kingdom, Ireland, Australia and New Zealand arranged
with SHOGAKUKAN.

TRANSLATION **TETSUICHIRO MIYAKI**

ENGLISH ADAPTATION **ANNETTE ROMAN**

TOUCH-UP ART & LETTERING **JAMES GAUBATZ**

COVER & INTERIOR DESIGN **ALICE LEWIS**

EDITOR **ANNETTE ROMAN**

Printed in the U.S.A.

Published by VIZ Media, LLC
P.O. Box 77010
San Francisco, CA 94107

10 9 8 7 6 5 4 3 2 1
First printing, October 2019

MEDIA

viz.com   shonensunday.com

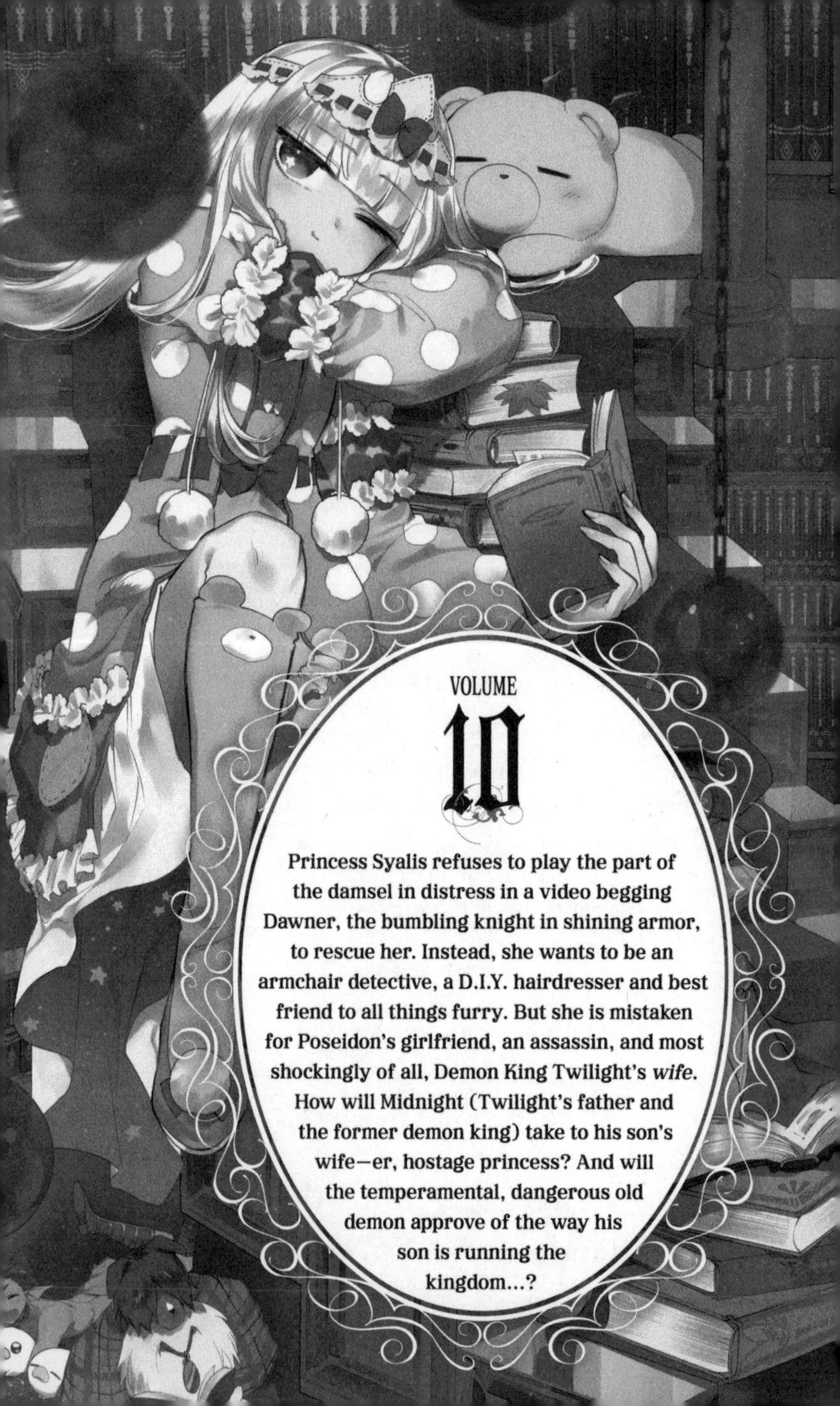
VOLUME
10
Princess Syalis refuses to play the part of the damsel in distress in a video begging Dawner, the bumbling knight in shining armor, to rescue her. Instead, she wants to be an armchair detective, a D.I.Y. hairdresser and best friend to all things furry. But she is mistaken for Poseidon's girlfriend, an assassin, and most shockingly of all, Demon King Twilight's *wife*. How will Midnight (Twilight's father and the former demon king) take to his son's wife—er, hostage princess? And will the temperamental, dangerous old demon approve of the way his son is running the kingdom...?

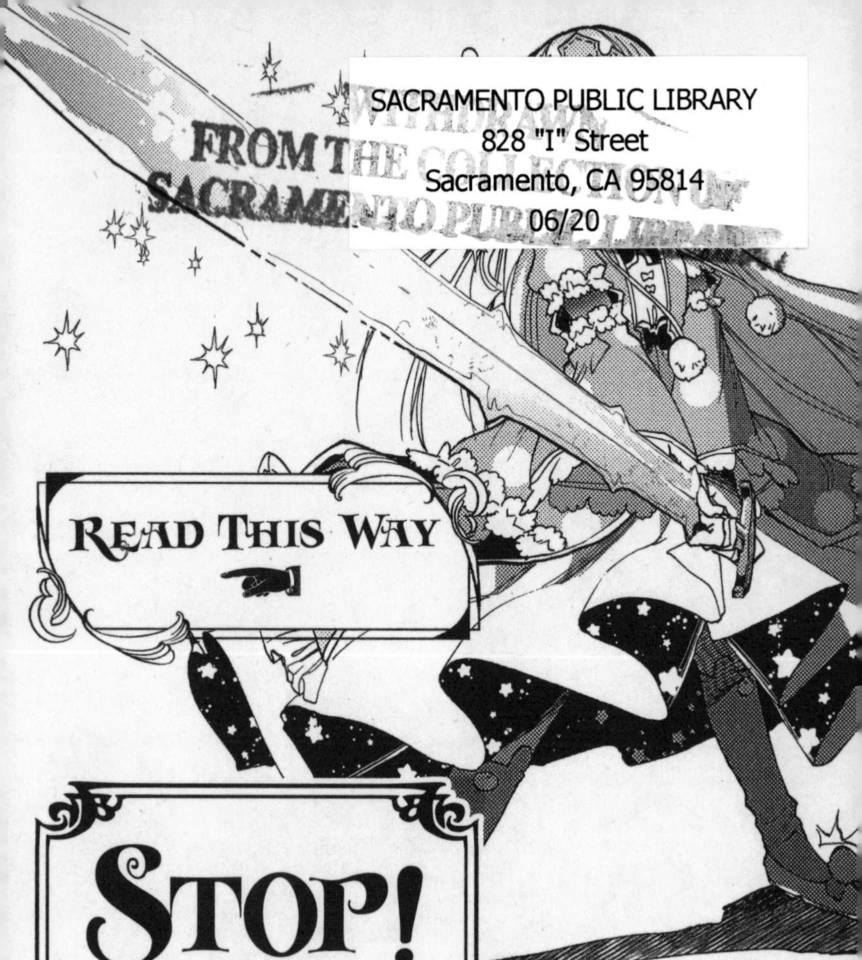
READ THIS WAY

STOP!

You may be reading the wrong way!

In keeping with the original Japanese comic format, this book reads from right to left—so action, sound effects and word balloons are completely reversed to preserve the orientation of the original artwork.

Check out the diagram shown here to get the hang of things, and then turn to the other side of the book to get started!

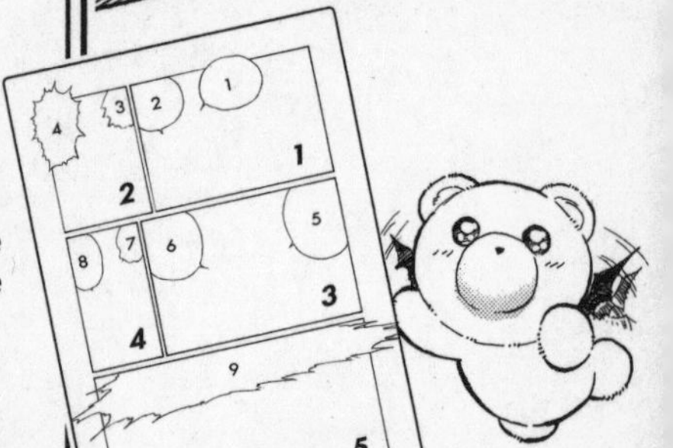
1
2
3
4
5